# The Norton Anthology of World Masterpieces

*Sixth Edition*

D0555633

## Volume Two

## Instructor's Guide

Maynard Mack, <u>General Editor</u>

Patricia Meyer Spacks

René Wellek

Sarah Lawall

Kim A. Herzinger

# The Norton Anthology of World Masterpieces

## SIXTH EDITION

### Volume Two

### Instructor's Guide

**W·W·Norton & Company**
New York · London

ISBN 0-393-96193-1

W. W. Norton & Company, Inc.
500 Fifth Avenue, New York, New York 10110

W. W. Norton & Company Ltd.
10 Coptic Street, London WC1A 1PU

1 2 3 4 5 6 7 8 9 0

# Contents

## Masterpieces of the Enlightenment

# Masterpieces of the Nineteenth Century
## Varieties of Romanticism

## Masterpieces of the Nineteenth Century
### Realism, Naturalism, and the New Poetry

## Masterpieces of the Twentieth Century
### Varieties of Modernism

## Masterpieces of the Twentieth Century
### Contemporary Explorations

# Preface

In this guide for instructors, we offer the many loyal friends of *The Norton Anthology of World Masterpieces* a systematic overview of useful class procedures. Most derive from our own experience, some from yours, which many of you through the years have been kind enough to share with us. We hope that you will continue to contribute whenever the spirit moves, for a collection of this kind is only valuable if it is alive, always hospitable to ideas that have proved their viability, always ready to jettison those that fail.

It goes without saying that not all the suggestions put forward here will work equally for all teachers, classes, or occasions. No teacher needs reminding how different various classes can be, or how different the same class on different days. Yet we like to think that there will be something in these pages to assist even the most seasoned voyagers among masterpieces, particularly when they are outside their familiar waters (certainly this has been the case with the seven of us!); and we firmly believe that there is much here to give confidence to the newcomer.

We include, for instance, summaries pointing up what seem to us the main characteristics of each work, not forgetting those qualities that constitute its claim to our attention, as well as background material, additional to that in the anthology introductions and headnotes, on the several factors that may have helped shape the work (*Backgrounds*). These are followed by generously full discussions of ways in which the work may profitably be approached under classroom conditions, and, likewise, of the difficulties we have found that students sometimes have with it, owing to social, political, cultural, or linguistic change (*Classroom Strategies*). Following this, we propose a number of points for class discussion or for writing that, at least in our own experience, can be counted on to engage student interest while at that same time lighting up the work in hand (*Topics for Discussion and Writing*). There is at the close a special annotated bibliography of writings likely to prove particularly helpful in preparing either a class lecture or a class discussion (*Further Reading*).

It is our conviction that this guide supplies an important addendum to our anthology, if used with imagination and good sense. It is not, and is not intended to be, a teachers' "answer-book." In the first place, because your own inspirations are what finally matter: ours will work best if they serve primarily as a warm-up for yours. And in the second place, because in the profound world of human feelings and failings, agonies and joys of which world literature treats, there are no "answers"—only understandings that are better or worse according as they do justice to the full reality of that impassioned image of ourselves which great works of art bring before us.

THE EDITORS

# The Norton Anthology of World Masterpieces

*Sixth Edition*

**Volume Two**

**Instructor's Guide**

# Masterpieces of the Enlightenment

## JEAN-BAPTISTE POQUELIN MOLIERE
### Tartuffe

*Classroom Strategies and Topics for Discussion*

The biggest problem for students who are reading *Tartuffe* for the first time is likely to be the expectations they bring to the play. If they anticipate characters with realistically conceived psychologies, and events closely resembling what might occur in ordinary life, they will be bewildered and irritated. It is important, therefore, to explain in advance that the play depends on the particular forms of artifice we call *convention*.

In the first place, it relies on the set of *dramatic* conventions associated with the comedy of manners. These conventions include the use of type characters, figures differentiated by role rather than by psychology. Students can probably identify many of the types in *Tartuffe* themselves, once alerted to the presence of type characters: the hypocrite, the clever maid, the blustering young man, the foolish but tyrannical father, the naive young girl, and so on. Equally conventional is the structure of the plot, dependent not on plausibility but on the design of providing pleasure (including particularly the pleasure of surprise) by its ingenuity and of demonstrating the restoration of a just social order and the punishment of deviants from that order.

The play also assumes a set of *social* conventions. These have to do with the kind and degree of authority exercised by the father of a family. A father, for instance, has absolute power over his daughter's marital choices; he may be argued with but not refused. A wife's chastity is of paramount importance to her husband. A son's economic status depends entirely on his father's will. Thus the father's role in the family resembles the king's in the country—a point of some importance to the ending of *Tartuffe*.

It is especially useful in teaching this play to read aloud sequences with different members of the class assuming different roles. Only thus will students realize the brilliance of the verse, the wit of the language (e.g., "You deserve to be tartuffified") and rhymes (e.g., *fossil-docile*)—effects approximating in English the dramatist's achievement in French —the speed and economy with which Molière conveys necessary information and moves the plot along, the sheer *fun* of language and event. The first scene is a good place to start, both for reading aloud and for analysis. Mme. Pernelle's initial haste ("Come, come, Flipote, it's time I left this place": students should think about how the entrance would be staged, with everyone rushing to keep up with Mme. Pernelle) when contrasted with her leisure for denunciation, extending to everyone in the household except Tartuffe, of course creates comedy. One might ask whether it has also a serious point. It announces a theme that runs through the play: the degree to which people are driven by their own obsessions to be blind to the needs of others. If students are asked for examples of this pattern, they will probably mention Tartuffe and Orgon (perhaps the brilliant scene in which Orgon hears of his wife's illness but concerns himself only with "poor Tartuffe"), but Damis, Mariane, and Valere are also relevant. What else does the first scene accomplish? It introduces the presence of Tartuffe as a potential problem. Students might discuss the impression of Tartuffe they get from this scene; later in the discussion, they might pursue the ways that this impression is elaborated and modified as the play goes on. And the scene sketches, mainly from Mme. Pernelle's distorted point of view, characteristics of the play's persons. What notion does one get of each? It introduces Dorine as a young woman exceptionally willing to state her own opinions. Does one trust her view or Mme. Pernelle's more fully? What aspects of their accounts of other people make them seem more or less trustworthy?

Many individual scenes of the play reward similar analysis. Particularly rich are the farcical scene between Valere and Dorine (II.4) and the seduction scene, with Orgon under the table (IV.5) Analysis of almost any scene can lead to investigation of the play's larger issues. A few general points worth pursuing: *Is* this comedy in fact anti-religious, or does it only attack corruptions of religion? (Opinions may differ here; the point is to get students to support their opinions by reference to the text.) In Act IV, Scene 3, Elmire remarks, "My taste is for good-natured rectitude." Is "good-natured rectitude" the implicit value advocated by the play? How does the concept of rectitude relate to the common sense consistently exemplified by Cleante? (Cleante's role is worth extended discussion. What, exactly, does his common sense involve? What sort of view of human nature does he seem to have? Why does Orgon refuse to pay attention to him?) How serious a criticism of society does this play offer? In other words, is its purpose only to entertain or does it aspire to educate as well?

In working out answers to such questions, it is worth thinking about what causes characters to be deluded. The ridiculous misunderstanding between Valere and Marianne comes partly from the wish of each to have the other acknowledge need or desire first. If Valere proclaimed his love when Marianne was actually willing to marry someone else, he would appear weak; conversely, if Marianne says she won't marry Tartuffe because she loves Valere, she gives him the upper hand. Similar issues of power emerge in every situation. Orgon feels himself powerful in his role of benevolent patron to Tartuffe; he must believe in Tartuffe's goodness in order to believe in his own magnanimity. Tartuffe, to take the most obvious example, gains power by proclaiming his weakness and humility. This common element in the characters' motivation is worth emphasizing because it calls attention to the fact that the play lights up issues of perennial concern, not simply those inherent in a society with religious and political structures quite different from our own.

Some time should be spent on the question of plot and how it works here. Tartuffe's will to power (including the power of wealth) and Orgon's determination to indulge him are the motivating forces producing an intertwined sequence of events that seem inevitable, given the premises. Students might be asked at what points in the play they were surprised by what happened next. Any answers to this question would be worth pursuing, to try to ascertain whether surprise reflects a real failure of plausibility or a failure of expectation. The most likely moments of surprise are Tartuffe's attempt to seize the house, after he is unmasked and one expects all problems to be solved, and the final intervention of the king. Both are particularly useful to discuss. The first surprise derives from our expectations of comedy: we anticipate no really serious problems, we assume that difficulties will be readily resolved in a comic scheme. Molière's extra twist serves as a reminder that the problems announced in this play *are* in fact serious—and perhaps as a reminder that in the real world they are not so easily solved.

The matter of the king is more complicated. To twentieth-century sensibilities, this may seem an arbitrary intervention, or a piece of gross flattery; and perhaps it cannot be fully justified. But it can at least be argued that the introduction of the king as a force in the action serves as a reminder that the family is a microcosm for larger patterns of social organization. Order must be restored in the family for order to operate in the kingdom; and it is only by the exercise of authority, in this play, that order exists.

## Topics for Writing

1. The function of the mother-in-law (Mme. Pernelle)

2. The importance of seeing in *Tartuffe*

3. The voice of reason in *Tartuffe*

4. What kinds of emotion are important in the play?

5. Secrets and secrecy in *Tartuffe*

## Further Reading

See also the reading suggestions in the anthology, p. 10.

Gossman, L. *Man and Masks.* 1963.
Looks at Molière in his historical situation with emphasis on his continuing relevance to the present as well as on the way he embodies ideas important in his own time.

Guicharnaud, J., ed. *Molière, A Collection of Critical Essays.* 1964.
Exemplifies diverse approaches and includes a particularly valuable group of seven essays under the rubric, "The Art of Comedy."

Hubert, J. *Molière and The Comedy of Intellect.* 1962.
Particularly useful for teachers: studies the playwright's "achievement as a creator of dramatic and poetic forms," emphasizing the inner coherence and the moral vision of Moliere's work as a whole. The chapter on *Tartuffe*, "Hypocrisy As Spectacle," is rich in insight.

Jagendorf, Zvi. *The Happy End of Comedy*. 1984.
Treats Molière's comedies in relation to Shakespeare's and Ben Johnson's.

McBride, R. *The Sceptical Vision of Molière*. 1977.
Organized around the idea of paradox, with an introductory section about the relation between Molière as moralist and as comic artist followed by a detailed study of how the playwright's thought is embodied in his comedy.

Walker, H. *Molière*. 1971.
An introductory volume in the Twayne series which provides a brief biography, thematically organized analysis of the plays, and valuable bibliography.

# MARIE DE LA VERGNE DE LA FAYETTE
## The Princess of Clèves

*Classroom Strategies and Topics for Discussion*

This short novel lends itself readily to division into two assignments, with the first one ending at the end of the first paragraph on p. 70. The text, so different from the realistic novel with which most students are familiar, presents some obvious problems for the beginning reader. The class should perhaps be warned in advance not to expect the kind of circumstantial detail and leisurely narrative typical of more recent fiction. Instead, the story proceeds by a series of rather flat, rapid summaries of events, focusing attention on characters' inner responses rather than their external behavior. If students have been prepared to take note of the work's psychological complexities, they may have an easier time reading it.

Particularly if they have been told that this is a psychological novel, however, undergraduates are likely to be troubled by its stress on political detail. The first few pages, crammed with historical and political data, are therefore a good place to start discussion. The question of how the political relates to the personal has considerable immediacy for twentieth-century readers; de La Fayette's apparent assumption that the two cannot be separated challenges belief in the possibility of an altogether "private" life. It is easy enough to see that in a court, love might be mingled with politics and politics with love; as the novel develops, however, the reader begins to understand that love *is* politics. The opening pages' stress on beauty, wealth, and status as publicly accepted values prepares for the gradual revelation that the same values operate in private relationships as well. Students may be interested in discussing how romantic entanglements in the novel are revealed to involve balancings of power. Even the Princess's genuine concern with virtue becomes a means for her to dominate both husband and lover, although she has no apparent wish to dominate. Discussion of politics as the science of power, and of how private and public politics reflect one another, can help students see that the remote historical setting and formal diction of the novel only slightly disguise its preoccupation with issues that still concern us.

A specific episode useful to discuss in this connection is the story of Mme. de Tournon (pp. 95ff.), told by M. de Clèves to his wife. This tale of love, grief, deceit, and misunderstanding epitomizes the mistaken trust in appearances, the misdirected passion, the intertwining of public and private concerns that pervade the novel as a whole. (Students may find it interesting to trace other occurrences of these themes.) It also emphasizes processes of reinterpretation likewise typical of the entire work—and of students' everyday experience with their classmates. Sancerre is forced to understand his relation to his beloved in new ways; M. de Clèves reinterprets both Sancerre and Mme. de Tournon; Mme. de Clèves enlarges her comprehension of possibilities of female deceit. The telling of stories about other people is an insistent activity in this fiction; typically, these episodes (the story of Mme. de Tournon is exemplary in this respect too) remind their immediate hearers as well as the reader of the fact that what happens to a single member of a coherent society affects everyone else as well, if only by changing understanding. The past keeps changing as people find out new things about it; neither public nor private history remains static. The tale of Mme. de Tournon can provide a starting point for examining the reiteration of these points in *The Princess of Clèves*.

With the second assignment, discussion might turn to psychological issues: those suggested by the headnote and others as well. A possible starting point would be the Princess's act of deception in rewriting from memory the lost letter (pp. 125ff). Why, despite her virtue, is she willing without urging to engage in this deception? The act, which involves her in close association with her would-be lover, suggests her desire for such association; it hints a weakening in her rigid moral code, since she allows herself an interlude of pure pleasure with M. de Nemours; it illustrates the way the past keeps encroaching on the present and demanding reinterpretation. To think about the Princess's feelings here and how they are expressed leads readily to discussion of how those feelings develop in the course of the novel, from premarital repression through this brief interlude of expansion back finally to postmarital repression.

Talking about the Princess's emotional development may involve awareness of how much this novel emphasizes not the feelings conventionally associated with romantic love but rather such emotions as fear, embarrassment, and anxiety. It is worth discussing both the plausibility of such emotions, in the society evoked, and the nature of their importance. Among other things, the kind of embarrassment and anxiety here typical reflect the novel's assumption that the pressures of other people largely determine much individual experience. (A more abstract way of putting the same point would be to say that society is of the utmost importance to every person in it; there is no way to avoid its force.) To think about how people impinge upon one another in this fiction may lead to understanding of the Princess's final choice: she has removed herself from the arena of social pressure, thus ultimately declaring her individuality even when she seems to be suppressing it.

A question particularly likely to engage contemporary students is that of the novel's female authorship. Is there anything in the work that declares the sex of its author? Answers to such a question must necessarily remain highly speculative, but it is perhaps worth considering how characteristically the action here proceeds by indirect rather than direct means. People overhear one another, see one another from hiding, watch in mirrors, learn things by accident, rely on rumor and gossip, withhold crucial information. Another possibly "female" aspect of the fiction is its stress on pain as something to be concealed rather than to be displayed (compare Racine). Does the great attention to appearance have anything to do with the author's sex? Does this author's way of setting a private drama in a public context have the effect of subverting the importance of the public? Such unresolvable questions of course persist for modern authors as well.

## Topics for Writing

1. The Importance of Propriety in *The Princess of Clèves*

2. The Character of the Prince of Clèves

3. The Princess's Relation to her Mother

4. The Significance of Paintings in *The Princess of Clèves*

5. The Happy Ending of *The Princess of Clèves*

6. The Unhappy Ending of *The Princess of Clèves*

## Further Reading

See also the reading suggestions in the anthology, p. 70.

Gregorio, L. *Order in the Court: History and Society in* La Princesse de Clèves. 1986.
A sound historical investigation.

Haig, S. *Madame de La Fayette.* 1970.
Of the scanty literature in English on the novel, this is probably the most useful. It follows skillfully the usual Twayne formula of biographical introduction, critical analysis, and bibliographical survey.

Kuizinga, D. *Narrative Strategies in* La Princesse de Clèves. 1976.
A highly specialized treatment, with its focus indicated by the title.

Showalter, E., Jr. *The Evolution of the French Novel, 1641–1782.* 1972.
Places de La Fayette in the context of the developing tradition of realism.

Turnell, M. *The Novel in France.* 1951.
Includes biographical information and speculation and a short critical analysis of *The Princess of Clèves.*

# JEAN RACINE
## Phaedra

*Classroom Strategies and Topics for Discussion*

Even if they have already read Molière and de La Fayette, students may have trouble with the artifice and formality of Racine. To encounter characters who make pronouncements about their feelings in blank verse, with none of the comic relief familiar from Shakespeare, often proves a forbidding experience. The problems that preoccupy these characters seem remote from common twentieth-century life; the personages on the stage do not invite easy identification from the audience. But all is not lost. Although students should probably be told at the outset enough about seventeenth-century tragic convention to understand that they are to look at and learn from these characters, not instantly perceive them as analogues for the self, in fact it is possible to find in the long run important points of contact between the constructed world whose inhabitants concern themselves with conflicts of love and virtue and our own time and experience.

To achieve such a result demands attention to the play's detail. Although it is possible to read the entire drama as a single assignment, it lends itself well to a two-part division: the first three acts, and then the final two. A good place to start discussion is with Phaedra's first important speech, her explanation to Oenone, in Act I, of the source of her distress. Reading this speech aloud facilitates talk about the function of the play's sonorous verse. Even in translation, one can feel how the dignity and control of language and meter provide a counterpoint for the chaotic emotion they render. The dramatist is always in control, although the characters are not necessarily able to keep a sense of mastery, and the poetic authority of Racine's voice (behind Phaedra's) affirms the possibility of restored human order—that possibility clearly announced at the play's ending.

But the content of Phaedra's speech also deserves attention. Her initial characterization of her love for Hippolytus as "My ills" sets the tone for her utterance as a whole, with its emphasis on evil, pain, and misery. Students might be asked to find the metaphors in this passage. The imagery emphasizes war and sickness: metaphors that run through the play. Where else do such metaphors occur, you might ask; the answers will help students see how imagery creates and emphasizes unity. This speech also brings up the large question of Phaedra's responsibility for her own and other people's suffering. She sees herself as helpless ("Venus fastens on her helpless prey"); is she? This is not, of course, the kind of question that has a pre-established answer, but students should be urged to find evidence for their position on either side. If they believe that Phaedra's love has overcome her with no possibility for her to resist, is she to be held responsible for her further acts, for confessing her love to Hippolytus and condoning Oenone's terrible lie about him? How does one determine human responsibility in a world governed by gods and goddesses? Are we to take these deities simply as projections of human feelings? If so, Phaedra *is* responsible. In that case, does she become villain rather than victim? The problem of moral responsibility is a powerful issue in the play, as in our lives. One way of understanding Phaedra's insistence that Venus is to blame is to recall our modern tendency to see criminals as "sick" rather than wicked, ourselves as formed by our heredity and environment rather than our wills. But no matter how much we blame our parents for what's wrong with us, we are left with a residue of feeling that it's all our fault. So is Phaedra. Discussion of the final two acts of the play should obviously involve attention to how Phaedra's suicide modifies our sense of her disclaiming responsibility.

Oenone's speech in response to Phaedra's revelation (after the interruption of Panope) brings up further large issues. The nurse speaks, typically, in a voice of common sense. She invokes public opinion, a mother's obligation to her child, tactics for appealing to Hippolytus. Of course her advice proves fatally wrong. Does this fact suggest anything about the value attached to "common sense" in the play? Why does common sense seem altogether irrelevant to the characters' real problems? To investigate such questions leads to understanding of how insistently the play claims that human dilemmas must be comprehended first of all in moral rather than in pragmatic terms. Oenone does not think primarily about right and wrong; Phaedra tries to, but often fails. Yet right and wrong remain the crucial issues of this drama.

To speak of "right and wrong" brings up the whole matter of "virtue," allegedly Hippolytus's defining characteristic. Why is Hippolytus so completely vulnerable, a teacher might ask. The answer must surely involve the character's claim to virtue. He knows himself to be good and believes goodness to be sufficient protection; the innocent, he fancies, must triumph. But he is wrong—not only mistaken because he inhabits a corrupt world, but mistaken because his smugness about his own virtue involves ignoring the claims and the feelings of other people. Oenone observes to Phaedra (III.3), "You must give up, since honor is at stake, / Everything, even virtue, for its sake"; she values the reputation of virtue more highly than the thing itself. She is wrong too: neither honor nor virtue is sufficient in itself.

Such general formulations are less important than the means of reaching them: by close attention to the language of the text, which provides material for many kinds of formulation. Other large questions that discussion might engage include these: Why and how is the past important in this play? The past figures as both public history (the history of rulers and governments) and private (the history of families, frequently and emphatically alluded to). It is also involved in allusions to gods and goddesses: in the background is a history of relations between deities and mortals. Such stress on the past emphasizes the fact that here, as in *The Princess of Clèves*, no act occurs in isolation. People cannot act independently of other people, as Hippolytus must tragically learn, and they cannot cut themselves loose from what has happened before them. Why is there so much stress in the play on Theseus's womanizing? Sometimes this seems an aspect of his heroism; sometimes it seems a flaw. Hippolytus' attitude toward it emphasizes both his own inadequacy and his moral superiority. It underlines the whole problem of sexual feeling which lies at the drama's heart. Sexuality appears to be the primary source of human vulnerability: it gets Theseus into trouble; it kills Phaedra and Hippolytus; it makes Aricia miserable. It seems to lie outside the control of reason—a fact that must be taken into consideration in any discussion of the function of reason as an ideal in this action. How do issues of power become part of issues of love here? As in *The Princess of Clèves*, private politics reflects public. Not only do actual and potential sexual alliances literally affect government, they too involve complex patterns of dominance and submission which can be traced through the play. And finally, what about the play's ending? Does one believe in the reconciliation that Theseus proposes? How does one feel about Phaedra's final "purity" (the last word she speaks)? Again, there is no "right" answer, but discussion of such problems calls attention to the fact that the play demands, and usually receives, complicated emotional responses from its readers. Such responses reveal that the problems it engages remain dilemmas that concern us all, even though we typically put them in less elevated terms.

## Topics for Writing

1. The role of Oenone

2. The meaning of Hippolytus' death

3. Theseus as a father

4. The emotional effect of any single speech and how it is achieved (for example, Phaedra's speech to Hippolytus, pp. 186–87; Hippolytus to Aricia, pp. 202–03)

5. Phaedra as a strong woman

6. Phaedra as a weak woman

## Further Reading

See also the reading suggestions in the anthology, p. 170.

Burnley, A. M. *Lilith Raging: The Gender Crisis and Alienation in the Theatre of Jean Racine.* 1989.
Strong feminist interpretation.

Cloonan, W. *Racine's Theatre: The Politics of Love.* 1977.
A study of the conflict between the personal emotion of love and the socially accepted ideal of glory which examines the "quest for reconciliation between personal needs and the legitimate obligations which society must impose upon its members."

Goldmann, L. *Racine.* Trans. by A. Hamilton. 1972.
A Marxist analysis which reviews biographical data and studies the development and structure of Racine's drama.

King, R. *Racine: Modern Judgments.* 1969.
Includes pieces on structure, detail, style, and tradition.

Turnell, M. *Jean Racine, Dramatist.* 1972.
A thorough and illuminating study of the "dramatic experience"

Racine provides, with attention to versification and staging as well as theme and structure.

Weinberg, B. *The Art of Jean Racine*. 1963.
An investigation of Racine's dramatic development which demonstrates how the art of each play builds on that of its predecessors.

# SOR JUANA INÉS DE LA CRUZ
## Reply to Sor Filotea de la Cruz

*Classroom Strategies and Topics for Discussion*

Perhaps the most interesting aspect of Sister Juana's polemical *Reply*, from the point of view of modern readers, is its use of autobiography as an element of argument. A class discussion of the work can profitably be organized around this topic.

Such a discussion might start with a question about what the author is arguing for in the essay as a whole—or, as usefully, what she is arguing against. Students may conclude that she wishes to defend the right of women to learning; alternately, that she wants to defend herself against charges of presumption, impiety, or unwomanliness. Other formulations of the grounds of argument are possible, but all will probably fall into one or the other category: arguments about Sister Juana's own role, arguments about the position of women in general. The relation between the two categories—women in general, Sister Juana in particular— provides a way to focus discussion.

The first few pages of the *Reply* consist mainly of apologies, couched in a tone of extreme deference ("my clumsy pen"; "your most prudent, most holy, and most loving letter"). What purpose do they serve in the piece as a whole? Whether or not they are asked to make such a judgment, students are likely to volunteer that Sister Juana does not sound "sincere." Such a comment supplies a useful opening. Is it possible that Sister Juana doesn't *wish* to sound sincere, that she is heavily ironic in her insistence on her own comparative inadequacy and that she wants the irony to show? She thus dramatizes the posture of humility expected of women and suggests her own discontent with it. Increasingly as her essay continues, the reader is forced to realize the discrepancy between her elaborate pose of ignorance and her rhetorical skill.

The autobiographical section of the *Reply* begins with Sister Juana's assertion of her "vehement . . . overpowering" inclination toward learning. It concentrates mainly on her intellectual life—but the intellectual and the emotional merge for this writer, and in a sense that merging is the subject of the autobiography. Students can be asked to locate the various ways and places in which the writer conveys her intense feelings about learning. Does she also communicate emotions about other matters? What is she trying to establish in her "autobiography"? Most autobiographies dwell on a sequence of experience; Sister Juana appears less concerned with experience than with character. She primarily wants us to know not what she has done or what has happened to her, but what kind of person she is. What kind of person *is* she? If students disagree on this matter, the disagreement can be made the starting point for detailed discussion not only of what kind of character emerges from this narrative but of the strategies Sister Juana uses for conveying character.

Autobiography in effect merges with argument at various points—for example, in the paragraph where Sister Juana speaks of the inspiration she has found in books and lists the gifted women who appear in the Bible. Such a passage not only tells us of Sister Juana's reading and her reaction to it, it also contributes to a larger argument about the capacities and rights of women. You might invite your students to locate other passages in which the writer's personal experience—particularly her experience of books—is recorded in ways suggesting her views about the nature of women.

Sister Juana's career is obviously an unusual one, and she presents herself as a phenomenon among women. What makes her "special"? The question is worth considering in some detail: Perhaps one might conclude that her intellectual enthusiasm and capacity are no more remarkable than is her relative lack of interest in the ordinary social life of the convent. Her revelation of genuine passion also helps to define her specialness: the sheer intensity of her feeling, and her willingness to make it known, differentiate her from other women.

But if Sister Juana differs dramatically from others of her sex, the question recurs: How does her autobiography relate to her argument about the status of women in general? A remarkable aspect of the *Reply* is its combination of assertions of uniqueness with the implication that many women, given the opportunity, might display comparable capacities. Indeed, the repeated allusions to the author's inadequacies emphasize her insistence that many women, despite social restrictions, have demonstrated their ability to rule, to teach, to write. She narrates her own struggles to learn as part of an argument that women should routinely receive opportunities for education. What makes her "special," she implicitly argues, is not her intellectual gifts so much as her will to develop them. Her desire for learning which she alludes to as a "torment" and as an "ungovernable force" drives her to surmount the limitations imposed on women.

The *Reply* makes a powerful case for the value of learning in itself—a value equally great for men and for women. Love of wisdom, Sister Juana maintains, constitutes a ground for persecution: people hate the person who claims intellectual authority, who demonstrates intellectual vitality. But the writer herself has been willing to endure obloquy for the sake of her endless mental activity. How does she make the reader feel that the pleasure of thought and writing is worth the pain of social disapproval? It might be worth drawing attention to the passages in which children playing spillikins. Both provide instances of Sister Juana's indefatigable spirit of inquiry; they exemplify the nature of intellectual inquiry in general at the same time that they tell us of this woman's special ways of pursuing it.

### Topics for Writing

1. Examine Sister Juana's use of specific detail as an element in her argument.

2. What is Sister Juana's attitude toward the power of language? How does she convey this attitude; how important is it in her argument as a whole?

3. What is the dominant emotion of the *Reply*? Self-pity? Pride? Anger? Write a paper maintaining the primary importance of one emotion in Sister Juana's essay.

4. Discuss the functions of biblical allusion in the *Reply*.

5. Write an essay in which you use some element or elements in your own experience as the foundation for a serious argument.

### Further Reading

See also the reading suggestions in the anthology, p. 211.

Apart from the Twayne volume cited in the anthology, virtually all the available English-language material on Sor Juana occurs in the context of broader discussions.

Anderson-Imbert, Enrique. *Spanish-American Literature: A History.* Revised by Elaine Malley. Vol. I. Detroit, 1969.
Sets Sor Juana's writing in its historical context.

Henriquez-Urena, Pedro. *Literary Currents in Hispanic America.* Cambridge, Mass, 1945.
Given as the Norton Lectures at Harvard, these essays offer a good introduction to Sor Juana in relation to her contemporaries and her successors.

Montross, Constance M. *Virtue or Vice?: Sor Juana's Use of Thomistic Thought.* 1981.
A fairly technical study of Sor Juana's theological position.

Torres-Rioseco, Arturo. *The Epic of Latin American Literature.* New York, 1942.
Another general treatment which sets Sor Juana in her literary context.

# JONATHAN SWIFT
## Gulliver's Travels

### *Classroom Strategies and Topics for Discussion*

Students may well be bewildered by the sometimes bland, sometimes ferocious tone of *Gulliver's Travels*, Book IV and by such questions as, what is Swift attacking? why? what does it have to do with us? and—most troubling of all—how can we be sure?: exactly the questions that have disturbed generations of critics. It may be useful at the outset to point out that a minimal definition of satire is "attack by indirection" and to discuss the possibility that one important satiric function, often, is to generate just the kind of trouble the students are presumably experiencing. *Gulliver's Travels* creates uncertainty partly because of society's constantly changing assumptions about what is important, what is *good*, for human beings. Swift concerns himself with such fundamental values. If he can make his readers inquire about their own assumptions, as well as about how matters should be, he has achieved part of his aim. His kind of satire does not produce certainties, it produces difficulties.

One can profitably organize discussion around a series of large and obvious questions, with special attention to the need to support hypotheses from the text. First of all, what is the relation between the Yahoos and humankind? In answering (or attempting to answer) this question, one must consider the development of Gulliver's attitude toward them. At the outset, he says, "I never beheld in all my travels so disagreeable an animal, or one against which I naturally conceived so strong an antipathy (p. 248). This response suggests that the Yahoos belong to an alien species. But Gulliver's convictions change, influenced partly by the assumptions of his Houyhnhnm hosts, who believe him to be of the Yahoo kind. The episode in which the young Yahoo girl pursues Gulliver with lustful intent might suggest that they belong to a single species. By the end, Gulliver believes all the rest of humanity to be Yahoos, but appears to exempt himself. He is, at any rate, a Yahoo educated in a way no other human being has enjoyed. If we accept Gulliver's view, we must understand this volume of *Gulliver's Travels* as constituting an unrelenting and total attack on humankind.

The problem of how far we can accept Gulliver's view must be dealt with fairly early in the discussion; it will certainly come up in the course of considering the Yahoo question. Evidence for Gulliver's state of mind after his sojourn with the Houyhnhnms comes from the book's final chapters and from the prefatory letter to Gulliver's cousin Sympson (which students should be urged to read, or to reread, *after* reading the narrative proper). The question can be formulated as one of delusion: is Gulliver deluded after his journey? does his attack on pride only conceal his own pride, his overweening desire to escape the limits of the human situation? In trying to decide how far we can accept his judgment (e.g., his judgment that human beings are Yahoos), one must try to assess the forces possibly operating to distort his judgment: for example, the pressures inherent in the master-slave relationship in which he finds himself.

The obvious corollary to the Yahoo question is the Houyhnhnm question. Whether or not people and Yahoos are the same, do Houyhnhnms represent an ideal for humanity? Considering this matter implies not only further speculation about Gulliver's dependability but direct assessment of the evidence. What are the characteristics of this race? Most salient, of course, is their allegiance to reason. They believe that reason is sufficient guide for a reasonable being. Is this conviction relevant to the realities of human existence? How does one respond to their lack of literature, to their difficulty in finding subject matter for conversation (Gulliver provides useful material for their talk), to such activities as their threading of needles, to their attitudes toward their young? If one has negative responses to any of their manifestations of commitment to reason, do such responses declare something wrong with them or something wrong with us?

The part of the book dealing with Gulliver's activities and responses after leaving the Houyhnhnms deserves particularly close attention. What does it mean, in Swift's satiric structure, that he is wounded by the arrow of savages? Certainly this fact suggests that man in the state of nature is brutal and far from being governed by reason and benevolence. But the character of the Portuguese captain also demands attention. Here is civilized man, acting with generosity and sympathy in the face of Gulliver's boorishness. Does the existence of such a man refute the identification of humanity with the Yahoos? What differences does it suggest between humanity and the Houyhnhnms? If Gulliver seems wrong (misguided) in his response to the captain's kindness, how does this fact bear on our assessment of his judgments?

I have suggested no answers for this series of questions because the answers are largely indeterminate. This fact itself, as I've already indicated, must become an issue for discussion. It brings up a historical problem: does our difficulty in ascertaining where Swift stands come simply from the time that has elapsed since he wrote? One must suspect that shifts in general assumption between the eighteenth and the twentieth century help to account for the problematic aspects of this satire, but the difficulty in determining the exact scope of the attack is also partly built into the text. The historical problem, however, also creates an opportunity to raise the question of how far Swift's satire remains relevant to our own time, in which wars and lawyers and doctors and politicians continue to provide manifestations of folly and vice and in which questions about the human capacity for reason and virtue continue to present themselves.

One problem about teaching *Gulliver's Travels* (it's a problem in teaching everything, of course—but particularly here) is that of time. The general issues I have sketched are peculiarly compelling; and they are *essential* to minimal understanding of the narrative. But Swift's local effects also deserve attention. If time permits, it is useful to take up such episodes as Gulliver's early conduct toward the Houyhnhnms (his assumption that they are to be won by bracelets and mirrors) and his recital to his master about the nature of civilized life. Students need to understand that in the structure of the narrative, Gulliver's account demonstrates considerable distortion and exaggeration, attributable to his desire to impress his master in various ways; and also that, in the structure of the satire, it exemplifies exactly the kind of distortion that generates emotional power. If it is not always clear what designs *Gulliver's Travels* has on the reader in the most general sense, it *is* clear that it attacks specific corruptions of eighteenth-century English society in a way that makes it relevant to our own.

## A Modest Proposal

*Classroom Strategies and Topics for Discussion*

Virtually all teachers have in their repertoire at least one anecdote about trying to teach *A Modest Proposal* to a class all of whose members insisted on taking it straight, unable to comprehend the nature of Swift's irony. As the horrors of the twentieth century multiply, it becomes harder and harder to appeal to universal standards of decency, to insist that of course we all know that no one would really think of eating children. Human skin has been made into lampshades; why shouldn't babies be made into meat? The problems of teaching this work, then, are clear-cut: to help students find the clues to Swiftian irony, and to make them understand what as well as how the satirist attacks.

One way to start is with the character of the speaker. What sort of person does he seem to be? Undergraduates can readily be brought to recognize his self-image as a practical, sensible man, fond of statistics ("three, four, or six Children") and of economic solutions ("a fair, cheap, and easy Method"), not devoid of vanity (he would like to have his statue set up as a preserver of the nation), both self-confident and ambitious (see paragraph 3). Students should be asked to read the opening paragraphs with particular care, and asked what is the first word that begins to make one suspicious about this projector. For most readers, it is *Dam*, in the fourth paragraph, with its suggestion that the speaker thinks of human beings, if they are poor, as identical with lower animals. One can trace further evidence of the projector's inhumanity, his incapacity to imagine the poor (or at least the Irish poor) as beings like himself, throughout the satire.

The speaker objects to his friend's proposal of butchering starving adolescents on the grounds that it might be censured as "a little bordering upon Cruelty." Why does he not think of his own proposal as cruel? This topic is worth extended consideration. One can examine the various ways in which the projector demonstrates the need for drastic measures; the cruelty of the existing state of things, he implicitly and explicitly argues, far exceeds that of his scheme for remedying the situation. Particular attention should be paid to the italicized paragraph of "other Expedients" that Swift would in fact advocate. What are these expedients like? It should be noted that they combine the practical and the moral, that they demand clear perception, concerted action, and steady moral awareness. The speaker's doubt that there will ever be a sincere attempt to put them in practice therefore suggests Swift's criticism of the Irish people as well as of their English oppressors.

This text of course provides abundant opportunity for talking about the classic problems of satire. Students might be interested to discuss the question of whether such writing as this implies any real purpose of reform or whether it constitutes only attack; and they might wish to talk about how the satire makes them feel, and why. (Indeed, such an apparently naive approach to the work might be a profitable way to start.)

### Topics for Writing

1. The importance of Gulliver's initial situation (how he is cast ashore) to the narrative

2. How Gulliver sees himself

3. A specific object of attack and how it is criticized

4. Why are horses (rather than some other species) made creatures of pure reason?

5. A definition of a Yahoo

6. A modest proposal for our time

7. Has Swift any hope for Ireland?

### Further Reading

See also the reading suggestions in the anthology, p. 242.

Donoghue, D. *Jonathan Swift: A Critical Introduction.* 1969.
An interpretation that seeks to avoid relying on irony as the governing mode of Swift's work. Offers detailed exegesis of *Gulliver's Travels* as "an anatomy of human pride."

Ehrenpreis, I. *Swift: The Man, his Works, and the Age.* 3 vols. 1962–1983.
The definitive critical biography. Vol. III, Dean Swift, contains detailed treatments of *Gulliver's Travels* and *A Modest Proposal*: accounts of their composition and publication as well as critical analysis.

Quintana, R. *The Mind and Art of Jonathan Swift.* 1956.
An accessible introduction to Swift. Provides both biographical data and a critical survey of thought and technique.

Reilly, E. J., ed. *Approaches to Teaching Swift's* Gulliver's Travels. 1988.

Immensely useful, pedagogically focused collection of essays.

# ALEXANDER POPE
## The Rape of the Lock

*Classroom Strategies and Topics for Discussion*

This fanciful narrative of trivial pursuits uses its account of a belle's pleasures and conflicts to suggest the moral flaws and the aesthetic values of early eighteenth-century English social life. Its allusions to epic imply intent to comment on the preoccupations of a society—not, of course, "society" in its largest sense, the community of humankind, but the limited aristocratic society of eighteenth-century London, concerned with appearance and with luxury rather than with genuine accomplishment, cut off from realities of human suffering, yet miniaturizing the same desires that drive the heroes of the *Aeneid* or the *Iliad*. One problem you face is to ask students to discover connections between eighteenth-century London society and its twentieth-century American counterpart.

The glittering smoothness of Pope's verse, concealing complexities of thought, sometimes creates the illusion that the poetry is easy to read. It isn't, of course, given its density of meaning, but first-time readers have to be shown that it's worth struggling with. I have found it useful on occasion to spend a good part of a class hour working on a single short passage: for example, the toilette scene at the end of Canto I (121–48). By exploring in depth the implications of such a phrase as "the sacred rites of Pride" (128), one can demonstrate what close attention Pope's language demands, and what rewards it offers. Why are these rites "sacred"? And why, for that matter, are they "rites"? As students begin to realize how completely Belinda (and her society, and ours, and we ourselves) has ritualized everyday procedures, they come to understand why the trivial receives so much emphasis in the poem, and in our own lives. The necessity for putting on make-up is never questioned in Belinda's world, as the order of religious rituals is never questioned. The sequence of rouge and powder and eyeshadow is unvaried, unchallenged. Like other "rites," this one of make-up provides a stay against confusion, an assertion of continuity and of power. Such rites are "sacred" because they participate in a religion of self-love belonging not only to Belinda herself but to the community in which she participates. And they are *called* "sacred" in the poem to remind us of other more significant rites which they trivialize.

If it is possible to spend two class hours on this poem, students might be asked to read it in its entirety for the first meeting, which could concentrate on close reading of a relatively short sequence; the class might read the poem again for the second meeting, and then engage in more general discussion of the poem as a whole.

Students often find the couplet structure monotonous and uninteresting. The best way to disabuse them of the notion that Pope engages in a kind of automatic writing is to ask each to compose a single couplet. The experience of trying to condense meaning into two rhymed pentameter lines usually proves both chastening and enlightening.

Sometimes students assume that *The Rape of the Lock* is as trivial as its subject matter. But of course the trivial can be highly revealing, in Pope's time and in ours. A character who mingles Bibles and love letters on her dressing table bears some resemblance to the student who reads Milton while listening to rock music: incompatible commitments jostle in all our minds. To call attention to such jostling does not imply the commentator's frivolity, but it's usually necessary to spend a good deal of time demonstrating how Pope enforces his criticism of a group which has lost its sense that some values are preferable to others, as well as time talking about why mere "silliness" matters in the moral scheme.

Students can become quite involved in the problem of how to ascertain the poet's precise targets of attack. The famous couplet, "The hungry judges soon the sentence sign, / And wretches hang that jurymen may dine" (p. 314) provides an obvious example of satiric attack, in which the extreme discrepancy between the motivation of judge and jury and the fate of the "wretches" they condemn calls attention to something wrong in society. Discussion might move from this sort of obvious satiric instance to other kinds of discrepancy: between staining one's honor and one's dress, for example, or between the stately elephant and the comb to which its tusks are converted. Pope's discrepancies typically alert the reader to "something wrong"; figuring out just what is wrong and why often proves a valuable enterprise.

One more difficulty troubling to many readers of Pope is that of ascertaining positive value in *The Rape of the Lock*. What does the poet believe in? This is by no means a simple question to answer, but it is a useful one to confront. Clarissa's counsel of good sense provides one standard by which to judge the deviations from the sensible that pervade the poem, but it is not the only standard. Why is the lock taken up into the heavens, why does the poem conclude with stress on its own permanence, why is Belinda's world evoked with such poetic beauty? The answers to all these questions are surely related: the poet, too, appears to believe in the aesthetic, in the necessity and the lastingness of the art that transforms the trivial into the stuff of poetry (or of constellations).

## Topics for Writing

These develop readily from the kinds of discussion suggested above. A few possibilities:

1. The Function of Clarissa's Speech

2. The Importance of the Sylphs

3. The Concept of Manhood in *The Rape of the Lock*

4. What's Wrong with Belinda?

5. Why the Cave of Spleen?

# An Essay on Man

## Classroom Strategies and Topics for Discussion

Students—like other people—often have trouble with the very idea of a philosophic poem: the notion of the "philosophic," they seem to feel, opposes that of the "poetic." The teacher's problem, then, is to demonstrate (or to help the class discover) how Pope reconciles the two modes—a task made more difficult by the fact that the *Essay on Man*, unlike *Paradise Lost*, presents no sustained characters.

As usual, a good place to start is at the beginning, with the introductory section. Students can be asked to locate Pope's images: maze, wild, garden, field, "Nature's walks," "Folly" and "Manners" as birds to be hunted. Then they can discuss how the images' implications expand. Why, for example, is the garden "tempting with forbidden fruit" (8)? The world is thus made analogous to Eden, and humankind, by implication, is in danger of recommitting the original sin of Adam and Eve. Thinking about the rest of Epistle I, students might speculate about what this sin constitutes, how it might be repeated. As the Epistle develops, it increasingly emphasizes the human tendency to pride (and the degree to which this tendency often seems inherent in the very act of presuming to philosophize). Eve too, as readers of *Paradise Lost* may remember, was victimized by pride: the desire to assume a place closer to that of Deity. The introductory section of the *Essay on Man* thus foretells the epistle's argument in specifically metaphoric terms. Reminded of the particular allusion to *Paradise Lost* in line 16, students may wish to reflect about how *vindicate* differs from *justify*, Milton's word: what a different (more combative, more skeptical) universe the change of a verb implies. Enough time should be spent on this section (the development of the hunting metaphor, with its casual tone and purposeful rhetoric, also repays attention; and the conversational, almost joking tone of the opening couplet) for the class to realize that Pope has established a situation and an atmosphere not at all predictable for philosophic verse, and that he has done so by relying on traditional poetic devices.

Students will probably be eager to discuss, even to argue about, the nature of Pope's thought. It is valuable to trace the argument as it develops, section by section, through the epistle, pausing on the question of how connections are made between one point and the next. A useful way to link Pope's method with his subject is to look for persuasive devices. How does the poet seek to convince his audience of the rightness of his view? Aspects of the poem likely to attract comment in this connection include the use of example, both brief images ("die of a rose in aromatic pain" [200]) and more extended vignettes (the poor Indian, or the lamb licking the hand of its slaughterer), and of the sheer power of sound and rhythm as persuasive devices (the concluding passage, for instance). Discussion of the poem's shifting tone would also be appropriate. If asked, after talking about such matters, whether Pope relies more heavily on intellectual or on emotional arguments, students are likely to agree at least that emotional persuasion forms an important part of his agenda: that he works, in this respect, more like what they might expect of a poet than what they might expect of a philosopher.

Another fruitful subject for discussion is the relationship, or series of relationships, established between the narrator and the reader. The section numbered I, for instance, begins in a measured, reasoned tone suggesting the opening of a set of intellectual propositions. By the end of the 18-line section, the narrator is beginning to insult the reader ("Is the great chain, that draws all to agree, / And drawn supports, upheld by God, or thee?" [33–34]) by calling attention to that reader's insignificance in the universe; the next section, emphasizing humankind's pettiness, begins, "Presumptuous Man!" Alternations of didacticism, insult, a kind of cooperative reasoning (see Section V), and inspirational rhetoric (Section VIII) continue through the poem, shifting with bewildering rapidity. Asked to think about this technique in relation to Pope's purposes here, students might conclude that the poet's rhetorical agility calls attention to exactly the problem the epistle's title announces: "The Nature and State of Man, with Respect to the Universe." The dilemma about humanity's nature and state involves the poet as speaker and the reader as listener: neither poet nor reader, it seems, can securely know his or her position. Sometimes the poet appears to understand everything; sometimes he shares the humility he enjoins for the reader; sometimes he substitutes awe for comprehension. Always he dramatizes the human position.

Specific passages worth special attention include the short sequence on the passions (165–72), interesting to discuss as exemplifying Pope's emotional and ideological commitment to necessity for action: the passions may be good or bad in themselves, but they *function* for good because they make things happen. The lines beginning, "All are but parts of one stupendous whole" (267–80) are important for defining Pope's view of the universal scheme in terms that will be useful when one gets to Wordsworth.

## Topics for Writing

1. Why the poor Indian?

2. How the satiric impulse is expressed in the *Essay on Man*

3. A specific image and how it works

4. What does Pope mean by *order*?

5. The function of animals in the poem

## Alexander Pope—Further Reading

See also the reading suggestions in the anthology, p. 306.

Damrosch, L. *The Imaginative World of Alexander Pope.* 1987.
    Fresh and provocative new readings of the poems.

# FRANÇOIS-MARIE AROUET DE VOLTAIRE
## Candide, or Optimism

*Classroom Strategies and Topics for Discussion*

Its combination of metaphysical and social satire makes *Candide* both exciting and problematic. What is the connection between pointing out the barbarities of war and of organized religion (themes also of Swift in *Gulliver's Travels*) and calling attention to the possible fatuities of philosophic optimism (by exaggerating and simplifying ideas like those in the *Essay on Man*)? How does Voltaire persuade us to tolerate, and even to laugh at, recitals of incredible horror? If such questions are too large and forbidding for students (or anyone else), answers to them can at least be approached by discussing specific aspects of *Candide*.

To begin with the first chapter: a useful exercise is to try collectively to separate sentences with satiric bite from those (like the first) that seem intended quite seriously. There will probably be dispute about at least a few examples—a development that can profitably lead to questions about how one decides. Even if everyone agrees about everything, the group can discuss how they know what is straightforward and what satiric. Such discussion should include consideration of the matter of assumed common standards. We all agree, presumably, that for a woman to weigh three hundred and fifty pounds is not sufficient reason for her to be respected, and that the congruity of noses and spectacles is not part of the order of nature. What is worth emphasizing is that we share these assumptions, and many others, with Voltaire, and that he can and does draw on them in constructing his satiric fiction: moreover, that without at least some vestige of such shared standards, we would be unable to recognize satire. This point is important for students to understand, both because it helps them to realize that the gap between the eighteenth and twentieth centuries is not in every respect so great as they imagine and because it is absolutely fundamental to an understanding of satire.

Candide's experiences in the Bulgar army typify central patterns of Voltaire's work. You might call the class's attention to the enormous speed of the narrative (other sequences of the fiction would of course work equally well to demonstrate this aspect of Voltaire's technique). Detailed discussion of effects generated by this speed is likely to prove profitable. For instance, it's worth pointing out that the failure to linger over gruesome details helps to suggest that they are not too serious after all. Their lack of apparent "seriousness" of course depends on their emphatic fictionality: because the narrator himself seems unconcerned, seems to think these things don't matter much, we are reminded that they belong to the realm of imagination. If they had really happened, they would horrify the narrator and the reader alike. The speed of movement also has a comic effect: the sheer incongruity between the dreadfulness of what allegedly happens and the gusto and rapidity with which reports of the dreadful pile up makes us smile. Consideration of this sort of effect enlarges understanding of the workings of satire, which typically depends on exaggeration and unmistakable distancing from the actual to enforce its comments. In this connection, it is perhaps worth inquiring whether the literal horrors of twentieth-century war, far in excess of anything Voltaire has imagined, have any effect on our response to Voltairean satire.

A large question that will both interest students and draw them closer to the workings of this fiction concerns the functions of sex in the narrative. What purpose does the stress on sexual feeling and action serve? As in *Phaedra*, although of course with tonality as different as possible, sexuality makes people vulnerable. It is a form of feeling all men and women share, a defining aspect of animal nature but also, in some of its specific expressions, of human nature. The relation between animality and humanity is a recurrent theme of *Candide*; students might be asked to find examples of it. In this respect and others, the sexual expressiveness of men and women epitomizes kinds of paradox that interest Voltaire. Sexuality involves both weakness and strength, pleasure and pain, physical disease and psychic health, human connection and violation, and so on. Students can find instances of apparently contradictory values associated with sex, and can move from these to realization of how *Candide* constructs a notion of humanity far too complicated to be contained in a Panglossian scheme of things.

What keeps one reading this narrative? Answers to this question are likely to differ greatly from responses to a comparable question in relation to *Rasselas*. Voltaire generates genuine suspense, not so much about his characters (who, as students will readily see, are almost as devoid of individuation as are Johnson's), as about the workings of his imagination. What will he think of next, what further excess will he conjure up? What explanation will he find for the fact that the old woman has only one buttock? Our interest in the operations of the satirist's fancy intensifies satiric effect: as we realize that we are enjoying images of rape, murder, treachery, violence, we are presumably led to reflect on the real occurrences of such phenomena in our own world, on how we respond to them (when, for example, they are reported on TV), and on the implications of our capacity to tolerate horrors when they happen to other people.

But another point that should be discussed is the incursions of realism into this text. In what ways, to what extent, does Voltaire rely on realistic insights? In Chapter 14, Candide laments, "Cune'gonde, brought from so far, what will ever become of you?" "'She'll become what she can', said Cacambo; 'women can always find something to do with themselves; God sees to it; let's get going'" (p. 361). Cacambo's kind of practicality accepts the limitations of a fiercely competitive world and acknowledges the need for dealing with the given. (Her attribution of women's instinct for self-preservation to God is another matter, more closely related to Voltaire's satiric pattern.) The kind of comment we might call "realistic" is here typically a general observation on human nature or habits drawn from the exaggerated experience of the protagonists. Students can easily multiply examples. In this way—by offering generalizations of which we recognize the cogency—Voltaire keeps his satire rooted in truths we can acknowledge. (Again, the matter of shared assumptions between author and reader is relevant.)

Increasingly toward the end of the tale, the narrative dwells on human corruption (e.g., the shooting of admirals, the deposing of kings, the various operations of avarice, lust, envy, competitiveness). In the last chapter, "Pangloss asserted that he had always suffered horribly; but having once declared that everything was marvelously well, he continued to repeat the opinion and didn't believe a word of it" (p. 400). By the time we are told directly that Pangloss doesn't believe his own philosophic contentions, we have been brought to realize that philosophic optimism (here parodied as the view that everything is for the best in this best of all possible worlds) itself amounts to one of the constructions human beings make to protect themselves from reality—like Pococurante's belief that nothing is of value, Candide's declarations of love for Cune'gonde; and like the human propensity for war, thievery, and rape, all of which constitute modes of asserting or acquiring power and importance. Political arrangements and philosophic beliefs, the work has shown, have a good deal in common. It is useful to compare the ending of *Candide* with that of *Rasselas*, to try to define the nature of achieved wisdom in each text and how its achievement is managed.

## Topics for Writing

1. Could Voltaire satirize Hitler?

2. An exercise in Voltairean satire (i.e., student attempts in the mode)

3. What Candide learns

4. A moment of comedy and how its effect contributes to the satire

5. The function of some minor character

6. The relation of the conclusion to the beginning

### Further Reading

See also the reading suggestions in the anthology, p. 336.

Aldridge, A. *Voltaire and the Century of Light.* 1975.
The biographical treatment emphasizes both personality and thought, "combining the methods of comparative literature and the history of ideas."

Torrey, N. *The Spirit of Voltaire.* 1938.
Provides a biographical treatment with emphasis on Voltaire's intellectual life and development.

Wade, I. *The Intellectual Development of Voltaire.* 1969.
Supplies an exhaustive examination of Voltaire's intellectual life.

Waldinger, R., ed. *Approaches to Teaching Voltaire's* Candide. 1989.
This collection of essays by many authors, published by the Modern Language Association, is designed to help teachers in the classroom.

# SAMUEL JOHNSON
## Rasselas

*Classroom Strategies and Topics for Discussion*

What often makes *Rasselas* puzzling to modern readers is the nature of its status as fiction. On the one hand, it offers a fanciful setting at the outset, a kind of latter day Eden, and presents a series of clearly imaginary characters traveling and having diverse experiences in a way familiar to any reader of picaresque fiction. On the other hand, the characters all sound roughly the same—their voices are not really differentiated—and nothing that happens to them makes much difference: it only provides material for elaborate semi-philosophical reflection. The best way of tackling this problem, I suspect, is to confront it directly, to ask students to think about what kind of fiction this is. The terminology doesn't matter (to explain that this is a "philosophical tale" only obscures the difficulty of reading it); what matters is trying to figure out what Johnson is doing here and why.

So a good place to start is to ask how the characters are distinguished from one another. It's useful to read aloud, say, a speech by Nekayah and one by Rasselas, and to inquire how one tells the difference. In some instances (as when Nekayah investigates private life and Rasselas public), difference in immediate experience produces differences in what they say, but there is little contrast in the way they say it. Similarly, Imlac differs from the others in having had more experience before the escape from the Happy Valley, but only in that respect. One has little sense of distinct personality in any of the travelers. What degree of interest do their adventures generate? The only real suspense concerns their efforts to find out what they should do in life, and it comes as little surprise that they reach no firm conclusion.

Once a group agrees, as it almost certainly will, that Johnson's characters all sound alike and that their adventures elicit no suspense to speak of and little excitement, the next obvious question is what Johnson is trying to accomplish here. He does not appear to have conventional fictional purposes; it is not hard to decide that his intent is didactic. But what is he trying to teach, and why does he choose this particular method of instruction?

These large questions may be announced fairly early, but they will only be answered by close attention to what is going on in the text. The Happy Valley section offers some interesting problems. Does one feel that Rasselas is wise or mistaken in wanting to get away? How does the language of the narrative generate a feeling of uneasiness about this idyllic setting? Students can be asked to find the words that suggest something wrong here—words like *imprisonment* and *tediousness*. It's useful to call attention to the degree of effort that seems to be involved in making the place attractive for its inhabitants. Rasselas's experience of boredom is convincingly rendered. But if one sympathizes with the young man's desire to escape his benign environment, what does such sympathy mean? Is the point that humankind, in its imperfection, cannot be happy with perfection? Or is there really something wrong with the Happy Valley? Perhaps the best answer to these questions is Imlac's observation, in relation to his own life, that "some desire is necessary to keep life in motion" (p. 410).

Imlac's narrative of his past experience is worth close attention. He reaches the conclusion, in one of Johnson's best-known formulations, that "Human life is every where a state in which much is to be endured, and little to be enjoyed" (p. 417). Although the actual events of his earlier life bear little relation to those the travelers will undergo, it can be argued that his brief autobiography is a miniature version of what happens later in the narrative. Students can be asked to support or refute this contention by reference to the text. A specific point worth attending to is the famous dissertation on poetry. How does that relate to what happens later, to the argument as a whole? It announces the discrepancy between the imagined and the actual which the rest of the story will reiterate in many different ways; when students see that point, they will begin to see how ingeniously Johnson has enforced a consistent vision of life.

To substantiate that vision is, of course, the didactic function of the tale. If class discussion does not arrive at the conclusion that *Rasselas* is primarily concerned to explore the power and the danger of the imagination, the instructor can suggest this view as a hypothesis. Then the group can look at any single episode, or any group of episodes, to see how the idea is embodied (the philosopher unable to face the death of his child—he has constructed a set of theories with no relation to actuality; the mad astronomer, who has a vision of himself equally unrelated to the real; the pyramids, which show the imaginative boldness of an ancient people vainly trying to surmount the limitations of mortality; and so on). Even at the narrative's end, when the protagonists are disillusioned, they retain shreds of their own imaginative compulsions. (Any adequate discussion of this tale will of course confront the problem of the ending: what does it mean that the travelers return to Abyssinia? Are they going back to the Happy Valley? If so, why?)

But the final question remains: if this is in fact a treatise on the imagination, why cast it in the form of a fiction? If earlier discussion has concluded that characters are differentiated largely on the basis of their experience, the matter of experience is worth returning to at the end. Johnson's differentiations imply that experience is essential to the making of a human being. Experience is an important value in *Rasselas*; the gaining of experience—experience of events and of other people—appears to be the only way for people to combat in themselves the hunger of imagination. The mad astronomer, after all, loses his delusion only by associating with others. Johnson's use of a fictional form, a form dependent on the idea of characters if not of individually distinguished character, declares his conviction that abstract truths have no meaning: they mean only as they are experienced. He demonstrates (or at least outlines) the process of learning in his characters; he hopes to induce a comparable process in his readers, who have the benefit of vicarious experience through the fictional model.

### Topics for Writing

1. Johnson's arguments against the pursuit of happiness

2. Rasselas as an idealist

3. What does Rasselas learn?

4. The importance of the pyramids in the narrative

5. How happy is the Happy Valley?

### Further Reading

See also the reading suggestions in the anthology, pp. 404–05.

Bate, W. J. *Samuel Johnson.* 1977.
    Likely to remain the best biography since Boswell, exhaustive in critical exploration of Johnson's work as well as in supplying data

# Masterpieces of
# the Nineteenth Century
## Varieties of Romanticism

## JEAN-JACQUES ROUSSEAU
### Confessions

*Classroom Strategies and Topics for Discussion*

The aspect of Rousseau's autobiographical writing likely to interest students most, even in a fragmentary selection, is the author's determination to create a mythology of the self. Class time can profitably be occupied in tracing elements in Rousseau's systematic development of a self-image that coincides with his notion of what a man should be. Most important, perhaps, is his emphasis on his "passions" as defining a central aspect of his nature. Students may be asked to locate occurrences of the word and the concept of passion. The writer claims for himself "unique" knowledge of the passions as a child-reader; he celebrates his own passion for music; he characterizes himself as "a man of very strong passions," which take total command of his personality; he suggests that no one has ever possessed passions "at once more lively and purer" than his own; he boasts his "lively and tumultuous passions"; and so on. Everyone has passions (meaning strong feelings), of course; why does Rousseau believe his own feelings so important? As students speculate about this question, it would be worth suggesting that they think back to the eighteenth-century texts they have read, and the very different valuation of the passions expressed or hinted in them. In *Phaedra*, for example, passion is the enemy of reason and of civil order; in *Gulliver's Travels* IV, it belongs only to Yahoos; in *The Princess of Clèves*, it is something to be rigidly controlled. If *An Essay on Man* indicates that passion generates action, it also suggests the need for restraint. Such reminders will emphasize that Rousseau's self-glorification on the basis of his own intense and uncontrollable passion implies a new value-system. Possible answers to the question about why Rousseau assigns such importance to his passions include the hypothesis that strong feelings are associated with "naturalness" and with authenticity. Even when Rousseau says of himself that he is marked by "sluggishness of thought" along with his "liveliness of feeling," he describes himself as a man whose thought readily becomes inextricably mixed with feeling; the resulting "agitation" testifies once more to his status as a being un-corrupted because uncontrolled.

Other aspects of his personality that Rousseau emphasizes include his imagination, his attachment to nature, his commitment to impulse, his interest in the common people. Each of these characteristics could also become subjects of discussion that might dwell on how this writer differs from his eighteenth-century predecessors. Possibly even more fruitful would be examination of the idea of uniqueness in the *Confessions*. The book opens, of course, with the author's claim of absolute distinction ("If I am not better, at least I am different" [p. 452]). In Book II, however, Rousseau observes, "I have been reproached with wanting to pose as an original, and different from others. In reality, I have never troubled about acting like other people or differently from them" (p. 455). And in Book VI, instead of asserting his difference, he *wonders* about whether others share his ideas. Is it possible to reconcile these claims? One can, of course, emphasize the verb *pose* in the second sequence: Rousseau doesn't want to *pose* as an original, he simply *is* one. But the question of posing or acting is a useful one to bring up in connection with the *Con-fessions*. Is all Rousseau's self-presentation perhaps a form of posing? His wondering about other people acknowledges the mystery of unique-ness. In fact, no one can possibly know whether he or she is different from everyone else. So to claim difference, as Rousseau does at the outset, necessarily involves a kind of posing. But is that necessarily a bad thing? Such questions can obviously lead to consideration of the perplex-ing problem of what autobiography as a genre implies.

Rousseau himself directly brings up the problem of autobiographical narrative in the selection quoted from Book VI. He suggests the difficulty of communicating the source of feeling, the impossibility of making narrative equivalent to memory. Students may be asked to assess the de-gree to which he in fact solves these problems. Does he convincingly evoke feeling and memory? If so, how?

## Topics for Writing

A useful paper assignment is to ask students to write a fragment of their own "confessions." Other possibilities:

1. The place of imagination for Rousseau

2. Rousseau's evocation of Paris

3. A description of the child Rousseau

## Further Reading

See also the reading suggestions in the anthology, p. 452.

Crocker, L. *Jean-Jacques Rousseau.* 2 vols. 1963.
An exhaustive and perceptive treatment of Rousseau's life and works.

France, P. *Rousseau, Confessions.* 1987.
A critical study entirely focused on the *Confessions.*

Gremsley, R. *Jean-Jacques Rousseau: A Study in Self-Awareness.* 1961.
Provides psychological analysis of Rousseau's personality.

Guéhenno, J. *Jean-Jacques Rousseau.* Translated by J. and D. Weightman. 2 vols. 1966.
Another excellent critical biography (its treatment of the *Confessions* is confined to volume II).

Havens, G. *Jean-Jacques Rousseau.* 1978.
In the Twayne series. A rather pedestrian but useful general introduction.

# JOHANN WOLFGANG VON GOETHE
## Faust

*Classroom Strategies and Topics for Discussion*

As the "type characters" in Molière and Johnson are likely to create problems for student readers, so are the personages of Goethe's *Faust*. You can simplify the task of reading this work (probably in two assignments, the first one ending just before the first appearance of Margaret, p. 519), by explaining that *Faust* can best be read as a philosophic poem. Its characters exemplify positions rather than display developed personalities. Such positions, however, can be very complex indeed; a good place to start discussion of the play is by trying to elucidate together the set of attitudes and assumptions that Faust himself embodies.

What, first of all, about his attitude toward knowledge? Those who know Marlowe's *Dr. Faustus* (in volume I of the anthology) or other versions of the Faust legend may anticipate that the protagonist will seek intellectual grasp or comprehension of the universe. In fact, it is Faust's rather foolish and obtuse assistant Wagner who "should like to know all." Faust, on the other hand, proclaims that "We can know nothing." He adds immediately, "It burns my heart" (p. 467). Does he mean that the knowledge he has gained all seems irrelevant to his purposes? or that none of it means anything? or what? Detailed analysis of his first speech will announce the chief problems of his role. *Why* can he not presume to make use of his learning, or open his mind to improve humankind? No answer is immediately given in the text; students should be urged to support speculations based on later passages and actual textual evidence. They may well conclude—even on the basis of the first speech as a whole—that Faust cannot use his learning or improve humankind because learning has nothing to do with reality and because people exist only in individual isolation.

As the first speech continues, it becomes ever clearer that Faust wishes not to gain more knowledge but to escape the knowledge he has acquired. He wants to stop "rummaging in phrases," to unite himself with nature, "casting dusty knowledge overboard," to participate in the world rather than deal with "skeletons" (books and theories). A useful question is how the concepts that seem important to Faust compare with those apparently important to Rousseau. Nature and imagination are key ideas here too; the common people are valued (in the scene where Faust walks in the village), and so is feeling. But Faust dwells on these ideas in more meditative and detailed fashion than does Rousseau. Rousseau assumes their authority; Faust comes closer to arguing it. The question of his heroic stature is perhaps best postponed until students have finished reading the entire play, but it is worth inquiring even at the outset what kind of impression his passionate investment in his own convictions makes on first-time readers.

An important early piece of action is Faust's near-suicide. What impels him to kill himself? One way of answering this question (there are of course others, and students should be encouraged to find them) is to say that he cannot tolerate the gap between his capacity to imagine and his capacity to act. He can conceive of great possibilities for himself, but the realities of experience and of other people keep frustrating them. (This source of pain is best articulated in the soliloquy beginning "Hope never seems to leave those who affirm" p. 473.) The choir of angels he hears saves him from self-destruction; why? Its meaning seems less to concern religion than memory— "these chords, which I have known since infancy." Memory involves reminiscences of past faith, and perhaps of past community.

Faust, like Rousseau, considers himself unique, superior to others. Mephistopheles presents himself as "the spirit that negates," and Faust, accepting him, implicitly denies himself association with his kind. An important issue for class discussion of the first reading assignment is Faust's pact with the devil. Why does he voluntarily accept death and damnation if ever he stretches himself on a bed of sloth? This is a complicated and important question. In assessing why Faust in effect equates sloth and death, students should be urged to think, for example, of the scene in which he amends the Bible, denying the power of the Word as originating force, replacing Word with Mind, then with Force, then with Act. As Faust says shortly after making his compact, "Restless activity proves a man." A little later, he makes it clear that he values no effect that fails to result in "new strength within." The class should consider such statements (and others) as evidence for the high value Faust attaches to *effort* and *force* and *action* as defining characteristics of the truly human. His aspiration involves the need constantly to *do*, without much regard for what the doing specifically involves.

When Margaret enters the play, its emphasis changes. Discussion of the second assignment might begin with the figure of Margaret. In her first appearance, she seems rather spunky ("I . . . can go home without your care" p. 519), but once Mephistopheles begins plotting on Faust's behalf to get her, she loses obvious force of character. What is her function in the play? Neither great beauty nor great intelligence is assigned her; she epitomizes virtue but falls easily to Faust. One way of understanding her (students may generate this hypothesis themselves, or be asked what they think of it) is as a projection of Faust's desires. What does he want in a woman? He rhapsodizes over the neatness of her room; he praises her as an "angel." If he himself wants to act and desire without ceasing, he appears to wish for a woman who will do neither except in response to him. Margaret fills his needs because she so readily makes him the center of her universe (he is already the center of his own). But at the end of Part I, she transcends his construction of her. Is her refusal of his rescue attempt psychologically and morally plausible? The question admits of much debate. One can at least argue that her reaffirmation of the moral authority of her religion and her community both fits with her previously demonstrated need for self-subordination and shows how, in the play's logic, a sense of guilt (which Faust is only beginning to develop) can be liberating. Certainly the voice from above that pronounces her "redeemed" suggests that her misery results in a happy ending.

Obviously important to the structure and the argument of *Faust* is Mephistopheles, worth attention both for the way that his moral position is established and elaborated and for the relation of that position to Faust's. A crude way to put the contrast between him and Faust might be to suggest that he always takes a cynical view of experience and Faust often takes an idealistic one. Discussion of this point might begin with investigation of the dialogue just before the scene in Martha's garden, where Faust, in Mephistopheles's summary of his viewpoint, speaks his "soul's profoundest love" and his devilish companion suggests that such talk is only a way to "Deceive poor Gretchen" (p. 530). Faust protests his truth and declares his flame of love "everlasting"; Mephistopheles insists that he, the cynic, is right; and Faust concludes, "You are right, because I have no choice." Faust believes himself to be making only a verbal concession; he doesn't deeply acknowledge his companion's rightness. But one brilliant aspect of this play is the way it demonstrates the partial accuracy of many points of view. Faust's conviction of the absolute authenticity and authority of his own feelings is from one viewpoint naive and self-centered; from another, it affirms the value of the emotional capacity that presumably helps to differentiate humanity from the lower animals. Conversely, Mephistopheles's cynicism is entirely too easy—

everything in experience is obviously susceptible to his kind of criticism; the value of feeling and aspiration can in the nature of things never be proved. But it also calls attention to the equivalent "easiness" in Faust's protestations. Students can be led toward an understanding of the relationship of cross-commentary between Faust and Mephistopheles by beginning with an apparently simple but engaging question: How do you feel toward Mephistopheles? The next question, obviously, is: Do your feelings change? If so, when, and why? The various answers such questions will generate will lead the group back to the text to look particularly at the various sequences of dialogue between Faust and his betrayer.

Other issues worth attending to include the importance of the supernatural in the play—What is gained by casting this drama in terms of God and devil? Could the same story be told as well in other terms?—and the function of the various minor characters.

### Topics for Writing

1. Why the witches?

2. How does the figure of Martha clarify that of Margaret?

3. Is Faust a hero?

4. How does Margaret affect Faust?

5. The importance of feeling

6. The importance of imagination

7. What nature means in this play

### Further Reading

See also the reading suggestions in the anthology, p. 464.

Dieckmann, L. *Johann Wolfgang Goethe.* 1974.
  In the Twayne series. Particularly good, "intended as a guide to close reading," and offering a chapter on Faust.

Fairley, B. *Goethe as Revealed in His Poetry*. 1932; reprinted 1963.
Includes two chapters on Faust, one arguing that the entire play
rather than merely its hero must be understood as dramatizing a
process of development, the other on Faust as a manifestation of
Goethe's lyricism.

Friedenthal, R. *Goethe: His Life and Times*. 1965.
Concentrates on the poet's life and his social and historical context
rather than on his works.

McMillan, D. J., ed. *Approaches to Teaching Goethe's* Faust. 1987.
Varied and useful essays.

Stearns, M. Goethe: *Pattern of Genius*. 1967.
Predominantly biographical in emphasis, also offers detailed
analysis of Faust.

# WILLIAM BLAKE

### *Classroom Strategies and Topics for Discussion*

In teaching Blake, as with all lyric poets, one must spend a good deal of time—probably, most of the available time—attending to local effects. But there are also large matters that attract attention. It is often useful to students (because it provides a kind of orientation that helps in reading individual poems) to point out in advance that Blake's lyrics are marked by their mixture of social and metaphysical awareness. If students have heard this suggestion before they read the assignment, they may be prepared to begin discussion by pointing out specific examples of the combination. (Good ones occur in "The Little Black Boy," "The Chimney Sweeper" [both versions], "London," and "And Did Those Feet.") Then the class can talk about how Blake achieves this unusual merging of concern, and how successful it is. Such discussion will lead naturally to detailed investigation of individual lyrics. Here are a few questions I have found useful for some of the poems.

### "Introduction"

It is enlightening to consider the "Introduction" to *Songs of Innocence* and that to *Songs of Experience* together, seeking similarities and contrasts between them. Both poems define a poet's role. How does that role differ in the two poems? Matters worth attention are the poet's subject matter and tone in each case ("happy" songs—the word occurs three times, along with related terms like "pleasant glee," "laughing," "joy"— about a Lamb or about "chear," versus visionary songs from a "weeping" Bard who sings in order to appeal to "the lapsed Soul"); the kinds of communication anticipated (to "Every child" or to Earth and the Soul); the imagined function of poetry (to create emotional effect, to redeem the fall of man). Students might be asked about the differences in the level of diction and syntactical complexity, and about the effects generated by these differences. Finally, one might inquire what kind of volume each introduction appears to introduce.

## "The Lamb"

This lyric is useful as a basis for discussing what "innocence" means in Blake's mythology. The lamb, as students should know or be told, is a traditional symbol of Christ. It is also, like the little child, associated with innocence. What is the effect of the childlike diction and repetition in this poem? They create a kind of incantatory effect which almost forces the reader to attend to the speaker's sense of a wondrous universe. The simplest phenomena, to a child's sensibility, can seem astonishing; Blake tries to recreate the feeling of innocent astonishment. Innocence thus becomes a mode of perception—as it appears to be in all the poems of the volume. Discussion can move on in this way to other poems: What is the perspective of innocence in each case? How does it work?

## "Earth's Answer"

The combination of abstract and concrete diction here may interest students. Such phrases as "grey despair" and "Starry Jealousy" (extremely difficult to explicate) exemplify the way that Blake tries to make abstractions part of the physical world. This is a very hard poem to understand. It's valuable, therefore, to show students that they probably understand more than they think they do. One can go through the lyric, stanza by stanza, asking what impression each leaves. Most readers will comprehend the general situation—this is a lamentation by imprisoned Earth. To what does it "answer"? The "Introduction," just before, ends with an appeal to Earth to "Arise" and participate in a process of redemption. This answer involves Earth's explanation of why she cannot arise—because of emotional, not political, enemies which oppose love and growth.

## "The Tyger"

The poem is convenient to consider in conjunction with "The Lamb" as a transformation of the same sense of wonder into terms of experience rather than innocence. What kind of emotion does it generate in the reader? What is the effect of the peculiar syntax in line 12 ("What dread hand? & what dread feet?")? How does the rest of the poem account for the change in verb in the last lines of the first and the last stanzas (*could* to *dare*)?

## Topics for Writing

1. One of Blake's characters (e.g. the chimney sweeper, the child on the cloud, or the speaker in any of the poems)

2. What is the city like?

3. Blake's use of nature

## Further Reading

See also the reading suggestions in the anthology, pp. 571–72.

Frye, N. *Fearful Symmetry*. 1947.
Sees Blake as developing a unified myth through his poetry. (See Hirsch, cited in the anthology, for an opposing view.)

Gleckner, R. *The Piper and the Bard*. 1959.
Treats *Songs of Innocence* and *Songs of Experience* as dividing naturally into groups organized by common images and themes.

Gleckner, R. F. and M. L. Greenberg, eds. *Approaches to Teaching Blake's* Songs of Innocence and Experience. 1989.
Another invaluable collection.

O'Neill, J., ed. *Critics on Blake*. 1970.
A work specifically intended for undergraduates. Includes a smattering of criticism from 1803 to 1941 as well as several later essays; its essays concentrate on *Songs of Innocence* and *Songs of Experience*.

# FRANÇOIS RENÉ, VICOMTE DE CHATEAUBRIAND
## René

*Classroom Strategies and Topics for Discussion*

To consider *René* as narrative is one way of directing attention to the work's special qualities. What elements in the piece maintain the reader's interest? This might be a provocative opening question; it of course risks the answer that *nothing* holds one's interest, that *René* is boring to read. Even this response, however, provides a useful starting point for discussion. Here, after all, is a story turning on incestuous feelings between a brother and a sister—a sensational theme. Yet Chateaubriand appears to go out of his way to make his tale as unsensational as possible; he buries the information about the sister's desires so completely that the inattentive reader might miss it altogether. Why does he seem actively to suppress the narrative elements that, from a modern point of view, would seem the most likely ways to engage a reader?

An obvious answer might be that the writer cares more about conveying certain ideas and attitudes than about telling a story. Why, then, does he choose to use a story as his means of communicating them? Or, to put the question in other terms, what ideas does he express in this way that he would have difficulty expressing in any other? Any discussion of these issues must of course begin with an effort to define what ideas and attitudes emerge as centrally important in *René*. Possible formulations might include: the corruption of society, the superiority of uncivilized to "civilized" existence, the pleasures of melancholy, the necessary isolation of the sensitive individual, the imaginative power of nature, the self-sufficient value of emotional intensity, the impossibility (for the sensitive soul) of finding full satisfaction on earth. Clearly, abstract discussion of such issues could hardly be as persuasive as a treatment that evokes a *specific* "sensitive individual" and dramatizes his or her plight. All the ideas articulated and implied in *René* concern the nature of personal experience; they depend upon the assumption that only individual experience matters. The way that the city impinges on a young man's consciousness concerns Chateaubriand; the activities, architecture, sound of the city in itself interest him not at all. Indeed, even the accounts of nature in this narrative are strikingly generalized: nature doesn't matter either; what matters is how it affects René. So the presence of a *character* is obviously essential to Chateaubriand's purposes, and the existence of a character implies that something will happen to him—a minimal basis for story. Some such minimal sense of the meaning of narrative seems implied by this account. But why introduce the sensationalism of incestuous feeling? What, in other words, does incestuous feeling mean in the context here established?

The sister's inadmissible desire for her brother, never acted upon, never openly acknowledged, dramatizes the impossibility of emotional fulfilment for such fine spirits as René and Amelia. Other elements in the narrative reiterate the same sense of impossibility. René cannot find contentment no matter what he does. The wilderness satisfies him hardly more than the city; following his counselor's advice does him no particular good. When he thinks Amelia doesn't care about him, he feels melancholy; when he knows she cares about him entirely too much, his sadness only changes its focus. *René* might be described as a narrative of impossibility—a fact helping to account for its curious languidness of tone, which expresses the futility of attempting to engage energy toward any particular objective in a world guaranteed to frustrate attempts.

Yet this work contains a certain amount of social commentary. What is the relation between its insistence that meaningful action always proves impossible and its critical orientation toward what humanity collectively has done? The individual with delicate feelings—exemplified not only by René but by the narrator who tells his story—is capable of perceiving the evils of a corrupt society but not of remedying them. The power of perception has value in itself; it derives partly from the emotional capacity that René demonstrates in his every response. Chateaubriand celebrates consciousness—the consciousness that generates story, that creates feeling.

### Topics for Writing

1. Discuss the importance of René's two interlocutors in conveying the effect and communicating the meaning of Chateaubriand's story.

2. Discuss the techniques by which Chateaubriand evokes natural scenes here. Try to specify the purposes served by each particular strategy you locate.

3. To what extent does René have a specific character? Discuss the ways in which he is characterized and possible reasons for the traits he is assigned.

4. Try to define the predominant feeling evoked by *René* and to indicate the ways in which this feeling is conveyed.

### Further Reading

See also the reading suggestions in the anthology p. 580.

Call, M. J. *Back to the Garden: Chateaubriand, Senancour, and Constant.* 1988.
Treats Chateaubriand in relation to other French writers, emphasizing the issue of social change.

Sieburg, F. *Chateaubriand.* 1961.
Translated from German, a thorough critical study.

Switzer, Richard. *Chateaubriand Today.* Madison, Wis., 1970.
Studies in French and in English reassessing Chateaubriand in relation to the twentieth century.

Switzer, Richard, ed. *Chateaubriand: Proceedings of the Commemoration of the Bicentary of the Birth of Chateaubriand.* Geneva, 1970.
Essays by various authors treating many aspects of Chateaubriand's work.

Walker, T. C. *Chateaubriand's Natural Scenery.* 1946.
As the title indicates, this study stresses the complex importance of nature in Chateaubriand's work.

# WILLIAM WORDSWORTH

*Classroom Strategies and Topics for Discussion*

As some students may know already, William Wordsworth has a special position as the announcer of Romanticism in England (in the preface to *Lyrical Ballads*). You should probably suggest before they begin reading that they will find in his poetry an even more emphatic stress on nature than Rousseau and Goethe offered, and equivalent attention to the importance of the self and its feelings. Students might also be alerted in advance to the significance of memory and of childhood as Wordsworthian themes. A few suggestions about the two long poems follow.

## "Lines Composed a Few Miles Above Tintern Abbey"

As so often with poetry, it is illuminating to read a passage aloud at the outset and to talk about the effect of the verse form. If students have just been reading Blake, they will hardly be prepared for the leisurely, ruminative rhythms of the blank verse which by its very movement helps to establish the contemplative tone of the poem. Talking about the introductory section (1–21), you might inquire about the speaker's attitude toward appearances created by human beings as opposed to those of nature. The orchard tufts that "lose themselves / 'Mid groves and copses" epitomize a pattern as the poet subsumes human artifacts into the natural world, making the hedge-rows seem like bits of wood, the farmhouse smoke seem like a hermit's smoke, and so on. Observation of this fact prepares readers for the complicated attitude toward the human that develops as the poem goes on. One can trace throughout the poem the ways in which the speaker approaches and retreats from connection with the human: he speaks of acts of kindness and of love, but immediately moves on to something "more sublime"—a mood which enables him to forget the body, become all soul, and see into the life of things. The "fretful stir" of the third section suggests real antipathy to the human. Nourishment comes from the natural ("in this moment there is life and food / For future years" [64–65]); Nature guards the heart and soul and moral being. But the poem is resolved by an address to his sister. The ending is worth dwelling on: Does it in fact resolve the problems the poem has established? What are those problems? One of them, certainly, is the speaker's relation to others of his kind. Another is the loss implicit in growing up (students can be asked to find evidence for this notion). Yet another is the difficulty of preserving in memory what is lost in experience. How does the final section answer these problems? Or does it only evade them? How convincing is Wordsworth's evocation of nature as a moral force? How does his vision of "something far more deeply interfused" (96) compare with the evocation of universal "oneness" at the end of the first epistle of *An Essay on Man*?

### "Ode: Intimations of Immortality"

To a considerable extent, the themes of this poem duplicate those of "Tintern Abbey." Students may find it interesting to begin by trying to locate ideas that the two poems hold in common, going on to analyze ways in which differences in expression and context have the effect of altering meaning. Specifically, it may be valuable to compare the sense of past versus present in the poems, and the function of nature, which here appears to be more emotional than moral. The word *glory* (along with *glories* and *glorious*) occurs at least seven times in this ode. "There hath past away a glory from the earth," line 18 proclaims. Considering the different occurrences of the word and its cognates, what does *glory* appear to mean here? It will not be possible to define it precisely, but a group can talk about its associations (with royalty, with divinity, with splendor, beauty, radiance, for example) and about the range of meanings suggested by the word's various uses in the ode. It might be hypothesized that the word's value for the poet comes partly from its vagueness and its breadth of association. The poem is trying to articulate something that cannot be precisely located; it tries to make the reader understand this "something" by playing on the reader's feelings. A passage particularly repaying close attention is the account of human development in stanzas VII and VIII. What does this theory of development involve and imply? It glorifies the preconscious and deprecates maturity; it implicitly argues that human association (the heavy, freezing weight of "custom") contains the seed of the soul's destruction. Compared with the view of "Tintern Abbey," this seems more extreme, more somber. What about the resolution of this poem? Is it more or less satisfactory than that of its predecessor? Does it solve the emotional problems that have been evoked? Why is the last word *tears*? Does that fact suggest anything about the atmosphere of this ending as opposed to the other?

## Topics for Writing

1. Sunshine and clouds in the "Immortality" ode

2. An impression of the "sister" in "Tintern Abbey"

3. The morality of "Tintern Abbey" (or of "Immortality")

## Further Reading

See also the reading suggestions in the anthology, p. 602.

Bewell, A. *Wordsworth and the Enlightenment.* 1989.
   An anthropological approach to Wordsworth and his historical
   context.

Davies, H. *William Wordsworth.* 1980.
   A highly readable biography, with splendid plates.

Davis, J., ed. *Discussions of William Wordsworth.* 1965.
   An exceptionally useful collection of essays which exemplifies
   many points of view.

Ferry, D. *The Limits of Mortality.* 1959.
   A study of Wordsworth's major poems that places those included
   in the anthology in the context of the poet's other work.

Hall, S., with J. Ramsey, ed. *Approaches to Teaching Wordsworth's
   Poetry.* 1986.
   Pedagogically invaluable essays.

Noyes, R. *William Wordsworth.* 1971.
   In the Twayne series. Provides thoughtful criticism as well as a biographical introduction and bibliography.

# SAMUEL TAYLOR COLERIDGE

*Classroom Strategies and Topics for Discussion*

Coleridge's poetry is likely to interest students by its capacity subtly to differentiate states of emotion, and also to find compelling ways to suggest the nature of an emotional condition. If undergraduates think his tone sometimes overwrought, they can often be brought by close attention to the text to understand the precision of his poetic effects and how richly they are used in poetic structures.

"Kubla Khan"

Absolutely sure-fire as a way of engaging student attention is the problem of automatic writing brought up by Coleridge's account of the composition of this poem. You should point out that the footnote calls attention to the dubious authenticity of this account, but then go on to invite speculation about why the notion of the poet as inspired creator is so compelling to the imagination. Why should we like to think that poetry issues from unconscious depths, without effort, discipline, or re-writing? Certainly this view contradicts ordinary experience of what it is like to write anything at all; good writing, most people find, is hard work. It is then valuable to point out how the vision of the poet as natural seer comes into the poem itself. You might inquire about the "damsel with a dulcimer" and how she figures in "Kubla Khan," and about the "I" at the poem's end and what others are alleged to "cry" about him. What do the final lines ("For he on honey-dew hath fed, / And drunk the milk of Paradise") mean and imply? The poet here emerges as an awe-inspiring figure, set apart from others, mysteriously dangerous, nourished in other ways than ordinary mortals, possessed of essentially magic powers ("And all who heard should see them there"). Another kind of question worth pursuing in relation to this poem is the power of scene to evoke feeling. Students can be asked to specify the various individual scenes summoned up by description, and to talk about the kinds of emotion they call forth.

"Dejection: An Ode"

The poem is worth going through stanza by stanza, to specify what is happening in each stanza and how each relates to its successor. If time forbids such detailed examination, here are a few matters to investigate. What is the relation between the conversational tone of the opening lines and the rhetorical intensity of, say, Stanza III? In other words, how does the speaker make plausible his movement from one tone to the other? In effect he documents that movement in the course of Stanza I: The casual observation about the weather leads him to think about the prospect of bad weather that would fit with his mood; by Stanza II it has become apparent that the remark about the weather was in the first place only an effort to disguise the mood of depression. How is *scene* used in this poem (perhaps in comparison to "Kubla Khan")? Here too one can trace precise correlations between scene and feeling. Special attention should be paid to the idea that the human experiencer gives meaning to nature, announced at the end of Stanza III and the beginning of Stanza IV; students might be asked to trace the intertwining of subjective and objective through the poem. What is the meaning of "Reality's dark dream" (100)? The speaker seems to have in mind fantasies stimulated by the dark realities around him; the rest of Stanza VII specifies such fantasies. What psychic purpose do they serve? They enlarge the reference of the depression which tends to isolate the person who feels it; in the development of the poem, they prepare for the invocation in Stanza VIII, which declares the speaker's capacity to concern himself for others. Finally, what is the role of the "Lady" in the poem, and how does it compare with the role of the "Sister" in "Tintern Abbey"?

### Topics for Writing

Writing topics can develop from any of the questions suggested above; it is also often useful to ask students to write about the function of a single image and how it is developed in the poem. See also *Topics for Writing* for Shelley, below.

### Further Reading

See also the reading suggestions in the anthology, p. 613.

Bygrave, S. *Coleridge and the Self: Romantic Egotism.* 1986.
   A psychologically focused essay.

# PERCY BYSSHE SHELLEY

*Classroom Strategies and Topics for Discussion*

One aspect of Shelley's poetry likely to interest undergraduates is his combination of lyric impulse with political and social passion—a version of the same linkage found in Blake.

### "England in 1819"

This sonnet is a useful place to start discussion—partly because it is likely to contradict any expectations students might come with about Shelley as a poet. In the next to the last line of the sonnet, *graves* become a summarizing image for all the phenomena previously evoked. The point of the grave appears to be that a "glorious Phantom" may burst out of it. But graves are also, above all, places where someone (or, by extension, something) is buried. In what sense can kings, princes, armies, and the rest be said to bury something? In other words, how does the metaphor of graves enlarge or illuminate what has come before? Among other things, all the realities Shelley has evoked seem in his view to represent ends to hope, belief, or possibility; this is one reason his tone is so angry. Before all the early references are summed up as constituting "graves," however, they are also characterized by a wealth of individual metaphors. What are some of these metaphors? Students will presumably mention *dregs, mud, leeches, sword, book, statute.* Do these metaphors have anything in common? Typically, they reduce something human to something nonhuman, thus preparing for the final reduction of everything to the grave. A line students are likely to find particularly difficult, because of its extreme condensation, is line 10—"Golden and sanguine laws which tempt and slay." (The footnote helps, but not a whole lot.) It is worth spending some time on elucidation here, working out what it might mean to imagine laws as tempting and slaying. Do golden laws tempt and sanguine ones slay? Or are laws in general being imagined as both golden and sanguine? What kinds of laws might tempt? How do they slay? A particular reason for attending to this line is that it is likely to lead to a perception of how relevant Shelley's indictment might be thought to be to our own time.

"Ode to the West Wind"

How does the high value attached to *energy* in this poem compare with the valuing of energy in *Faust*? One might remark, in this connection, the degree to which Shelley attaches the idea of energy to that of *purpose*. What is the relation between the poet's dwelling on description and his apparent belief that the poet can provide "The trumpet of a prophecy"? It might be argued that the luxurious descriptions here exemplify an important aspect of the poet's power: to evoke, to make real, to generate the force of incantation. These are the methods he (or, for that matter, she) can use to inspire and to prophesy.

"A Defence of Poetry"

It is entertaining to compare Shelley's account of poet and poetry with Imlac's version in *Rasselas* (Chapter 10), to which Rasselas responds, "Thou hast convinced me, that no human being can ever be a poet." Would the same response be appropriate to Shelley's version? How does the emphasis on power in this essay compare with the stress on energy in "Ode to the West Wind"?

*Topics for Writing*

The exercise on an image would work well here too. Other possibilities:

1. Compare Shelley and Coleridge on dejection

2. Use the *Defence* as a means of characterizing one of the other Romantic poets

*Further Reading*

See also the reading suggestions in the anthology, p. 621.

Chernaik, J. *The Lyrics of Shelley*. 1972.
    Contains new texts of many Shelley poems and offers thoughtful readings of the lyrics in the anthology.

---

Duerksen, Roland. *Shelley's Poetry of Involvement*. 1988.
Shelley as social commentator.

Reiman, D. *Percy Bysshe Shelley*. 1969.
Provides an excellent short general biography and critical introduction, with useful bibliography.

White, N. *Shelley*. 2 vols. 1940.
The standard biography, monumental and exhaustive.

Hall, Spencer, ed. *Approaches to Teaching Shelley's Poetry*. 1990.
Another useful MLA volume.

# JOHN KEATS

## Classroom Strategies and Topics for Discussion

If students enjoy poetry at all, they usually like Keats for the incantatory and evocative power of his verse (although they wouldn't put it that way). Class time can usefully be spent on trying to elucidate how he achieves his effects. For example (a few poems):

### "La Belle Dame Sans Merci"

This narrative poem begins with a question, a statement of a problem. How is the question finally answered; i.e., what, exactly, *does* ail this knight? How has the woman injured him? Or is it his total absorption in love that has damaged him? What about the kings, princes, and warriors who appear to him—what exactly do they warn him about? Such questions will emphasize the fact that one element in the poem's power is the presence of what is *not* said, the suggestions of a narrative behind the explicit narrative, which the reader must figure out. Descriptively, there is considerable stress on seasonal signs of cold and on the contrast with what has gone before (the withered sedge and silent birds call to mind their opposites). How does this technique reiterate the poem's theme? Certainly the denuded form of external nature echoes the sense of psychic deprivation the knight feels, and underlines the fact that his deprivations depend on the fact that he previously had—or thought he had—what now he lacks.

### "Ode on a Grecian Urn"

In many ways the representations on the urn appear to be superior to what real life has to offer. What are some of these ways? One might mention the degree to which art offers stimulus to the imagination (unheard melodies, which must be imagined, are sweeter than those actually heard; and the sequence of questions emphasizes the imaginative inquiry set in motion by the sight of the urn's shapes); the impossibility of disappointment for characters embedded in artistic form; and, most important, the permanence of art, comparable to eternity. Increasingly, the poem stresses this element of permanence and its effect on mortals. What kinds of effect does it have? Specifically, what does it mean that the urn can "tease us out of thought" (44)? Perhaps it makes us feel rather than think; perhaps it makes us surpass thought, entering a realm of intuitive knowledge; perhaps, as other lines suggest, it helps us avoid ordinary kinds of thought by removing us from commonplace experience. The ode's final lines can of course supply much matter for debate. The fundamental question here, beyond what it means to identify beauty and truth, is why this should be sufficient knowledge for humankind.

### "Ode to a Nightingale"

What sort of "happiness" is it that creates numbness and heartache? This is a point worth dwelling on, trying to define the sort of emotion Keats here wishes to evoke—by no means an easy matter. What is the poem's attitude toward ordinary human experience (Stanza III)? How does the function of art as suggested in this poem differ from that implicit in "Ode on a Grecian Urn"? Art, here, is epitomized by "Poesy," whose "viewless wings" carry the hearer of the nightingale's song to imaginative union with the bird. The "dull brain" (34) creates obstacles to such fusion, as "thought" appears to generate problems in the previous poem. Here too, then, art enables mortals to transcend their limitations, but by a rather different process from that suggested by "Grecian Urn." What is the importance of death in the poem? The poet declares himself "half in love with easeful Death" (52) and imagines death while listening to the bird as a rich and satisfying experience, but also imagines it as a state of deprivation in which he would "become a sod" (60). The bird's power, like that of the urn, comes partly from the possibility of imagining it as free of the threat of death—not, of course, in its own literal body, but because nightingales have always existed and will continue to exist and to become the substance of imagination. So there seems to be a contrast here between two views of death: the literal death that makes people and birds alike into mere pieces of earth, and an imagined kind of death that becomes itself a form of fulfillment. Why is the "self" unsatisfactory in the final stanza? The self seems a being deprived of imagination because existing in isolation, separated from the bird which has enabled the speaker to transcend his own sense of limitation.

## "Ode: To Autumn"

In relation to this poem of lush description, possibly the most useful question is the simplest and most obvious: How does it make you feel? If students can specify emotional responses, one can work backward from such responses to their stimuli in the text. It's essential to pause on the personification of Autumn in the second stanza, to inquire how that works in the poem. Autumn becomes a person deeply enjoying the experiences that only this time of year offers: the sense of luxurious ease. The "music" of autumn, specified in the final stanza, has less obvious power than "the songs of Spring" (22). What is attractive about this kind of music? One might wish to mention its multiplicity, both of source and of sound, and the impression it gives of the unity of all nature.

### Topics for Writing

1. The function of nature in a single poem

2. A comparison between a Keats poem and one by Shelley

3. A single emotion that attracts the speaker—and why

### Further Reading

See also the reading suggestions in the anthology, p. 628.

Dickstein, M. *Keats and His Poetry: A Study in Development.* 1971.
Supplies a particularly detailed reading of "To a Nightingale."

Gittings, R. *John Keats.* 1968.
An excellent recent biography which makes use of new material.
Gittings attempts to provide factual substantiation for every detail
of the poet's life; Bate and Ward (cited in the anthology) offer
critical as well as biographical interpretation.

Vendler, H. *The Odes of John Keats.* 1983.
Offers brilliant, exhaustive interpretations of all the odes.

Watkins, Daniel P. *Keats's Poetry and the Politics of the Imagination.*
1989.
Keats as social commentator.

# HEINRICH HEINE

## *Classroom Strategies and Topics for Discussion*

There is, of course, no substitute for close reading of poetic texts. Only by paying careful attention to the details of individual Heine poems can students begin to realize the sources of his power. Even in translation, the lyrics particularly lend themselves to attentive reading. "The Rose, the Lily, the Sun, and the Dove," for instance, presents a deceptively bland surface; students are likely to think that they "understand" it in a first rapid reading. But they may find it difficult to answer even an apparently simple question about the poem. Why, for example, the particular objects of love specified in the first line rather than, say, the stars, the moon, the ocean, and the sky? The rose, like the moon, is a clichéd symbol of natural beauty; unlike the moon, (and the stars, ocean, and sky), it is literally graspable, something that can be held in the hand. On the other hand, like the lily and the dove the rose is relatively fragile —it blooms only briefly. Only the sun, of the first line's images, is powerful, permanent, a source of energy. But the speaker's linking of the sun with the other entities suggests his lack of discrimination. He understands all four only as objects of his "rapture of love," and is hardly capable of distinguishing among them. The incongruity of the four images, in other words, may be part of the point of their conjunction.

The relation between the "maiden" (4) and the nouns of line one provides a useful subject for further analysis. The three adjectives applied to the maiden seem closely connected because of their rhymes. How do they remind the reader of the first line? "Slight" recalls the fragility of the flowers; brightness alludes to the sun, whiteness to the dove. The maiden, then, is "the source of love" partly because she recapitulates the beauties the speaker has previously found elsewhere.

The allegation that the maiden is the source of love appears to be an objective statement about her. What in the poem qualifies the reader's sense that this assertion tells us something about the maiden? In fact, like such Romantic works as *René*, "The Rose, the Lily, the Sun, and the Dove" primarily concerns itself with one individual's emotional life. Although the lyric refers to traditional sources of beauty outside the self, its true subject is the way that personal perception reshapes the universe.

The speaker's "rapture" suggests his need to love; his love must find an object. The maiden constitutes a more satisfactory object than her predecessors: Why? Partly because she unites in a single "source" qualities previously dispersed. Yet the capsule history of emotion here presented hints the potential fragility of this love as of the earlier one. If human consciousness must create for itself an object of devotion, it can destroy as well as make. The undertone of sadness typical of Romantic utterance derives partly from awareness of this double aspect of consciousness, and of the impossibility of controlling it.

Heine's reliance on simple sentence structure, obvious rhymes, and naiive diction establishes a tension reiterating that implicit in the poem's double consciousness. On the one hand, he appears to offer simple, confident assertions. Yet the confidence is subtly undermined by the implications suggested above. The effort to state simple truths, like the effort simply to love, is a difficult endeavor; and, like its counter-part, it may finally prove inadequate.

The theme of consciousness provides a useful starting point for other Heine poems as well. One might ask about the effect and the meaning of attributing consciousness to a spruce tree; or about how the folk-theme of the Loreley is personalized in Heine's treatment of it; or how "The Silesian Weavers" propose to destroy God, king, and fatherland (presumably by altering the people's understanding—or "consciousness" of what these concepts mean in actuality). Given this perspective, students may be brought to see a fundamental unity of approach in even the most apparently disparate of Heine's works. If you or a colleague speak German well, one or two of the shorter poems read aloud in the original will convey aspects of this unity not easily got at through discussion.

### Topics for Writing

1. Compare any two lyrics by Heine in their use of imagery.

2. Do the political attitudes of "The Silesian Weavers" and "The Migratory Rats" have anything in common? Discuss the nature of these attitudes and how they are communicated.

3. Discuss the concept of death implied in one, two, or three of Heine's poems.

4. How does the idea of the past figure in Heine?

See also the reading suggestions in the anthology, p. 638.

Brod, Max. *Heinrich Heine: The Artist in Revolt*. New York, 1957.
A study of the poet's literary career.

Fairley, B. *Heinrich Heine: An Interpretation*. 1977.
Scholarly and thorough.

Kohn, Hans. *Heinrich Heine: The Man and the Myth*. New York, 1959.
Short lecture offering suggestive definitions of Heine's characteristics as a poet.

Liptzen, Sol. *The English Legend of Heinrich Heine*. New York, 1954.
A lucid account of the shifts of Heine's literary reputation in England.

Perraudin, M. *Heinrich Heine*. 1988.
A general critical study.

Roche, M. W. *Dynamic Stillness*. 1987.
Treats the importance of quietness as a theme in Heine and other major German poets.

Rose, William. *The Early Love Poetry of Heinrich Heine: An Inquiry into Poetic Inspiration*. New York, 1962.
As the title suggests, this work concentrates on analysis of Heine's early lyrics and of their sources.

Spencer, H. *Heinrich Heine*. 1982.
A fairly elementary introduction in the Twayne series. Useful bibliography.

# GIACOMO LEOPARDI
## The Broom

*Classroom Strategies and Topics for Discussion*

A provocative issue in this poem is the relation between its large ideas (about history, nature, humankind) and its specific details. Students, typically, are far more eager to talk about big ideas than about how they emerge from the text; you should help them understand that the mode of communication constitutes part of the meaning.

A good starting point is the flower that gives the poem its title. What does one learn within the poem itself about what the flower is like? It blooms in "dead tracts"; it has a sweet smell; it grows in "stalks with . . . grave silent presence"; it is "fragile." Leopardi personifies it as "yielding," "innocent," "gentle," and finally as "wiser and less weak" than a man. He emphasizes both how easily it is destroyed, by lava flows or natural upheavals, and how indomitably it inhabits waste places. The paradox of fragility coexisting with strength is central to the poem. How does it illuminate the nature of humanity? One might argue that the human paradox precisely reverses the one asserted of the flower: Humanity declares its strength while demonstrating its weakness; the broom presents itself as weak but consistently survives and returns.

Large sections of this long poem are marked by their tone of anger; here too it might be asserted that the speaker's consciousness is as much his subject as is anything external to himself. Why is anger an important emotion here; what is the speaker angry about? Students might be asked to trace the progesssion of the speaker's assertions about humanity in order to locate with precision the sources of his rage. The poem's first allusions to human achievement seem sympathetic: "The plough, and villas, and laughter . . . ." Then humanity figures as victim of nature; the thought of this inevitable victimization leads to the first hint of ironic rage, with the phrase, "grand destinies and progressive hopes." Gradually the speaker becomes more and more angry, moving from the laughter of line 71 to an increasingly specific sense of human pretension and hypocrisy.

The vision of human nature that emerges emphasizes people's propensity to hide behind elevated language and conventional sentiment, using rhetoric as self-deception. "The truth displeased you," Leopardi writes (I. 79). This is the heart of his indictment; he perceives unwillingness to face the truth as an unforgivable and unnecessary weakness. The flower, in constrast to humanity, accepts (according to this vision) the truth of its own condition: hence its "wisdom."

Leopardi's treatment of the human situation draws specifically on nineteenth-century actuality. Students might be asked both to locate the explicit historical allusions of the of the poem and to reflect on the degree to which the description and emotion here offered apply also to times and places quite removed from the poet.

The speaker frequently refers to himself as "I" (e.g., I. 158ff.), and he alludes also to "you" (I. 183): the "seed of man." Students might be interested in the question of how and why he separates himself from the rest of humankind. In his apparent assertion of uniqueness, he recalls other Romantic writers, but his claim of specialness appears to rest more on thought than on feeling. He differentiates himself from others on the basis of his willingness to see and acknowledge the truth. Yet feeling accompanies seeing, from his point of view—"Laughter" and "Pity" as well as anger. Emotional capacity is implicit in the kind of intellectual honesty the speaker claims.

### Topics for Writing

1. Compare the use of natural imagery in Leopardi with that in one of Heine's poems.

2. Analyze the importance of the poem's speaker as an element in its effect.

3. Try to describe and evaluate the logical or the emotional progression of this poem.

4. Discuss the various symbolic meanings of Vesuvius in the poem.

### Further Reading

See also the reading suggestions in the anthology, p. 646.

Carsaniga, G. *Giacomo Lombardi: The Unheeded Voice.* 1977.
   A fairly recent reassessment that places Leopardi in his social and historical context.

# ALEXANDER SERGEYEVICH PUSHKIN
## The Queen of Spades

*Classsroom Strategies and Topics for Discussion*

One provocative aspect of Pushkin's great story is the way a reader's expectations are systematically manipulated and violated. To trace the ways in which anticipation is generated, only to be thwarted, may help students realize the artistry of this narrative.

What does the opening scene lead one to expect? A story about gambling, perhaps, about winning and losing. Its central character, one might think, will be Tomsky, the only person who speaks at any length and the one who offers judgements on others ("Hermann's a German: he's cautious—that's all"). After he tells the story of his grandmother, none of the responses suggest that those who make them will have any narrative importance. Chapter Two in its first section divides the interest between Tomsky's grandmother and the girl Lisaveta, promising a romantic fairy tale on the order of *Cinderella*—the poor abused underling will find her prince. When Hermann reappears, at the chapter's end, we may suspect that he will be the prince, although his intense interest in money already has disturbing overtones. Chapter Three begins by suggesting a sexual denouement but ends with the Countess's death; the tale has changed direction once more. Chapter Four exposes Hermann in his full heartlessness and leads one to expect that this will be a story of complete frustration; no one will achieve what she or he desires. Chapter Five turns into a ghost story, focusing our interest on whether the dead countess has revealed the truth; Chapter Six leaves that question unresolved (has she deliberately named the wrong third card or has she by supernatural intervention switched the cards?). The "Conclusion," contradicting all previous suggestions, gives everyone but Hermann— and Hermann is, after all, the princpal character—his or her heart's desire.

Why does Pushkin adopt such techniques of playing with the reader? Students may find it interesting to ask why we have the kinds of successive expectations suggested above. When we try to locate a story's main character on the basis of who has the most to say, when we allow ourselves to expect a romantic story or a sexual one or to focus our attention on exactly how a ghost has dealt with a human being, we demonstrate the degree to which we read every piece of writing in relation to other literary works we have experienced. Not what we know about life but what we know about literature leads us to think that Lisaveta might find her Prince Charming; we may not "believe" in ghosts, but we've all read enough ghost stories to know the kinds to questions one should ask about the operations of such beings. Pushkin, by manipulating our expectations, calls attention to their nature. He thus suggests the possibility that in reading a work of fiction we both expect and want something quite different from what we find in our actual lives. Of course the characters Pushkin creates also want, within the fiction, something different from what their lives offer them. Everyone dreams of a way of escaping from the dissatisfactions of his or her existence. Hermann—who intentionally calls Tomsky's tale of his grandmother a "fairy-tale"—in his actual confrontation with the old woman says to her, "the happiness of a man is in your hands." His imagination has indeed created for him a world of happiness dependent only on the winning of money; his earlier doctrine that "Economy, moderation and industry . . . are my three winning cards" has vanished in fantasy. A young man of "fiery imagination," Hermann exemplifies in extreme form what the story's other characters also reveal—that imagination disguises harsh or boring actuality by project-ing into the future the fulfilment of desire. When Hermann entreats the Countess "by the feelings of a wife, a lover, a mother" to grant his request, he suggests that even authentic tender feelings can become merely instruments of the imagination's insatiable hunger, words to be invoked rather than emotions to be experienced. Pushkin arouses the reader's desires in various ways only to frustrate them; he assigns satis-factions to his charactrs in almost random fashion, as though to mock longings for a universe controlled by justice.

This way of investigating "The Queen of Spades" implies that the story has dark social and moral implications. The point, of course, might be argued; you can inquire of students whether they believe Pushkin to be offering a serious social indictment. What human qualities and social arrangements does the story criticize? What evidence does it provide for the author's outrage at, perhaps, human self-deception, self-absorption, heartlessness? or at the maneuverings for wealth and position that society encourages? or at inequities of rank and power? How does Pushkin enforce his attitudes?

Students may find it useful to reflect on the narrator's importance in this fiction—and the reader's. Since the story reveals the emotional and moral inadequacies of all its characters, it in effect makes a hero of the storyteller, who alone demonstrates his awareness of what is really going on in a corrupt society. And this storyteller, through the manipulations of the reader discussed above, brings that reader to comparable awareness. If he denies us the obvious sorts of literary satisfaction, he provides a kind of moral satisfaction by placing us, finally, in a position of superiority to the characters. Our consciousness has been altered; we have been made to understand something. And the narrator's consciousness has guided us to understanding.

The story repays close attention to detail; almost any paragraph can be analyzed as attentively as a lyric poem to reveal its structural relation to the whole. A deceptively simple way of engaging student interest in Pushkin's larger purposes is to concentrate on his use of concrete detail. For example, you might wish to consider the description of the furniture in Lisaveta's bedroom and in the Countess's, Lisaveta's clothing and the Countess's, or the various allusions to flowers.

## Topics for Writing

1. Discuss the importance of Tomsky as a character in the story.

2. How appropriately does the "Conclusion" conclude the narrative? Consider how each of its details has been prepared for in the fiction as a whole.

3. Analyze the character of Lisaveta, making sure to support your analysis by specific reference to the text.

4. Discuss the importance of Hermann's moralizing in "The Queen of Spades" as a whole. Why do you think Pushkin conceives him as a German?

## Further Reading

See also the reading suggestions in the anthology, p. 655.

Barta, P. and U. Goebel, eds. *The Contexts of Aleksandr Sergeevich Pushkin*. 1988.
A collection of essays that attempt to place Pushkin in his historical and literary setting.

Lavrin, Janko. *Pushkin and Russian Literature*. London, 1947.
A short study primarily concerned with the historical background and setting of Pushkin's work, this establishes a useful context in which to consider the writer.

Magarshack, David. *Pushkin*. New York, 1967.
A biography with emphasis on its subject's literary development.

Petrie, Glen. *The Fourth King*. 1986.
Critical exegesis of Pushkin's accomplishment in many genres.

Simmons, Ernest J. *Pushkin*. Cambridge, Mass. 1937
A sound biography offering little literary analysis.

Todd, W. *Fiction and Society in the Age of Pushkin: Ideology, Institutions, and Narrative*. 1986.
As the title suggests, this study examines the social implicaions of Pushkin's fiction.

# VICTOR HUGO

*Classroom Strategies and Topics for Discussion*

As one of the great exemplars of the Romantic movement in Europe, Victor Hugo merits attention not only for the remarkable range of his individual accomplishment but for his consistent embodiment of the principles of Romanticism. Glorification of imagination—indeed, of consciousness; attention to the phenomena of the natural world; indignation over social oppression; interest in the illuminations provided by detail; an effort to re-imagine and re-see the everyday—such manifestations of the Romantic spirit appear everywhere in Hugo. Any of them might provide a starting point for investigation of the group of poems in the anthology.

Particularly rewarding, perhaps, is the subject of consciousness, most complexly explored in "Et nox facta est." The shorter poems, too, reveal versions of this concern. Often it manifests itself in awareness of alternate possibilities dependent on different states of consciousness. Thus "Reverie" develops from reflection on the possibilities of diffrent ways of seeing the world; "Tomorrow, At Daybreak" is structured around what the speaker imagines himself as rejecting and as accepting on the following day. Much of the latter poem depends on negatives: "I cannot stay far from you," "Seeing nothing outside me, hearing no sound," "I shall not look." Such allusions remind the reader of alternate situations—of another hypothetical setting in which the speaker might in fact see and hear and look in quite different ways. The poignance of the situation evoked, in other words, derives partly from allusions to other possibilities. "Memory of the Night of the Fourth" generates emotion partly by contrasting the actualities of the dead child and grieving, uncomprehending grandmother with the fact of Napoleon and his fantasies of power; the speaker, conscious of both pieces of reality (the humble scene of grief, the distant scene of power), feels helpless anger at the ironic conjunction.

You might ask students simply to locate, in any individual poem, allusions to the possibility of alternative ways of feeling, thinking, or seeing. The discovery of such allusions can often lead to awareness of the ways in which Hugo conveys complex emotional states through deceptively simple structures.

"Et nox facta est" offers a more manifestly intricate treatment of consciousness. Students will think at first that "consciousness," in this poem, alludes only to Satan's mental states; and indeed Satan's emotional progress provides an appropriate starting point for investigation. If your class has read *Paradise Lost*, comparison with Milton's Satan—who, like Hugo's, declares his hatred of the sun—is one way to elucidate the problem. It can be argued that Hugo's defier of God is a more nearly sympathetic figure than is Milton's. At any rate, you might offer this hypothesis to the class and invite them to support or refute it by reference to the text. But the question of how one is invited to feel about Satan can also be considered without reference to Milton. How do such adjectives as *aghast* and *dumbfounded* and *sad* make one feel about Satan? How does one respond to his desperate flight after the dying star? to his "Quiver" at the growing of his "membraned wing," his shivering at the loss of two suns? These instances of apparent invitations to pity must be considered in relation to such terms as *bandit* and *monster* and to Satan's declaration of hatred for God; certainly no case can be made for sympathy or pity as *adequate* responses to this being. Hugo insists that one understand Satan both as victim and as villain, and that one reflect about the relation between the two reactions.

Thus the poet invites alternative states of consciousness in the reader. He also tacitly contrasts Satan's state with God's ("absorbed in being and in Life"); the meaning of the perverted archangel depends on awareness of the state from which he has fallen. Finally, providing a complicated retrospect on the entire poem, Hugo's concluding section introduces the question of the writer's consciousness and its meaning. Students should be asked to speculate about the importance of this section (11. 213–230) in the poem as a whole. It calls emphatic attention to the fact that the narrative we have just read is and must be entirely a product of imagination, since it alludes to "Cycles previous to man, chaos, heavens," about which no human being can possibly have direct knowledge. The "sage," the "thinker," the "wise man"—in other words, the poet—undertakes a superhuman moral search, "further / Than the facts witnessed by the present sky." His effort is described in heroic terms. What is the connection between his grand, impossible, necessary undertaking and that of Satan, which the poem has just described? This question cannot be answered with certainty, but speculation about it is sure to prove fruitful in leading to an understanding of the mysterious, dangerous power which the Romantics believed inherent in the poetic act.

## Topics for Writing

1. Select a single detail from one of Hugo's poems and demonstrate as fully as possible how it functions in the poem as a whole.

2. Discuss Hugo's use of color in two or three short poems.

3. In what respects is Hugo's Satan a heroic figure? Describe in detail how the impression of his heroism is developed through the course of "Ex nox facta est."

4. What is the importance of the white feather in "Et nox facta est"? Consider the allusions to feathers and to wings of various sorts in the poem as a whole; do not rely on the explanatory footnote as a guide to the feather's *significance*.

## Further Reading

See also the reading suggestions in the anthology, p. 677.

Grant, Elliott M. *The Career of Victor Hugo*. Cambridge, 1946.
A useful literary biography.

Guerlac, S. *The Impersonal Sublime: Hugo, Baudelaire, Lautreamont*. 1990.
This treatment of Hugo in conjunction with other important French poets emphasizes his modern aspects.

Houston, J.P. *The Demonic Imagination: Style and Theme in French Romantic Poetry*. Baton Rouge, 1969.
Section on Hugo relates his "demonic imagination to that of other French Romantic poets.

Porter, L. *The Renaissance of the Lyric in French Romanticism*. 1978.
Places Hugo in his immediate literary context and stresses his importance as lyricist.

Swinburne, Algernon. *A Study of Victor Hugo*. London, 1886.
An important English poet reacting to an important French poet.

# ALFRED, LORD TENNYSON

## Classroom Strategies and Topics for Discussion

The narrative interest of the Tennyson poems included in the anthology should involve student readers. Even *In Memoriam* implicitly tells a story about the domination and then the weakening of grief; the two shorter poems more vividly elucidate narratives of human feeling. "Ulysses," the more readily comprehensible of the two, is a good place to start.

### "Ulysses"

Students might be asked what they think the purpose of the poem is. The answer most likely to emerge, finally, is that it both establishes and celebrates a particular kind of human character. What seems to be the precipitating cause of Ulysses' monologue? He appears to be at a point of decision about his life; Tennyson's rendering reveals how and why he proposes to change course. What, exactly, do we learn or deduce about Ulysses' character? This is of course the most obvious subject of discussion, but it is a fruitful one, as students find support in the poem itself for their understanding of its central character. Related, and almost equally important, is the question of what makes Ulysses a hero in Tennyson's view. If students have read the *Odyssey* (in volume I of the anthology), they will remember Homer's version of Ulysses' character and will realize that it only tangentially coincides with Tennyson's. The poem's final line, of course, epitomizes the attitudes here held up for admiration. The contrast with Telemachus (33–43) is worth dwelling on. What, precisely, does Ulysses mean by "his work" and "mine"? How does he make the reader feel about the opposition between them?

### In Memoriam

A large question that can focus the entire discussion of the poem is how Tennyson manages to unite public (social, intellectual, theological, scientific) and private concerns in what purports to be an extended record of his grief over a personal loss. (Since the potential selfishness of dwelling on one's own feelings concerns many adolescents and adults alike, the question is one of large interest.) Finally in *In Memoriam*, the dead young man Hallam becomes representative of a higher human species approaching realization, but originally his importance comes only from his close friendship with the poet. To trace the stages by which his significance is enlarged, and the correlation between this enlargement of meaning and the diminishment of grief, is probably sufficient enterprise for any class.

A few more local issues that may prove illuminating (and that often can call attention to larger problems): The Prologue purports to be a statement of faith, but in fact it expresses great uncertainty. How is uncertainty conveyed? It is worth noting a sequence of ambiguous verbs: *thinks* (11), *seemest* (13), *know not* (15), *cannot know* (21), *trust* (23). Also relevant are the contrast between the assertions of faith, or the appeals to God (e.g., "Let knowledge grow from more to more," 25), and the statements of fact (e.g., "They are but broken lights of thee," 19; "these wild and wandering cries," 41). As students attend to the varying rhetoric of this piece of the poem, they should come to see that it establishes a kind of drama, an internal conflict between faith and perception that in fact runs through the poem as a whole (and can be traced, if there's time).

Section 3: Personified Sorrow dominates this section; her "whisper" epitomizes one aspect of the speaker's struggle. Why does the speaker perceive what she says as both sweet and bitter? This allegation suggests that he finds perverse comfort in the notion that all of Nature simply duplicates the sense of futility that he himself experiences, given his loss. It is particularly important because it provides one answer to the question of how Tennyson unites small and large concerns; here he demonstrates the psychological pattern by which human beings can make the universe subordinate to their own feelings, turning Nature itself into an objectification of personal emotion. What is the effect of the final stanza? It emphasizes the continuing ambiguity of the speaker's responses; he cannot decide whether it is comforting ("natural good") or destructive ("vice of blood") to allow himself this kind of interpretation.

Section 5: This section raises the question of poetry and its function. What *is* its function in this passage? Concealment is emphasized more than revelation: poetry's discipline helps to numb pain and to obscure the intensity of feeling. Why is it "half a sin" to write poetry about this subject? By implication, because it falsifies in being unable to reveal all. Students might be asked to seek other passages in which the poet speaks about the function of poetry.

Section 21: Here the function of poetry comes up again, in relation to imagined responses to it. Why does the poet imagine various others reacting to his poem? Perhaps he is thus suggesting his own doubts about what he is doing. The specific things that are said are worth examining and summarizing: that such dwelling on grief fosters weakness in others, that it constitutes self-indulgence and seeking after fame, that concern with the private has no validity in a time of public upheaval and of dispute over the revelations of science. How is the problem of negative response resolved? The poet claims the spontaneity and naturalness of his song, and his compulsion to sing it; he cannot help himself, as a bird cannot help himself. If students are asked whether this resolution seems adequate, they are likely to say no—and I think they would be right. The weakness of the resolution is part of the continuing structure of doubt; the poet cannot yet fully justify what he is doing.

Section 95: This poem contains the moment of revelation that most clearly resolves the problems previously articulated. What is the importance of the natural setting? Earlier, Nature in a large, abstract sense seemed to echo the poet's sense of futility; now specific details of nature generate a sense of calm. But it could be argued that the most significant fact here is that the speaker is now able fully to notice what lies outside him; he is no longer locked in his own grief. What is the stimulus to the visionary experience? Looking at the leaves (Stanza 6), the poet is reminded of natural cycle, and of the fact that even fallen leaves may remain green, as Hallam's memory remains green for him. The speaker thinks specifically of the dead man, and of his qualities of character; this leads to the revelation. What does that revelation consist of? The poet announces that it cannot be fully stated in words (yet another glance at the problem of poetry's function), but he conveys a recognition of universal pattern making sense of Time, Chance, and Death, those apparent obstacles to human happiness. Then he returns to the natural scene. Why? The calm continues, but it is a calm involving movement and process; dawn comes to foretell the day, symbolizing the new day of acceptance and possible happiness in the poet's experience.

## Topics for Writing

1. Science in *In Memoriam*

2. An analysis of one section of *In Memoriam*

3. The use of animals in *In Memoriam*

4. Water in *In Memoriam*

5. Tithonus and Ulysses as characters

### Further Reading

See also the reading suggestions in the anthology, p. 688.

Bloom, H., ed. *Alfred Lord Tennyson*. 1985.
Miscellaneous, often provocative, essays.

Culler, A. D. *The Poetry of Tennyson*. 1977.
Supplies a particularly fine treatment of *In Memoriam*, analyzing the poem's form and thought and giving detailed accounts of specific poetic effects.

Kissane, J. *Alfred Tennyson*. 1970.
In the Twayne series. Centers on treatments of the poet's work in various genres: lyric, narrative, and drama.

Tennyson, C. *Alfred Tennyson*. 1949.
The standard, thorough biography.

# ROBERT BROWNING

*Classroom Strategies and Topics for Discussion*

The question likely to interest students most in any reading of dramatic monologue is that inherent in the form: How does an imagined character reveal himself or herself without any apparent intention of doing so? The question, in relation to the bishop ordering his tomb, has two obvious aspects: what do we learn of his personal history? and what do we learn of his character?

The two matters, of course, are closely connected. From line 3 ("Nephews—sons mine . . . ah God, I know not!") on, the reader is increasingly forced to realize the interdependence of history and character. The fact that the bishop does not know the nature of his relationship to the men around the bed reveals that he has had promiscuous relations with women—a revelation both of character and of experience. As students call attention to the details that show the bishop's nature and uncover his past, you can ask them to think more deeply about the implications of almost any line. The clergyman's lack of knowledge about his children, for instance, speaks of more than his promiscuity: it suggests his lack of concern for human ties in general, in his failure to keep track either of his women or of their offspring.

Lines especially worth attention include line 14, "Saint Praxed's ever was the church for peace," an example of a trick frequently repeated in the poem. The speaker appears to declare something he values— "peace"—only to reveal as he goes on that he has done everything possible to contradict this value: he has fought every inch of the way. Then there is the bishop's description of his setting, particularly the columns of "Peach-blossom marble": how does the description reveal him? The conjunction of "Peach-blossom," "red wine," and "mighty pulse" suggests the degree to which he attributes vitality to the realm of sensuous satisfaction, conveying more affection for stone than for women (or putative offspring). Lines 56–61, about the frieze the dying man imagines, are also worth attention: they demonstrate his detailed aesthetic awareness and how that dominates any religious feeling, as religious and pagan references mingle for the sake of an imagined spectacle in stone.

Specific questions about the bishop's character may lead students more deeply into the poem. For example, in what terms does he understand other people? His interpretation of Gandolf and of his "sons" suggests that he can only grasp the nature of others by thinking them like himself. (Of course, the poem offers no evidence than they are *not* like himself: we see only through the bishop's eyes, and through his eyes everyone emerges as grasping and competitive.) What is the bishop's attitude toward language? He appears to be an obsessive talker, but he also thinks about language: for example, "marble's language, Latin pure, discreet" (98). Language becomes for him an aesthetic phenomenon like marble itself, and a woman's "talking eyes," which speak a non-verbal tongue, seem no more appealing than "Choice Latin, picked phrase."

The last line of the poem reiterates line 5; how has its meaning and effect changed, given all that has come between its two occurrences? As we learn more and more about the bishop, we realize that he thinks of a woman as like a piece of lapis lazuli or a statue: her value, too, is purely aesthetic. The only ground for envy he can imagine concerns the possession of aesthetic objects.

At the end of the poem, the bishop appears to have achieved a certain peace, as he rests in "the church for peace." What accounts for his apparent emotional shift? He knows that his sons will follow not his will but their own, that he will not have the tomb he desires; he knows that he is dying. But his past aesthetic triumphs continue to comfort him: even if he possesses nothing now to arouse Gandolf's envy, he possesses his past, his perceptions and the memory of his perceptions. He contents himself at last with what he securely has.

"My Last Duchess," which appears to constitute a less complicated narrative, provides a particularly useful focus for discussion because it allows students to tease out meanings from the apparently direct and simple. Questions of character are obviously at issue in this poem. Although a teacher may wish to begin discussion by making sure students understand the situation and the past happenings that have taken place (To whom is the duke speaking, and why? How did the duchess die? What does she look like in the portrait?), such concerns quickly lead to more subtle matters of characterization. What was the duchess like as a person? This obvious question can generate intense classroom exchange, as it leads to the related problem of the duke's nature. Why does the poem emphasize works of art to insistently? Is there any relation between the duchess's portrait and the bronze statue of Neptune (1.54)?

Does the word *fair* (1.52) have any special importance by the time the duke uses it here? What is his attitude toward money?

Finally students may find it interesting to contemplate why Browning would choose to tell his story in verse rather than prose. The narrative could provide the substance of a short story or even, conceivably, a novel. Here, though, the story is told in retrospect and allusively. What are the advantages and disadvantages to such a method? How does the use of couplets contribute to the poem's meaning and impact?

"Childe Roland to the Dark Tower Came,'" a more obviously difficult poem, also tends to generate lively controversy—usually over the fundamental issue of what the poem is *about*. It should probably be acknowledged at the outset that no definitive answer to this question is likely to present itself: critics have debated for many years whether the poem has allegorical meaning. The instructor might direct discussion by asking students to specify what, exactly, the poem allows its readers to *know* (e.g., we know that someone is looking for something; we know that he has been searching for a long time; that many before him have failed in the quest; that he follows the cripple's advice . . . ). Many facts emerge from the narrative; what crucial facts remain missing? Students may decide that they feel deprived of important information about what the point of the quest is, why so many have undertaken it, what the Dark Tower "stands for." Next they might think about why the poet would choose to omit so much information. In other words, what poetic effects are achieved by the omissions?

One way of trying to define the poem's mood and its effect on the reader is to trace the speaker's uncertainties, which multiply steadily as the poem goes on, from his doubt about whether the cripple lies through his doubt about his own fitness, his questions about whether the horse is alive or dead—on and on. How do these uncertainties affect the reader.

Discussion of the poem's ambiguities may lead to larger issues about the workings of poetry. Students may wish to discuss whether definable meaning is essential to a poem, whether creating a mood is sufficient goal for a poet, what besides clear meaning determines poetic impact.

### Topics for Writing

1. The five senses in "The Bishop Orders His Tomb"

2. The importance of conflict in the poem

3. Why I admire the bishop

4. Why I feel contempt for the bishop

5. Why the duchess's portrait is behind a curtain.

6. The duke's "skill in speech" (cf. 11.35–36)

7. The importance of the title to "'Childe Roland to the Dark Tower Came'"

8. The similes in "'Childe Roland . . . .'"

### Further Reading

See also the reading suggestions in the anthology, p. 712.

Bloom, H. and A. Munich, eds. *Robert Browning: A Collection of Critical Essays.* 1979.
Useful for suggesting varied critical approaches.

Burrows, L. *Browning the Poet.* 1969.
Presents itself as an introductory study; it contains a useful detailed reading of "The Bishop Orders His Tomb."

Thomas, D. *Robert Browning: A Life Within Life.* 1982.
A well-written recent biography.

# FREDERICK DOUGLASS
## Narrative of the Life of Frederick Douglass, An American Slave

*Classroom Strategies and Topics for Discussion*

This personal account of self-discovery, survival, and escape translates into narrative terms the linked concern with the social and the emotional that we have encountered in the work of such poets as Blake and Shelley. Douglass's story has obvious historical interest, but it also generates vivid awareness, still relevant today, of the emotional realities of oppression. Although students may find Douglass's language on occasion uncomfortably "high-flown," they will probably be caught up in the drama of his efforts to escape conditions that appear inescapable.

Because the shift to prose narrative constitutes such a startling change from the poetry that surrounds this work in the anthology, it's probably useful to begin by talking about autobiography as a form. Students can be either told or asked about what it means to tell a story of the self. The important point here is that telling such a story involves imaginative activity comparable to that involved in writing a poem. The facts of a life are given, but the appropriate way of imagining the self is not. The autobiographer must decide, consciously or unconsciously, how to present him or herself—as hero or victim, as unique individual or as representative of a group, as defined principally by childhood experience or as self-creator. Selections must be made among the many events remembered; one cannot set down *everything*. Such self-imagining, such selection form the story. Another way of putting the same truth is to point out that many different stories can be told of any individual; students might be asked to think about how many different life stories they can imagine for themselves.

As for Douglass's story, it divides itself naturally into two teaching units, the first one extending to the beginning of Chapter X (p. 755). It's useful to ask students when they read to try to decide what the center of each chapter is, in terms of narrative or emotional interest. I shall make a few suggestions, chapter by chapter, of how classroom discussion might be focused.

## Chapter I

It's worth spending some time on the first paragraph, concentrating on the question of what that paragraph establishes, how it prepares us for the book that succeeds it. Points worth mentioning: the stress on deprivation, on what the narrator does *not* know; the linkage of slaves to the natural cycle (they locate their birthdays by planting-time, etc.), the degree to which the narrator identifies himself with his social class, the mention of contrast between the situation of blacks and that of whites as a source of consciousness, the definition of the narrator as someone who figures things out (his way of estimating his own age). The tone is matter-of-fact, yet emotion permeates the paragraph. Where does it come from? One might comment on the emphasis on the negative (no knowledge, no memory, want of information, "could not tell," not allowed, etc.) and on the explicit reference to early unhappiness. The episode in the chapter receiving the greatest emotional stress is Douglass's concluding account of watching the whipping of his aunt. Why, one might ask, does this episode merit such extended attention? It is directly stated to be "the first of a long series of such outrages"; in other words, it has representative meaning. It announces themes that the rest of the text will reiterate—not only the irresistible power and brutality of white masters, but the degree to which sexual issues are intertwined with those of slavery. And it suggests the way in which Douglass as a child felt himself directly implicated in the persecution he saw, not for altruistic but for selfish reasons: "I expected it would be my turn next."

## Chapter II

This chapter concerns Colonel Lloyd and his household; its most emphatic detail has to do with the songs the slaves sing. "To those songs," Douglass writes, "I trace my first glimmering conception of the dehumanizing character of slavery." Can we understand why the songs affect him thus? Douglass stresses the mixture of joy and sadness in the songs; the joy is associated with going to the Great House Farm. There is pathos, thus, in the very cause of joy, pathos in the fact that slaves achieve their satisfaction out of such impoverished stimuli. The importance of the invariable undertone of deep sadness is of course primary: Douglass insists that there is no joy without sadness in the slaves' lives, but that in spite of their oppression they manage to find causes for qualified happiness.

## Chapter III

The episode of the two Barneys is central here. Why? The arbitrary punishment meted out to them by an unjust master, and his greater concern for his horses than for the slaves who care for those horses, epitomize the dehumanization of slavery.

## Chapter IV

The series of murders toward the chapter's end best express the theme. It is worth commenting on the relation of Chapters II, III, and IV to one another—a steadily intensifying emphasis on slavery's injustice. Why, the class might be asked, has Douglass thus far said so little about himself, except as observer? Obviously, he wishes to insist as forcefully as possible on his identification with his people: Whether or not he is actually murdered, he participates emotionally in the plight of the victims.

## Chapter V

"I look upon my departure from Colonel Lloyd's plantation as one of the most interesting events of my life," Douglass writes. Why? He attributes to this event the possibility of his subsequent escape, and he attributes the event itself to the interposition of Providence. Why is this important? It places the narrative as a whole in a religious context and suggests in a muted way an issue that will later become explicit: How can Christians reconcile themselves to slavery?

## Chapter VI

The key event of this chapter, and perhaps of the book as a whole, is the abortive reading lessons Douglass receives from his mistress (see the headnote). Their importance is directly stated in the text and is quite obvious, but nonetheless worth discussing. But the chapter ends with the story of Mary's mistreatment. Why? Douglass wishes to emphasize that even in the best possible situation for slaves, injustice and oppression remain, and remain impossible to withstand.

## Chapter VII

This chapter dwells almost entirely on reading, and on the degree to which learning to read from white children intensified Douglass's consciousness of the intolerable difference of situation between him and his white contemporaries. The most important theme here is the way the child moved from consciousness of his particular plight to awareness of generalizations that could be made about it. Why is the capacity to generalize perceived as a source of strength? The boy's interest in the term *abolition*, his reading of *The Columbian Orator*, even his conversation with the Irishmen all enlarge his comprehension. The ability to go beyond himself, to understand himself in a social context, is crucial to Douglass's self-freeing. Students might be asked about the relation between his interest in books and his ability to figure out how to learn to write. Both aspects of his character declare his capacity to make use of what lies outside himself, a capacity of enormous value to him.

## Chapter VIII

This chapter reports Douglass's enforced leaving of Baltimore and of his relatively kind master. Its central episode, however, is the partly imagined story of his grandmother, who, if she now lives, "lives to remember and mourn over the loss of children, the loss of grandchildren, and the loss of great-grandchildren." Douglass goes on to envision, however, her solitary death, and to insist that a righteous God will punish those responsible for such a situation. Why is this episode so important in the narrative economy? Talking about this problem will provide a way of discussing the degree to which this autobiography builds itself up by the use of symbolic events, events not necessarily directly autobiographical. If one tries to describe what kind of person Douglass is (and the effort to do so makes a useful classroom exercise), it is necessary to dwell on the fact that he is a symbol-maker, someone who sees experience in symbolic terms. Just as the whipping of his aunt symbolizes for him one aspect of injustice, the isolation of his grandmother symbolizes another. Her alienation in old age, however, assumes special symbolic importance because, as this book increasingly makes clear, the sense of community among slaves is their greatest resource; isolating the old woman in the woods deprives her of this community. Douglass's way of writing resembles a poet's method of creating events: He uses individual happenings to stand for kinds of happening, and to evoke the emotion associated with other events of the same order.

## Chapter IX

Now Douglass finds himself at the mercy of a hard master. This chapter is very short; at its heart is the matter of Southern Christianity. Why does Douglass linger on this aspect of his culture? He thus finds another way to emphasize the injustice of his situation: It is injustice considered in relation to the human obligation to God as well as that to other people. He is gradually enlarging the scope of his concern and his claim.

## Chapter X

In this first chapter of the second assignment, the scale of the narrative changes. Chapters X and XI together occupy almost as much space as the nine preceding chapters. All the rest, from one point of view, is background; now the autobiographer moves toward the crucial—the absolutely central—event of his escape, showing what emotional forces made escape feel a necessity, and what contributed to making it a possibility. Chapter X summarizes the narrator's experience with three different masters. Its central episode is the failed attempt at escape, important both in relation to what led up to it (the increasingly intense abuse in Douglass's life) and what it leads to (increased determination to escape successfully). But it is worth asking also about the importance of other events, most notably the "magic root" that protects Douglass from being whipped, the Sabbath school he establishes, and his experience as a caulker in Baltimore. An effort should be made to establish both his intensifying sense of personal integrity and independence and his increasingly emphatic sense of community.

## Chapter XI

Now the escape actually takes place, but this chapter, more than any previous one, emphasizes emotional rather than external event—an effect made more emphatic by the author's deliberate suppression of the literal details of his escape. Instead, he talks about his feelings. It's useful to discuss what feelings are most important—the sadness at the thought of breaking the ties of affection with his slave friends, exhilaration at freedom, suspicion of white and black men alike, wonder at the prosperity of the North, excitement at earning his own money. And time can profitably be spent on delineating the relation between these emotions and those earlier evoked in the book—to what extent these feelings confirm or develop from earlier ones.

### Appendix

Here Douglass makes most explicit the larger meaning of his narrative. He claims not to be talking about a single life but to be discussing a problem with its bearing on religious professions and practice. Yet the *Narrative* ends with his reassertion of his own name and identity. The large question of how this book integrates its concern with the individual and with the social must be confronted finally—in writing or in class discussion.

### *Topics for Writing*

1. A single episode and how it relates to the whole

2. What kind of man was Douglass?

3. A way in which this narrative relates to late twentieth-century problems

4. The importance of songs and hymns

5. A single character (apart from Douglass) and his or her importance in the story

6. What whipping means in this narrative

### *Further Reading*

See also the reading suggestions in the anthology, p. 726.

Huggins, N. *Slave and Citizen: The Life of Frederick Douglass.* 1980. Offers a short but comprehensive biography for the general reader, with a bibliography of historical sources.

McFeely, W. S. *Frederick Douglass*. 1990.
Biography with extensive historical content.

Preston, D. *Young Frederick Douglass: The Maryland Years*. 1980.
Concentrates on Douglass's youth, with a section on his late-life
return to Maryland; Preston provides a thorough, lucid account.

Stepto, R. "Narration, Authentication, and Authorial Control in
Frederick Douglass's Narrative of 1845," *Afro-American Litera-
ture: The Reconstruction of Instruction*, ed. R. Stepto and D.
Fisher. 1978.
*and*
Stone, A. "Identity and Art in Frederick Douglass's Narrative,"
*College Language Association Journal 17*. 1973. p. 192–213.
Two essays that explore Douglass's work as narrative and
specifically as autobiography.

Sweet, L. *Black Images of America, 1784–1870*. 1976.
Places Douglass's thought in the context of intellectual history,
with stress on his concept of nationality.

# WALT WHITMAN

*Classroom Strategies and Topics for Discussion*

*Song of Myself*

The notion of the self as inherently fascinating dominates much literature of the Romantic period. One may think, for example, of the Rousseau of the *Confessions*, or of the character of Faust. Since college students themselves are in a developmental stage of intense self-concentration, concerned to define and to understand their own identities, they are likely to be readily interested in the problems of what it might mean to write a "song of myself"—and what in fact it *does* mean in Whitman's version. Does any notion of the self emerge from the selections printed in the anthology? Certainly one would have to comment on the idea of the self as infinitely inclusive, not defined by difference (as most of us define ourselves) but by comprehension. It is worth pausing to specify some specific varieties of comprehensiveness here suggested: geographical, political, vocational, sexual ("I am the poet of the woman the same as the man," [21.4]), emotional. Are these claims of vast inclusiveness equivalent to Rousseau's insistence on his uniqueness? It might be argued that Whitman, on the contrary, tries to unite himself with all the rest of humanity—all the rest, that is, of American humanity. Yet, paradoxically, such an attempt at union underlines the speaker's specialness—he alone has the capacity for such inclusiveness. It might be worth pausing to discuss what the poet's notion of containing all kinds of people within himself really means. It is obviously not literal. Does he, perhaps, mean that he has a large capacity for sympathy and empathy? Is this another way of celebrating the poetic imagination, directed now not toward birds and urns but toward other human beings?

One way of getting at important aspects of *Song of Myself* is to inquire in what ways it might be peculiarly American. Published only five years after *In Memoriam*, it of course reflects a very different sensibility. The difference can be explained in terms of Tennyson's and Whitman's personalities, but also in relation to the divergencies between English and American culture in the mid-nineteenth century. Obvious answers to the question about "American" aspects of the poem might begin with the specific geographical allusions that abound. Almost equally apparent are the references to American occupations—planter, raftsmen, fancy-man, rowdy, and the like. It is yet more illuminating to note Whitman's enormous emphasis on the idea of democracy. This is both explicit ("I speak the pass-word primeval, I give the sign of democracy," [24.10]) and implicit, in the reiterated idea of the equality of humankind. (Why should the "primeval" be associated with democracy? The poet appears to imply that democracy constitutes the natural state of humanity—a favorite notion of the Romantics.) Whitman's diction is often insistently American: "Shoulder your duds dear son" (46.15). (Students might be asked to seek other instances of especially "American" language.) And his verse form deviates dramatically from the developed conventions of English poetry, deliberately risking prosiness, working in leisurely rhythms. Even the idea of unity through diversity, here imagined as epitomized in a single person, can be understood as an American concept, a personalized version of a national ideal.

"Out of the Cradle Endlessly Rocking"

This extended lyric particularly invites comparison with previous Romantic poetry. An obvious point of connection is Whitman's use of nature. How does the speaker's attitude toward the birds compare with, say, Keats's toward the nightingale? Whitman appears to be more interested in evoking the birds in themselves, imagined in terms of the birds' situation rather than only in relation to the speaker's needs. The bird song, for Whitman, has more specific emotional meaning, with more detailed narrative background associated with it. The speaker's sense of identification with the bird is more emphatic. The experience he reports has taken place in the distant past; Keats creates the illusion that he speaks of the present. (This is a point worth dwelling on: What differences are generated by the speakers' different locations in time? It is interesting to consider the relative poetic values, and the different poetic functions, of immediacy versus the impression of meditated meaning.) Both poems stress emotional contrast; both stress the melancholy of the bird song. Death becomes in both lyrics an important issue: What is the difference in their treatment? (It might also be valuable to compare Whitman's musings on death here with Shelley's in "Stanzas Written in Dejection.") To Whitman, death seems to comprise a kind of literary temptation ("The word of the sweetest song and all songs," 180), a "delicious" word, the "key" to all poetry—but not even at the level of fantasy an invitation to suicide. Students might be asked to look for the evidence the poem supplies of its speaker's great vitality. He identifies his own energy with that of his impulse to write verse ("A thousand warbling echoes have started to life within me, never to die," 149), and he defines himself, in Faustian fashion, with infinite wanting ("The unknown want, the destiny of me," 157; "O if I am to have so much, let me have more!" 159). Knowledge of death, in his apparent view, is necessary to the capacity for full expressiveness of life. Why does he evoke the sea as "savage old mother," "fierce old mother," "some old crone rocking the cradle"? The idea of the sea as mother of humanity, the origin of all life, is a Romantic commonplace, but Whitman through his adjectives suggests a common source for life and death: The principle of life contains, inextricably mingled, that of destructiveness.

## Topics for Writing

1. Whitman's relation to his reader (in a single poem)

2. The personality the poet creates for himself (in a single poem)

3. The importance of a single image from nature

4. Whitman's optimism

## Further Reading

See also the reading suggestions in the anthology, p. 791.

Allen, G. *Walt Whitman Handbook.* 1946.
   Provides useful biographical and critical background.

Asselineau, R. *The Evolution of Walt Whitman.* 2 vols. 1960–1962.
   Consists of a biographical volume subtitled *The Creation of a Personality* and a critical volume, on *Leaves of Grass*, called *The Creation of a Book.*

Kummings, D. D. *Approaches to Teaching Whitman's* Leaves of Grass. 1990.
   Stimulating collection representing varied approaches.

# HERMAN MELVILLE
## Billy Budd, Sailor

*Classroom Strategies and Topics for Discussion*

The sheer suspense of this psychological narrative will keep students involved in reading the story, but—like professional critics—they will probably have trouble with its complexities and ambiguities. As the headnote suggests, such "trouble" can itself supply a source of interest. In any case, it is helpful, before the first assignment (the narrative naturally divides at the end of Section 17, p. 836), to suggest that readers concentrate on trying to fathom the characters of Billy, Vere, and Claggart, and on thinking about the voice of the storyteller, what it's like and what it contributes to the story's effect. The first discussion may well concentrate on just these matters.

The obvious first question for a class, though, is why Melville includes at the beginning the detailed account of the black sailor in Liverpool. This is, of course, only the first of many "digressions" apparently designed to insist on the broad implications of Billy's story. Billy belongs to a type, the narrator suggests; we should understand what happens to him in relation to the function of that type. The black sailor is the center of his companions' attention; he seems to have an enviable role, and to foretell just such a position for the hero of this story. The episode is worth returning to at the end of the discussion of *Billy Budd*, as a good example of Melville's irony.

Subtle and important points can emerge from class conversation based on such apparently simple and straightforward questions as: What is Billy like?, What is Claggart like?, etc. In arriving at a consensus on such matters, it is obviously important not to let the discussion stray too far from the text. Students might wish to talk about the imagery used to characterize Billy. On the one hand, he resembles "a dog of Saint Bernard's breed," or an "upright barbarian"; on the other, he turns out to be the kind of barbarian Adam may have been before the Fall. How does one reconcile the apparently degrading and the apparently exalted metaphors associated with Billy? Is it possible that to be a barbarian or a dog might be a good thing, given the nature of civilized society? In Chapter 16, Billy is said to be ignorant, simple-minded, unsophisticated.

Such qualities precipitate his destruction. Are they therefore to be condemned? Like all questions associated with *Billy Budd*, these have no definitive answers, but pursuing them will help readers realize the complexity of the narrative.

The characterization of Vere also presents difficulties. What are we to make of the explanation of his being called "starry Vere"? The matter-of-fact account of the epithet associates him with a long tradition of English heroism, but also suggests that the adjective is a kind of joke. Is it a good thing or a bad one that he loves books? (This manifestly unanswerable question is worth raising because his scholarly nature becomes relevant later on.) Students should particularly note the stress on his social conservatism, and the imagery ("a dyke against those invading waters") associated with it.

You should make sure that students understand the nature of Claggart's job on the ship, to which Melville gives considerable stress. It becomes important that he is the officer in charge of discipline. The storyteller suggests that he is impossible to characterize adequately ("His portrait I essay, but shall never hit it," p. 819). Why? Worth noting particularly is the emphasis on covert suggestions of "something defective or abnormal" about him, suggestions summed up, on the social level (they are also relevant on the psychological level), by the persistent stories of a criminal past. What is the source of the antagonism Claggart feels for Billy? Speculation about this matter provides much of the substance of Chapter 12; does this speculation resolve anything? What would it mean to say that this is the fundamental antipathy of evil for good? Can we believe in this sort of antipathy? Would the Bible support such belief?

The voice of the storyteller in some ways presents the greatest difficulties of all. Passages that should be considered in assessing it include the observation at the end of Chapter 2 that Billy is not a conventional hero and his story no romance (what does *romance* mean here? is the narrator simply claiming realism for his tale?); the apology for digression at the beginning of Chapter 4, with the association between digression and sinning (why? is this simply a joke? does it raise questions about the nature of "sin" in the story itself?); and (particularly important) the discussion in Chapter 11 about Claggart's antipathy, which suggests and rejects the possibility of inventing an explanation. This last sequence implicitly insists that the storyteller does not finally have control over his story, and other passages echo the point. It makes a claim of truth for the narrative, and it argues that reality is more "mysterious" than invention.

Students should be asked how they respond to such a claim. Does it make them trust or distrust the narrator? It could certainly be argued that the storyteller goes out of his way to hint that he is not a dependable or adequate guide through the intricacies of his own story; why should he do such a thing? Perhaps he is trying to make his readers reflect on the final incomprehensibility of their own experience, and of all human experience, and to tell us that the difficulties of his story correspond to those of life.

The second class should perhaps begin with renewed discussion of the imagery associated with Billy. There is, of course, increasing stress on Biblical reference, most of which associates Billy with innocence or virtue. Melville renews his allusions to Billy as child, as barbarian, and as dog; he adds, at a crucial moment (just before the hanging), the singing bird. How does this imagery control or affect our developing impression of Billy? Does it convey the storyteller's clear judgment? Students will be interested in the large moral questions raised by the second half of *Billy Budd*. For example, does Billy receive a fair trial? Both possible answers to this question should be fully explored. If Captain Vere's arguments are taken with full seriousness, the answer will probably be yes; if one believes that morality rather than legality or practical considerations should operate in legal proceedings, the answer will be no. In Melville's account, considerable stress is placed on the influence of Vere's "unshared studies," which, along with his superior intellectuality, differentiate him from the other men. Is the point that Captain Vere's is the more well thought-out position? If this *isn't* the point, what is?

The problem of the storyteller's role also recurs more emphatically in the second half. For example, he claims not to know what happened in the final private interview between Billy and Captain Vere; he can only "conjecture." This device reiterates the claim of truth for the narrative; it may also renew the reader's uneasiness. It's worth asking once more why the narrator, the inventor of characters and action alike, should disclaim his own authority. Do the questions he implicitly raises about authorial authority extend to other kinds of power? Or does one come to believe in the truth of the story he tells? Another question about the way the story is being told may arise with the "Digression" after the hanging: what is the point of introducing these speculations about why Billy's body didn't move? Do they suggest something supernatural about his death? Does the reader find him- or herself trying to come up with other explanations? Do we believe that the problem matters at all?

A few more large questions that might prove stimulating: Do the three principal characters conduct themselves in the crisis in ways you would anticipate from their characterizations in the first half? Claggart is the villain, but he alone does not cause Billy's death. Who or what should be blamed? Captain Vere? "Society"? War? Chance? How do you feel about Billy at the end? Is he saint or simpleton? Can you think of comparable instances, in public or in private life, of conflicts between legality and justice that are very difficult to adjudicate?

### Topics for Writing

Most of the questions that have been raised here would provide good material for essays, whether or not they have been discussed in class. (Since this work is so richly interpretable, everyone can have individual opinions differing from ones arrived at collectively.) Some other possible topics:

1. Why does the action occur during the French Revolution?

2. Billy as a passive hero

3. Billy's effect on others

4. Captain Vere: the tragedy of the educated man

5. Claggart's motives

### Further Reading

See also the reading suggestions in the anthology, pp. 804–05.

Milder, R., ed. *Critical Essays on Melville's* Billy Budd, Sailor. 1989.
Representative group of critical essays.

Miller, E. *Melville.* 1975.
Both biographical and critical, stressing Freudian interpretation.

Parker, H. *Reading* Billy Budd. 1990.
Focused on the difficulties of interpretation and their significance.

Stafford, W. *Melville's* Billy Budd *and the Critics.* 1969.
    Offers an enormous amount of useful information, containing texts
    of Melville's story and of the play made from it; an essay on the
    Hayford-Sealts text; and a collection of early and recent criticism
    from several points of view, including treatments of characters,
    sources, digressions, tradition, theological implications, and a
    valuable bibliography.

# EMILY DICKINSON

*Classroom Strategies and Topics for Discussion*

First-time readers of Emily Dickinson typically have trouble under-standing why such tiny poems should be taken seriously. Because Dick-inson makes no loud claims for herself, because her lyrics do not elabo-rate their emotional arguments, perhaps even because of their eccentric punctuation, students may make the mistake of thinking these are easy and obvious poems. Your first task, therefore, is to demonstrate how much goes on beneath the surface of apparently simple verse—and for this purpose, there is no substitute for close attention to a specific text. A class can easily spend an hour exploring implications of a single short poem; to do so provides the best way to demonstrate the complexity of Dickinson's achievement.

If time limitations forbid such leisurely analysis, one may use a more general approach. You could point out, for example, that at least five of Dickinson's lyrics here printed deal centrally with death (216, 449, 465, 712, 1564). Beyond this theme, the five poems have little obviously in common. Yet it is illuminating to compare them with one another—say, 216 and 712. Do they share any images? Students might notice immedi-ately that both suggest connections between graves and houses: "a House that seemed / A Swelling of the Ground," "Alabaster Chambers." Are these associations reassuring or disturbing? This question should gene-rate considerable discussion—possibly even controversy. The solidity, beauty, security of alabaster, satin, stone (216, stanza 1) might be cited as forms of positive suggestion; and the apparent affinity to nature of the "House" in 712. On the other hand, the fact that the alabaster chambers remain untouched by morning and noon (with the past participle repeated for emphasis) is more ambiguous. One could argue that being untouched by diurnal sequence implies existence beyond time, transcendence—or, with very different emotional tone, that it implies the cessation of ex-perience. Similarly, the "Centuries" that have elapsed since the speaker in 712 set out on her journey with Death may convey the positive associ-ations of "Immortality" or the terrifying possibilities of "Eternity." Does the speaker convey a consistent attitude toward death in each case? The effect of 216 depends on the contrast between its first and second stanzas. Is that contrast mainly between the ignorance of breeze, bee, and birds and the "sagacity" of the dead? Perhaps so—but the sagacity has already "perished," so "the meek members of the Resurrection" in their sleep can oppose no wisdom to the "ignorant cadence" of the birds.

The noun *Resurrection* in 216, like *Immortality* in 712, suggests a Christian view of the afterlife. Does anything else in either poem substantiate this view? The predominant images, in both cases, are secular—in 216, details of tomb, coffin, and natural world; in 712, items of clothing and scenes that recapitulate stages of human life. Why, then, the Christian allusions? Generations of critics have debated this problem, and no definitive answer is likely. Students might, however, find it interesting to think about the degree to which both poems achieve their effects by juxtaposing incongruous points of view without mediating between them. The most obvious example is the imagining of Death as a gentlemanly figure stopping his carriage for a lady and of the journey through eternity as an exercise in civility. To think of gossamer and tulle in relation to death, or of horses and eternity, also strains the imagination by invoking sharply different focuses of perception. The abstractness of *Immortality* contrasts with the concretely imagined scene of two figures in a carriage. To think of the dead as "members of the Resurrection" conflicts with thinking of them in their graves; to turn attention to what happens in the air makes it hard to think simultaneously of what happens under ground; and to sum up the dead as having embodied "sagacity" violates the expectations that the poem has established.

The techniques students will discover by trying to figure out the relation of these two poems recur in many others. In other lyrics too they can find unpredictable juxtapositions of abstract and concrete and of opposed perspectives; gaps in meaning that both demand and elude interpretation (what, for example, is the relation, on the narrative level, between the "House" before which the travelers pause in 712 and their continued journey? What does the grave have to do with eternity?) and the shock value of unexpected words (e.g., *omnipotent* in 585, *infirm* in 1129, *enabled* in 1207, *Pangless* in 1564). The effect of the punctuation is worth discussing: Often a dash at a poem's end suspends meaning, implying that a thought or feeling is only interrupted, not completed; often dashes in the middle of lines force pauses that demand attention for a phrase suddenly made fresh by being perceived as a small, contained unit. And you may wish to call attention to Dickinson's slant rhymes (*away* and *civility*, *chill* and *Tulle*). True rhymes in a quatrain structure create effects of finality, order, closure. These near-rhymes, like the dashes, suggest that matters cannot quite be closed off, that no statement comprehends the significance of any phenomenon.

Rhetoric, rhythm, and punctuation reiterate the same implications of open meaning. These poems demand active involvement from their readers. Their predominantly simple language, their way of contemplating the ordinary until it becomes strange (think of the buzzing fly in 465), suggest that everyday experience also invites active involvement, active interpretation, and that all meaning depends on interpretation. One can imagine the dead as buried or as resurrected (or as both at once), one can imagine a train as an animal or a star (585). Such acts of imagination make the world simultaneously comprehensible and mysterious.

## Topics for Writing

1. Animal life in Emily Dickinson

2. A "feminine" aspect of Dickinson's poems

3. Who is the speaker (and what is she like?) in any poem?

4. Dickinson's sense of humor

## Further Reading

See also the reading suggestions in the anthology, p. 866.

Fast, R. R. and C. M. Gordon, eds. *Approaches to Teaching Emily Dickinson's Poetry*. 1989.
An exceptionally useful and varied collection.

Juhasz, S., ed. *Feminist Critics Read Emily Dickinson*. 1983.
Collects valuable examples of feminist approaches.

Pollak, V. *Dickinson: The Anxiety of Gender*. 1984.
Analyzes the life and work with emphasis on her experience as a woman.

Sewall, R. *The Life of Emily Dickinson*. 2 vols. 1974.
———, ed. *Emily Dickinson: A Collection of Critical Essays*. 1963.
A thorough, readable, and interesting biography, and a group of essays illuminating in their diversity.

# Masterpieces of the Nineteenth Century
## Realism, Naturalism and the New Poetry

## GUSTAVE FLAUBERT
### Madame Bovary

### *Backgrounds*

*Madame Bovary* is the story of Emma, a young woman living in Normandy in the 1840s. She has received a convent education that has filled her head with romantic dreams of luxury and love. She marries a country doctor, Charles Bovary, an awkward, dull, but honest and loving young man, and bears him a daughter. Quickly disappointed and bored by her marriage, she resists the advances of a shy student, Léon, but then becomes depressed and revives only when Charles manages to move into a larger village, Yonville. There she quickly succumbs to the advances of a dashing landowner, Rodolphe. She wants to elope with him, but he deserts her in the last moment. On a trip to Rouen where she attends the opera, she again meets Léon, now a law clerk, and becomes his mistress. Her clandestine meetings and the luxuries she purchases involve her in debt to a local, usurious merchant. When he presses her and all attempts to get help from her lovers fail, she commits suicide by arsenic poisoning. Only after her death does Charles discover her infidelities.

Flaubert wrote the novel after his return from a trip to the Orient, deliberately choosing a low and commonplace subject and a heroine whose vulgarity he despised. He felt he had to make a new beginning as all his early writings had been lyrical and romantic. He worked assiduously at the novel, describing his slow progress and his "agonies of composition" in letters to his friend Louise Colet.

Flaubert's treatment of sexual encounters, frank for his time, and his description of the ceremony of extreme unction caused an attempt by the government of Napoleon III to suppress the book as obscene. The defense won acquittal on the argument that the story actually shows the wages of sin and even metes out harsh punishment for Emma's adulteries. The success of the book was thus assured. What Flaubert wrote, however, was neither a salacious book nor a warning against adultery but a supreme work of art, which today is generally regarded as the first modern novel, clearly set off by its objectivity from the earlier moralizing novels of writers such as Balzac, Dickens, and Thackeray.

### Classroom Strategies

Flaubert divided the novel into three parts, which can be taught in three assignments. If necessary, Part 2 may be divided after Chapter VIII (which ends on p. 989) and Part 3 after Chapter VI (which ends on p. 1083), making five assignments.

The main difficulties of the book come from defining the author's ambiguous attitude toward Emma, which obviously includes condemnation of her lying, her lust, and her improvidence, satire on her romantic illusions, and compassion for her sufferings. As the headnote indicates, Flaubert's point of view is not as detached and completely objective as the reputation of the book might suggest. The story begins in the schoolroom with a teller who speaks of "we" as if he were one of the boys in the class, but then the point of view shifts to omniscience: much that is represented could not possibly have been seen or felt by Madame Bovary. Occasionally Flaubert comments disapprovingly on her "hardhearted and tightfisted peasant nature" or her "corruption". But at the end, in his description of the extreme unction, he solemnly pronounces forgiveness even for her sensuality and lust. One must keep alert throughout for shifts in perspective of this kind. For example, the ball at the castle of the Marquis (Chapter VII of Part 1) is drenched in the atmosphere of Emma's own dreams and longings. The agricultural fair on the other hand, which has been called "polyphonic" in reproducing the speeches of the pompous officials alternating with the love-talk of Rodolphe, is viewed not through Emma's eyes, but with the satirical and ironic detachment of the author.

Other valuable points for discussion are the satirical picture of the whole society (particularly as represented in the odious pharmacist Homais, who is the target of Flaubert's dislike of the ideas of progress, science and democracy) and the character of Charles Bovary, who opens and closes the book and whose final judgment "It was decreed by fate," (p. 1120) is endorsed by the author even though Rodolphe finds it slightly ridiculous.

The technique of building the book around striking pictorial scenes should also be discussed. The ball, the agricultural fair, the ride in the woods, Emma receiving Rodolphe's letter and climbing to the attic, the opera (*Lucia di Lammermoor*) in Rouen, the visit to the Cathedral, the cab ride, the scenes in the hotel with Léon, and finally the suicide print themselves indelibly on one's memory, and it pays to ask by what means Flaubert has accomplished this. Often small details are used almost symbolically, as in the little scene of Charles and Emma having supper, he eating boiled beef, she drawing knife lines on the oilcloth on the table: a scene used by Erich Auerbach in *Mimesis* to stress the novelty of Flaubert's impersonal realism. Or to take another example: the wooden napkin rings of Binet and the whirr of the lathe, which saves Emma from falling to her death. Such details serve to point out the estrangement between husband and wife while emphasizing also the role of little things, the chances of life.

### Topics for Discussion and Writing

1. Discuss the character of Emma and the author's attitude toward her.

2. Discuss the social picture and social types of the novel: the husband-physician, the landowner, the law clerk, the pharmacist, the merchant-usurer, the beggar, etc.

3. Discuss Percy Lubbock's statement in *Craft of Fiction* that this is "the novel of all novels which no criticism of fiction can overlook" (p. 60). Comparing it with other novels you have read—*The Princess of Clèves*, for instance—what features do you discover in it that might justify Lubbock's praise?

4. Discuss the implied philosophy of life or scale of values. Do you agree with Martin Turnell (*The Novel in France*) that this novel is "an onslaught on the whole basis of human feeling and on all spiritual and moral values"? Think also of the "positive" figures: Emma's father, the pharmacist's apprentice, the old peasant woman at the agricultural fair who got for fifty-four years of

service a medal worth twenty-five francs, or of Dr. Larivière, who comes too late to save Emma.

5. Discuss some particularly clearly visualized episodes such as the agricultural fair and the scene in the Cathedral. Both contrast the trivial lovetalk with the pompous rhetoric of an official or a guide. What is the effect of this?

6. Ask how far the story transcends its local setting in time and place and, particularly, how far its scenes, persons, actions, emotional and mental attitudes may be applied to our own time. Emma is sometimes thought of as a typical dreamer like Don Quixote, but in fact the two are very different. Don Quixote does something about it, however foolish, while Emma can only plan a trip to Italy. Homais has become the type of the conventional small town man who has accepted all the commonplaces of nineteenth-century progress, faith in science and democracy, and is, in the last words of the book, rewarded with the order of the Legion of Honor. Do we still find this type today?

## Further Reading

See also the reading in the anthology, p. 889.

Auerbach, Erich. *Mimesis: The Representation of Reality in Western Literature*. Translated by Willard Trask. Princeton, 1953.
"In the Hotel de la Mole" has luminous pages.

Bart, Benjamin F., ed. Madame Bovary *and the Critics: A Collection of Essays*. New York, 1966.

James, Henry. *Notes on Novelists*. New York, 1914.
Throws doubt on the choice of subject.

Levin, Harry. *The Gates of Horn: A Study of Five French Realists*. New York, 1963.
The chapter "Flaubert" gives a general appraisal of *Madame Bovary*.

Lubbock, Percy. *The Craft of Fiction.* New York, 1921.
In Chapters 5 and 6, Lubbock stresses the role of telling and the point of view.

Steegmuller, Francis. *Flaubert and Madame Bovary.* New York, 1939; new ed. 1950.
Good on the biographical background and the genesis of the book.

Turnell, Martin. *The Novel in France.* London, 1950.
Criticizes Flaubert from a moral point of view.

# FYODOR DOSTOEVSKY
## Notes from Underground

### *Backgrounds*

*Notes from Underground* consists of two distinct parts. First comes the monologue of a lonely, spiteful former clerk who lives in a garret in St. Petersburg and states his hatred of humanity, progress, science, and determinism. Next follows a kind of memoir in which the same man reminisces about events in his earlier life. An attempt at self-assertion has led to his jostling an officer; an intrusion into the company of former schoolfellows has resulted in humiliating altercations and finally in a visit to a brothel. There he in turn humiliates the prostitute Lisa by depicting her future terrible fate. Deeply moved and determined to change her life, she calls on the Underground Man, only to find him engaged in a disgraceful scene with his servant. Newly humiliated, he seeks vicarious revenge by sexually assaulting the girl and forcing money on her. She flees, throwing the money away. The Underground Man remains in his hole, alienated, mortified, disgusted with himself and everything around.

The story, written in 1864, reflects the beginning of Dostoevsky's conversion to a conservative creed. He had, as explained in the headnote (see p. 1125), taken part in an underground circle, which the government of Tsar Nicholas considered subversive, but which was mainly a discussion group interested in the Utopian Socialism of Fourier. Dostoevsky was arrested, tried, taken to be shot, but reprieved on the place of execution to ten years penal servitude in Siberia. Four years he spent in a stockade in chains and six as a common soldier on the frontier of China. He returned to Petersburg in 1859, a changed man.

*Notes from Underground* is a departure from Dostoevsky's early manner as a social novelist, and anticipate the later great novels beginning with *Crime and Punishment* two years later.

### *Classroom Strategies*

Two assignments or three. Part 2 can be divided after Chapter 5 (which ends on p. 1178), if three are desired.

The first part, the monologue, presents difficulties to students in that it contains a searing attack on the assumptions of their tradition. The whole Enlightenment cherished by the West—including the ideas of perpetual progress, of scientific truth, of a well-organized, rational society "in pursuit of happiness"—is not only questioned, but jeered at. Students are apt to discount the whole diatribe because it is put into the mouth of a despicable being, who himself declares that he is motivated by resentment at his failure in human relations. Such a dismissal would be an enormous mistake: the Underground Man is right in Dostoevsky's eyes in asserting human freedom, which seems to him the essential prerogative of our species. He feels that he is robbed of it by deterministic science, which forbids him to argue that two plus two may be five, and by the Utopian schemes of socialist world-improvers who would force humanity into an artificial collective paradise. Through the mouth of his unlovely speaker, Dostoevsky attacks all rationalism, all Utopianism, all illusions about natural goodness. He does not believe that men and women follow their enlightened self-interest as the Utopians hoped. Rather, in his view, they are creatures of passion, even senseless and destructive passion. The human species is bloodthirsty, and history is a record of butcheries. Our nature, as history shows, craves chaos and destruction, even suffering and pain. The intellectual position of the Underground Man can be seen as an anticipation of Existentialism, which in the writings of Jean-Paul Sartre and Albert Camus asserted indeterminism, the freedom of the will, and choice. It can also be seen as curiously prophetic of the terrifying inhumanities we have witnessed in our own century.

## Topics for Discussion

The whole question of optimism vs. pessimism about the fate of mankind will properly take center stage. Questions about the brutalities of humankind both past and present will make for exciting debate. Our own modern fear of totalitarianism is raised as the Underground Man revolts at the thought that the individual soul might become a member of an ant-heap, a mere cipher, a piano-key, an organ-stop (as he says in many variations).

The second part, in particular, raises psychological questions: Dostoevsky depicts a personality dominated by resentment, who doubts the stability of human personality and who himself oscillates between pride and humility, the desire to humiliate others, and the hardly concealed desire of being humiliated. The scenes with Lisa are the best illustrations.

A literary question is raised by the dramatic monologue, which at times is almost like a stream of consciousness, in its relation to the confessions of the second part, which buttress and justify the tone and content of the first part. The parody of the rescue of a prostitute is the most striking example. The whole story, told by an "anti-hero," may at first strike us as purely negative; yet it is one of the paradoxes of Dostoevsky's art that he uses his most doubtful characters as spokesmen for his most cherished ideas. Though Dostoevsky complained of the suppression of a chapter by the censor, hinting at a religious solution that he found later, we may at this stage of our knowledge of Dostoevsky's writings remain baffled by the blind alley in which the Underground Man has lost himself.

A further point of discussion is raised by the peculiarly Russian setting of the person and events of the story. Dostoevsky considers the Underground Man, in his alienation from society, to be representative of the generation of the forties and the fifties. The story particularly attacks the Utopianism of such novels as that by Nikolay Chernyshevsky, *What is to Be Done?* (1863), which much later was highly admired by Lenin, and jeers at the materialist progress reflected in the Crystal Palace at the London Universal Exhibition, which Dostoevsky saw in 1862. Polemics against Russian radical critics of the sixties color the speech of the Underground Man. The nature of the reflections on romanticism, which here means "dreaming" or vague "idealism," and the picture of the stratified society (clerks, bureaucrats, military officers, prostitutes) date the story to the same extent as the wet snow and the fog localize it in a Petersburg winter.

### Topics for Writing

1. Discuss the attack on the idea of progress, on the natural goodness of humankind, on the benefits of science, and on rationalism and optimism generally.

   [Clues to possible answers are suggested in the headnote and the *Topics for Discussion*, but may be different for different students.]

2. Discuss the view that humanity's history shows our cruelty: that we *want* to suffer and inflict pain. Do not exclude current and recent history.

   [In psychiatry the term "sado-masochism" would describe this condition. In the story, the scenes with Lisa are perhaps the best examples.]

3. Discuss humanity's "terrifying freedom." Are you convinced by the argument against determinism and for complete individualism, even caprice? Are you any more convinced by the converse of these views? Why or why not?

4. What does the term Underground Man imply?
[In Russian, *podpolie* means "below the floor." The Underground Man is compared to a mouse living in a cellar-hole, but the actual protagonist lives in a garret with a servant. The answer is suggested by the whole tone of resentment, isolation, and alienation.]

### Further Reading

See also the reading in the anthology, pp. 1125–26.

Carr, Edward Hallett. *Dostoevsky, 1821–1881: A New Biography.* Boston, 1931.
Sober and factual.

Dostoevsky, Fyodor. *Notes from Underground.* Edited by Robert G. Durgy; translated by Serge Shishkoff. 1969; reprinted 1982.
Contains a section of modern criticism.

Frank, Joseph. *Dostoevsky: The Seeds of Revolt, 1821–1849.* Princeton, 1976.
———. *Dostoevsky: The Stir of Liberation, 1860–1865* (the Period of *Notes from the Underground*). Princeton, 1986.
———. *Dostoevsky: The Years of Ordeal, 1849–1859.* Princeton, 1984.
The best up-to-date, well-written biography.

Jones, Malcolm V. *Dostoevsky: The Novel of Discord.* London, 1976.
A good recent introduction.

Simmons, Ernest J. *Dostoevsky: The Making of the Novelist.* London and New York, 1940.
Provides a reliable digest of Russian scholarship.

# LEO TOLSTOY
## The Death of Iván Ilyich

### *Backgrounds*

*The Death of Iván Ilyich* is the story of a Russian judge in the 1880s who, from an accidental fall while climbing a ladder to fix a curtain, contracts an illness that leads to a lingering, painful death. In the course of dying, Iván Ilyich recognizes that he has led a wrong life, yet at the very end he feels he has defeated death. There is a light at the bottom of the black sack into which he is being pushed.

The story (1886) was written after Tolstoy's "conversion" in 1879 and reflects his lifelong preoccupation with death and dying and his ambition to found a simplified religion together with his criticism of city civilization.

The story differs sharply in its bald manner of telling from the earlier epic novels, *War and Peace* and *Anna Karenina*. Its tone is rather that of a parable: "Iván Ilyich's life had been most simple and most ordinary and therefore most terrible" (p. 1215).

### *Classroom Strategies*

The story is so unified that it is difficult to divide it. If two assignments are needed, the end of Chapter III (p. 1125) would be a breaking point.

The story is so straightforward that students cannot misunderstand it. It is intended to remind us forcefully of the inevitability of death and the loneliness of every human being when confronted with his or her own death. Tolstoy brings home the contrast between the triviality of the life and activities of the average person (Iván Ilyich in Russian sounds like John Smith) and the sudden, awesome awareness of death and dying. One could argue that he stresses this contrast because he resents the hypocrisy with which the fact of death is usually swept under the rug and wants to hold out some hope of another life in the symbol of the light at the bottom of the black sack.

Readers may have difficulties with the harsh satire upon doctors, the institution of marriage, and the courts of law, as well as with the possibly not clearly motivated final acceptance of death that Iván achieves. Possibly an explanation of the Russian class system may help to explain details: the bureaucracy sharply divided from the peasantry of which Gerasim, the assistant of the butler, is the lonely representative. He alone has genuine compassion for his dying master and is able to speak of death, while all the upper-class characters are hidebound in social conventions and hypocrisy.

## Topics for Discussion

Compare the attitude to death and dying with representative American attitudes. What do our current substitutions of *funeral director* for *undertaker*, *casket* for *coffin*, *deceased* for *dead man* or *woman*, and *passed away* for *died* have to do with Tolstoy's theme? In Tolstoy the ritual of the orthodox church is satirized: the confession, the display of the corpse in an open coffin, the concern of the widow for the price of the burial plot, but mainly the hypocrisy of the people surrounding the man—all these are exposed. So are the annoyance of the family at their own inconvenience (the girl is eager to marry), the callousness of the doctors interested in the diagnosis of the illness (floating kidney or vermiform appendix?) rather than in the suffering of the patient, and the hardly concealed pleasure of Ilyich's supposed friends at the news of his death, since it will vacate a position at court. But Tolstoy wants primarily to convey our need to recognize the majesty of death and the triviality of the life of the average man.

A powerful vein of realism runs throughout this story. Ugly details usually excluded from conventional fiction bring before us the smell of the disease, the processes of elimination, the sound of screaming in excruciating pain. Yet there is also a degree of contrivance almost too neat in the way the characters are typed and their lives and the beginning and end contrasted. Small satirical details like the creaking of the hassock or the full bosom "pushed up by her corset" of Iván Ilyich's wife (p. 1242) will seem too artful, and the final image of the black sack with the light at its bottom is obviously a symbol with a manifest design on our feelings. Suspense is deliberately eliminated by the title and the first scene of the funeral service.

The story can be seen as a miniature educational novel. Ilyich slowly comes to recognize that what we all know in theory (that human beings are mortal) is going to happen to *him*. He slowly progresses to a recognition not only of the inevitability of death, but to a rejection of his former

---

life and finally to a dim hope for transcendence and even redemption.

## Topics for Writing

1. What is the attitude to death and dying of the main character, Ivan Ilyich, and of the author?
   [Clues to an answer are found in the comments above.]

2. What elements in the story are unrealistic?
   [See the comments above.]

3. Trace the main events and changes in Ivan Ilyich's life discussed above.
   [Details of Ivan Ilyich's earlier life appear in the reminiscences he evokes.]

4. Describe the society implied in the story (the group in the law courts, the family doctors, the servants). What elements appear to you peculiarly Russian or late nineteenth–century? What elements seem universally applicable?
   [However blunt Tolstoy's attack on society and its hypocrisy, it is well to recall that his main concern is to enforce the universal truth of man's mortality and the falseness of living without consciousness of the end.]

## Further Reading

See also the reading in the anthology, p. 1208–09.

Maude, Aylmer. *The Life of Tolstoy.* 2 vols. New York, 1917.

Simmons, Ernest J. *An Introduction to Tolstoy's Writings.* Chicago, 1968.
Elementary and informative.

# HENRIK IBSEN
## Hedda Gabler

### Backgrounds

This is the tragedy of a beautiful, proud woman, the daughter of a general (whose picture presides over the scene). At thirty, when in straitened circumstances, she marries a scholar, George Tesman, who takes her on an extended honeymoon trip from their Norwegian town (Christiana, now called Oslo) to the Continent to further his research, "The Domestic Industries of Brabant in the Middle Ages." The play begins with their return home.

They have rented a splendid house in the expectation that Tesman will soon be appointed Professor, but this turns out to be uncertain. A rival, Eilert Loevborg, has just published a survey of the history of civilization and might thus win in a competition for the chair. Eilert, however, who has courted Hedda in former times, has a drinking problem, from which he has (for the time being) been rescued by a former schoolmate of Hedda's, Mrs. Thea Elvsted, during a stay in the country. When he returns to town, Thea leaves her husband to follow him, fearing his relapse into alcoholism. As soon as Eilert meets Hedda, he begins to court her again passionately and abandons any idea of challenging Tesman for the Professorship. He now dismisses his published work as trivial and is absorbed in writing a book on the future of mankind, the manuscript of which he carries with him.

Hedda is violently jealous of Eilert's relation to Thea and considers the new abstinence a sign of weakness and of subservience to the other woman. A friend of the house, Judge Brack, arranges a drinking party, which Hedda taunts Eilert into joining. The party is a disaster for Eilert: he gets drunk and late in the night goes off to a brothel, losing his manuscript on the way. When Tesman finds it and brings it back to the house, Hedda in her jealousy burns it. It is somehow, she feels, Eilert and Thea's child. This striking scene ends the third act. In the fourth act, we hear that Eilert has not only gotten into trouble with the police, but has killed himself with the pistol that Hedda had given him. The Judge, who also has designs on Hedda, threatens to testify that she supplied Eilert with the pistol unless she gives herself to him. Trapped by her marriage, by the prospect (which she scorns) of bearing Tesman's child, and by the fear of local scandal, she shoots herself.

In his youth, Ibsen had written romantic verse plays such as *Peer Gynt*, but established his reputation as a writer for the stage with his social plays. These advocated causes such as the emancipation of women (*A Doll's House*) or discussed taboo topics like hereditary venereal disease (*Ghosts*). *Hedda Gabler*, unlike the rest, seems to have no direct social purpose, unless it is to celebrate the dilemma of the rebellious individual who must die to escape societal constraints. The play, extremely effective on the stage, has allowed many famous actresses to display their art.

### Classroom Strategies

The play can be taught in two class periods.

The greatest difficulty of the play lies in explaining the character and behavior of Hedda. We must assume that she is desperate on returning home, hating her dull, somewhat obtuse, and even ridiculous husband, and further disgusted by the prospect of bearing a child—in particular, his child. Her playing with the pistol in threatening the Judge and later giving one of the two pistols inherited from her father to Eilert, thus practically ordering him to commit suicide, forecasts her own final decision. She is not, however, a blameless heroine. She behaves with cold contempt toward her husband, callously and maliciously toward his harmless aunt, with cattish jealousy toward Thea, and with violent, domineering passion toward Eilert, who has to prove himself in her eyes by drinking and returning "with a crown of vine-leaves" in his hair. When he fails, she sends him to his death quite unconcerned. At the same time, she is strangely hemmed in by conventions. She yearns for luxuries—a liveried footman, a thoroughbred horse, a grand piano—and has ambitions to play hostess. She is unwilling to commit adultery, though she flirts with Judge Brack, and she is deeply upset by the prospect of a police investigation and a local scandal. Her main trait is a fierce individualism: pride in her family, her beauty, and her independence. The fear that she might have to yield to Judge Brack is the last straw in motivating her suicide. There is something grotesque and a little sick in her insistence that a beautiful death consists of putting a bullet through the temple and that Eilert has bungled his by shooting himself in the abdomen. Still, we are asked to admire her beauty, pride, and yearning for freedom and to pity her as the victim of the dull, limited, or cowardly people around her.

The only problematic character besides Hedda is Eilert. We must assume that he is something of a genius. Ibsen contrasts what seems to him Tesman's dull, antiquarian subject, "The Domestic Industries of Brabant in the Middle Ages" with Eilert's allegedly brilliant speculations about the future course of civilization. At least in the imagination of Hedda, he is an almost Dionysian figure, whose collapse and ignominious end come as a terrible blow to her.

The construction of the play demands attention. We may notice the deliberately misleading optimism of the beginning. By the end of Act I, Hedda has bested both her husband and his aunt and by hypocritical blandishments extracted the secret of Thea's relation to Eilert. In Act II, she proves her power over Eilert by inducing him to join the Judge's party. The act ends with Eilert leaving and the two women, Hedda and Thea, left alone waiting for his return late into the night. Act III is the turning point, the *peripeteia*. It ends with Hedda burning the manuscript of Eilert's new book. Act IV brings a speedy resolution. The story of the horrible end of Eilert, the disappointing recognition that Eilert's manuscript can be pieced together again from notes preserved by Thea and Hedda's own husband, the threat of Judge Brack all add intensity and suspense to the final moment when, playing a "frenzied dance-melody" on the piano, Hedda ends her life with a pistol shot. The comments of the two survivors: Tesman screaming "She's shot herself! Shot herself in the head! By Jove! Fancy that!" and Judge Brack's commonsensical "But, good God! People don't do such things!" (p. 1313) make a grotesque, almost parodic point.

### Further Reading

See also the reading in the anthology, p. 1254.

Bentley, Eric. *In Search of Theatre.* New York, 1953.
Contains a good chapter on Ibsen.

Brustein, Robert. *The Theatre of Revolt: An Approach to the Modern Drama.* Boston, 1964.
A survey of modern drama containing chapters on Strindberg, Chekhov, Brecht, Pirandello, and others. Chapter 2 (pp. 35–85) deals with Ibsen.

LeGallienne, Eva. "Preface to Ibsen's Hedda Gabler". London, 1953.
Praise from a famous American actress.

Northam, John. *Ibsen's Dramatic Method: A Study of the Prose Dramas.* London, 1953.
Concentrates on Ibsen's stagecraft.

# ANTON CHEKHOV
## The Cherry Orchard

*Backgrounds*

Chekhov's plays have the reputation of being plotless, static, a mere string of scenes held together by a mood. But this is not true of Chekhov's last play, *The Cherry Orchard*. It has a clear plot-line: Madame Lubov Ranevskaya returns to her estate in the provinces of Russia after an absence of five years. With her are her seventeen-year-old daughter, Anya; the governess Charlotta; and a footman, Yasha. They are greeted by the brother of Lubov, Leonid Gayev; a maid, Dunyasha; and a merchant, Yermolay Lopahin, who is the son of a serf on the estate, but who has made money—even become wealthy—cultivating poppies. He soon reminds the arrivals that the estate will be up for sale unless they can raise the money to pay the heavy debts. The great cherry orchard will have to be cut down to make room for country houses. It is spring now: the orchard is in bloom, all white, a symbol for Lubov of the innocence of her childhood, which she betrayed when, after the death of her husband and the accidental drowning of her other child, the boy Grisha, she left for Paris with a lover, who has since robbed and betrayed her.

The second act in the open air provides relief in an idyllic setting. The "eternal" student Petya Trofimov, who was the tutor of the drowned boy, courts Anya and grandiloquently talks about the backwardness of Russia and the bright future of humanity. The merchant Lopahin reminds Lubov of the impending sale, which she faces helplessly.

The third act is the turning point. Recklessly, just on the day of the auction, Lubov gives a dance: at the end, Lopahin comes back from town and awkwardly announces that he has bought the estate when another bidder seemed about to acquire it. He has paid 90,000 rubles for it above the mortgage.

The fourth act returns to the scene of the first: the nursery where the company assembles ready to depart. Lubov and her brother have somewhat recovered from the blow of the sale. Lubov is returning to Paris to look after her ill lover, who has been bombarding her with telegrams. Leonid has gotten a job in the local bank. Anya will go to Moscow to study. The house will be locked and eventually demolished. One hears the sound of the axes cutting down the cherry orchard.

## Classroom Strategies

The play has four acts; two assignments should suffice.

The most controversial question, still being debated, is about the pervasive tone of the play. Is it a tragedy or, as Chekhov insisted, a comedy? The headnote discusses the issue at length (see p. 1315). There is an undoubted pathos in the sale of the orchard and in the situation of old Firs, age 86, left alone in the abandoned house. (It is possible but not necessary, however, to think of him as dying. One may surmise that Lopahin, who goes off to Kharkov, instructs his clerk Yepihodov to look after the house.) There is also sadness in the passing of the old order, in the destruction of the beautiful orchard, and the acquisition of the estate by an upstart developer. The end can be seen as an example of the twilight of Tsarist Russia or more accurately of its land-owning class.

But the economic and social theme is made purely personal and possibly trivial by the passive resignation of Lubov, who feels that she must pay for her sins, and even more by the grotesque fecklessness of her brother Leonid. Though Lubov can say "without the cherry orchard life has no meaning for me," she accepts the solution. Her brother says that "we all calmed down and even felt quite cheerful." Lubov, in fact, is sleeping and feeling well and is now off to Paris to live on the money of a great aunt, which she knows will not last long. There are so many comic and even farcical characters and scenes in the play that the gloom of the main event is considerably lightened.

Anya, a serious decent girl, is the only character who is not ridiculed. Even Trofimov, the student who plays court to her and who pronounces famous, grandiloquent speeches on the backwardness of Russia and the need for expiating the sufferings of the serfs in the past, is himself a good-for-nothing who has never done any work. His speech promising a bright future for mankind sounds hollow, as does his pompous assertion of being "above love." Lubov punctures this boast by scolding him: "At your age not to have a mistress!" (p. 1343). The relation to Anya fizzles out.

Lubov's brother, Leonid Gayev, is similarly a figure of fun: effete, limited, even stupid. He drinks and eats and talks too much, telling the waiters quite inappropriate stories of the decadents in Paris. He plays imaginary games of billiards on all occasions, loudly giving commands in the jargon of the game. The adopted daughter of Lubov, Vanya, is a poor, awkward spinster who spoils her last chance of marrying Lopahin in a painful scene where she speaks of a broken thermometer. Charlotta, the governess, plays card-tricks and is a ventriloquist who lugs a dog around. The neighboring landowner with the comic double name Simeonov-Pishchik (something like Squealer) is as broke and irrepressible as the owners of the cherry orchard, but is rescued by an Englishman turning up out of the blue to pay him for the lease of some white clay found on his estate. Having swallowed a whole box of pills of Lubov's, he falls suddenly asleep and talks knowingly about Nietzsche's advocating the forging of banknotes. The clerk, Semyon Yepihodov, is an even more grotesque figure. He is unlucky, constantly knocks over things, finds a cockroach in his drink, and quite irrelevantly drops the name of Buckle, a British historian. The maid, Dunyasha, is a foolish girl in love with the one definitely repulsive character, the valet Yasha. Firs, the old man-servant who remembers with nostalgia the days of serfdom, is a pathetic figure, hard of hearing, shuffling, ludicrous in his loneliness. One has to conclude that the play is a mixture of comedy and pathos.

## Topics for Discussion

1. The picture of Russia at the turn of the century is a topic of interest. The play presents the landed gentry with their hangers-on and servants, the new merchant-developers risen from the serf class, and the ineffectual, verbose student intelligentsia.

2. The technique of the play deserves discussion, especially the contrasts of the four acts. These are spring, summer, a day in August, and, shortly after, the day of departure. There is the white bloom of the cherries in Act I juxtaposed against the sound of the axes felling them in Act IV. Action shifts quickly from one speaker to another, and small incidents interrupt any semblance of a consecutive argument or mood.

## Topics for Writing

1. Is the play a tragedy or a comedy? How does Russia look, as seen in this play? What message is implied, if there is one?
   [Chekhov's attitude is not that of a reformer or revolutionary, but is also not reactionary. It is an attitude of deep human sympathy for almost everybody, coupled with a dim hope for progress. While

extravagance is obviously condemned and the merchant Lopahin depicted favorably (as Chekhov's letters insist), the playwright also excuses real passion, even guilty passion—or at least shows understanding for it.]

2. Can one define the role of symbolism in this play?
[The cherry orchard dominates obviously. More puzzling is the sound of the broken string. This, when it first sounds out of doors in Act II (p. 1330), is explained as possibly due to the fall of a bucket in a distant mine or perhaps as the cry of a heron or the hooting of an owl, but its repetition at the very end of the play (p. 1355) has an unexplained, ominous, weird effect. Attempts have been made to trace it to a childhood memory of Chekhov's or more simply to the general superstition that a broken string, say on a guitar, presages ill luck or even death.]

*Further Reading*

See also the reading in the anthology, p. 1317.

Barricelli, Jean-Pierre, ed. *Chekhov's Great Plays: A Critical Anthology.* New York, 1981.

Chekhov, Anton. *Anton Chekhov's Plays.* A Norton Critical Edition. Translated and edited by Eugene K. Bristow. New York, 1977. Contains several useful critical essays.

Hingley, Ronald. *Chekhov: A Biographical and Critical Study.* London, 1950; New York, 1966.

Jackson, Robert Louis, ed. *Chekhov: A Collection of Critical Essays.* Englewood Cliffs, N. J., 1967.

Magarshack, David. *Chekhov the Dramatist.* London, 1951; New York, 1960. Has a chapter arguing for the comedy of *The Cherry Orchard.*

Valency, Maurice. *The Breaking String.* New York, 1966. A general study of Chekhov's themes.

# CHARLES BAUDELAIRE

## *Backgrounds*

His contemporaries would have been amazed to know that Charles Baudelaire, a dandyish Parisian poet and art critic whose disturbing *Flowers of Evil* earned him a court fine in 1857, would continue to inspire writers, critics, and even rock groups for more than a century after his death. Baudelaire's fascination with questions of good and evil, his passion to explore the unknown (especially forbidden topics), his combination of crude realism and escapist dreams, and the insistent sensuality of his tormented love relationships strike chords in readers everywhere. These are not necessarily *pleasant* chords in, despite occasional peaceful and harmonious lyrics, for Baudelaire distrusts prettiness. He tries to shock us into clearer insights by undermining conventional attitudes: addressing his beloved as a potentially rotting carcass in "A Carcass," or accusing his reader of being—like himself—full of vices and fundamentally hypocritical. Baudelaire's modern appeal, however, derives from more than shock effects. Speaking from his own anguished subjectivity, the poet describes broadly human concerns: the fear of death and decay, the need for love, a painful alienation from others and from society. In response, he desires to create beauty, to understand relationships ("correspondences"). and to find answers. Such themes are reinforced by a precise and disciplined style that coordinates classical meter and rhyme schemes with extraordinarily subtle interrelationships of images, associations, and logically-developed argument.

"To the Reader" functions as a traditional preface, introducing the book's themes and establishing a common ground with its reader; however, there, convention stops. This preface is also a direct attack on the reader, who in included—along with the poet—in a lurid sermon on human sin. The catalogue of sins culminates unexpectedly in "BOREDOM," seen as a destructive apathy that is worse than conventional vices because it refuses to become involved and merely "swallows the world in a yawn." Images of the devil as scientist in his laboratory boiling off human willpower, or as puppet-master controlling our strings, underscore this fundamentally religious vision in which free will is of paramount importance. The riddling seventh stanza launches a long, two-stanza sentence suggesting that one supreme sin remains to be mentioned. That sin is finally identified as boredom, described literally as a monster smoking a water-pipe or hookah (used for smoking opium). In a line that continues to be quoted to this day, the poet accuses himself and his reader of complicity in this worst of evils.

"Correspondences" is an anchor point in Baudelaire's work, a classically perfect Alexandrine sonnet proclaiming that everything is interconnected (corresponds) at a subterranean level which the poet, a seer, is specially qualified to perceive. Baudelaire insists on connectedness throughout, repeating the French word *comme* ("like" or "as") six times in the two middle stanza; moreover, he strengthens the impact of this link-work by giving it two syllable instead of the usual one. (In classical French verse, the mute *e* is sounded separately when it precedes a consonant.)

The sonnet develops its argument in logical stages of hypothesis, explanation, and illustration. At the beginning, Nature is seen as quasi-divine, a living temple in which only humankind wanders blindly. In this basic unity of all life, explains the second stanza, the five sense—specifically, scents, colors, and sounds—are fused (literally, "answer one another"). The third stanza offers examples of these five reciprocal senses in perfumes (*smell*) that are fresh as (literally) a child's flesh (*touch*), sweet as oboes (*taste* and *sound*) and green as prairies (*color*). The overwhelming tones of youth and immaturity in these images prefigure the maturing of perfume images into rich, over-ripe ("corrupt"), expansive odors that dizzy and transport the senses. It is this ecstasy of the mind and senses that fascinates Baudelaire, a motif he will evoke in different images throughout his poetry.

In the love poem "Her Hair," Baudelaire celebrates his mistress's head of hair as another route to ecstasy. The poet's recurrent theme of the *voyage* blends with erotic escapism as Jeanne Duval's tresses become a perfumed sea of ebony, a black ocean whose sensual pleasure invites him to dream of a sea voyage to exotic tropical climes. (Compare the less erotic but similarly ecstatic voyage in "Invitation to the Voyage.") This richly colorful dream dominates the whole situation, for clearly Jeanne herself—hair, oasis, and gourd of wine—disappears under the weight of the dream-evocation which she has inspired.

"A Carcass" intends to shock the reader with its brutal description of an animal carcass swarming with maggots—a carcass, moreover, that the poet ends by comparing with the woman he loves. The contrast of ideal femininity and physical mortality was familiar to the Romantics; Baudelaire is treading familiar paths when he parodies Petrarchan imagery ("star of my eyes" etc.) and the *carpe diem* tradition (claiming in the last stanza that he has preserved "the form and divine essence / of my decomposed loves"). He has pulled off a surprising poetic gamble, nonetheless, in transforming images of decay into images of new life, the hum of flies and maggots into the more acceptable music of waves, running water, wind, or a thresher winnowing grain. By this transformation, the poet has demonstrated the power of artistic imagination (eighth stanza) before returning to the cruder image of the hungry dog, and the final, aggressive emphasis on universal decay—inevitable for all but the art of poetry.

"Invitation to the Voyage," written for Marie Daubrun, is celebrated for the musicality of its verse and the peaceful beauty of its visionary trip to an idealized Holland: the Holland of Dutch interiors painted by Vermeer, for example, or the Holland that collected objects of Eastern splendor through its seafaring empire. It is a dream of harmony, as embodied by a woman addressed as "child" or "sister" rather than the erotic images of other love poems. This harmony is also the profound unity of "Correspondences," in which beautiful sensuous images combine to address the soul in its sweet and secret native tongue."

"Song of Autumn, I" is the first of two short poems written in the same month: October, 1859; the second poem is a love poem addressed to Marie Daubrun. The scene is Paris; winter approaches, and Baudelaire (who detests cold) hears the customary October delivery of cordwood in the courtyard. Wintry passions will enter his soul. His heart, chilled to a frozen red block by despair and hard work, is compared to a setting sun frozen in its own arctic hell. The poem is especially accessible through the ascending sequence of images based on the sound of falling logs: Baudelaire imagines the regular thumps as the construction of an executioner's scaffold, the blows of a battering-ram destroying a tower, or nails being driven into a coffin. Autumn's dull knocking does not announce an arrival; instead, it heralds a departure into winter and, by association, death.

The three "Spleen" poems evoke this same melancholy in an even more concentrated fashion. They may be taught individually or as a group, expressing different facets of the speaker's alienation and despair. You may wish to compare the world-weariness of Chateaubriand's *René* (p. 580), or the bitterness of Dostoevsky's narrator in *Notes from Underground* (p. 1126). Like "Song of Autumn, I," each "Spleen" employs both realistic details and larger abstract or fantastic visions, and each depicts a progression of images. The best-known, "Spleen LXXXI," pursues a series of confinement images from covered pot, dungeon, and barred prison to the enclosures of brain and skull. A series of water-related images dwindling gradually from city to playing cards characterizes "Spleen LXXVIII," while the first half of "Spleen LXXIX" accumulates images of the dead past to evoke the poet's numb despair at the meaningless passage of time. Before students become too discourages by the theme of gray misery, remind them that these are virtuoso performances, developments on a theme just as is the peaceful dream of "Invitation to the Voyage." Baudelaire considers it a kind of redemption to be able "to produce a few beautiful verses" ("One O'Clock in the Morning"), and he finds in art a counterweight to the boredom and sense of helplessness called *spleen*.

"The Voyage" assumes a number of familiar Romantic themes, such as the deception of everyday life in a world too petty and cramped for the human spirit, the desire to escape by travelling to exotic and unknown realms, and the lure of the infinite. Although contemporary students may be struck chiefly by its colorful allegories of the human condition, its attack on organized religion (VI, ll. 206–09) and on political structures (VI, ll. 203–04) was so pointed that the poem was rejected by the journal scheduled to publish it. Writing to his friend Charles Asselineau on February 20, 1959, Baudelaire predicted that "The Voyage" would cause "nature to shudder, and especially lovers of progress."

The poem's eight sections fall into three general movements: the first describing a human craving (felt already in childhood) to voyage toward an intuited ideal realm (I–V), the second depicting the sin and corruption which the traveler encounters everywhere on earth (VI), and the final sequence reiterating the experienced traveler's compulsion to continue—realizing this time that the real voyage leads beyond mortal experience and into the only remaining unknown region, death.

Although there are scattered examples of short poetic works written in prose before Baudelaire, the appearance in 1862 of twenty-one *Little Poems in Prose (Paris Spleen)* by the French poet marked the first time that the genre had been named as such. For Baudelaire, these poems filled a different role from *The Flowers of Evil*: based in everyday experience, they offered a broad range of "impressions of the street, Parisian events and horizons, sudden starts of consciousness, languorous daydreams, philosophy, dreams themselves, and even anecdotes." In his dedication, he envisioned the ideal prose poem as a "poetic prose that would be musical without rhythm or rhyme, supple yet irregular enough to adapt to the lyric movements of the soul, to fluctuations of reverie, to sudden starts of consciousness." The prose poem is no less poetic for not being written in verse; it manifests the same internal rhythm and intricate organization of theme and image that we associate with lyric poetry. In Baudelaire's eyes, this supple and rhythmic prose was uniquely suited to expressing shifts of consciousness. It is easy to see how not only poets but also twentieth-century novelists exploiting stream-of-consciousness techniques (e.g., James Joyce, Virginia Woolf, and William Faulkner) are indebted to Baudelaire's example.

## Classroom Strategies

Two days will allow you to give a good sense of what Baudelaire is about and why he has been such a powerful influence on later literature; three days will allow you to look closely at a number of poems. There are several ways to enter the subject, depending on your own and your students' preferences. The autobiographical stance of the four prose poems make them especially accessible to students who are "afraid of poetry," and they allow easy entry into Baudelaire's characteristic themes. The picture of the harassed poet alienated from a commercialized society ("One O'Clock in the Morning") is a familiar theme, to be paired with the escape wish in "Anywhere Out of the World" (students appreciate the humorous realism of the hospital image, too). Alternately, you may wish to begin with the longer thematic poems ("The Voyage" and "A Carcass") and move to a selection of shorter lyric pieces. Another possibility might be to structure the days according to selected thematic contrasts ("Spleen and Ideal," a grouping in *The Flowers of Evil*; or dream and reality, beauty and ugliness, escape and a feeling of being trapped, eroticism and childlike harmony).

## Topics for Discussion

1. Baudelaire combines aspects associated with Realism and Romanticism. How far can he be considered as belonging to the Age of Realism? In what ways may he be considered a Romantic? Discuss this in light of the general introductions to the relevant sections.

2. Discuss the theme of the *voyage* throughout Baudelaire's poetry.

3. Discuss the appearance of an urban (as opposed to rural or pastoral) sensibility in Baudelaire's poetry.

4. Baudelaire is often claimed as the first Symbolist poet, although Symbolism as such did not develop until mush later in the century. What elements in his poetry support this claim?

5. Compare and contrast the world represented by Baudelaire's speaker with (choose) 1) Petrarch's; 2) Hamlet's; 3) Pope's in "The Rape of the Lock"; 4) Mme. de La Fayette in *The Princess of Clèves*; 5) the narrator in *Notes from Underground*.

6. How are women imagined and characterized in the poems you read? What attitude is implied? Is it dual or contradictory? Does Baudelaire give similar weight to the description of men? Discuss.

7. Compare the picture of women in Baudelaire and in (choose) 1) Pope, "The Rape of the Lock"; 2) Voltaire, *Candide*; 3) Goethe, *Faust*; 4) Flaubert, *Madam Bovary*. How are women presented? What definitions of womanliness are depicted, affirmed, or criticized in each work?

8. Discuss the theme of art, and of the role of the artist, in Baudelaire's poetry. You may wish to compare your findings with similar themes in Wordsworth, Coleridge, Keats, and Shelley.

*Further Reading*

See also the reading suggestions in the anthology, p. 1359.

Auerbach, Erich. "The Aesthetic Dignity of *Les Fleurs du Mal*," from *Scenes from the Drama of European Literature: Six Essays*. 1959. Impressive stylistic analysis.

Benjamin, Walter. *Charles Baudelaire: A Lyric Poet in the Era of High Capitalism*. Translated by Harry Zohn. 1973.
An imaginative theoretical treatment by a forerunner of deconstructionist criticism. See also the chapter on Baudelaire in his *Illuminations*, 1968.

Bersani, Leo. *Baudelaire and Freud*. 1977.
An interesting discussion of Baudelaire's poetry, arranged according to Freudian terminology.

Caws, Mary Ann and Rifferaterre, Hermine, eds. *The Prose Poem in France: Theory and Practice.* 1983.
Studies in the French prose poem from Baudelaire to modern times.

Eliot, T. S. "Baudelaire," 1930, from *Selected Essays,* 1932.
A discussion focused on Baudelaire's religious views.

Poulet, Georges. *Exploding Poetry: Baudelaire/Rimbaud.* Translated by Françoise Meltzer. 1984.
Contains an extended essay on Baudelaire's consciousness or worldview by a major phenomenological critic.

Raymond, Marcel. *From Baudelaire to Surrealism.* 1957, reprinted 1961.
A major critical work that contains a discussion of Baudelaire and his influence on modern poetry.

Rees, Garnet. *Baudelaire, Sartre and Camus: Lectures and Commentaries.* 1976.
A brief volume of accessible, popularized lectures.

Sharpe, William Chapman. *Unreal Cities: Urban Figuration in Wordsworth, Baudelaire, Whitman, Eliot, and Williams.* 1990.
An interesting discussion of Baudelaire and other city-oriented poets of the modern age.

# Masterpieces of the Twentieth Century
## Varieties of Modernism

## SIGMUND FREUD

### Backgrounds

If there is a single twentieth-century figure about whom people generally feel that they should know something, that figure is Sigmund Freud. Freud, after all, demonstrated that there was an unconscious life of the mind governing many of our daily activities; he proposed methods for recognizing these buried impulses; he held out the possibility of a systematic self-knowledge that was hitherto only hinted at in literary works from Saint Augustine's *Confessions* to Dostoevsky's *Notes from Underground*. Freudian vocabulary has become common currency for describing human behavior; terms such as "repression," "defense mechanism," and "self-love" have lost any visible connection to the founder of psychoanalysis but continue to be used in describing how people relate to one another. Scrutinizing the self has become a staple of art, literature, philosophy, medicine, and science. Self-scrutiny itself cannot be attributed to Freud, of course; Socrates claimed in fifth-century Greece that the "unexamined life" was "not worth living," and Romantic writers commonly developed the theme of self-knowledge, but Freud stands out as the modern figure who most crucially symbolizes an attempt to understand the phenomenon of human behavior.

When "Dora" (Ida Bauer) became Freud's patient in October, 1900, the psychoanalyst was still indignant at the poor reception of his recently-published *Interpretation of Dreams* (November 4, 1899; publisher's date 1900), which found few readers and was attacked by conservative members of the medical establishment. In the partly-autobiographical study, Freud had not only reviewed previous literature on dreams and dreaming as if investigating a serious topic but—more upsetting to neurologists—he had also developed a theory of dream interpretation that included a theory of how the mind works. Dreams were a way of representing and dealing with material that could not safely be brought to consciousness; as he explained in the prefatory remarks to *Dora* (omitted in this selection), they were *"one of the détours by which repression can be evaded."* Freud claimed that he learned "how to translate the language of dreams into the forms of expression of our own thought-language." He intended the case study of *"Dora"*, initially titled "Dreams and Hysteria," to be read as a response to criticism of the *Interpretation of Dreams* and a practical demonstration of its theories. Its combative preface reasserted that "a thorough investigation of the problems of dreams is an indispensable prerequisite for any comprehension of the mental processes in hysteria and the other psychoneuroses, and that no one who wishes to shirk that preparatory labor has the smallest prospect of advancing even a few steps into this region of knowledge. . . . What is new has always aroused bewilderment and resistance."

If critics attacked the *Interpretation of Dreams* as too speculative and abstract, *Dora* would earn their criticism for being too specific—an invasion of privacy in the particularly sensitive field of personal sexuality. Freud predicts this criticism in his Prefatory Remarks, and indeed he goes out of his way to justify his procedures. If, as he believes, the causes of neurosis are to be found in the patients' psychosexual life and repressed wishes, then completely elucidating such neuroses does reveal personal secrets that a "person of delicacy" would refuse to betray. However, Freud continues, "the physician has taken upon himself duties not only towards the individual but towards science as well"; thus it becomes "a disgraceful piece of cowardice" not to expose what he knows. Readers who have noted Freud's disappointment at Dora's termination of the treatment may agree with his principles but find the attitude ambiguous—the writer reminds us that he

> naturally cannot prevent the patient herself from being pained if her own case history should accidentally fall into her hands. But she will learn nothing from it that she does not already know; and she may ask herself who besides he could discover from it that she is the subject of this paper.

In the next paragraph, Freud speculates on that very matter. Although he has changed names and only his friend Wilhelm Fliess knows Dora's identity, Freud is aware that "many physicians (revolting though it may seem) choose to read a case history of this kind . . . as a *roman à clef* [a novel with 'real-life' references intended to be deciphered] designed for their private delectation."

Freud anticipates another reproach: impropriety. He expects his readers to be startled at the frankness with which he discusses sexual matters with a young woman, especially since "the organs and functions of sexual life will be called by their proper names." Scientific inquiry, however, requires such frankness; he claims for himself "the rights of a gynaecologist" and adds that it would be "a singular and perverse prurience to consider that such conversations excite or gratify sexual desire. Overall, Freud is very aware of his readers' foreseeable response as well as of his own aims; he states in a letter that *Dora* "is the most subtle thing I have yet written and will produce an even more horrifying effect than usual."

*Dora* continues to be read as a major case history, but interpretations of *what* one reads differ. In the traditional view, Freud progressively uncovers Dora's real motivations and fails to effect a cure only because she prematurely terminated the analysis. In a view gaining increasing currency today, Freud himself is implicated in the tale of Dora and the reader's analysis must be brought to bear on both main character; the analyst, who is determined to uncover the truth and reveal it in a coherent explanatory narrative, and the analysed, who resists the author-physician's attempt to write her story for her.

There are many indications of Freud's personal interest in this story, among them his presentation of the case history as a "practical application encompassing plot despite (or, through the interpretation of) Dora's resistance. "Story" and "narrative" are terms that recur throughout the case history. After noting his patients' generic "inability to give an ordered history of their life in so far as it coincides with the history of their illness" (p. 1390), Freud assumes the responsibility of drawing up that ordered account: "At this point the physician is usually faced by the task of guessing and filling in what the analysis offers him in the shape only of hints and allusions" (p. 1406). An inquirer must not "rest content with the first 'No' that crosses his path" (p. 1395) but must pursue an explanation which the patient is trying to conceal.

To a certain degree this pursuit seems only reasonable, but it is accompanied by an extraordinary insistence on the correctness of Freud's interpretation. He is hot on the trail of truth—"I was obliged to point out . . . ," "there could be no doubt . . . ," "it could be none other than . . . ," "the truth of this statement can invariably be relied upon," "I could not avoid the assumption that . . ."—while patients ideally "arrive at a sense of conviction of the validity of the connections which have been constructed during the analysis" (p. 1445). Dora and the reader must be persuaded, as the former seems to realize towards the end: "And Dora disputed the fact no longer" (p. 1437). Readers encounter a constant obbligato of footnotes, supplemented over the years, that support Freud's argument by elaborating a particular judgement, adducing other works, or referring backward or forward in the text to confirming passages. The Postscript, added fifteen months later, proposes a further explanation. Dora's case was a failure because Freud (as he now realizes) had not taken fully into account the phenomenon of transference; Dora had transferred to Freud her feelings of betrayal by her father and Herr K. In short, it remains extremely important to Freud that this "Fragment of a Case," which was terminated abruptly by the patient in what he calls "an unmistakable act of vengeance on her part" (p. 1440), result at some point in a successful explanation.

Another common issue in contemporary discussion of *Dora* is the extent to which Freud's interpretation is colored by the patriarchal bias or nineteenth-century Viennese society. Although the analyst does not accept the father's view without qualification, he certainly uses it as a point of departure. Her father is "a man of unusual activity and talents . . . a man of some perspicacity . . . shrewdness which I have remarked upon more than once" (p. 1391, 1395). We hear a great deal about Dora's relationship with her father, but very little about the mother whom both father and daughter consider "an uncultivated woman and above all a foolish one"—a perfect example of what Freud calls the "housewife's psychosis" (p. 1392). Freud also seems predisposed in Herr K's favor and is quite ready to consider Dora, at age fourteen, "entirely and completely hysterical" for failing to be excited by his kiss. "I happen to know Herr K., for he was the same person who had visited me with the patient's father, and he was still quite young and of prepossessing appearance" (p. 1397–98). Small wonder that Dora should come to associate Freud with her father and Herr K.; all three play the role of male authority figures who challenge her credibility in a sensitive situation where she is crucially involved. That it is in fact a challenge and not merely analysis emerges from the way Freud's own image of Dora evolves according to circumstances; although he initially appreciates her intelligence and "engaging looks" (1394), his descriptions become harsher and more critical the more she disputes his interpretations. While Dora's nervous disorder is undoubtedly real, and severe enough to cause physical symptoms, the rhetorical structure of this "Fragment of a Case of Hysteria" reveals a male-oriented perspective that can only have augmented her dilemma. The conceptual discoveries that Freud was able to make on the basis of this analysis did not accompany a successful treatment, and Dora chose to put her own end to the story.

*Dora* begins with a brief discussion of Freud's theories in *The Interpretation of Dreams*, followed by a relatively detailed summary of the patient's family situation. Dora's real name was Ida Bauer; her father was a well-to-do manufacturer and a dominating figure to whom she was devoted from early childhood. The father had suffered many illnesses: tuberculosis when Dora was six years old, a detached retina when she was ten, and two years later the confusion and partial paralysis for which he sought Freud's help. Freud attributed the father's illness to syphilis, a disease which he had apparently passed on to his wife, now estranged from both husband and daughter, who spent her time obsessively house-cleaning. Dora fell ill at age eight with a dyspnoea (difficulty in breathing) that Freud calls an early neurotic symptom; we learn later that she also wet her bed around this time. At age twelve she began to have migraine headaches and a nervous cough which sometimes led to a complete loss of voice for three to five weeks at a time. When she was seventeen she had a feverish attack that was diagnosed as appendicitis. All these symptoms Freud would later relate to emotional causes, and indeed Dora's father brought her to Freud when she was eighteen after discovering a suicide letter in her desk.

Dora's depression, explained her father, was due to an unreasoning dislike of Herr K., who she said has propositioned her when they were walking by a lake during summer vacation. She was also jealous of her father's friendship with Frau K. Dora's version of events was quite different. Herr K. had first kissed her by surprise when she was fourteen, the episode by the lake was quite real, and her father had been having an open affair with Frau K. ever since the latter took over his nursing during a serious illness. Dora was not only outraged by her parents' refusal to believe her, but she resented being—as she felt—bartered to Herr K. in compensation for his wife.

Freud's treatment consists largely in asking Dora to tell the story of these relationships in increasing detail, and to examine her own feelings. He comments on everything she says, interpreting her words, her actions (e.g., the nervous opening and closing of her small purse, 1427), and the two dreams, whose words and images are given rigorous analysis. Throughout the case history, there are extended passages of self-reflexive psychoanalysis in which Freud explains Dora's behavior, his own procedures, and the various concepts he is in the process of formulating. Step by step, he obliges his patient to recognize in her actions and dreams an unconscious attraction to Herr K., as well as to her father. In an extraordinarily complex network of interrelated images, word-play, and ambiguous associations, Freud elucidates a series of repressed desires that are at the base of Dora's depression and physical maladies. His patient, however, has imperceptibly been deciding to discontinue treatment, a decision she announces to the analyst's surprise on December 31, 1900, only eleven weeks after their first session. Freud brings the analysis to a conclusion in a final set of interpretations to which Dora listens "without any of her usual contradictions" (p. 1440), but his disappointment and hurt are evident in the Postscript. In January, 1901 he wrote up the case, though its unfinished nature continued to plague him, and he published the "Fragment" and its Postscript in 1905.

### Classroom Strategies

Given the cultural significance of Freud's work, and the length and complexity of *Dora*, you will probably want to allot four days to this piece. Students will very likely have strong ideas about "Freudianism" even if they have not read Freud, and you may find it useful to begin by finding out what these presuppositions are. Some will know a few terms (Oedipus complex, defense mechanism, repression, narcissism, etc.), others will be intrigued by the thought of uncovering hidden motivations, others may be concerned by the preoccupation with sexuality, and still others may be acquainted with the feminist "anti-Freud" debate and be ready to denounce him.

It will probably be useful at this point to emphasize the balance of *scientific inquiry* and *fictional portrait* that will carry you through the discussion of *Dora*. Students will be aware of Freud's standing as a scientist and founder of psychoanalysis; you can, therefore, suggest that they treat this assignment as another novel with a given cast of characters and a first-person narrative point of view—in fact, the conventional "unreliable narrator." Draw contrasts with previous works in this volume that offer similar novelistic paradigms (the adulterous affairs of Emma Bovary, the descriptions of family relationships in *The Death of Iván Ilyich*), or with other books they have read. Point out the dual nature of the narrative point of view; on the one hand, Freud has just completed *The Interpretation of Dreams* and is now working on his *Psychopathology of Everyday Life*, so he is feverishly engaged in formulating some basic insights into human behavior; on the other hand, he is consciously arranging events to tell a story while proposing a particular version of the truth. Remind your students that Freud was quite aware of literary structures and of the way his own case histories read like stories; encourage them to follow the thread of this "fragment" by using familiar literary-critical techniques (e.g., analyzing the narrative point of view, discussing the relationships of major and minor characters, following the cumulative stages of the plot and the duel of the two major characters, Freud and Dora).

There are many ways of organizing the material. You might use the first day to establish the setting: Freud's identity as psychoanalyst and author of *The Interpretation of Dreams*, Dora's family background, the way that she came to be Freud's patient. Ask the students what they think is going to happen, and what their evaluation of the narrator's reliability is, on the basis of this initial information. In the second day, you might begin to develop the alternate aspects of this case history: the increased understanding of Freudian psychoanalysis as it takes shape in the very course of the analysis, and concurrently, the developing picture of Dora as she becomes a flesh-and-blood character engaged in a duel of competing interpretations with her analyst. The third day might well be devoted to the dreams as examples of the dream analysis that is Freud's real interest in this work: the first, longer and more narrative, and the second, shorter and more complicated. Finally, the last day could be a wrap-up of the whole piece focused on the Postscript, which makes clear Freud's continual involvement with the case and also the way he continues writing and rewriting the story. If you have a colleague in Psychology or Women's Studies who might be willing to join in a general discussion of *Dora*, this would be a good time to schedule such a visit.

### Topics for Discussion

1. Why is it part of the psychoanalyst's duty, according to Freud, to compose a coherent story from the patient's disjointed memories? [Compare, if you like, Freud's statement that he is like "a conscientious archaeologist," one of those discoverers whose good fortune it is "to bring to the light of day after their long burial the priceless though mutilated relics of antiquity. I have restored what is missing, taking the best models known to me from other analyses . . ."].

2. How, according to Freud, do dreams work to allow repressed

impulses and memories a way to express themselves?

3. Explain and give examples of such Freudian concepts as repression, displacement, somatic compliance, overdetermination, sublimation, symptomatic acts, and the importance of word play or "switch-words."

4. Why did Dora's father bring her to Freud for analysis? Did Freud fulfill his expectations? Did he intend to?

5. What does Freud mean when he says, "There is no such thing as an unconscious 'No'"? (p. 1414)

6. How many instances of betrayal would Dora have felt in the course of the case history?

7. What is "transference" and how does Freud feel that it played a part in the case history's unsuccessful conclusion? Do you agree with his interpretation, given in the Postscript, of what he should have done? (1446)

8. What evidence do you find of Freud's ability as a creative writer? [Among other examples, you might point to the second paragraph in which the patient's account is described as an "unnavigable river whose stream is at one moment choked by masses of rock and at another divided and lost among shallows and sandbanks."]

9. To what extent, in your opinion, has Freud located the causes of Dora's depression and physical maladies?

10. How successful is Freud in maintaining an objective point of view?

11. Speculate on what the analysis might have looked like if Dora's mother had been the patient. What evidence do we have of Freud's attitude toward this possibility? (See p. 1392)

12. Comment on the following statement made by Thomas Mann in 1936:

We shall one day recognize in Freud's life-work the cornerstone for the building of a new anthropology and therewith a new structure, to which many stones are being brought up today, which shall be the future dwelling of a wiser and freer humanity.

## Further Reading

*Diacritics* (Spring, 1983).
A special issue, "A Fine Romance: Freud and Dora," includes Sarah Burd's translation of a short play called *Portrait of Dora* by French feminist scholar Hélène Cixous.

Forrester, John. *The Seductions of Psychoanalysis: Freud, Lacan and Derrida* (1990).
Contains a section on the "Dora" case.

Freeman, Lucy and Herbert S. Strean. *Freud and Women* (1981).
An introduction with a biographical approach and brief summaries of individual cases.

Gay, Peter. *Reading Freud: Explorations and Entertainments* (1990).
Offers a series of eight essays on different aspects of Freud's work and thought.

Mahony, Patrick J. *Freud as a Writer* (1987).
Analyzes Freud's literary style as a key to his habits of mind.

Storr, Anthoy. *Freud* (1989).
Offers a brief overview of Freud's life and chief concepts situated in critical perspective; it includes a section on contemporary psychoanalysis and a short annotated bibliography.

# WILLIAM BUTLER YEATS

## Backgrounds

We continue to read W. B. Yeats because he wrote incontestably great poetry of widely differing types for over fifty years; because the various phases he passed through mirror the course of modern poetry as a whole; and because his work both charms the unsophisticated reader and challenges the sophisticated. He is the one modern poet who most forcefully suggests to students something of the possibilities of poetry. The nine poems selected here are among the most famous and most representative of his work.

### "When You Are Old"

"When You Are Old" is one of the five love poems that Yeats copied out in manuscript and presented to Maud Gonne, who inspired many of his poems and much of his imagery. The central themes of the five poems have to do with threats to love—pity, tears, exhaustion, death, and, in the case of "When You Are Old," age.

The poem is relatively without difficulty until the last stanza, when the speaker of the poem presents the figure of Love pacing upon mountains and hiding "his face amid a crowd of stars." Here, the figure of Love has fled from the physical realm to the Olympian—the realm, that is, of poetry. Like other poems of Yeats's, this one features the sad recollection of the physical passion of youth from the perspective of wise age, which must replace sweet but fleeting passion with the eternal beauty of art. "Sailing to Byzantium" raises similar issues, as does Keats's "Ode on a Grecian Urn."

The author expects us to see that he has based his poem on one by the sixteenth-century French poet Ronsard, but with a difference. Whereas the speaker in Ronsard's poem stresses the fast fading joys of youth to strengthen his argument that the beloved should yield to him now, Yeats takes the argument to an entirely different plane of feeling, with a love that has fixed itself forever among the stars.

"Easter 1916"

To convey the state of mind—and of Ireland—out of which this poem rises, it may be useful to hand out copies of Yeats's "September 1913," in which the poet insists that the money-minded middle class (the paudeens) have so completely taken over that the romantic spirit of the Irish revolutionaries is dried up: "Romantic Ireland's dead and gone / It's with O'Leary in the grave."

By the time of "Easter 1916," an appropriate time of year for thoughts of rebirth, Yeats's views have changed. The Irish spirit and "all the delirium of the brave" have revived with the Easter Rebellion. And for Yeats, all has "changed, changed utterly: / A terrible beauty is born." The first stanza of the poem delivers an Ireland reminiscent of "September 1913"—it seems a fool's country, meaningless, a "casual comedy" in which all heroism is dead. Stanza two enlists a number of Yeats's friends and acquaintances who played prominent roles in the Rebellion—Con Markiewicz, Patrick Pearse, Thomas McDonough, even John MacBride (the estranged husband of Maud Gonne)—to suggest how the meaningless Ireland of "September 1913" has been transformed utterly.

Stanza three is truly extraordinary. It contrasts mutability with stasis, the living stream and the seasons with the "stone" that the poet associates with the fatal revolutionary purpose of his friends. The imagery of the stanza seems governed by the compelling forward-motion of the changes these friends brought about. The stanza surges with activity, plunging forward with increasing speed and power, dazzling the ear. The whole of the natural world participates in this motion, enchanted into action, so to speak, by the single-mindedness of the revolutionary vision—perhaps in the same way that a stone in a stream generates ripples, eddies, even cascades.

But the single-minded passion necessary to create such an active transformation can "make a stone of the heart." In stanza four Yeats raises the questions which must be asked about the consequences of any passionate action, especially revolutionary action. Where will it end? Was it necessary? Was it excessive? Was it worth it? Yeats raises the questions, but—and we can be thankful for this—declines to answer them. That, Yeats says, "is Heaven's part, our part / To murmur name upon name" and to "know their dream; enough to know they dreamed and are dead." Yeats's response to the Easter Rising is, then, complex. The last lines of the poem, the refrain, shift from a comparatively simple celebration of change into something celebrative but simultaneously deeply ambivalent. The words "terrible" and "beauty" in the refrain have picked up important new connotations; they are now as highly charged with apprehension as with celebration.

### "The Second Coming"

With the possible exception of "Sailing to Byzantium," this is Yeats's most famous poem. To expound its implications fully it will be necessary to introduce a brief description of Yeats's theory of history, which is discussed in the headnote (p. 1451). But this introduction should be kept brief and pithy or the poem will get lost in the theory. It is enough to say here Yeats implies that a second coming is at hand, not literally the coming of the Christian Antichrist, but of a new era which will have characteristics opposite to those of Christianity—an era that Yeats imagines beginning around the year 2000. The first stanza describes the disintegration of the Christian era: It has lost coherence, unity, order; the "centre cannot hold; / Mere anarchy is loosed upon the world;" the falcon whirls beyond the control of its master. At the end of this era, then, the order and ceremony of Christianity will be reversed. Lines 5 and 6 suggest an explosion of violence—an inverted baptism, with inverted results; the innocent will be drowned in their own blood.

Stanza two declares the meaning of this incoherence: "Surely some revelation is at hand; / Surely the Second Coming is at hand." As a symbol of the new era Yeats imagines a kind of Sphinx, "a shape with lion body and the head of a man," which is just beginning to move as "indignant" desert birds reel above it. Their presence recalls the uncontrolled falcon which begins the poem, and thus confirms the link between the end of the old era and the beginning of the new. The poet's ability to visualize this new beginning then ends: "The darkness drops again." But he knows what he has "seen," and he knows its meaning. The new pitiless cycle of history has been waiting its turn, "vexed to nightmare" by the twenty centuries of the Christian era. Its time now has come; and Yeats leaves us with his final question—"What rough beast, its hour come round at last, / Slouches toward Bethlehem to be born?"

There is no definitive answer of course. There is no more poem. But the implications of "The Second Coming" are that the new order will reverse the values of the exhausted Christian era; the new era will be violent, "blank and pitiless," where only "the worst" will have the intensity to carry out their convictions. And, since the traditional answer

---

to the riddle of the Sphinx has always been "Man," the "rough beast" may be Man himself. And Yeats doesn't like the look of what he sees.

### "Leda and the Swan"

"The Second Coming" deals with the end of the Christian era and the beginning of a new one; "Leda and the Swan" deals with the beginning of the classical era that preceded the Christian, but a classical era that many take to be a metaphor for our own. As the descent of the Dove upon Mary announces a scheme of things that in "The Second Coming" is nearing the end, so the rape of Leda by the swan announces a scheme of things that includes the Trojan War (fought for Helen, one offspring of this union) and the murder of Agamemnon by Clytemnestra (another of its offspring). You may well find that your students are concerned by this mythologized glorification of whit is, in fact, the rape of a terrified girl. The powerfully sensual description of that rape is pursued right up to the last two line, when attention is directed to a more abstract issue: "did she foresee the future? how far in *this* instance did the divine suffuse the human?" The combination of these two aspects can be a strong catalyst for class discussion.

### "Sailing to Byzantium"

With "The Second Coming," this is probably Yeats's best-known poem and, except for Eliot's "The Love Song of J. Alfred Prufrock" and one or two of Robert Frost's pieces, it is perhaps the best-known modern poem in English. Although "Sailing to Byzantium," like "The Second Coming" and "Leda and the Swan," requires some knowledge of Yeats's personal mythology to be fully understood, you must again be on guard against losing the poem amid symbolic baggage.

Reading of the poem is best begun by comparing "that country" which the speaker is leaving (Ireland, perhaps) with the place he is going—Byzantium. Both are symbolic places, and idiosyncratically so, since the meaning Yeats means to give them is true only insofar as we accept the poet's claims for them. They cannot be better understood by reading more about Byzantium or the mating habits of the early-Modern Irish; they can be understood as symbols only by reading more Yeats. "That" country is the country of the young, the passionate, the fertile; it is a place "caught in sensual music," a place of generation and, therefore, of the inevitable decay that comes with mortality. Byzantium, on the other hand, is a city of the soul, especially of the artist's soul; it suggests changelessness and immortality. It is that place where the spiritual and secular meet in art.

Stanza two establishes the poem's speaker as an "aged man" who must "sing louder," that is, insist on the primacy of spirit over body as he becomes older. And since the spirit is best represented in art, the speaker has "sailed the seas" to reach Byzantium. Once there, he asks the city's "sages" to instruct him, to become the "singing-masters" of his soul, to gather him into the "artifice of eternity" that only art can make.

In the last stanza, the speaker makes known his desire—that he shall never again take bodily form except, perhaps, as a work of art, a golden bird upon a golden bough who will sing "To lords and ladies of Byzantium / Of what is past, or passing, or to come" (31–32). Thus if the poem concentrates on the speaker's desire to leave the world of mortality in order to achieve an immortality of the spirit through art, it should also be noticed that the last line suggests its opposite—the world of mortality, the very world the speaker has renounced. (So likewise in "Lapis Lazuli," the Chinese elders look out upon a world in turmoil from their secure place in art, and their glittering eyes are untroubled, tranquil, gay.) The last line echoes "Whatever is begotten, born, and dies" in stanza one and thus serves to remind us, as Yeats always reminds us, that when something is gained, something is lost. "Sailing to Byzantium" looks back at earlier poems such as "The Stolen Child" and "The Dolls" (both of which might be usefully handed out to students), and ahead to "The Circus Animals' Desertion," in which Yeats insists that the ladder of his vision, and of all art, starts in the "foul rag-and-bone shop of the heart." Like Keats in "Ode on a Grecian Urn," Yeats recognizes that the immortality of art is cold; it derives from and serves life—the one thing it cannot be. "Sailing to Byzantium" can very easily be read as being "about" the desire of the aged to transcend the decay of the body in favor of the eternality of art, but the ambiguity of the poem should not be ignored.

## "Among School Children"

This poem, like "Sailing to Byzantium," begins with the question of old age, the contrast between current decrepitude and remembered youth, and then moves to a consideration of how age and final decay come to everyone, no matter how wisely one has worked to find an ideal world to pit against the imperfections of reality. Plato, Aristotle, and Pythagoras, like the speaker and the rest of us, become old scarecrows—"Old clothes upon old sticks to scare a bird."

As if to mock humankind's inevitable decay and to put off thoughts of it, "nuns and mothers worship images"—nuns worship religious icons as mothers worship idealized versions of their children. The invocation of these visions (both icons and fantasies are a kind of art), leads Yeats to his final stanza. Here Yeats again insists on the necessity of combining real and ideal, mortal and immortal, life and art. The ideal worlds of Plato and Aristotle are achieved only by denying an important part of what life is; they bruise the body to "pleasure soul." Instead, Yeats appears to say, images and theories cannot be separated from life itself— "How can we know the dancer from the dance?"—and the actual world and the visionary world, the world of mortal imperfection and artistic perfection, must exist in concert. The "comfortable old scarecrow" and the child he once was are one thing, much as the chestnut-tree is always its past and future as well as its present, a synthesis of leaf, blossom, and bole.

### "Byzantium"

In this poem Yeats stresses particularly the mutual dependence of the changeless, perfect world of Byzantium and the mortal world of "all that man is . . . The fury and the mire of human veins." "Byzantium" exploits the same contrast as its predecessor, but what existed as a rather ambiguous implication in "Sailing to Byzantium" becomes the central issue here.

After four stanzas which describe the spirit world of Byzantium, and how the mortal becomes immortal, Yeats gives the final stanza over to images, as one critic puts it, "not only of the eternal world, but also of the world of nature which is feeding it." In this poem, then, the natural and spiritual are inseparable; one can never be entirely abandoned for the other.

Students will find Yeats's imagery—the dolphins, the mummy, etc.— significantly more problematic here than in "Sailing to Byzantium," but most of their troubles will be addressed in the footnotes.

### "Lapis Lazuli"

When "Lapis Lazuli" was written, in 1936, Europe was both emerging from an economic depression and heating up for war. Hitler and Mussolini were gathering themselves in Germany and Italy, and the Spanish

Civil War was running its course toward Franco. It was not just "hysterical women" who must have told Yeats that they were sick of art, or that he should use his considerable powers for political purposes. In these years, public affairs were intruding on private visions so forcefully that almost all of the important younger British poets and novelists of the period (Auden, Spender, Day Lewis, MacNeice, Isherwood, Orwell, Warner, etc.) were engaged in writing books which were emphatically political. Poetry, especially as it was being written by High Modernists, was seen as a kind of luxury, too obscure and resistant to the needs and desires of the public to do the work in the world that these writers, and Yeats's "hysterical women," thought needed to be done. "Lapis Lazuli" constitutes Yeats's answer to them.

The first stanza presents the accusation: Art is no longer enough. Commitment is needed, because if "nothing drastic is done" war will break out. Yeats's use of a popular seventeenth-century ballad to describe war has enticed some critics to claim that Yeats was ignoring political realities. Indeed, the scornful phrase "King Billy bomb-balls" does have the effect of deflating the seriousness of what might, and did, happen. But Yeats surely intended this deflation, because it serves to place the war to come in the larger context of all wars, in the larger context of the rise and fall of civilizations (many of which are now remembered or understood only through, and because of, their art), a subject with which Yeats, like Eliot and Pound, was much obsessed.

Stanza two suggests that in the play of civilizations even the greatest of actors do not betray the tragic parts they play, though they and we know they are participating in tragedy. Instead they retain a "gaiety" which "transfigures all that dread." They commit themselves but remain themselves. They empower the play they are in and, at the same time, transcend it by displaying the proper heroic reaction to catastrophe. And these "actors," Yeats suggests in stanza three, are the ones who make civilizations. Their work may fall, may not last out the day, their "wisdom" may go "to rack," but "All things fall and are built again, / And those that build them again are gay."

Stanzas four and five locate that transcendent gaiety in one seemingly unspectacular work of art, a piece of lapis lazuli "carved by some Chinese sculptor into the semblance of a mountain with temple, trees, paths, and an ascetic and pupil about to climb the mountain." In it, Yeats discovers all their civilization, now available only through art. He imagines them seated between mountain and sky, surveying "the tragic scene" below. And their "ancient, glittering eyes, are gay." They have, through art, survived, immortalized, and thus transcended the civilization from which they emerged. Through them, through art, their civilization retains the only meaning left to have. If King Billy's bomb-balls are pitched in, if Yeats's civilization is "beaten flat," his art—if it is really art—will remain, preserving its world for the instruction and delight of future men and women, perhaps even "A young girl in the indolence of her youth, / Or an old man upon a winter's night." ("On Being Asked for a War Poem," ll. 5–6)

## "The Circus Animals' Desertion"

"The Circus Animals' Desertion" was written in the last year of Yeats's life, and it serves as a kind of final survey of his career, a map of his imagery and thinking, and a declaration about the source of his art. The "circus animals" are, of course, the images that Yeats has used throughout his poetic life, during that "winter and summer till old age began." Here again are all the "stilted boys" of his imagination: Oisin, Niamh, Countess Cathleen, Cuchulain, the various faces of Maud Gonne, "Lion and woman and the Lord knows what." In his insouciant litany of his "masterful images," Yeats admits—a bit sadly, one feels—that it was the images themselves that finally enchanted him, not "those things they were the emblems of."

In the final stanza, Yeats speculates, as he had so often in his earlier work, about the source of his art. And he discovers it, as we knew he must, in the "mound of refuse," the noisy and filthy thing, that life is. No matter the heights to which imagination may climb, the ladder of vision necessarily stands planted in mire of earth. And now that the ladder is gone, he "must lie down where all the ladders start / In the foul rag-and-bone shop of the heart"(39–40).

### Classroom Strategies

If you plan to teach all nine of the poems, you should probably allow at least two—better yet three—days for the purpose. Yeats's poems tend to build on themselves, the meaning and imagery of one informing the meaning and imagery of the next. Hence it is wise to keep them in their chronological order, though it will be difficult not to make "Sailing to Byzantium" and "Byzantium" into a matched pair.

Should you choose to teach a representative sample of the poems, I would recommend "Easter 1916," "The Second Coming," "Sailing to

Byzantium," "Among School Children," and "Lapis Lazuli." The middle three poems here are among his most famous as well as his best, and introduce some of his most persistent poetic concerns, while at the same time providing a kind of unity to your students' experience of his work.

The most difficult immediate problem for students will lie with the "allusive imagery and symbolic structure" (see the headnote, p. 1449) of Yeats's work, especially his best work. Not only are many of his most suggestive images and symbols derived from sources well out of the mainstream of Western thought—occult texts, Irish myths and legends, personal friends and unrequited lovers, etc.—but they are also filtered through Yeats's own fertile imagination and given their applicable meanings *only in the context of Yeats's own work.* That is to say, the only way students can fully understand Yeats's images and symbols is to read more Yeats, though as suggested in the critical discussions above, these can be understood and appreciated without plunging deeply into Yeats's personal mythology. A brief description of his most important mythical structure—Yeats's cyclical model of history—appears on page 1451. Yeats's historical "gyres," or spirals, might best be represented in the following way:

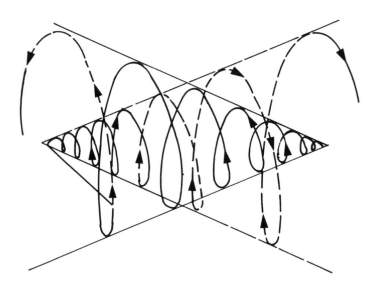

It is important to notice that the gyres interpenetrate, that a new one begins only as its opposite concludes, that each gyre represents a cycle of history covering approximately 2000 years, and that—though one is always dominant—the opposing gyres exist simultaneously, one always implying the other. (His "Byzantium," therefore, exists at that mid-point—A.D. 1000—of the gyres' interpenetration.) Yeats's use of this model, as well as his related use of the "phases of the moon," is personal in the extreme, but can be related to other cyclical versions of history, such as those of Vico, Spengler, and Toynbee.

To get students in the mood to discuss such matters, it is useful to point out that all of us have and maintain versions of history, whether we realize it or not. To mention some of them—the Christian version; the "wave;" evolutionary meliorism, or the idea of progress; the strictly linear (Aldous Huxley's "one damn thing after another")—will always evoke discussion and soften up the doubters. Teachers who wish to know more about Yeats's particular version should consult *A Vision*, surely one of the most arcane and, in some ways, difficult books ever seriously offered by a major writer.

Students will very likely recognize Yeats's technical prowess after they are advised of it, but they are unlikely to respond to it on their own. Yeats himself once said that poems should be "packed in ice or salt," meaning that they should retain traditional, formal structures. Like Frost, he felt that writing poems without formal complications was like playing tennis without a net. It should come as no surprise, then, that each of the poems here is highly structured.

"Sailing to Byzantium" uses four stanzas of eight lines apiece, and each stanza maintains a rhyme scheme of *a b a b a b c c*. This very tight formal structure is at the same time relaxed in the sense that it is almost invisible; it seems not to intrude at all on the development of the poem's meaning. Each stanza suggests a movement in space, from "that country" to "Byzantium," which corresponds to the speaker's movement of mind, from engagement in nature to engagement in spirit. The first stanza, one of Yeats's most memorable, is as rich and sensual as the natural world it observes. The phrase "Those dying generations" calls up one of the central issues of the poem—that in the world of nature whatever is born must inevitably die—in fact is always in the process of dying. This phrase, and the notion it suggests, is immediately called up again by the "salmon-falls," which salmon climb to spawn and die. The richness of organic life, "fish, flesh, or fowl," re-echoes in a phrase summarizing its rich but also limiting processes: "Whatever is begotten, born, and dies."

And this is echoed again, with extended meaning, in the last line of the poem. Thus the first stanza describes the "sensual music" of the natural world while it sings the very music it describes.

In "Among School Children" (eight stanzas of eight lines each with a rhyme scheme of *a b a b a b c c*), the formal structure of the poem again reflects its interwoven thoughts and images. The movement of the thought is supported by recurring imagery—the scarecrow, Leda (and swans), history, Plato, "image," and "dream." Thesis and antithesis (age/youth, reality/dream, mortal/immortal) finally achieve synthesis. The assurance of Yeats's formal structure gives a certain credence to the assurance of the poem's final resolution.

## Topics for Discussion

1. In what ways is "When You are Old" like "Sailing to Byzantium"?
   [See *Backgrounds*, "When You are Old."]

2. What is Yeats's attitude toward the Easter Rebellion of 1916 and the people who were involved in it? Are his feelings mixed? How do we know?
   [See *Backgrounds*, "Easter 1916."]

3. How do the images in stanza three of "Easter 1916" relate to the poem as a whole?
   [See *Backgrounds*, "Easter 1916," paragraph 3.]

4. How does stanza two of "The Second Coming" answer stanza one?
   [See *Backgrounds* on "The Second Coming."]

5. What are gyres? What have they to do with Yeats's idea of history? How are they used in the poem? Does Yeats seem to think that the coming era will be better or worse than the last? How do we know?
   [See *Backgrounds*, "The Second Coming," and paragraphs 3 and 4 of *Classroom Strategies*.]

6. What is going on in the first stanza of "Leda and the Swan"? How long does it take to realize that Yeats is alluding to a classical myth? What use does he make of that myth? What do the last two lines mean, and why is the beak finally "indifferent"?
   [See *Backgrounds*, "Leda and the Swan."]

7. What is the crucial difference between "That country" and Byzantium? Why does the speaker wish to sail to Byzantium in "Sailing to Byzantium"? What does he want to do once there?
   [See *Backgrounds*, "Sailing to Byzantium."]

8. Through what details does Yeats conjure up the natural world in stanza one of "Sailing to Byzantium"? Why these details? What are his feelings about the world of "sensual music" that he renounces? From what evidence in the poem do we infer these feelings?
   [See *Backgrounds*, "Sailing to Byzantium," and paragraph 7 of *Classroom Strategies*.]

9. How are Keats's "Ode on a Grecian Urn" and "Ode to a Nightingale similar to "Sailing to Byzantium"?
   [Both contrast the sensual, temporal world to a world of immortality and timelessness. Both use a bird as a symbol of that immortality.]

10. What is Yeats's point in "Among School Children"? How are the images worshipped by "nuns and mothers" similar? What other poems by Yeats help us to understand this one?
    [See *Backgrounds*, "Among School Children," as well as the last two paragraphs of *Classroom Strategies*. "Leda and the Swan," "Sailing to Byzantium," "Byzantium," and "The Circus Animals' Desertion" can all be usefully related to "Among School Children."]

11. How does "Byzantium" answer "Sailing to Byzantium"?
    [See *Backgrounds*, "Byzantium."]

12. What would Yeats's answer be to those who want him to write poems about present-day concerns? What does Yeats mean by "gaiety" in "Lapis Lazuli"? Doesn't Yeats take the possibility of war seriously?
    [See *Backgrounds*, "Lapis Lazuli."]

13. In what ways is "The Circus Animals' Desertion" a review of Yeats's poetic career? Where does it locate the source of art?
    [See *Backgrounds*, "The Circus Animals' Desertion."]

14. What are the major thematic concerns in Yeats's work? Is he consistent in the positions he takes on matters that concern him? Where can apparent contradictions be found? Is he ambivalent about many of these matters? Should Yeats be consistent or certain?

## Further Reading

See also the reading suggestions in the anthology, p. 1452.

Archibald, Douglas. *Yeats*. Syracuse, 1983.
An overall study, but especially interesting on Yeats's work with regard to politics and public life.

Bloom, Harold. *Yeats*. New York, 1970.
Yeats's achievement discussed and judged in the context of the Romantic tradition, especially the work of Blake and Shelley.

Diggory, Terence. *Yeats and American Poetry*. 1983.
The impact of individual poems on the "tradition of myself" in American poetry. Poets discussed include Eliot, Stevens, Tate, Ransom, Warren, MacLeish, Roethke, and Robert Lowell.

Donoghue, Denis. *William Butler Yeats*. 1988, © 1971.
A fluent, generalized thematic discussion of Yeats's relationship to European Romanticism, exploring ideas of self, imagination, will, action, symbol, history, world, vision, and self-transformation.

Ellmann, Richard. *Yeats: The Man and the Masks*. New York, 1948; revised edition, 1978.
A very fine, short critical biography.

Finneran, Richard J. *Editing Yeats's Poems: A Reconsideration*. 1990.
A scholarly companion to Finneran's 1989 revised edition of Yeats's *The Poems*, containing new material.

Henn, T. R. *The Lonely Tower*. London, 1950.
A thorough and influential study of all of Yeats's work.

Kinahan, Frank. *Yeats, Folklore, and Occultism: Contexts of the Early World and Thought*. 1988.

Longenbach, James. *Stone Cottage: Pound, Yeats, and Modernism*. 1988.
Situates Yeats inside the modernist movement.

Lynch, David. *Yeats: The Poetics of the Self*. 1981.
A more specialized psychoanalytic study emphasizing the analysis of the self practiced by Heinz Kohut.

Stallworthy, Jon. *Between the Lines: Yeats's Poetry in the Making*. Oxford, 1963.
Displays various drafts of Yeats's work in process.

Stanfield, Paul Scott. *Yeats and Politics in the 1930s*. Another discussion of Yeats's relation to politics.

Timm, Eitel. *W. B. Yeats: A Century of Criticism*. Translated by Eric Wredenhagen. 1990.
A survey of Yeats criticism structured according to early, middle, and late works that describes critical tendencies and approaches and includes debates over specific works.

Zwerdling, Alex. *Yeats and the Heroic Ideal*. New York, 1965.
Yeats's vision of heroism and its expression in his poetry.

# LUIGI PIRANDELLO
## Six Characters in Search of an Author

### Backgrounds

Pirandello's plays are so important to modern drama as a whole that it is almost impossible to imagine what it would have been like without him. His theoretical concerns—the inability of language to say what one most wants to say; the difficulty a person has in establishing germane communication with another; the variability of personality; the relation of life-illusion to stage-illusion; the relativity of perception to time, place, mood, personality, and even the state of one's digestion—anticipated almost every important development of the modern theater. He is humorous, exasperating, fascinating, profound—a true genius of the theater.

*Six Characters* is about fictional and dramatic "characters." These differ from human beings in that they are embodiments of feelings, ideas, or overpowering emotions, and trapped in their embodied roles. Unlike human beings, they are also possibly immortal; "whoever has the luck to be born a character," says The Father in *Six Characters*, "can laugh even at death. Because a character will never die" (p. 1474). Thus characters have a life of their own—they live on eternally but only so far developed as their creator has made them. Our six characters, having been abandoned by their author, are so overpowered by emotion that they are compelled to come to the theater and plead with the professional actors (who are rehearsing Pirandello's play *Mixing It Up*) to reenact their drama. The Father says: "The play is in us: we are the play . . . the passion inside us is driving us on," (p. 1474). The characters have been created but left stranded, with no play or novel to house them; their vitality has no context in which to live. They can reach their completion only as parts of a play.

Discovering a ready-made setting for their "existence," they insist that their tragedy is more important, more urgently in need of expression, than the Pirandello play being rehearsed. The drama of their lives is simple enough, though complicated at the end by the question of what has happened as opposed to what is happening. What has happened takes up almost the entire first act, and can be outlined as follows: The Father is a rationalist who married beneath himself. He notices the interest that his secretary takes in his wife, and that it is returned. It is a platonic relationship, but the Father senses their love and sends them off together, though he keeps his young Son with him. The wife obediently leaves with the secretary and they raise three children of their own. The abandoned Son grows up resentful and arrogant; he has been raised away from his father by a wetnurse. The Father keeps up with his wife's new family, even going so far as to watch the Stepdaughter as she comes and goes from school. The secretary eventually takes his family and leaves town. Years pass and the secretary dies. His wife and children, destitute, move back to their original town, but they do not contact the Father. The Mother gets a job with Mme. Pace, a dressmaker who runs a call-girl ring from her shop. Mme. Pace lures the Stepdaughter into her service. The Father patronizes the establishment and unwittingly ends up in the arms of the Stepdaughter, only to be interrupted by the screams of the Mother ("just in time," according to the Father; "almost in time," according to the Stepdaughter). The Father is horrified and reunites the family under his roof. His own Son opposes the reunion, and becomes excessively bitter toward all of them, especially his Mother. There is an explosion of emotions in the house; the Mother agonizes over her Son's bitterness, and the Boy—the wife's middle child by the secretary—despises being what he sees as a charity case.

But this is not all. To this point, we know the history of the family by watching it filled in, piece by piece, by the characters. The inner action now merges with the outer action of the play (Act III) when the wife's youngest child falls into a garden fountain and drowns, and the Boy, who watches in horror as it happens, draws a revolver and shoots himself. Because this last takes place after the actors and the Producer (who were rehearsing the Pirandello play) have prepared the scene for the play the characters want to perform, the question of what is "real" and what is "illusion" becomes even more tenuous. The characters "perform" the final acts of their history, but when the shot rings out confusion reigns; the Boy lies on the ground while some of the actors cry, "He's dead!" and others claim, "It's all make-believe. It's a sham!" The Father rejoins: "What do you mean, make-believe? It's real"(p. 1510).

The play deals with various planes of "reality," and does so in such a way as to place the entire notion of reality under suspicion. That the theater is an illusion is not at issue here, although the degree to which the theater is simply unable adequately to reflect reality certainly is. When the actors, who have adopted conventional stage mannerisms, attempt to act out the parts the characters have provided for them, the characters—whose "real" drama is about to be enacted—can hardly recognize themselves; they laugh satirically.

> THE FATHER: [*Immediately, unable to restrain himself.*]. Oh, no!
> THE STEPDAUGHTER, *watching* THE LEADING ACTOR *enter this way, bursts into laughter.*]
> THE PRODUCER: [*Furious.*] Shut up, for God's sake! And don't you dare laugh like that! We're not going to get anywhere at this rate.
> THE STEPDAUGHTER: [*Coming to the front.*] I'm sorry, I can't help it! The lady stands exactly where you told her to stand and she never moved. But if it were me and I heard someone say good afternoon to me in that way and with a voice like that I should burst out laughing—so I did.
> (p. 1495–96)

Pirandello is suggesting the wide gulf which inevitably separates life from its recreation on stage. Robert Brustein has pointed out that when the "Producer transforms the sordid, semi-incestuous happening in the dress shop into a romantic and sentimental love scene between the Leading Man and the Leading Lady . . . the Father understands how the author came to abandon them—in a fit of disgust over the conventional theatre."

But if one of Pirandello's central concerns is the theater's inability to catch reality as it is, an even more central concern is his seemingly paradoxical notion that theater is "truer" than life. He expresses this by contrasting the fixed reality of literary characters with the ever-changing reality of human beings. Fictional characters are "less real," perhaps, "but truer." It is the characters' tragedy that they are fixed within immutable bounds, often in one disastrous moment of their lives, or that, like The Boy and the Little Girl in *Six Characters*, they may have personalities and histories that are barely developed. Still, though they may be frustrated by their ineffective attempts to extend their fixed identities, they do not—like the human beings they imperfectly imitate—have to experience the yet more frustrating attempt to unify the multiple aspects of their personalities. As the Father tells the Producer in the play:

> But [our reality] doesn't change! Do you see? That's the difference! Ours doesn't change, it can't change, it can never be different, never, because it is already determined, like this, for ever, that what's so terrible! We are in an eternal reality. That should make you shudder to come near us.
> (p.1403)

The Father's argument here is also Pirandello's: Human beings—unlike the imaginative creations of human beings—are merely a series of moods, impressions, beliefs, idiosyncrasies, and social masks which can never be fully integrated. The human tragedy—and comedy—is that we keep trying to unify these disparate elements, and are disconsolate at our failure.

Many of the most important of Pirandello's works, including *Six Characters*, were written during the most insecure and troubled period of his life. His wife's insanity began in 1903, after the birth of their third and last child and the loss of the family fortune. Pirandello refused to institutionalize her. She remained at home torturing the family with her insane rages while Pirandello suffered in silence, his wife beating at his door while he wrote. Among other things, she accused him and their daughter of incest, an accusation which so unsettled the daughter that she attempted suicide.

It is not difficult to imagine why artifice held such attraction for him, or why it struck him as being so obviously different from reality. His writing was his only release. Pirandello once wrote to a friend that he would sometimes sit in his study all day "at the service of the characters of my stories who crowd about me, each one wanting to come to life before the others, each one with his particular unhappiness to make public." His "madmen" characters provided a way to shout and revolt at his predicament. *Six Characters* is one of many plays which reveal Pirandello's torment as well as his genuine pleasure in the immortal fixity of his creations, creations which would not cringe at his wife's accusations, and which could strut, immortally undemoralized, out the door and into an eternal future.

Two of the most significant influences on Pirandello were Henri Bergson (1859–1942) with his theory of "psychological" time and his emphasis on the mutability of personality, and Henrik Ibsen, with his grasp of the inner life. More interesting, perhaps, is the degree to which Pirandello himself has touched subsequent dramatists and fiction writers. Only Shakespeare and Ibsen, it has often been said, have been more influential. Anouilh, Sartre, Camus, Beckett, Ionesco, Giraudoux, O'Neill, Pinter, Stoppard, Albee, Wilder, Wesker, and Genet all show Pirandello's influence in one way or other. Though there is no discernible direct influence, it is worth noting that the text in the anthology which bears the closest theoretical similarity to *Six Characters*, Woolf's "An Unwritten Novel," was also published in 1921.

## Classroom Strategies

Because of the peculiar problems of *Six Characters*, it may need to consume two class periods and, for best effect, should be taught in tandem with other self-reflexive works—especially the more accessible "An Unwritten Novel."

Like the stories of Borges, John Barth, or Robert Coover, Pirandello's play will be a fascinating puzzle to some and a positive headache to others. It will be important to establish the context of *Six Characters* before discussion of its theoretical implications swamps the class. We have "real" actors putting on a "real" play in a "real" theater, interrupted by "fictional" characters who want to act out their "real" "fictional lives," or to have them acted out by the "real" actors. The melodrama of these characters' lives can, and should, be outlined for the students—perhaps in a handout distributed at the first class. During the first day of discussion, this melodrama—what we have here called the "inner action" of the play—should be established. Since the characters' story is mainly revealed in Act I, you may wish to limit discussion to that act on the first day. Acts II and III will provide discussion of the "outer action" of the play, with the theoretical and philosophical implications it raises. Although there are many possible approaches, the central theme of reality and illusion—in part because it is so thematically central to much modern drama—will probably be the most fruitful. The last few paragraphs of *Backgrounds* are intended to suggest some of the most significant theoretical questions raised by Pirandello.

It may be difficult to persuade students of Pirandello's humor, in part because it does not translate very well and in part because students are unlikely to be amused when they are confused. The notion of humor was basic to his writing (he wrote an essay on the subject which insists on the its importance in comprehending and coping with suffering), and will be basic to students' enjoyment of the play. You should read appropriate passages or, perhaps more effectively, have students take parts and do a reading in class. There is a 55-minute videotape available from Films for the Humanities, a compressed but lively version of the play, which would be extremely useful for students to see.

## Topics for Discussion and Writing

1. In the original stage directions Pirandello says of the characters:

> A tenuous light surrounds them, as if radiating from them—it is the faint breath of their fantastic reality.

In the revised edition he states that in order for the six characters to be distinguished from the actors of the company, the characters should wear semi-masks:

> The six characters must not appear as phantoms, but as "created realities," immutable creatures of fantasy. They are more real and consistent than the voluble actors.

Why did Pirandello make this change? What does it have to do with his theory of characters and his notions about human personality? In what ways can a character achieve independence from its author? Is this just a literary notion or does it have some application to everyday life?

[Characters are fixed while human beings are not, and it is human beings who feel cheated and disappointed at their predicament.]

2. In what ways is the play about the problem of illusion and reality? What is "real" in the play? Are there *degrees* of "reality" in *Six Characters*?

[See *Backgrounds* for discussion.]

3. What purpose does the "play-within-the-play" serve? What other plays use this technique?

[A look back at *Hamlet* may be useful here.]

4. What do you make of the end of the play? Is the Boy dead? In what ways is he dead? In what ways is he not dead?

[We cannot, perhaps, definitively resolve the question of the Boy's death. We can say that he is dead insofar as the play ends, that he is not dead insofar as the play may be put on again.]

## Further Reading

See also the reading suggestions in the anthology, p. 1467.

Bishop, Thomas. *Pirandello and French Theater*. New York, 1960.
Contains a helpful chapter on "Ideas in Pirandello's Theater."

Brustein, Robert. *The Theatre of Revolt*. Boston, 1964.
An illuminating and cogent discussion of the play.

Giudice, Gaspare. *Pirandello: A Biography*. Translated by Alastair Hamilton. London, 1975.
A good, short biography.

Lorch, Jennifer, "The 1925 Text of 'Sei Personnaggi in Cerca d'Autore' and Pitoëff's Production of 1925," from *Yearbook of the British Pirandello Society*, 2, 1982, pp. 32–47.
Gives a detailed discussion of Pitoëff's innovative production of *Six Characters* and its impact on later versions of the play (see Introduction).

Oliver, Roger. *Dreams of Passion: The Theatre of Luigi Pirandello*. New York, 1979.
Discusses *Six Characters* and four other plays, as well as Pirandello's aesthetics.

Vittorini, Domenico. *The Drama of Luigi Pirandello*. New York, 1957.
A thorough study, first published in 1935, which Pirandello himself approved.

# MARCEL PROUST
## Remembrance of Things Past

### Backgrounds

In the eyes of many, twentieth-century writing after 1913 is merely a footnote to Marcel Proust. It was Proust's massive novel, *Remembrance of Things Past*, which gave literary definition to the concept of "human time"—a subjective or *bodily* experience of living in time that would represent human existence far more accurately than the "clock" time of exterior, scientific measurement. Proust shows his narrator, Marcel, carefully building a picture of his "whole" self out of layers of buried memory; each glimpse of an earlier "Marcel" brings with it a forgotten world of experience, and makes clear the emotional and intellectual links between past and present identity. The detailed description of sense perceptions (the smell of a book or stairway, the taste of a small cake and tea) becomes a key to uncovering a past which is actually a series of layers creating the present. Proust's ability to convince us of the reality of these experiences derives in large part from his use of concrete details —details which follow a stream of psychological association and seem to espouse the rhythms of the remembering consciousness itself. Both the richly remembered scenes and the example of the narrator's associative memory have provided a compelling example for later writers, themselves haunted by the question of knowing the self and the difficulty of representing it in language. The extraordinarily complex architecture of this multi-volume novel, and its complex symmetry of themes and metaphors, has also proved a fruitful example for modern novelists who emphasize organization by themes or mental associations rather than by linear or chronological construction. While the appreciation of Proust's aesthetic constructions will take more than one reading, students usually feel—often to their surprise—a strong identification with his description of sensuous memory, and with the search for the past as a way of giving meaning to the present.

The title "Overture," introducing a book whose title translates literally as *In Search of Lost Time*, sets the tone for a chapter which examines the meaning of memory itself. It is Marcel's process of associative memory which is at stake, from the beginning where he talks about the state of half-consciousness and blurred perceptions when he is going to sleep, to the end where he describes the successful recall of his childhood world. Marcel is attempting to "gradually piece together the original components of my ego" (p. 1518), and he finds that the memory of physical sensations is an indispensable part of this process. His dreams and confused memories are shaped by the physical position of his limbs in bed; later on, it will be the taste of *madeleine* soaked in tea that calls up a world the conscious mind has forgotten. "My body . . . loyally preserving from the past an impression which my mind should never have forgotten . . ." allows the narrator to recapture scenes, events, and emotions which were otherwise lost to consciousness.

After the introduction in which the older narrator recalls (among other things) his childhood experience of going to sleep, we move into the years at Combray when Marcel's bedtime hours were dominated by his Mamma's goodnight kiss. The child Marcel appears as a sensitive, highly nervous boy whose devotion to his mother is coupled with a lively imagination and the need for reassurance and familiar surroundings: He is disturbed by the way the slide-projected story of Golo and Genevieve de Brabant becomes superimposed on the appearance of his familiar bedroom, and confused by the way Golo's cloak or face seems to share the reality of down-to-earth objects like the doorknob.

The initial description of the narrator's ambivalent state of consciousness now moves to a series of embedded stories that center on themes of love and loss: Marcel's anxious wait for Mamma's kiss, and Swann's similar anxiety during his earlier love for Odette (a piece of information known to the older Marcel, and alluded to here as he narrates events in full perspective). The narrative center of these tales is the dinner party from which Marcel is sent to bed without his accustomed goodnight kiss—a dinner where Proust's famous capacity for character sketches and social satire emerges especially strongly in the portraits of the two sisters, Flora and Celine, and their inability to thank Swann directly for his present of a case of Asti wine. Throughout the evening, Marcel undergoes alternating hope and despair as he appeals to his mother through a message carried by Françoise, is humiliated when she refuses to respond, decides to stay up for her no matter what the cost, and is unexpectedly allowed her company for the night when his indulgent father recognizes the child's real misery. The "Overture," however, is not merely a story of Marcel's successful attempt to obtain his goodnight kiss. The sequence of memories also culminates in Marcel's first realization that his mother is excusing him as a "nervous" child, not truly responsible for his actions and psychologically flawed. This realization, which is accompanied by feelings of guilt at having thus "traced a first wrinkle upon her soul" (p. 1544) but also by Marcel's determination to enjoy the evening's unrepeatable indulgence to the hilt, forms a climax after which there is a sudden break and the narrator concludes with a meditation on the role of memory.

The picture of Proust that remains in the mind is of an extraordinarily sensitive aesthete and intellectual who lived most of his adult years shut up in a heated, cork-lined room in Paris because he suffered from asthma. The disease that attacked him at the age of nine sharply limited his activities; nonetheless, he was able to transform personal experience—seaside vacations at Cabourg, country visits to Illiers and Auteil, a year's military service at Orleans, participation in Parisian salon society, protests during the Dreyfus affair, and his relationship with Albert Agostinelli into a complex panorama of Parisian society around the turn of the century.

Many readers like to compare Proust and the philosopher Henri Bergson, author of the influential *Essay on the Immediate Data of Consciousness* (1889). Bergson stressed the importance of "duration," or lived time, as the direct intuition of consciousness—to be valued over the sterile mathematics of measurable "clock time." While the comparison is often illuminating because of the similarity between Proust's and Bergson's rejection of positivist explanations of human experience, it remains a comparison rather than a causal link.

### Classroom Strategies

Your students will enjoy Proust more if you devote two class periods to the "Overture"—one discussing the psychological drama of Marcel's going to bed, another examining the famous Proustian style that calls up buried memories. Since Proust is traditionally associated with the project of recapturing forgotten layers of memory, we recommend using this aspect as an opening wedge. Here there are two easy approaches: examining a short but significant passage as a "laboratory sample," and asking students to think about the processes of memory—their own and those described at the beginning of the book.

You may find it useful to start with the last sentence, and read aloud the famous description of the Japanese flowers that are only crumpled bits of paper until they expand in water and become a miniature land-

---

scape. Some students may have seen these flowers, and those who have not can still appreciate the gradual unfolding of the description as the bits of paper "become wet, stretch and twist and take on colour and distinctive shape, become flowers or houses or people . . . " (p. 1551). You may then wish to read back into the preceding page and take up the episode of the *madeleine*, and its contrast between the "intellectual memory" that preserves "nothing of the past itself" and the memory of the senses— "taste and smell alone" (p. 1550)—that enables one to call up buried worlds.

Another possibility is to examine the description of consciousness and memory at the beginning, asking students to compare their own experiences with the narrator's account, and pointing out the use of this relaxed or open consciousness to link different stages of life: "I had drifted back to an earlier stage in my life . . . only the most rudimentary sense of existence . . . (I) would gradually piece together the original components of my ego" (pp. 1516–18). Once you have established the role of involuntary (bodily, sensuous) memory in calling up past experience, you are ready to describe the rest of that experience: Marcel's adoration of his mother, his misery as he ascends the staircase, his alternate hope and despair as he waits for her kiss, and the rest.

There are a number of passages that lend themselves well to discussion: the magic lantern, the dinner party, the sending of the letter via Françoise, Marcel's mixed feelings as his father tells his mother to stay with the boy, the descriptions of the grandmother (her love of the outdoors, her relationship to the great-aunt, her choice of books).

The chief difficulty that students encounter is the length of the sentences and paragraphs. Perhaps they should be reassured that the long sentences are not a quirk of translation, but an integral part of Proust's style—a style that consciously sets out to imitate the rhythms of a mind caught up in its many memories. Encourage them to read fast, and to read aloud. They should not stop and wonder about each image and allusion (on first reading, at least), but read quickly through the sentences and paragraphs to get the drift of the whole. Once they realize, for example, that the first two pages are a series of associations by a mind drifting in and out of sleep, they will be more comfortable about the shifting, digressive pattern of the prose. Only then should each image be taken up for what it contributes to the whole picture.

A second difficulty may come with Proust's habit of embedding stories within stories. Students may be confused by what seems constant digression from the topic, and they should be encouraged to read quickly through to the end of the passage where the digression finally makes thematic sense. You may wish to meet the problem head-on by examining the embedding or associative technique with the class. Two useful examples come in the passage where Marcel's anguish is compared with that of Swann's unhappy passion for Odette (which then becomes a generalized description of unrequited love in Parisian society), and the description of the grandmother's character in the midst of a scene where Marcel's mother reads him a book (p. 1544ff.).

## Topics for Discussion and Writing

1. What are the two kinds of memory, according to Proust, and how do they work?
   [The "voluntary" or intellectual memory and the "involuntary," spontaneous memory associated with the senses. See the first and second paragraphs of *Backgrounds*.]

2. In what sense is Marcel a "nervous" child? How does his account of the evening illustrate this quality? Will he outgrow it?
   [See paragraphs 3–4 of *Backgrounds*. "Nervousness" in this sense is the quality of being high-strung and over-imaginative; it appears in Marcel's sensitivity to colors, smells, and in his anxiety over the ambivalence of reality and fantasy in the magic-lantern picture on his wall as well as in his anxious dependence on his mother. The adult Marcel—our narrator—seems equally sensitive to sense perceptions and the nuances of memory.]

3. Comment on Proust's use of digression.
   [See paragraphs 5–6 of *Classroom Strategies*. Digression is not only a technique of the associative memory, but also an excellent way to introduce short sketches of intrinsic interest that add to our knowledge of characters or situations.]

4. From what point of view is the story told?
   [See the third paragraph of *Backgrounds*. Proust blends the still-naive experiences of the younger Marcel with the informed perspective of the older Marcel who is narrating the novel.]

5. Are there any comic elements in the story?
   [See the fourth paragraph of *Backgrounds*. In addition to the

almost caricatural pictures of the two sisters, students may note the constant frustration of any conversational thread, and the way the grandfather is thwarted in his desire for gossip.]

6. Compare Proust's associative technique with that of other writers known for use of the "stream of consciousness." (In this anthology, the selections by Woolf and Joyce will provide examples.)

### Further Reading

See also the reading suggestions in the anthology, p. 1515.

Bloom, Harold, ed. *Marcel Proust.* 1987.
More general, with some overlap, than Bloom's collection, *Marcel Proust's* Remembrance of Things Past; it contains some useful essays.

Bowie, Malcom. *Freud, Proust, and Lacan: Theory as Fiction.* 1987.
Discusses and compares the theories of knowledge underlying each writer's work.

Deleuze, Gilles. *Proust and Signs.* Translated by Richard Howard. 1972.
Post-structural, semiotic criticism of the novel as a "machine producing signs of different orders."

Ellison, David R. *The Reading of Proust.* 1984. A more specialized theoretical discussion of the narrative self, questions of readability and influence, and Ruskin's influence on Proust.

Fowlie, Wallace. *A Reading of Proust.* 1963; reprinted 1975.
A useful guide.

Painter, George. *Marcel Proust: A Biography.* 1959, new edition, 1989.
A readable, anecdotal biography.

Poulet, Georges. *Proustian Space.* Translated by Elliot Coleman. 1977.
A study of Proust's fictional world-vision in terms of time and space.

Proust, Marcel. *Selected Letters.* Translated by Ralph Manheim; edited by Philip Kolb. 1983.
and
—, "On Reading." Translated and edited by Jean Autret and William Burford. 1971.
Proust's views on the psychological experience of reading.

Zurbrugg, Nicholas. *Beckett and Proust.* 1988.
An interesting source of comparative topics for discussion, despite a rather mechanical organization of ideas.

# THOMAS MANN
## Death in Venice

### Backgrounds

Thomas Mann often used the figure of the artist in society as a vehicle for examining cultural crisis, and *Death in Venice*—describing the fall of writer Gustave von Aschenbach—is a complex tracery of political, artistic, psychological and ethical issues. Published two years before the beginning of World War I, portraying a cosmopolitan Europe that is already collapsing under the weight of economic and political rivalries, the novella describes in realistic detail a particular moment of European society. Yet this historical aspect fades into the background before larger themes: the role of art and the artist and the balance that human beings must preserve between reason and impulse, discipline and spontaneity, conscious and unconscious life. Mann himself noted that an important turn in his work had occurred with the writing of *Death in Venice*. Works after this period regularly incorporate a dual meaning-structure, a system of entwined references which endow characters and events with both psychological and broad historical or mythic significance.

Mann wrote *Death in Venice* in 1911, shortly after he had taken a brief vacation in Venice to recover from nervous exhaustion. Correspondence with his older brother, the already-established Heinrich Mann, shows that he was frustrated at being unable to finish a series of planned works, much less the masterwork of which he felt himself capable. Obsessed by his image of the artist's tormented but prophetic role, struggling to define his own lofty concept of art over and against contemporary stress on innovative form, Mann produced the story of a writer many of whose anxieties are close to his own. Yet Aschenbach is not a hero, and while Mann sympathizes with his predicament, he also criticizes him for several kinds of betrayal.

The Gustav von Aschenbach who is introduced at the beginning has earned his respected position (and the honorific *von* before his name) by hard labor at his craft, by a search for dignified expression, and by the repudiation of uncontrollable depths—that is, the fatal knowledge and profound emotions of the "abyss." (Compare Baudelaire's *The Voyage*, where the true artist plunges "to the bottom of the abyss" to find some-

---

thing new.) Mann's ironic description of the way this "master of his trade" has fought his way to a conventional, uninspired style in a quest for perfection prepares the ground for a shattering reversal. Challenged by the sight of a pugnacious traveler outside the mortuary chapel, the exhausted Aschenbach starts thinking about a foreign vacation to reinvigorate his creative powers. He imagines escaping from the monotonous, confining routine of his European life, and sees that escape in Eastern landscapes with lush swampland, tigers, and bamboo thickets. Venice, finally, is the place to which he retreats: "half fairy tale and half tourist trap" (p. 1595), combining East and West, past and present, art and commerce, all with an odor of corruption—an "impossible and forbidden place" that "bewitched him, relaxed his will, gave him happiness" (p. 1582, 1585).

The happiness that Aschenbach encounters in Venice is accompanied by complete disorientation that begins on the initial ferryboat ride when he feels "that something not quite usual was beginning to happen, that the world was undergoing a dreamlike alienation . . ." (p. 1566). He beholds with horror a garishly painted and bewigged old man among a crowd of young excursionists; yet he himself will later undergo a similar cosmetic rejuvenation when he pursues the Polish youth Tadzio.

Aschenbach's relationship with Tadzio fuses two main themes: erotic love and the artist's worship of beauty. He is drawn to the youth's classic beauty, which recalls the perfection of Greek sculpture and especially busts of Eros, the god of love. Gradually, as Aschenbach watches Tadzio on the beach and in the dining room, the references to godly beauty increase; so, too, does his attraction which he now defines as a "paternal fondness, the tender concern by which he who sacrifices himself to beget beauty in the spirit is drawn to him who possesses beauty" (p. 1578–79). Only when the writer is accidentally prevented from leaving Venice does he realize that he is in love with Tadzio. It is worth noting that Mann does not criticize Aschenbach's love itself but rather his response to it. The writer accepts doom for himself and for others rather than separation from Tadzio and a return to a life of humdrum toil; even after discovering that plague has stricken the city (and that the authorities are concealing it), he does not warn Tadzio's mother. His obsession with Tadzio also leads him to define a despairing view of art—and a personal submission—that precisely negate the Platonic position he appears to adopt.

References to Greek culture permeate *Death in Venice*, partly because they express Aschenbach's traditional German admiration for Greek art and philosophy and partly because the web of allusions supports the development of other themes in the novella. Eros (the Roman Cupid), god of love; Hermes, patron of travelers and "soul-summoner"; Semele, who perished in the flames of her lover Zeus, king of the gods; Helios, fiery god of the sun that "turns our attention from spiritual things to the things of the senses" (p. 1587); the boatman Charon, who ferries souls to the world of the dead; Narcissus, who drowned in his own reflected image; Hyancinthus, doomed object of Apollo's love; Dionysus, the "stranger god" whose orgiastic revels drive out reason; Eos; Pan; Poseidon; and others all have symbolic roles in Aschenbach's journey towards death. The allusions become more significant towards the end, as he seeks to understand his attachment to Tadzio in terms of Greek homosexual love (the *ped-erasty* that is literally the love of an older man for a youth, generally with implications of leading the youth towards adulthood) and especially Platonic views of art.

Aschenbach's discourse on love and the artist, in which he imagines himself speaking to the young Phaedrus of the Platonic dialogue, derives from several sources. The most obvious reference is clearly the *Phaedrus*, where Socrates counters a speech on love by the sophist Lusias with two of his own. Another well-known Socratic speech on love occurs in Plato's *Symposium*—a much-annotated copy of which was found in Mann's library after his death. The philosopher Arthur Schopenhauer, whose discussion of the artist's nature greatly interested Mann, linked both dialogues with Plutarch's *Erotikos* (*Dialogue on Love*) in the forty-fourth chapter of his *The World as Will and Representation*. Despite apparent similarities, however, there are sharp differences between Socrates' address to Phaedrus and that of Aschenbach. Where one talks about the artist, the other talks about knowing the beautiful. Aschenbach focuses on the necessary "self-debauchery" of the artist, who is doomed either by a knowledge and understanding that sympathizes with the abyss through intoxication with sensuous beauty (p. 1608–09). Socrates, conversely, interprets physical beauty as a sign of the ideal, and describes how love of a beautiful youth can draw the mind to contemplate concepts of ideal beauty and moral perfection. Aschenbach's despairing conclusion in *Death in Venice* is that the world of the senses will inevitably lead the artist astray. It is a conclusion prefigured by his earlier dream of a Dionysian orgy, when his last effort of will is insufficient to protect him against the onslaught of the Stranger-God, "the enemy of the composed and dignified intellect." From then on, he is enslaved by the world of earthly experience (p. 1604–05), submitting to the barber in an attempt to make himself more attractive and pursuing Tadzio wherever he goes.

Aschenbach dies in his beach chair with the ambiguous image of Tadzio-Hermes before his eyes, trying vainly to follow the "pale and lovely soul-summoner" into the immensity before him but sinking back into mortality and death.

Mann employs a series of leitmotifs and oppositions to organize thematic patterns throughout *Death in Venice*. There are smaller recurrent themes, such as the leitmotif in Tadzio's "twilight-gray eyes," the reddish hair and snub nose that belong to obscurely menacing character, or Aschenbach's repeated eating of strawberries which, shortly before the plague strikes him down, are "overripe and soft." More prominent themes include the figure of a traveler-guide, beginning with the traveler by the mortuary and continuing in the ship's purser, the Charon-like gondolier, and the various references to Hermes. There are also individual passages that echo each other, such as the description of the painted old man on the ferry and Aschenbach's transformation by the barber; or the writer's return to the little square where he rests again on the edge of a fountain; or his early "longing for the unarticulated and immeasurable" (p. 1576) echoed in the ending scene where he recognizes Tadzio-Hermes beckoning him into "an immensity rich with unutterable expectation" (p. 1610). Yet the broadest and most persistent contrast is that of Apollo and Dionysus as opposed rational and irrational forces—a famous opposition which Mann would have known from Friedrich Nietzsche's *Birth of Tragedy*. Reinforcing this contrast is a second thematics of East and West, in which the West is associated with order and discipline, with bourgeois habits and dignity, and with Apollo as the god of light and rationality. Conversely, the "stranger god" Dionysus comes from the East (as is clear in Euripides' play *The Bacchae*, which Aschenbach's dream recalls). Death also comes from the East; the plague afflicting Venice is an Asiatic cholera originating in the Ganges delta (pp. 1602). *Death in Venice* is a highly structured composition that demonstrates Mann's desire to create, in prose, a "musical complex of associations."

### Classroom Strategies

*Death in Venice* can be taught in two or three days, depending on how thoroughly you wish to explore its thematic patterns. It is probably easiest to begin by considering Aschenbach the man—his dedication to his work, his ambition, the willpower and self-control (and repression) that have come to dominate his life—before moving into questions of literary style and its implied moral choices. Once students have a good picture of what Aschenbach has become, and what he has sacrificed to reach that pinnacle, you can ask them if they have any predictions about what will happen to him, and whether his "moral resoluteness" indeed signifies "a simplification, a morally simplistic view of the world and of human psychology, and thus also a resurgence of energies that are evil, forbidden, morally impossible" (p. 1563). Get them to talk about their ideas of art (e.g. its moral and social function; the importance of form; the relative importance of spontaneity and discipline) and you will be launched into the second strand: Aschenbach the writer, who has devoted his life a certain concept of beauty.

It may be interesting at this point to broaden the discussion with references to other works in the volume, comparing different styles and concepts of art (see the Introductions to Realism, Naturalism, and the New Poetry; Modernism; and Contemporary Explorations). At this level, it is not merely Aschenbach's concept of art that is relevant, but Mann's own practice: his psychological realism, use of myth, almost musical organization of themes and motifs, *and* the critical distance from Aschenbach himself.

The stages of Aschenbach's infatuation with Tadzio are relatively clear; what remains to be explored is the degree of self-knowledge (or delusion) the writer attains, and also the secondary mythic plane of interpretation created by classical allusions having to do with human nature and the search for absolutes. Students may find the picture of Aschenbach repellent, but they should recognize that he constantly attempts to deal with fundamental issues. They may find the opposition of Dionysus and Apollo over-simplified, too (one hopes); this in itself is another subject for discussion.

Since Mann is such a complex writer, it will be helpful to focus on certain key passages as microcosms of intertwining themes. The most obvious possibilities are the Dionysian dream and the final "Phaedrus" soliloquy. The latter may be difficult for students to follow without guidance, not only for its philosophical distinctions but also because they may be expecting a more direct description of Aschenbach's death from plague at that point. There are, in addition, many useful passages or symbolic scenes throughout the novella, some of which are mentioned in the last paragraph of *Backgrounds*.

### Topics for Discussion

1. Why is it important that Aschenbach see Tadzio first as an incarnation of ancient Greek sculpture?

2. How does Mann bring out the *successive* stages of Aschenbach's infatuation with Tadzio?

3. Do you agree that the artistic form is "two faced," "at one and the same time moral and immoral"? (p. 1563) How does this concept determine Aschenbach's career as a writer?

4. What are several reasons for Aschenbach's unwillingness to tell Tadzio's mother about the plague?

5. Describe and contrast the two "Phaedrus" passages (pp. 1587–88, 1608–09).

6. Discuss the importance of mythological references for an understanding of *Death in Venice*.

7. How does Mann's description of Venice make it an appropriated place for Aschenbach's downfall and death?

8. Where else have you seen the concept of "abyss" used in reference to art? (See *Backgrounds*, third paragraph.)

9. Describe the combination of psychological realism, historical detail, and symbolic allusions in *Death in Venice*.

10. How does the contrast of East and West, Dionysus and Apollo, underlie issues in *Death in Venice*?

11. Discuss the theme of the traveler throughout *Death in Venice*; in what sense does Hermes preside over Aschenbach's journey into infatuation and death?

***Further Reading***

See also the reading suggestions in the anthology, p. 1554.

Bloom, Harold, ed. *Thomas Mann.* 1986.
    Twenty-one essays on themes, texts, and techniques in a range of Mann's work, including two pieces on *Death in Venice*.

Ezergailis, Inta M., ed. *Critical Essays on Thomas Mann*. 1988.
Fourteen essays on a range of broadly-focused topics.

Hatfield, Henry. *From The Magic Mountain*. Ithaca, 1979.

Jonas, Ilsedore B. *Thomas Mann in Italy*. Translated by Betty Crouse.
University, Alabama, 1979.
A discussion of Mann's use of Italy and his depiction of Italians
throughout his work.

Lesser, Esther H. *Thomas Mann's Short Fiction: An Intellectual
Biography*. 1989.
The stories read individually and as part of Mann's intellectual
development.

Lukács, Georg. *Essays on Thomas Mann*. Translated by Stanley
Mitchell. 1965, reprinted 1979.
Important essays by a major twentieth-century critic.

McWilliams, James R. *Brother Artist: A Psychological Study of
Thomas Mann's Fiction*. 1983.
Especially relevant to the theme of the artist in Mann's work.

# RAINER MARIA RILKE

*Backgrounds*

Rilke's exceptional lyric gifts make him the most prominent German poet of our century. His work, *The Duino Elegies* especially, speaks to the modern sense of a fragmented universe with "all that was once relation so loosely fluttering hither and thither in space"—a universe in which communion constantly gives way to solitude. Yet Rilke's vision is redemptive as well as tragic. Sharing with Joyce a highly developed sense of the artist's mission, he sees art as a way to combat chaos by lending shape to the invisible, and to transform suffering and unify life and death in the context of eternity.

"Archaic Torso of Apollo"

Apollo is just one of the statues in Rilke's poetic museum, but as god of poetry and light he assumes pride of place. "Archaic Torso of Apollo" displays for the first time the typical Rilkean sonnet form: *abba abab cddc cdcd eef gfg.* The volume it begins is dedicated to Auguste Rodin, and in fact it can be said that the poem aspires to the condition of the statue it describes—seeking heft, palpability, the power to confront its observer directly and irresistibly (its second-person form of address at the close has this effect) and to move him out of complacency: "You must change your life." The maimed statue embodies both the incompleteness of human art and its transcendence in spite of all: "We cannot know his legendary head / with eyes like ripening fruit. And yet his torso / is still suffused with brilliance from inside, like a lamp . . . ."

Light, Apollo's attribute and imperium, endows this stone with being. The glow of life, of animal warmth and sexual heat, irradiates the poem, shining from breast bone and shoulder, from the center of procreation (at the poem's physical center), its exuberance finally breaking out "from all the borders of itself" and spilling beyond form. Such is the role of art, creating a beauty whose impact reaches beyond its own formal boundaries.

*Duino Elegies*

"The First Elegy"

If the presiding genius of "Archaic Torso of Apollo" is light, that of "The First Elegy" is music—harmonies giving themselves to the wide air. According to J. F. Hendry, before his stay at Duino Rilke "had never set much store by music as an art," but was gradually converted by the Beethoven he heard played on the great terrace there by the Quartetto Triestino. Born of intense creative longing, "The First Elegy" constitutes a long reaching toward the sublime invisibility shared by music and death. It is a protracted questioning: "Ah, whom can we ever turn to / in our need?" There is the old chaos of Night, its "wind full of infinite space" that consumes us. There are lovers who, all unknowingly, hug emptiness. The poet harangues himself and, by implication, his readers: Are we equal to earth's gifts (spring, star, wave) or art's (a violin)? Can we recognize them? Lines 36–55 celebrate the beauty of unrequited love, love that has transcended its object "as the arrow endures the bowstring's tension, so that / gathered in the snap of release it can be more than / itself." Such love—which for Rilke was an almost exclusively female accomplishment—is free of space and time, and thus immortal. Rilke himself was unable to sustain loves more mundane: his marriage to Clara and his numerous other romantic liaisons were better sustained by absence and letter-writing. One of his lovers suggested that he was half angel, half man: partaking of earth and heaven, but at home nowhere.

The Elegy's next surge of empathy is for the dead, free almost before they know it of human custom and expectation, without wishes or names. But the boundary seems firm only from *this* side: "the living are wrong to believe / in the too-sharp distinctions which they themselves have created." The poet's angelic vision embraces both worlds, and his song—like the sculptor's art—creates transcendent harmony out of mortal life and death.

"The Ninth Elegy"

"The First Elegy" asks the questions; it is gestation. "The Ninth Elegy" moves beyond questions; it is a bringing forth. It begins with a contrast between the weight of human Destiny—which we flee and yet which fascinates us—and the simple life of a laurel leaf (a *specific* one, with tiny waves on its border). We persist in trying to enact a further destiny, but what *can* be carried into death? "Nothing." But in the next breath a correction: sufferings, "the heaviness, / and the long experience of love," and things that can be told by their names, "some pure word, the yellow and blue / gentian." When the poet *names*, he revives earthly things into the invisible yet transcendent life of the imagination. Things, in their turn, depend on *us* for their transcendence, want us to be their artists, to "change them, utterly, in our invisible heart, / within—oh endlessly—within us!"

Finally the Elegy turns directly to Earth, asking it "isn't this what you want," questioning it in the urgent and playful accents of a lover: "Unspeakably I have belonged to you, from the first" and offering death as its "holiest inspiration," "our intimate companion." (Rilke says elsewhere that it is necessary "to confirm confidence toward death out of the deepest delights and glories of life: to make death, who never was a stranger, more distinct and palpable again as the silent knowing participant in everything alive.") The Elegy ends with the poet's exuberant announcement that past and future stand undiminished; infinity lives in his heart.

In connection with "Archaic Torso of Apollo" it is important to remember Rilke's long association with Auguste Rodin, who served as patron, employer, friend, and exalted example. Rodin's enormous industry and initiative provided a model that Rilke—plagued as he was with an impossible double hunger for solitude and love, barraged by the shapes of his fevered imagination—could not hope to match. The sculptor, according to one of the characters in Rilke's story "The Last," enjoys special mastery:

A song, a picture you notice, a poem you like—all have their significance and value, the same, I think, for him who first creates it as for him who recreates it. The sculptor creates his statues only for himself: but . . . he also creates space for his own statue in the world . . . . Art raised man to God.

Rilke's poem can be said to recreate the sculptor's creation. To it belongs the joy of renewing the triumph of light (form, life) over chaos.

"The First Elegy," a rush of urgent speech that begins with an appeal to the angels, was born complete on a day of cold winds. Castle Duino was a place of spiritual fulfillment for Rilke. He wrote of it, "Duino is the cloud of my being"—but as always, solitude held demons: "I creep about for the whole day in the thickets of my life and scream like a savage and clap my hands:—you wouldn't believe what hair-raising creatures then fly up." Influenced by his friend Lou Andreas-Salome and his wife Clara, Rilke was considering psychoanalysis. But he held serious reservations about its effect on his art: "I always have the idea that my work is really nothing but a self-treatment of this kind." A letter to Andreas-Salome written on January 20th, the day before he began the Elegies, suggests that "something perilously close to a disinfected soul" might result from what he terms (in a letter to Clara) "this correcting of all the pages life has hitherto written." Though his irrational anguish tortured him, it was its cry that awoke an angel—an angel both beautiful and terrible, an angel of life and of death. A 1904 letter to Franz Kappus writes: "We know little, but that we must hold to what is difficult is a certainty that will not forsake us; it is good to be solitary, for solitude is difficult; that something is difficult must be a reason the more for us to do it."

At Chateau Muzot, Rilke finally found himself in a position to complete the work begun ten years earlier, on the other side of World War I (during which Duino Castle had been bombed and destroyed). The inspiration to complete the Elegies—and to write the wholly unanticipated *Sonnets to Orpheus*—came from an account of the death of a young girl—his daughter's friend, Vera. This event served Rilke as a wellspring of emotion—emotion aimed at contact with what he calls, in a letter to the Polish translator of the Elegies, "the center of that kingdom whose depth and influence we share, boundlessly, with the dead and the unborn." The Elegies finished, he writes to Andreas-Salome: "Now I *know* myself again. It was like a crippling of my being that the elegies were not there."

Influences on Rilke include Poe (particularly his linkage of terror and beauty, as seen in the opening of "The First Elegy"), Baudelaire (see the headnote), and Rodin (see above). Rilke also admired the lyrics of Holderlin and translated Valéry. Impressionist painting—Cezanne's work in particular—affected his way of seeing as well as his energies. Of Cezanne he wrote:

"I notice by the way Cezanne keeps me busy now how very different I have grown. I am on the road to becoming a worker, on a long road perhaps and probably only at the first milestone . . . . This consuming of love in anonymous work, which gives rise to such pure things, probably no one has succeeded in doing so completely as old Cezanne."

## Classroom Strategies

The three selections may be taught during two class periods. It would be helpful to start with "Archaic Torso of Apollo," not only because it is first chronologically, but because its relative compactness and formality make it most manageable. This poem can serve as a convenient introduction to Rilke's conceptions of the artist and of art. Students who are able to read the original German text (p. 1615) should be encouraged to read aloud to the class and to comment on any effects (rhythmic, verbal, imagistic) that they find specific to the German original. Fortified by discussing the shorter poem, students will be ready to plunge into "The First Elegy," with all its urgent questionings; and to discover "The Ninth Elegy" as its answer and fulfillment. With its emphasis on the sensuous phenomenal world, its palpable message, "The Ninth Elegy" may well appear to students as a relief and refreshment.

The most pressing difficulty may well be Rilke's conception of the Angels in the *Duino Elegies*. They are *not* the Christian angels students will want to make them. "The Angel of the Elegies," Rilke wrote in a letter to his Polish translator, "is the creature in whom that transformation of the visible into the invisible we are performing already appears complete.... The Angel of the Elegies is the being who vouches for the recognition of a higher degree of reality in the invisible.—Therefore 'terrible' to us, because we, its lovers and transformers, still depend on the visible." The Angel represents a sublimation of the human which can be imagined as human intensities continuing apart from flesh and time.

Students may also be disconcerted by the fragmentary nature of the *Elegies*—a fragmentation akin to that of the damaged torso of Apollo, demonstrating perfection in imperfection. It might be helpful to present the two Elegies as poems which are themselves a process of understanding (instead of a result); as poems which both explore and dramatize the shifting relationships between life and art.

The intense spiritual struggles embodied in the *Elegies*, struggles which might seem beyond the experience of youthful readers, actually are quite closely related to their experiences on the threshold of adulthood—their struggles to reach a sense of purpose in life, to be the artists of their destinies. The state of unrequited love which Rilke exalts will perhaps also be familiar to many students. Rilke's lovers may be profitably compared and contrasted with those who appear at the beginning of

Yeats's "Sailing to Byzantium."

## Topics for Discussion and Writing

1. What is the role of light in "Archaic Torso of Apollo"?
[See *Backgrounds* for further discussion.]

2. Why does Rilke choose to emphasize the sexuality of the statue?
[In a letter to Kappus, Rilke says that "artistic experience lies so incredibly close to that of sex, to its pain and its ecstasy, that the two manifestations are indeed but different forms of one and the same yearning and delight." See *Backgrounds* for further discussion.]

3. What does "Archaic Torso of Apollo" say (and demonstrate) about the role of art?
[See *Backgrounds* for discussion.]

4. How should we interpret the famous command at the end of "Archaic Torso of Apollo"?

5. If you read German, you may wish to read aloud or compare passages from the translation with the original poem (p. 1615). Students may also be encouraged to try reading the original text on their own, and to comment on the way the translation has or has not succeeded in grasping the German original. Some of the bolder ones may attempt their own translations, which will bring them closer to the text at the same time that it induces a healthy respect for the difficulties of translation.

6. In "Archaic Torso of Apollo" we are standing in a museum, in front of a statue from the past, experiencing the statue along with the poet. Where are the *Elegies* located in space and time?
[See *Backgrounds* on "The First Elegy" for further discussion.]

7. What does Rilke want from the angels? Who are they?
[See paragraph 2 of *Classroom Strategies* for discussion.]

8. What does "The First Elegy" assert as the task of the ideal lover?
[See *Backgrounds* for further discussion.]

9. What is the role of music in "The First Elegy"? Does it imply special importance for the artist as creator of music? [See *Backgrounds* for further discussion.]

10. What is the relationship between form and meaning in the *Elegies*?

11. What is the importance placed on naming things in "The Ninth Elegy"? (Saying them? Praising them?) What special mission does this afford the poet? Does this reverence for things recall "Archaic Torso of Apollo"? [See the headnote and *Backgrounds*.]

12. What is the tone of the poet's concluding address to Earth in "The Ninth Elegy"? [See *Backgrounds* for discussion.]

13. What makes possible the sense of wholeness at the end of "The Ninth Elegy"? [See *Backgrounds* for discussion.]

### Further Reading

See also the reading suggestions in the anthology, p. 1614.

Holthusen, Hans Egon. *Rainer Maria Rilke: A Study of His Later Poetry*. Translated by J. P. Stern. New Haven, 1952.
A short study which includes discussion of the *Duino Elegies*.

Mandel, Siegfried. *Rainer Maria Rilke: The Poetic Instinct*. Carbondale, 1965.
A useful introduction to Rilke's work.

Mason, Eudo C. *Rilke, Europe, and the English-Speaking World*. Cambridge, 1961.
Mason discusses Rilke's view of the English-speaking world, and its views of him.

Shaw, Priscilla W. *Rilke, Valery, and Yeats: The Domain of the Self.* New Brunswick, NJ, 1964.
Shaw discusses the relationship between self and world in Rilke, with particular reference to his view of the body and the world of objects.

# WALLACE STEVENS

## Backgrounds

Stevens is a poet of the drama of the mind, caught in its "double fate of self and world." He can be difficult, arcane, and even precious, but at his best he is elegant and resonant. He makes use of everything—images, parables, anecdotes, lectures, dialogues, monologues, aphorisms, and so on—to promote the life of the imagination. As Northrop Frye has said: "His poetic vision is informed by a metaphysic; his metaphysic is informed by a theory of knowledge; his theory of knowledge is informed by a poetic vision." But always, in Stevens, we come back finally to "poetry itself, the naked poem." It is the poet's responsibility, as he sees it, to renew a world under the constant threat of imaginative impoverishment, and he fulfills that responsibility in poems of extraordinary range and speculative brilliance.

## "Sunday Morning"

"Sunday Morning" is Stevens's most famous poem, and perhaps his best. It is a poem of contrasts—the female subject of the poem confronts two opposing views of paradise, neither of which is immediately satisfying: the earthly paradise, which she finds decadent and empty, and the mythological, religious paradise, to which she cannot commit herself. The woman, in whose highly civilized rooms we find ourselves, too sensitive to content herself with the decadent pursuit of earthly pleasure and too sophisticated to accept the religious idea of heaven. Her meditation on the matter, Stevens tells us, "is anybody's meditation."

The first stanza contrasts a luxuriously sensual natural world with "silent Palestine." But the objects of the sensual world—"late coffee," "pungent oranges," the "green freedom of a cockatoo"—"seem things in some procession of the dead." She is unable, emotionally, to commit herself to the physical or the spiritual. The second stanza develops the questions raised in the first. What does the natural world offer that can be "cherished like the thought of heaven"? The answer is that "Divinity must live within herself," through her experiences, and the memory of those experiences, in the natural world.

But if the earth—the natural world, the world of physicality—is to be "all of paradise that we shall know," she must then wonder what is to happen when the world of nature passes, to remain alive only in memory and desire. The sky may seem "friendlier" if paradise is invested in earth, but she still feels "the need of some imperishable bliss."

Stanza VI reconsiders the traditional view of paradise in a way that recalls Keats's "Ode on a Grecian Urn." It is static, a "cold pastoral," where rivers "seek for seas / They never find." It lacks beauty because it lacks death, and "Death is the mother of Beauty." Without death there can be no passionate pleasure.

In the last stanza, the woman relinquishes her desire for the paradise promised by religion; she finds that "The tomb in Palestine / . . . is the grave of Jesus, where he lay"—nothing more. We, however, must continue to live in "an old chaos of the sun," where death makes for beauty and sponsors the only paradise available to us, a place where:

> in the isolation of the sky,
> At evening, casual flocks of pigeons make
> Ambiguous undulations as they sink.
> Downward to darkness, on extended wings.
> (117–120)

## "Peter Quince at the Clavier"

Stevens wrote "Peter Quince at the Clavier" during the same period in which he wrote "Sunday Morning," and both poems evidence concern with the cyclical process of life and death in the natural world. In this poem, however, physical beauty not only becomes immortal through the memories of the living, but also by its transubstantiation into art. "Music is feeling," not mere sound, and it is music that in the first stanza brings the speaker to desire. The speaker compares his awakened desire for an unidentified woman of his memories to the "strain / Waked in the elders by Susanna," a "strain" which made their thin blood "Pulse pizzicati of Hosanna." Stanzas two and three recreate the Biblical story in a way reminiscent of paintings by Rembrandt and Tintoretto.

The last stanza recognizes that the passionate throbbing brought on by such beauty must, inevitably, die: evenings, gardens, seasons, maidens—all die. "Susanna's music touched the bawdy strings / Of those white elders; but, escaping / Left only Death's ironic scraping." But in memory, as in art, Susanna's music—her beauty and the desire it awakens—is immortal, and "makes a constant sacrament of praise."

### "Anecdote of the Jar"

"Anecdote of the Jar" can be, and has been, interpreted in two mutu-ally exclusive ways. One view of the poem finds that the jar represents the imposition of form by intellect, and that its introduction onto the hill destroys the "natural beauty" of the surrounding wilderness. Another view, perhaps less dedicatedly Romantic, notes that the wilderness is "slovenly" at first, but that the jar—which has form and is therefore representative of art—takes "dominion" and establishes order where before there was merely "wild" chaos. This second interpretation of the poem has the advantage of having a basis in Stevens's aesthetics—his insistence that art, because it has form, produces order and beauty in a world where flux and chaos otherwise predominate.

Both interpretations, however, assume that Stevens means to evaluate the wilderness, as well as the jar, either positively or negatively. Through the introduction of form, however undistinguished ("The jar was round upon the ground" hardly seems to suggest a particularly significant form), our perception of nature is inevitably altered.

### "The Emperor of Ice-Cream"

With the cold-blooded assurance of the child, the speaker of "The Emperor of Ice-Cream" registers the meanness and finality of death, and urges the reader to recognize that "The only emperor is the emperor of ice-cream." The ministrations over the dead become a kind of ugly carnival, the attempt at decorum is exploded by the recognition that it is, after all, merely empty formality—a pathetically inadequate illusion unappreciated by the one for whom it is being performed. Death is final, the hands that once embroidered fantails are still, the horny feet are cold. Death should be the end of the charade: "Let be be finale of seem."

### "The Idea of Order at Key West"

"The Idea of Order at Key West" illustrates the ascendancy of the poetic mind over the chaos and strength of the natural world, represented here by the sea. As in "Peter Quince," music is related to the desire to impose order upon the world. In "The Idea of Order," however, the female singer creates the world in which she exists through her song, and, more important, changes the world significantly for those who hear her. Nature attains a higher order of reality when it is organized by the artist, who speaks to and for her audience.

In the first line of the poem, it is apparent that the singer has powers greater than those of the sea. The sea possesses no ordering imagination; it moves and makes sounds, but they are movements and sounds without direction. It is the woman's song—not the "grinding water and the gasping wind"—that commands the speaker's attention. In comparison, the sea becomes a mere backdrop, a "place by which she walked to sing." The fourth stanza further emphasizes the idea that nature, without the creative imagination to order it, is beautiful but meaningless. Her voice gathers together not only the sea, but all that the sea apportions.

> It was her voice that made
> The sky acutest at its vanishing.
> She measured to the hour its solitude.
> She was the single artificer of the world
> In which she sang. And when she sang, the sea,
> Whatever self it had, became the self
> That was her song, for she was the maker.
>
> (34–40)

Because the singer is the "single artificer" of her world, the sea becomes, both for the singer and her audience, her particular vision of the sea—there is no "world for her / Except the one she sang and, singing, made."

When the singing ends, the speaker finds the world arranged, organized, gorgeous, in such a way as to be beyond the understanding of the aesthetician ("Ramon Fernandez"). The last stanza is a coda which pays tribute to the "rage for order" and to the inspirational quality of the art such a rage produces.

### "The Man on the Dump"

Once again, the central interest in "The Man on the Dump" is art—specifically the creation of poetry, and the problems of the poet as he imaginatively creates his world. "The dump is full of images," but these images are mainly exhausted, time-worn, obsolete, laughable; the poet sits atop the mound of the tradition's imagery and takes inventory—sifts, mocks, rejects. If the moon is going to come up at all in a poem, it will have to come up "as a moon" (not as a stale image of the moon) in an "empty sky" (a sky swept clean of all the trash the poet must reject). The process of rejection, the sloughing off of the trite, purifies and renews the imagination, and the poet is able to begin a new cycle of creativity. He beats "an old tin can" in order to create a fresh version of reality: "One beats and beats for that which one believes."

The poem ends with a series of questions which ask, essentially, why the poet has rejected certain images and why he continues to sit among them. The answer, if there is one, appears in the last line: The discarded images which now "torture the ear" were once fresh, once a direct apprehension of reality, the truth—"the the"—the thing itself. It is still the poet's job of work to find or re-find the image which offers the thing itself—"the the"—and reorder the world into beauty.

### Classroom Strategies

The six poems can be covered in two class periods. The most difficult aspects of Stevens's aesthetics and poetics are contained in "Sunday Morning" and "Peter Quince," so it would be useful to concentrate on these two during the first class meeting. If you can spend only one class period on the work, "Sunday Morning" and "The Idea of Order at Key West" are the most representative, significant, and telling poems to discuss. "The Emperor of Ice-Cream," however, is perhaps the most accessible.

Stevens's work offers both concrete imagery and abstract speculation, and the abstractions will cause most of the difficulty for students, who will want a definite meaning assigned to lines such as "Let be be finale of seem," phrases such as "The the," and images such as the jar in Tennessee. The more elusive these things are (and are intended to be) the more the student will insist on an assigned meaning—and decide, in its absence, that the poems are "not worth the trouble." This tendency will be exacerbated because of Stevens's continual use of art itself as his central subject. Some students find this fascinating, but many tend to doubt that it is an important enough subject for a poem, finding in it a certain self-absorption and an illusory self-importance. A discussion of literary language—tending as it does toward multiple meanings, as opposed to scientific language, which tends toward a sole meaning—can be useful in this context. So can the fact that Stevens worked as a successful insurance executive. Students find this duly surprising, but admirable. If a hard-headed businessman thinks poetry is so important, then . . .

Students might be directed to notice that quite often in Stevens's work there is a line in the poem with a truth that is demonstrated by the poem as a whole. In "Peter Quince," for instance, the speaker's claim that "Music is feeling, then, not sound" is confirmed by the poetic music which envelops each of the poem's characters. The coarse elders, for instance, are characterized by coarse poetic rhythms and images ("A cymbal crashed, / And roaring horns") or else pizzicati plucking intended to suggest their glandular excitement. The simpering Byzantine maids come and go with "a noise like tambourines." Susanna's music, however, is as "clear and warm" as she is.

In "The Idea of Order at Key West," visual and auditory imagery fortify Stevens's notion that the natural world, however beautiful, remains meaningless without the ordering power of the artistic imagination. The sea can only cry, grind, and gasp until it is transformed by the woman's song. Once again, the poem demonstrates its own claims.

## Topics for Discussion and Writing

1. What kinds of contrasts can be found in "Sunday Morning"? What purpose do they serve? How does Stevens exploit the traditional activities of a Sunday morning?
   [See *Backgrounds* for discussion.]

2. How does music function in "Peter Quince at the Clavier"? What is meant by "Music is feeling, then, not sound"? How is this thought demonstrated in the poem as a whole?
   [See *Backgrounds* and paragraph 3 of *Classroom Strategies*.]

3. What aesthetic position is suggested by "Anecdote of the Jar"? What other poems suggest a similar aesthetic position?

4. Both "The Emperor of Ice-Cream" and "Sunday Morning" concern themselves with death. How do they differ? Have they any similarities?

5. How does "The Idea of Order at Key West" illustrate the artist's ability to order the natural world? Do you believe any of this? Can you name any examples of art which have had the effect of causing us to reperceive the nature of the world? What did Oscar Wilde mean when he said that "Nature imitates art"?

6. Why does the poet in "The Man on the Dump" need to discard used-up images? Why do they become exhausted? Why would Stevens insist that it is important to discover new, fresh images?

7. Why does Stevens make such use of contrast? Locate and discuss examples of contrasting images, voices, settings, and points of view (see especially poems such as "The Idea of Order at Key West," "Sunday Morning," "Anecdote of the Jar," and "The Man on the Dump."

8. Compare Stevens's idea of the poet as creator of reality with Baudelaire (see especially "One O'clock in the Morning," "Windows," "A Carcass," "Her Hair" and "Correspondences").

### Further Reading

See also the reading suggestions in the anthology, pp. 1623.

Bloom, Harold. *Wallace Stevens: The Poems of Our Climate*. Ithaca, NY, 1977.
Intriguing commentary on his work, noting the "anxiety of influence" caused by similarities to Emerson, Whitman, Tennyson, Shelley, and others.

Doggett, Frank. *Stevens's Poetry of Thought*. Baltimore, 1966.
Clear, straightforward discussions of the poems.

Morse, Samuel French. *Wallace Stevens: Poetry as Life*, 1970.
An extended critical biography.

Pearce, Roy Harvey, and J. Hillis Miller, eds. *The Act of the Mind: Essays on the Poetry of Wallace Stevens*. Baltimore, 1965.
The essays by Morse, Pearce, Vendler, and Macksey are particularly useful.

Stevens, Wallace. *Letters of Wallace Stevens*. Edited by Holly Stevens. 1966.
Interesting letters that also contain observations on Stevens's own poetry.

# JAMES JOYCE
## A Portrait of the Artist as a Young Man

*Backgrounds*

Joyce's book remains one of the most rewarding of all novels for college students because they, in particular, identify with the struggles of Joyce's hero as he matures toward his vocation. Stephen's problems are their own; the fear and confusion of childhood and adolescence is still fresh in their memories. Stephen's experiences and concerns intersect at every point with theirs. In addition, the style is a masterful recreation, even documentation, of the formation of a sensibility—and a particularly interesting sensibility at that.

Joyce's *Portrait* is a *Kunstlerroman*, a story about the growing up of an artist. Unlike most of the artist-heroes in stories of this kind, Joyce's Stephen Dedalus is neither a genius—misunderstood and thus martyred by the society around him—nor a fool. One of the critical controversies generated by the book has to do with the attitude Joyce takes toward his hero, which can be, and has been, read as both sympathetic and ironically contemptuous. Readers of the excerpt we include will probably be more inclined toward the former, but later in the novel Joyce allows Stephen to appear an almost intolerable prig.

Joyce once wrote that "the past assuredly implies a fluid succession of presents" which should read like "the curve of an emotion." In *A Portrait of the Artist as a Young Man* the narrator creates that "succession of presents" by speaking in the changing voices of Stephen Dedalus at various stages of his development. At the beginning of this excerpt from the novel (pp. 1637–38), the narrator speaks with the voice of a very small boy, so small that he is yet unable to pronounce the words "rose" and "bloweth" (he sings, "O, the green wothe botheth"); he is at a stage where he is just beginning to assume his identity as a person separate from those immediately around him, especially his mother and father. One should notice that in the first paragraph the narrative is not in Stephen's voice at all, suggesting that he—as yet—has none; it is the voice of his father telling him a story. Stephen, then, first identifies himself with a character in a story ("baby tuckoo"), establishing the centrality that story-telling will have for him later. In the second paragraph, the father is identified—in a somewhat sinister way ("his father looked at him through a glass: he had a hairy face"). In the third paragraph Stephen is able to identify himself and begins, in the subsequent passages, to develop his own five senses: sight (the "hairy face"); taste ("lemon platt"); sound (the song); touch ("first it is warm then it gets cold"); and smell (a "queer smell"). Since the entire book is, in many ways, "about" coming to a sense of his identity, it is perfectly appropriate that it should begin with this process in microcosm.

Since much of the book concerns itself with establishing that identity as one different from, and often in opposition to, his social environment, it is appropriate that much of this excerpt presents us with Stephen's growing recognition that he is in some important way different from those who surround him. To do anything other than to escape (through "silence, cunning, and exile," as we are told later in the book) would apparently mean a life of subordination and humiliation for Stephen. Even in this early memory, at a point where Stephen is old enough to notice that there are others in the world (the Vances), and others with whom he might develop some kind of relationship (Eileen), Stephen finds himself in the position of being dominated; he hides under the table while Dante says "*Apologise, / Pull out his eyes, / Pull out his eyes, / Apologise*" (p. 1638).

Here Stephen attempts to establish who he is and what he wants to do (marry Eileen), and immediately finds himself set upon by those who are supposed to love him. Typically, his punishment has to do with his eyes, which throughout the book will be a source of humiliation and punishment. Furthermore, Stephen's sense of martyrdom (he is named for St. Stephen) is suggested here as is the underlying myth of Prometheus. Like Prometheus, Stephen wants to make a gift of fire, his artistic fire, his warmth and light, to his culture. Like another mythical figure, Icarus (the son of Daedalus), however, he may well fly too close to the sun (where there is too much heat, too much fire), his artistic wings will melt, and he will fall into the sea and drown.

These opening passages, then, establish a number of central notions that will be explored throughout the remainder of the excerpt and the novel as a whole: Stephen's difficult growth; his often exasperating attempts to come into some sense of who he is and what he should be in the world; and his presentation in a narrative which is close enough to Stephen to speak with his voice, but far enough removed to refuse to dictate what we are to think of him.

The second section of the excerpt charts Stephen's progress, or lack of it, at Clongowes School, and here again we find him at odds with his environment, desperately attempting to discover how to survive among schoolfellows who hold him in contempt ("He felt his body small and weak amid the throng of players and his eyes were weak and watery" [p. 1638]), and in a moral universe which offers him no absolute answers, even though he very much desires them. Stephen simply finds himself incapable of making absolute—or even adequate—distinctions. He doesn't know which is the right answer (should he kiss his mother or not? should he "peach" or not?), or which is the right "side" (green or maroon? York or Lancaster?), and it pains him that he cannot understand why people kiss, or where the universe ends. When Stephen turns to the flyleaf of his geography (p. 1644) we are reminded of precisely how small and insignificant, yet somehow central, Stephen feels he is.

Stephen's recognition of his own inadequacies, of which he is made painfully aware by life at Clongowes, is the source of his immense admiration for knowledge. It is knowledge, Stephen begins to feel, that makes assurance possible. "By thinking of things you could understand them," Stephen thinks later. Knowledge is seen as a stay against confusion; against his fears and questions; against the dark, the square ditch, the cold and slimy water, the ghosts of murderers, his own weak eyesight. He begins to associate knowledge with the only warmth and comfort he has ever known—home.

Home, however, as we see in the third section of the excerpt, is not a place where he will find adequate answers to his myriad questions. It is by no accident that Joyce places the raging argument between Mr. Dedalus and Mr. Casey (who support Parnell despite his indiscretions) and Dante (who does not) at the family's Christmas dinner, traditionally the warmest-spirited and most secure holiday that the Christian tradition has to offer. In Joyce's savagely ironic treatment of Christmas with the Dedaluses, the fragmentation and confusion that have been Stephen's burden at Clongowes erupt in the very place where he had hoped to find comfort and security. The argument at the table displays even this most small and intimate world as irreparably and angrily divided between two conflicting but equally adamant moral positions—one with its source in Catholic belief and the other in Irish nationalism. For Stephen, the priests must be right because the Church must be right, but his father must be right because he is his father. Once again, there are no answers; no one is right and no one is wrong. And Stephen once again finds himself "terrorstricken" amid chaos which he cannot control or understand.

In section four of the excerpt, which begins by dovetailing a schoolboy scandal with the Parnell scandal, young Stephen attempts to establish a kind of justice for himself, to take a stand against the undeserved humiliation which he has so often suffered. The section reinforces a number of the obsessions which inform the earlier sections: Stephen's obsession with words (his consideration of "Tower of Ivory" and "House of Gold," wine, and the sounds that cricket bats and pandybats make); his attempts to associate words and sounds with other sensory experiences; his wonder and confusion about those who live around him. The central incident of this section, however, once again features Stephen's humiliation and punishment—this time at the hands of a representative of the Catholic Church, Father Dolan. The pandybat scene (which, as usual, has its source in Stephen's weak eyesight; his glasses have been broken and he is unable to do his classwork) vividly registers Stephen's pain and his subsequent recognition of injustice: "It was wrong; it was unfair and cruel; and, as he sat in the refectory, he suffered time after time in memory the same humiliation . . . ." (p. 1670). Stephen's response to this injustice is to take his case to a higher authority, the rector, who agrees that Stephen has been unfairly treated and assures him that there is indeed justice. Stephen—for the first time—finds himself a hero among his schoolmates. Though our excerpt ends on this upbeat note, it needs to be pointed out that early in the next chapter Stephen discovers that his act of moral heroism was seen as nothing more than a great joke by the rector. "Father Dolan and I," the rector tells Stephen's father, "when I told them all at dinner about it, Father Dolan and I had a great laugh over it. *You better mind yourself, Father Dolan*, said I, *or young Dedalus will send you up for twice nine*. We had a famous laugh together over it. Ha! Ha! Ha!"

This sequence successfully reveals one of Joyce's central thematic concerns—Ego versus Authority—as well as one of the major structural patterns of the novel. Hugh Kenner has described this pattern by saying that "each chapter successively gathers up the thematic material of the preceding ones and entwines them with a dominant theme of its own, closing with a synthesis of triumph which the next destroys."

The way out of the impasses of Stephen's childhood, of course, is through art, and although it will take Stephen until the end of this book and, perhaps, on through *Ulysses* before he will become an artist able to forge "the uncreated conscience" of his race, the basis for his vocation is established early. Throughout this excerpt, Stephen shows an extraordinary concern and feeling for words—the medium of what will become his art; even in the midst of the horrible argument over Christmas dinner

Stephen feels a "glow rise to his own cheek as the spoken words thrilled him" (p. 1660). For young Stephen, all experience is intimately connected with words; to know and use words, to create with words, to feel the meaning and suggestion of words ("It was nice and warm to see the lights in the castle. It was like something in a book" [p. 1640]) is one of the few ways Stephen has to shore himself up against a world which otherwise terrorizes and humiliates him. Words will be the source of the knowledge and assurance he desires; they will provide him with his calling and give him the means to tell us, finally, who he is.

The excerpt of *Portrait* available here is based rather closely on Joyce's childhood, especially his school days, between 1882 and 1894. Most of the minor characters who make their appearance in these pages were an actual part of Joyce's childhood: Dante (his aunt, Mrs. "Dante" Hearn Conway); the Vances (including Eileen); Nasty Roche; Wells; Father Dolan (in reality Father James Daly); and Father Conmee, among others, were modelled very closely on their real-life sources. So too are events. His aunt "Dante" *did* warn the young James Joyce against playing with Eileen Vance; Joyce *did* attend Clongowes Wood College (from 1888 until 1891), where he was pushed into a cesspool and paddled by Father Daly; the controversy surrounding Parnell *did* rage during the time Joyce was at Clongowes. Joyce does, of course, distort, condense and otherwise reshape real characters and events in order to serve his imaginative purposes.

Perhaps the most important literary influences on Joyce were Henrik Ibsen, whose realistic dramas Joyce found particularly compelling; Gustave Flaubert, whose narrative control and ironic distance Joyce admired; and the French *symbolistes*, whose work stresses moments of revelation in what might otherwise seem to be ordinary experience. Scholars have mined *Portrait* for influences and have uncovered many others. Joyce's ability to assimilate and synthesize the languages and literatures of the Western world is legendary.

More important than the influences on Joyce, however, is his influence on subsequent literature. *A Portrait of the Artist as a Young Man* can be seen as a particularly central and representative work of modern literature for two essential reasons:

—Joyce's portrayal of the modern world as one without absolutes, a fragmented world in which the individual must discover for himself how best to live in it. This discovery ordinarily takes place in opposition to the larger world, rather than with its help. Modernism assumes that the beliefs, sanctions, and assumptions of the past have been exhausted, and that the individual soul (especially when that individual has the soul of an artist) will be required to forge ahead alone, to develop its own way of living and choosing, if it is to survive.

—Joyce's preoccupation with the inner life. Joyce did not invent the "stream of consciousness" or the other techniques that modern writers use to display interiority, but he—along with Proust, Woolf, Lawrence, Dorothy Richardson, and a number of others—believed that if there are, indeed, any truths to be told in fiction they are truths generated by the inner life, the life of the psyche. One of the most important tendencies of all modern literature is its insistence that what should actually constitute "life" in a character (or in the novel as a whole) cannot be adequately presented through the traditional means of describing what is outside of him—his job, his clothes, his social environment, etc.—but instead through the exploration of what goes on inside of him. Joyce, like almost all other major modern writers, had to develop a narrative technique which would allow these preoccupations to surface.

### Classroom Strategies

This excerpt of *A Portrait of the Artist as a Young Man* is perhaps best taught in at least three class periods. The excerpt divides itself rather easily into two sections: the beginning through the Christmas dinner, and the paddling incident and Stephen's subsequent attempt to secure justice for himself. The first class period might be given over to a discussion of Joyce's narrative techniques; a discussion of the first two pages of the text (with its catalogue of senses, its suggestion of the discovery of identity as a central theme, and its relentless insistence on a narrative voice keyed to Stephen's age and development) will offer the student a great deal to chew on.

Optimally, it might be wise to spend more than three class periods on the *Portrait* excerpt, since students will probably find its narrative mode rather difficult. For those of us who have read (or taught) *Portrait* before, or have read *Ulysses* or other books using similar narrative modes, *Portrait* probably seems simple enough. But to students who still assume that a narrative will be linear, *Portrait* will seem—at least at the beginning—almost indecipherable. You might do well to read certain passages out loud to the class, since the literal meaning of stream-of-consciousness narration often comes across more clearly when heard.

Reading Joyce always reminds us, if we need reminding, about the centrality of technique in literature—the *way* the work happens, rather than what it is "about." No one, at least no one in the last hundred years or so, would claim that Cezanne's paintings of apples or Matisse's flowers were unimportant because their subjects were not "profound" in themselves. What we are accustomed to look for in a painting—the painter's skill with his medium, no matter what the "subject"—is something that readers, especially student readers, tend to overlook or undervalue in responding to a work of literature. Joyce makes it almost impossible to overlook the fact that literature is made out of words, that those words form structures, that those structures make for content, and that we respond to the content that those structures make possible. It might be useful, then, to begin by emphasizing the word *portrait* in the title, and to relate it not only to the fact that this will be a book about the development of an artist, but also to the fact that in order to fully appreciate the book we will have to readjust the usual ways we read and talk about the significance of the literary medium itself.

The amazing thing about Joyce's narratorial adoption of Stephen's language at various stages of his development is that the narrative is very clearly that of a child, while at the same time it exhibits the extraordinary control and sophistication of an adult who is a master of his craft. Joyce will sometimes appear to write badly, but he risks this in order that the quality of Stephen's sensibility will be constantly on display. This is especially so in the sections of the book subsequent to this excerpt, when the adolescent and college-age Stephen is consumed by his pose as aesthete and his sensibility delivers itself in high-pitched purple passages.

It will not be difficult to convince students that, at the beginning of the book for example, the narrative reflects the world as seen by a child. Demonstrating the sophistication of Joyce's method, however, is another matter. It might be useful to concentrate attention on what is seemingly a randomly chosen song (yet "his song") which Stephen cannot yet sing correctly—"O, the green rose bloweth," which Stephen pronounces "O, the green wothe botheth." The song is actually *Lily Dale*, a sentimental Irish favorite, and the second line should be "On the little green grave," rather than "On the little green place." Commentators suggest that the word is changed because the song is being taught to a very small child, and the neutral "place" is thought to be more appropriate. More important, however, is the way this song is linked to Stephen's musings on the nature of things and his own nature. It is later remembered by Stephen in the midst of his confusion about the relative rightness or wrongness of things. "Lavender and cream and pink roses were beautiful to think of. Perhaps a wild rose might be like those colours and he remembered the song about the wild rose blossoms on the little green place. But you could not have a green rose. But perhaps somewhere in the world you could" (p. 1641). The point is that Stephen *can* have a green rose. He can have it in song, in art, but first he will have to "tell" it correctly. So here, in a book about how Stephen must learn to create a world that he can live in comfortably, Joyce uses this detail to plant his central theme in our minds.

The song is but one example of how Joyce consistently uses seemingly unimportant details to embody the major themes of the book. Following are some other examples of scenes, images, or events useful in discussing major aspects of the text:

1. "Once upon a time... ... (p. 1637): Our introduction to Stephen and his introduction to himself; significantly, it is through a story.

2. "Dante had two brushes in her press" (p. 1638): The introduction of split-vision in the book. For Stephen, there are always two sides to every question, two opposing ways to go: the Church or Parnell; saintly life or secular life; to kiss or not to kiss; etc.

3. "It would be nice . . . next his skin" (p. 1640): The pleasure of words (here clearly associated with fire and warmth) as opposed to the cold slimy water of the life available outside of words.

4. Lancaster and York (p. 1641): Stephen is again involved in a battle between two sides; appropriately, he is on the York (white rose) side, which Ireland supported during the Wars of the Roses—but which lost.

5. "Tell us, Dedalus . . ." (pp. 1642–43): A case of adolescent injustice, where there are no right answers.

6. Pages 1649–52: In the delirium of his sickness (Stephen has already told us that his real sickness is in the heart), Parnell's death, the songs and prayers of the Church, his life at home, his life at school, his loneliness, and his thousand fears all meet and mingle in these passages.

7. "A great fire . . ." (pp. 1652–53): Appropriately, this section on Stephen's return home for Christmas begins with the image of "a great fire." Such a fire can deliver warmth (which Stephen desires), or it can scorch (which it does).

8. "I'm blinded! I'm blinded and drownded!" (p. 1659): Here, in a story, are two very likely possibilities in Stephen's future. Like Stephen, the woman in the story has found herself on the "wrong" side, and is humiliated for it.

9. "They said: pick, pack, pock, puck . . ." (p. 1662): As is mentioned in the headnote, this phrase suggests the way Stephen's early experience merges "into the unified whole that underlies the *Portrait of the Artist as a Young Man*" (p. 1637). Chapter I ends with the same phrase, only slightly altered (p. 1675). Thus the two phrases, in effect, frame the material contained within and call our attention to the importance of this experience in Stephen's development.

10. "A cry sprang to his lips . . ." (p. 1669): Though Stephen is humiliated and punished in a very painful way, he will not apologize.

Students will have some difficulty with the many allusions to Irish national problems and history, and to Stephen's Jesuit upbringing. You will need to rely rather more heavily than usual on the editorial notes provided in the text, and you will need to remind students that although central themes are broadened and deepened by grasping the implications of the allusions, the book can be essentially understood without any special knowledge of them. You might rely on your own knowledge of Catholic tradition or ask the help of some of the students in class who have had a Catholic upbringing. The latter are invariably helpful with regard to some of Stephen's experiences, many of which strike non-Catholic students as merely curious or outdated. Although there are obvious differences between life at an Irish Catholic school and the often-written-about English public schools, reference to Orwell's well-known "Such, Such Were the Joys" or Cyril Connolly's "A Georgian Boyhood" might provide significant comparisons.

1. What are the implications of the words *portrait, artist,* and *young man* in the title?
   [See *Backgrounds*, especially the second paragraph, for a discussion of the book as a *Kunstlerroman*. See paragraph 3 of the *Classroom Strategies* for discussion of the word *portrait*.]

2. What are the similarities and differences between this book and other novels of childhood and adolescence? Compare *A Portrait of the Artist as a Young Man* with Dickens's *Great Expectations*, Meredith's *The Ordeal of Richard Feverel*, Butler's *The Way of All Flesh*, Lawrence's *Sons and Lovers*, Salinger's *Catcher in the Rye*, or any other appropriate work that students might be familiar with. Earlier stories by Joyce, such as "Araby," will be useful in such a discussion.

3. What is the effect on the reader of Joyce's narrative technique? How does this narrative technique work? How does it differ from traditional narratives?
   [See *Backgrounds, Classroom Strategies* and the Introduction to "Modernism" for a full discussion.]

4. Joyce was very careful to select names for his characters which were either "real" or perfectly plausible. Only the name of central character, Stephen Dedalus, seems blatantly symbolic. What are the implications of Stephen's name?
   [See paragraph 13 of *Backgrounds* for a discussion of Joyce's use of "real" names. See paragraph 5 of *Backgrounds* for a discussion of Stephen's name.]

5. What is Joyce's authorial attitude toward Stephen? Ironic? Sympathetic? Disengaged? How do we know?
   [See paragraph 2 of Backgrounds for discussion.]

6. What is the importance of the episode having to do with Eileen Vance? With Parnell? With Dante, his father, and Mr. Casey at the Christmas dinner? With Father Dolan? With the rector?
   [See *Backgrounds* for a full discussion.]

7. How does Joyce suggest that Stephen, from a very early age, is particularly interested in words, phrases, and stories? What reasons does Joyce suggest for Stephen's feeling that he is different from others? How do these differences help to form Stephen into the artist he eventually becomes? What kind of artist does Stephen eventually become?

[See *Backgrounds* for a fuller discussion. In addition, it should be said that it is easy to undervalue the usual psychological and sociological reasons for Stephen's development. Joyce gives us quite a bit of information which might help us to understand Stephen: his feelings of weakness and confusion, his weak eyesight, his pride, his family life, his Catholic upbringing and Jesuit education, his Irishness. Insofar as we can associate Stephen with Joyce, we know that Stephen becomes the kind of artist who writes *A Portrait of the Artist as a Young Man* in the form we have it, rather than in some other, more traditional, form (such as that of *Stephen Hero*, Joyce's first attempt at recreating his early life).]

8. In what ways does Joyce suggest that *Portrait* is a book about the formation of Stephen's identity?
[See *Backgrounds* for a full discussion.]

9. Discuss Joyce's descriptive technique in selected passages: for example, the beginning "babytalk" scene, Stephen's feverish imaginings when he is ill, the injured hands of the "pandybat" scene, or the peaceful evening of the last two paragraphs. How does Joyce combine references to the five senses to make a scene physically (rather than just intellectually) convincing? Compare, if appropriate, with Baudelaire's notion of "correspondences."
[See *Backgrounds*, third paragraph, and the anthology introduction to Baudelaire.]

### Further Reading

See also the suggestions in the anthology, p. 1637.

Beja, Morris and Bernstock, Shari. *Coping with Joyce.* 1989.
Presents four essays on Joyce himself as well as thirteen studies of specific works, including two feminist essays.

Bloom, Harold, ed. *James Joyce's* A Portrait of the Artist as a Young Man. 1988.
Collected essays.

Bradley, Bruce. *James Joyce's Schooldays*. New York, 1982.
A biographical study of Joyce's school years, with direct relevance to *Portrait*.

Brown, Richard. *James Joyce and Sexuality*. 1985.

Buttigieg, Joseph A. A Portrait of the Artist *in Different Perspective*. 1987.
A Nietzschean perspective.

Connolly, Thomas, ed. *Joyce's* Portrait: *Criticisms and Critiques*. New York, 1962.
A collection of essays, including particularly interesting pieces by Levin, Kenner, Van Ghent (see especially her "Problems for Study and Discussion" [pp. 307–18]), Ellman, Waith, Gordon, and Jack.

Ehrlich, Heyward, ed. *Light Rays: James Joyce and Modernism*. 1984.
Discusses Joyce's relation to modernism.

Goldberg, S. L. *James Joyce*. New York, 1962.
An extremely cogent introduction to Joyce, especially good on *Portrait* and *Ulysses*.

Henke, Suzette and Unkeless, Elaine. *Women in Joyce*. 1982.
Feminist criticism.

Kenner, Hugh. *Dublin's Joyce*. Bloomington, 1956.
A provocative study. *Portrait* is discussed on pp. 112–33.

Magalaner, Marvin, ed. *A James Joyce Miscellany: Second Series*. Carbondale, 1959.
See Maurice Beebe's essay on Joyce and the problem of autobiography.

McCormack, W. J. and Stead, Alistair, eds. *James Joyce and Modern Literature*. 1982.

Morris, William A., and Clifford A. Nault, eds. *Portraits of an Artist: A Casebook on James Joyce's* A Portrait of the Artist as a Young Man. New York, 1962.
A collection of essays. See especially those by Van Ghent, Redford, Friedman, and Prescott. Contains a good bibliography on *Portrait*.

Schutte, William M., ed. *Twentieth-Century Interpretations of A Portrait of the Artist as a Young Man: A Collection of Critical Essays*. Englewood Cliffs, 1968.
The essays by Ellmann, Booth, and Sharpless are especially interesting.

Scott, Bonnie Kime. *Joyce and Feminism*. 1984.

Staley, Thomas and Bernard Benstock, eds. *Approaches to Joyce's* Portrait. Pittsburgh, 1976.
A collection of essays. Those by Anderson, Mitchell, and Naremore are especially useful.
and
Staley, Thomas F. *An Annotated Critical Bibliography of James Joyce*. 1989.
Section G is devoted to *Portrait*.

Sullivan, Kevin. *Joyce Among the Jesuits*. New York, 1958.
Contains useful information on Joyce's school and university experiences.

# VIRGINIA WOOLF
## An Unwritten Novel

*Backgrounds*

Woolf's reputation has taken on a new dimension over the last decade as her work's scope and influence have become better known, enlarging an earlier image of her as a member of the Bloomsbury group who wrote brilliantly imaginative works of fiction. Not that critics have lost sight of her technical mastery, her psychological insight and genius for evoking moments of consciousness, and her ability to transform the raw data of reality into lyrical prose. Yet where she was long accepted chiefly as the author of major novels such as *To the Lighthouse* and *Mrs. Dalloway*, she is now also recognized as the consummate essayist whose works have had enormous influence on contemporary writers and on any discussion of women's experience, especially as writers, in Western society. The variety and brilliance of Woolf's fiction give her a place among the most innovative of modern writers, and the full range of her work has made her the century's single most important and influential woman writer in English.

Nothing happens in "An Unwritten Novel" except what "happens" in the mind of the writer, where everything happens. The situation is simple enough: the narrator/writer sits across from a woman in railway carriage and fabulates a life for her. Woolf used the same device in *Jacob's Room*, which appeared in 1922, and in "Mr. Bennett and Mrs. Brown" (1924), one of the most useful essays we have about the English modernists' reaction to the realist tradition they inherited. The device allows Woolf the opportunity to create a short piece of fiction—which involves an unhappy woman, a "crime," the booty of Sir Francis Drake, a traveling button salesman named Moggridge, Moggridge's drab family—as well as to reveal how that fiction comes into being. "Reality" (the word must be put in quotation marks, since the "reality" of the unnamed woman on the train, the object of the writer's speculations, is no more "real," of course, than Minnie Marsh or James Moggridge) is the starting point for the fiction. But from that "reality," and the writer's concrete observation of it—the look in the unnamed woman's eyes, her involuntary shudders, her rubbing the window pane with a worn glove, her few words—blossom

---

the writer's extraordinary fabulations, her attempt to create a plausible life-story for the woman whose story will otherwise never be told.

Throughout her career as a writer, Woolf was concerned with how one could create life in a fictional character; indeed, she was immensely interested in just what constitutes life. In "Mr. Bennett and Mrs. Brown" she rejects the Edwardian (and by extension the nineteenth-century realist) notion that life in the novel is best created by the close observation and reporting of facts. She tries it herself in the essay by creating a railway companion called Mrs. Brown. But she declares failure; she wasn't able to say what she meant:

> And to have got what I meant I should have had to go back and back; to experiment with one thing and another; to try this sentence and that, referring each word to my vision, matching it as exactly as possible, and knowing that somehow I had to find a common ground between us, a convention which would not seem to you too odd, unreal, and far-fetched to believe in. I admit that I shirked that arduous undertaking. I let Mrs. Brown slip through my fingers. I have told you nothing whatever about her. But that is partly the great Edwardians' fault. I asked them—they are my elders and betters—how shall I begin to describe this woman's character? And they said: "Begin by saying that her father kept a shop in Harrogate. Ascertain the rent. Ascertain the wages of shop assistants in the year 1878. Discover what her mother died of. Describe cancer. Describe calico. Describe——" But I cried: "Stop! Stop!"

For Woolf, and her Modernist contemporaries, "the Edwardian tools are the wrong ones" because they cannot render the inner life: the life of the psyche, the life of the pulses, where, she felt, truth—if there was a truth—was going to have to be found. She has to throw "that ugly, that clumsy, that incongruous tool out of the window." Life is exactly what is *not* to be found in the *Times*. The attempt to find "life," then, and to create a social and cultural context for it, is Woolf's special effort and her special pleasure. "An Unwritten Novel" reveals the process by which that effort may succeed.

First, the writer names her travelling companion Minnie and Minnie's sister-in-law, Hilda; she then names Hilda's children (Bob and Barbara) and pictures them with forks upright over their puddings; and then she creates a home environment for them (a typically drab lower-middle class home in Eastbourne, with its typically drab trappings). She follows Minnie upstairs, and imagines a God for her who looks "more like President Kruger than Prince Albert," a "brutal old bully" to whom, the writer imagines, Minnie must pray for forgiveness. But for what? A crime, of course, and since the writer has her "pick of crimes," she chooses the small crime of negligence, a brief moment of self-pleasure which Minnie once allowed herself, but which led to catastrophe. "She runs, she rushes, home she reaches, but too late. Neighbours—the doctor—baby brother—the kettle—scalded—hospital—dead—or only the shock of it, the blame?" (p. 1681) This is one of the most hastily contrived catastrophes in all of short fiction, but, as we are told, "the detail matters nothing." What matters is the effect it had on Minnie, on her life now: "It's what she carries with her; the spot, the crime, the thing to expiate, always there between her shoulders."

Having established Minnie's crime and its lasting effects the writer begins to nudge her toward madness (in a mode similar to that Woolf used for Septimus Smith in *Mrs. Dalloway*) until the "real" passenger insists on being "tethered to the shores of the world" by announcing "Eggs are cheaper" (p. 1682). The grasp that "Minnie" maintains on the mundane world of eggs and economics cannot, however, stop the writer from extending even these minute possibilities for fabulation:

Yes. And now you lay across your knees a pocket-handkerchief into which drop little angular fragments of eggshell—fragments of a map—a puzzle. I wish I could piece them together! If you would only sit still. She's moved her knees—the map's in bits again. Down the slopes of the Andes the white blocks of marble go bounding and hurtling, crushing to death a whole troop of Spanish muleteers, with their convoy—Drake's booty, gold and silver.

(p. 1683)

From here on, the writer's composing imagination is in full swing, and, as the headnote points out, "the process of composition appears in all its experiments, false starts, and corrections for tone and consistency" (p. 1677)—from the "dot, dot, dot" of ellipsis to the writer's urgent desire to get a "fling of red and white" into a fictional environment which would in "reality" accommodate only browns, grays, and greens.

When the woman who has become Minnie breaks the spell of the fiction by arriving at her destination and meeting her son (not Hilda, not Moggridge), the writer's "world's done for." She wonders: "What do I stand on? What do I know? That's not Minnie. There never was Moggridge. Who am I? Life's bare as bone" (p. 1686). But only momentarily. The new scene—mother and son—floods the writer anew. New questions must be asked, new environments populated, the "adorable world" must be reconstituted, all through the sympathetic embrace of the writer's liberating imagination.

It might be worth noting here that her home was just "past Lewes," in the tiny English hamlet of Rodmell. She often took the train down to Rodmell from London and, although there is no evidence that this particular woman ever sat across from her, such women are still such staples on British trains that it is difficult to imagine that no one like her ever took a seat across from Woolf.

The most obvious contemporary influence on Woolf was Marcel Proust, whose *Remembrance of Things Past* was, perhaps, her favorite book. Although she is often linked with Joyce, she did not—at least in her public statements—much like his work, which she called "indecent." Neither did she like the work of D. H. Lawrence, but the extraordinary similarities in their work should not go unnoticed. Joyce was mainly interested in using "stream-of-consciousness" techniques as a way of exploring the conscious mind; Woolf, like Lawrence, was interested in life below the level of consciousness, emotional life, and she used—as Lawrence did—all of her considerable creative powers to render and articulate that life. Woolf was also influenced by Henri Bergson's discussions of the immediate data of consciousness as it exists outside of clock-time. Dorothy Richardson, whose experiments in "stream-of-consciousness" pre-dated Woolf's, and Katherine Mansfield, whose sensibility and insight made Woolf envious, were also significant influences.

Woolf was at the center of what was perhaps England's most influential group of intellectuals during the 1920s and 30s—the Bloomsbury Group. It has often been noted by biographers of the Group and its individual members that their principles were derived from the Cambridge philosopher G. E. Moore, who argued, among other things, that "aesthetic enjoyment and the pleasures of human intercourse include *all* the greatest, and *by far* the greatest, goods we can imagine." Woolf went some distance in expressing these principles in life as well as literature.

### Classroom Strategies

"An Unwritten Novel" can be taught in one class period, perhaps in tandem with other pieces in which the reader's consciousness of the process of composition is very much heightened: Pirandello's *Six Characters* is an obvious choice, but the poems of Stevens, Joyce's *Portrait*, Borges's "The Garden of Forking Paths," and Robbe-Grillet's "The Secret Room" would also be extremely useful for purposes of comparison.

Once students are aware that the "story" here is not so much about Minnie Marsh and James Moggridge, but instead about the process of how a "story" comes into being, and about how "characters" like Minnie and James are created, they should have very few problems. A spirited and sympathetic reading aloud of certain parts of the text, especially those in which the fits and starts of creation are on prominent display, will be useful as well as interesting to those students who have difficulty "hearing" the voice of the writer/narrator. The paragraph describing Minnie's "crime," the sequence about the eggshells, and the paragraph beginning "To what, to where" (p. 1683) are particularly appropriate for this purpose. Similarly, sections of Woolf's essay, "Mr. Bennett and Mrs. Brown," in which she discusses some of the problems which attend the creation of character in fiction, might be handed out to students and referred to during discussion.

## Topics for Discussion and Writing

1. Is "An Unwritten Novel" a story at all? Why or why not?
[See *Backgrounds* for discussion.]

2. In what ways are Woolf's attempts at characterization different from those of other writers you have read?
[See paragraphs 2–3 of *Backgrounds* for discussion. "Mr. Bennett and Mrs. Brown" will be of great help in locating the differences Woolf herself saw between her characters and those of the realist tradition.]

3. Should we care about what "happens" to Minnie Marsh? Why or why not? Would it be useful to know the color of Minnie's eyes? Her hair? Her social class? Her job?

4. Does reading "An Unwritten Novel" provide an insight into how the creative mind makes use of "reality"? Does the piece make you think that literature reduces or expands "reality"? What is "reality" in fiction? What relation does it bear to everyday experience?

## Further Reading

See also the suggestions in the anthology, p. 1592.

Bell, Quentin. *Virginia Woolf: A Biography*. New York, 1972.
The definitive biography of Woolf, written by her nephew (the son of Clive and Vanessa Bell). It has been criticized for being too sympathetic with the Bloomsbury sensibility, but no one knows more about Woolf than Quentin Bell.

Gordon, Lyndall. *Virginia Woolf: A Writer's Life*. New York, 1985.
This biography moves back and forth between the life and the work, with special attention to the latter.

Woolf, Virginia. "Mr. Bennett and Mrs. Brown." From *Collected Essays*, vol. I. London, 1966.
An extremely important essay for understanding Woolf's approach to character in fiction, especially insofar as it differs from the English Edwardian realists.

————. *A Writer's Diary*. Edited by Leonard Woolf. London, 1953.
Although all of Woolf's diaries have now been published, this remains a good, short introduction to the writer at work.

# FRANZ KAFKA
## The Metamorphosis

*Backgrounds*

Even now, some seventy years after *The Metamorphosis* was written, students find it as fresh and contemporary as the latest story by Donald Barthelme, and as baffling and troubling as the last stories of Jorge Luis Borges. What still interests and excites contemporary readers and writers about Kafka is his ability to force us to look beyond the seemingly calm surface of the story for a symbolic or allegorical meaning, along with his persistent refusal to deliver such a meaning. As soon as we try to nail down Kafka, he gets up and walks away with the nail. Kafka frustrates our expectation that there is a final, unequivocal meaning to be found anywhere. Nevertheless, students will find Kafka's prose precise and objective, and they will find it especially enchanting because it appears to be in service to the inner life—dreams, fantasies, unconscious fears and desires—without straining their ability to understand what is being said. As baffling as Kafka often seems to be, he manages in his best work to present his world with the humanity, humor, and power that we expect from great writers of any era.

To say that someone is "like" a vermin, an insect, a bug—or to feel "like" that ourselves—is to say something that we all understand, meta-phorically. The metaphorical basis of Kafka's tale is rather simple; it is Kafka's matter-of-fact, almost journalistic, insistence on the *reality* of the metaphor that strikes us as being curious. In *The Metamorphosis* Gregor Samsa has been transformed into a metaphor that states his essen-tial self, but this metaphor in turn is treated as an actual fact. Gregor does not just call himself a vermin; he wakes up to find himself one. Kafka has transformed the metaphor back into fictional reality, and this counter-metamorphosis becomes the starting point of his tale. Such a fictional act seems simple enough, but it is extraordinarily radical, one of the most radical beginnings of any story anywhere.

Kafka confirms his intention to insist on the *fact* of Gregor's meta-morphosis by his use of absolutely ordinary language, a language purged of surprise, to describe it. The first two paragraphs of the story tell us a great deal about Kafka's method in *The Metamorphosis*. In the first

---

paragraph, Gregor is introduced already transformed—but he is introduced by a narrator who seems absolutely unsurprised by what has taken place, a narrator who presents this extraordinary moment with the cold objectivity and precision of a visiting zoologist. In the second paragraph, we notice that the narrator remains separate from Gregor's consciousness (and is thus able to make factual comments such as "Samsa was a traveling salesman"), but still identifies almost completely with Gregor, sees through his eyes and ears, removed only slightly farther away from things than the character himself. Such a narrative stance makes it impossible for us to read the story as if it were merely an hallucination or a dream. As importantly, and more intriguingly, the narrator seems curiously unhurried to explain what we are most interested in. When the narrator *does* evidence astonishment, it is not over Gregor's transformation at all, but instead over a vaguely erotic picture from an illustrated magazine which hangs on the wall of his room. "It showed a lady done up in a fur hat and a fur boa, sitting upright and raising up against the viewer a heavy fur muff in which her whole forearm had disappeared." The narrator refuses to be impressed by the same things that we are, and the frustration of our expectations—expectations which we probably did not know existed—is curiously humorous.

*The Metamorphosis* is also a family drama, a drama about the relationship between Gregor and his sister, his mother, and—especially—his father. Indeed, if we forget for a moment that Gregor is now a monstrous insect (although Kafka clearly doesn't want us to forget), his behavior resembles nothing so much as that of a monstrous infant, struggling unsuccessfully to establish a functional identity in an environment with which he is unequipped to cope, and in a family situation which continually reconfirms his lack of status. Gregor's family depend on him for their welfare, but as a "father"—the breadwinner, the one economically responsible for the family's welfare—Gregor feels himself to be a failure. He is such a minor functionary in his company that he can be mercilessly assailed by its manager, who arrives at the Samsa home only a few minutes after Gregor should have arrived at work. The manager berates Gregor "in the name of your parents and of your employer"—the two sources of authority, and therefore of punishment, in the story—in full view of his family, accuses him of doing unsatisfactory work, implies that he may have stolen money from company funds entrusted to him, and reminds him how easy it would be to be fired. He treats Gregor like the vermin that Gregor has, in fact, become, and exposes Gregor's sense of vulnerability and guilt.

The world of officials and the world of fathers appear to be essentially the same; both have authority and use that authority to punish Gregor, whose guilt attracts their attention and their desire for power. This is exacerbated by Gregor's own sense of insufficiency, which has stultified him spiritually long before his physical transformation. His literal imprisonment—in the body of a vermin, locked in his room, with employers and family members as jailers—is made even more intolerable by his horrible awareness of it. It has been suggested that Gregor's acceptance of his metamorphosis occurs because he recognizes that his present status as insect is about the same as his former status as human being.

In *The Metamorphosis*, every weakening of the son's position results in the strengthening of the father's. In the end, one will triumph, the other will die. Gregor makes three forays out of his room and into the world of his family, and these three forays constitute the central events of the three sections of the story. In Part I, Gregor struggles to open his door with his jaws, but when he emerges from his bedroom, he frightens away the manager and is finally driven back by his infuriated father, who wields a walking stick and a newspaper and stamps the floor in anger. In Part II, Gregor is overtaken by the desire to see his mother, but when his angry and exultant father, now wearing a uniform which suggests his new-found authority and power, discovers him outside his room, he drives him back by pelting Gregor with apples. In Part III, the starving, wounded Gregor comes out while Grete—the only one in the family who has shown anything resembling sympathy for his plight—is playing the violin; he is entranced by the music, but is driven back this time by a different, and more devastating, kind of attack: the stark indifference of his family. His mother sits still, his "eyes almost closing from exhaustion," and Grete, who has had enough of tending her brother, locks his door behind him and cries, "Finally!" Gregor dies alone, to be discovered in the morning by the charwoman. His father delivers Gregor's epitaph—"now we can thank God."

Gregor's treatment by his family—especially his father—is progressively more violent, fueled by their increasing disgust and annoyance at having to put up with such a creature in their house. In many ways, they become as monstrous, as parasitical, as Gregor looks. As long as Gregor filled the role of breadwinner, the family (especially the father) was moribund, but as soon as Gregor is reduced to a vermin, the family comes alive; Gregor's diminishment is in direct proportion to his family's advancement. For the family to thrive, Gregor must die. After his death, the family—suddenly and happily free of the burden that was their son—

decide to take a tram excursion into the country, which is "something they had not done in months." The last paragraph of the story is written in Kafka's most lilting cadences. It is springtime; the tram is "completely filled with warm sunshine"; they are free; and Grete, under the admiring gaze of her mother and father, demonstrates her own metamorphosis. Like a butterfly emerging from a cocoon, she has "blossomed into a good-looking, shapely girl." Mr. and Mrs. Samsa come to the conclusion that it would "soon be time, too, to find her a good husband. And it was like a confirmation of their new dreams and good intentions when at the end of the ride their daughter got up first and stretched her young body" (p. 1725).

It is easy, perhaps too easy, to read the central metaphor in *The Metamorphosis* as Gregor = vermin = modern man, and to insist that it is a parable about the human condition in the modern world. In many ways such a reading is perfectly justifiable; in other ways it extends the story's implications beyond what it can be reasonably expected to suggest.

Kafka's inability to assert himself, his overwhelming sense of shortcoming and consequently of guilt mark everything he ever wrote. Although he was a brilliant graduate in law, he never practiced, taking instead a position as a civil servant in the Austrian government. He was engaged several times and had several affairs (his meeting with Felice Bauer led directly to his writing *The Metamorphosis*) but could never bring himself to marry. Kafka even asked that his unpublished writings be destroyed upon his death. Fortunately for us, his literary executor, Max Brod, published them anyway.

Any analysis of Kafka's work must take into account the peculiarly poetic and tormenting character of Prague. As all biographers of Kafka agree, his Prague was perfectly suited to reflect his disposition—a place of Slavonic melancholy, weighed down by its history, where different traditions and tongues competed, and where desire for the unequivocal is persistently met by recognition of its impossibility. Because Kafka was a German-speaking Jew living in Prague, he felt even more powerfully the burden of his separateness, which reveals itself also in the very form of his stories. In his work—as in the Jewish tradition—time is a dimension which fuses past and present, eternity and the instant, just as it fuses the extraordinary and the mundane, the ultimate and the immediate. Authority is not represented by fathers alone, but also by Gentiles, who may turn from allies to enemies at any given moment. For Kafka's characters the world of authority—of Law—is closed but ambiguous, and nothing can be finally resolved. In the Jewish tradition, full resolution can take place only with the decisive return of the Messiah; until that time every one lives in the middle of an inconclusive history. We find this same "in the middle" effect in Kafka, where the story typically begins *after* the decisive event has taken place, where characters go through a gradual shifting of states of being, but are never granted a conclusive resolution to their problems.

*The Metamorphosis* was written in late 1912. It is one of the very few stories which apparently satisfied Kafka to the point that he wanted to see it published. Though it would be a mistake to interpret the story merely as a coded autobiographical document, *The Metamorphosis* does, of course, have a personal significance for its author. It quite evidently reflects his sense of personal inadequacy in comparison to his father—a strong-willed, self-made, authoritarian—who, as we know from reading Kafka's "Letter to His Father," once likened his son to a vermin. Kafka's tenderness toward his sister, Ottla, can be felt in his depiction of Grete, as can his frustration over his mother's inability to deal with his psychological difficulties.

After Kafka wrote "The Judgment" in 1912, a few months before he began *The Metamorphosis*, he wrote in his diary, "Thoughts of Freud, naturally." And it *was* natural; Kafka was intensely aware of the work of Freud and others working in the developing field of psychoanalysis, and he sometimes claimed that "the therapeutic claims of psychoanalysis" were an "impotent error" and that he was "nauseated" by them. Kafka had read some of Freud's work, had heard him discussed in various intellectual circles, and was personally acquainted with Otto Gross—a member of Freud's inner circle. The impact of Freud is evident in the importance Kafka attaches to the images of his inner life (as well as his talent for portraying them); his extraordinary interest in childhood experience and in the Oedipal situation in particular; and his awareness of his own neurotic symptoms.

The climate of thought which made his work possible is also evident in Expressionism, one of the most influential aesthetic movements of the early twentieth century. Its central tendency is to distort or magnify the shape of reality in order to suggest a higher order of emotional reality beneath the surface. It assumes, like many of the major movements of modern art and literature, that art based predominantly on visible reality is inadequate. If Robert Wiene's film *The Cabinet of Dr. Caligari* is available, it might be useful to screen it for the class, since it quite dramatically and enjoyably reveals a number of German Expressionism's essential features: the distortion of surfaces, the obsession with the inner life, and the relationship between individual and authority (especially the conflict between fathers and sons).

## Classroom Strategies

*The Metamorphosis* can be taught in as few as two class periods. The first discussion of the story could emphasize the nature of its narrative, while the second might concentrate on the relations between Gregor and his family, his feelings of guilt and inadequacy, the ambiguity of self-knowledge and values, and the relationship between the individual and authority.

The narrative of *The Metamorphosis* exploits the gap between a reader's expectations and his or her findings. Inevitably, then, students will find Kafka's narrative curious or even unacceptable. Though they may not know exactly why they find it so (they often accept events far more outlandish in a science fiction story), a close examination of the events described and of the tone the narrator uses will allow them to move beyond their initial confusion. In order to press the point home, it might be useful to read from other writers who use similar narrative strategies—Beckett, Borges, Donald Barthelme, Robert Coover, or Peter Handke, for instance. But perhaps the most telling comparison might be made between Kafka's narrative and everyday newspaper reports, which often describe the most extraordinary events in a tone of detached, journalistic objectivity. The cool, detached quality of such reports on unlikely events makes them bleakly humorous. In *The Metamorphosis*, the effect of such a narrative is first to establish the fictional reality of the metaphor: Gregor is an insect. But, like the newspaper stories, it also delivers humor, deriving, for the most part, from the apparent disjunction of the tone of the narrative from the events it describes. Teaching humor, beyond insisting that it's there, is very difficult, perhaps impossible; but there are particular moments in the text that might be used to establish Kafka's humor: Gregor's difficulty over getting up for the first time after his transformation and not feeling "especially fresh," along with his attendant worry over lying idle in bed and getting behind in his work (pp. 1690–91); Gregor's attempts to speak, which come out in an "insistent distressed chirping" (p. 1691); the manager's lecture on the nature of business (p. 1695); the three lodgers, who behave like performers in a vaudeville routine; or the cleaning woman, who appears to respond to

Gregor as if he were nothing more than a ridiculous obstacle to completing her work.

Henri Bergson—with whose work Kafka was familiar—has claimed that "We laugh every time a person gives us the impression of being a thing" and that the comic produces "something like a momentary anesthesia of the heart" which is brought on by "looking at life as a disinterested spectator." In *The Metamorphosis* Kafka meets these requirements, and our response is precisely what Bergson might have expected. Invariably, Kafka's grotesquely extravagant vision of people enmeshed in the sad absurdity of the universe evokes in us an uneasy laughter.

## Topics for Discussion and Writing

1. How does Kafka use his central metaphor in *The Metamorphosis*? In what ways is his use of it different from what we might expect to find?
   [Kafka's central metaphor, Gregor = vermin, is insisted upon as being literally true. The metaphor is treated as an actual fact. To get the response he evidently wants, Kafka exploits the gap between what the reader expects and what he finds. The reader's objections to Gregor's transformation into a monstrous vermin are undermined by the literalness, the journalistic objectivity, of the narrative.]

2. How does the apparent disjunction between tone and event create humor in *The Metamorphosis*?
   [See paragraph 2 of *Backgrounds* and paragraphs 2–3 of *Classroom Strategies* for a discussion.]

3. What is the relationship between Gregor and his family? What clues in the story suggest that his relationship with his family, particularly his father, is unsatisfactory?
   [See *Backgrounds*, paragraphs 4–7 for a full discussion. Besides the many evidences of Gregor's indifferent treatment in the story, students should note details such as his father's use of a newspaper (something we typically use to squash bugs) and a walking stick (a traditional symbol of paternal authority) to drive Gregor back into his room during their first confrontation. It is also worth noting that Gregor apparently feels it necessary to lock his room in his own home.]

4. Discuss the central events in each of the three sections of the story. In what ways do these events suggest that the weakening of Gregor results in the strengthening of the family as a whole? [See *Backgrounds*, paragraphs 6–7.]

5. What significance is attached to food in *The Metamorphosis*? [Kafka often uses food as an image of spiritual, psychic, or artistic fulfillment in his stories, just as he uses hunger and starvation to suggest unfulfillment. "The Hunger Artist" is the most famous example of his use of this formula. In *The Metamorphosis*, Gregor is first offered fresh food, which does not satisfy him; his sister, "in the goodness of her heart," then tries to satisfy Gregor by offering him half-decayed food from the family table. As his family becomes more indifferent, his sister merely shoves "any old food into Gregor's room with her foot," then clears it out "with a swish of the broom," heedless of whether it has been tasted or left untouched. Soon after, Gregor eats almost nothing while, by contrast, his family and the three boarders stuff themselves with meat and potatoes and make much of their satisfaction. Gregor thinks: "I'm hungry enough . . . but not for these things. Look how these roomers are gorging themselves, and I'm dying!" (p. 1717). On his last foray out of his room, Gregor trails "fluff and hairs and scraps of food" to listen to his sister play the violin. The music affects him greatly, and he feels "as if the way to the unknown nourishment he longed for were coming to light" (p. 1718). But it is too late. When Gregor's flat and dry corpse is discovered, the rotting apple thrown by his father still imbedded in his back, Grete says, "Just look how thin he was . . . . The food came out again just the way it went in" (p. 1723).]

6. What is the significance of the minor characters in the story—the manager, the three boarders, and the cleaning woman? [See paragraph 4 of *Backgrounds*. It should be noted that the family feels itself independent enough to dismiss the three boarders, and their demands, only after Gregor's death.]

7. What is the importance of the final scene in the story, the family's trip to the country? Why is it written so lyrically in comparison to the rest of the text?

[The lyricism of the last scene reflects the family's new dispensation, the revival of their prospects. Gregor's death allows them their release, and the language of this final scene embodies their new hopes. See paragraph 7 of *Backgrounds* for a fuller discussion.]

8. What other texts in the anthology might bear significant comparison to *The Metamorphosis?*
[One might usefully compare *The Metamorphosis* with "The Death of Iván Ilyich." In both works we are told of a character who moves toward death; in Tolstoy that death is redemptive, and it provides the central meaning of the text, but in *The Metamorphosis*, Gregor's death is remarkable precisely because it is without redemption. There are also comparisons which can be drawn between *The Metamorphosis* and *Notes from Underground*, especially with regard to the depiction of a psychological condition which suggests self-hatred. In *Endgame* we experience the same discrepancy between extreme unreality and the dry precision of its presentation, and we laugh with a similar uneasiness. In "The Love Song of J. Alfred Prufrock," the persona sings of his own insufficiency; in *A Portrait of the Artist as a Young Man*, Stephen Dedalus finds himself in a position with regard to authority which is much like Gregor's; and texts as different as "A Modest Proposal," *Candide*, and "The Garden of Forking Paths" all use a similar kind of narrative strategy to provoke the reader's response. It is important to note, however, that Swift and Voltaire both assume a firm and commonly understood series of values against which they measure their irony; Kafka has no such center and no such certainty.]

9. *The Metamorphosis* has been read and interpreted in many ways—as an example of existentialist philosophy, a depiction of man's condition in the modern world, a presentation of psychological neurosis, and as a theological parable. Discuss these various interpretive possibilities.

**Further Reading**

See also the reading suggestions in the anthology, p. 1689.

Anders, Gunter. *Franz Kafka*. Translated by A. Steer and A. K. Thorlby. London, 1960.
A well-known analysis of *The Metamorphosis* which examines Gregor's transformation as an extended metaphor for Kafka's view of the world "as it appears to a stranger."

Anderson, Mark, ed. *Reading Kafka: Prague, Politics, and The Fin de Siècle*. 1989.
Useful study of Kafka's relation to his time.

Benjamin, Walter. "Franz Kafka. On the Tenth Anniversary of His Death." In *Illuminations*, edited by Hannah Arendt, pp. 111–40. New York, 1968.
Benjamin describes clusters of related images, gestures, and motifs in order to suggest the nature of Kafka's world.

Bernheimer, Charles. *Flaubert and Kafka: Studies in Psychopoetic Structure*. 1982.
Employs contemporary critical theory to describe aspects of Kafka's work.

Corngold, Stanley. *The Commentators' Despair*. Port Washington, N.Y., 1973.
A useful annotated bibliography of works on *The Metamorphosis* (up to 1972).
and
————, *Franz Kafka: The Necessity of Form*. 1988.

Deleuze, Gilles and Guattari, Felix. *Kafka: Toward a Minor Literature*, translated by Dana Polan. 1986.
An important study of Kafka's many-sided alienation from his linguistic and social context.

Gray, Ronald. *Franz Kafka*. 1973.
Useful, brief studies.

Koelb, Clayton. *Kafka's Rhetoric: The Passion of Reading*. 1989.
Employs critical theory to describe aspects of Kafka's work.

Lawson, Richard. *Franz Kafka*. 1987.
Biographical study.

Robert, Marthe. *As Lonely as Franz Kafka*. Translated by Ralph Manheim. 1982.
Psychoanalytic criticism.

Robertson, Ritchie. *Kafka: Judaism, Politics, Literature*. 1985.
Describes Kafka's emerging sense of Jewish identity.

Sandbank, Shimon. *After Kafka: The Influence fo Kafka's Fiction*. 1989.

Stern, J. P., ed. *The World of Franz Kafka*. 1980.
Contains portraits and photographs.

Stric, Roman and Yardley, J. C., ed. *Franz Kafka (1883–1924): His Craft and Thought*. 1986.
Collected essays.

Thiher, Allan. *Franz Kafka: A Study of the Short Fiction*. 1990.

Udoff, Alan, ed. *Kafka and the Contemporary Critical Performance*. 1987.
Collection of essays.

# D. H. LAWRENCE
## Odor of Chrysanthemums

*Backgrounds*

Of all major twentieth-century writers in English, D. H. Lawrence is perhaps the most insistent in condemning what he sees as the ills of his civilization: its decadent spinelessness; its inability to accommodate energy and genuine passion; its rejection of the brightness of the natural world in favor of the grubbiness and mechanization of industrial organization. Lawrence sometimes harangues his readers, grabs them by the lapels and preaches to them; he often seems ham-handed because he rejects the cool delicacy of irony in favor of a cloying earnestness. Despite such objections, he writes with amazing vitality; he continually creates scenes as vivid and evocative as any in modern literature.

D. H. Lawrence was "discovered" by the influential English writer and editor Ford Madox Ford when, in 1909, Ford received in the mail the manuscript of "Odor of Chrysthanthemums." Ford later claimed (in *Portraits from Life* [1936]) that he read the first paragraph, laid the piece in the basket for accepted manuscripts, and then went to a dinner with H. G. Wells, G. K. Chesterton, and other Edwardian celebrities where he announced to the company that he had discovered another genius. Stories from this perior are part of this trun twards increased realism, and Lawrence revised them several times. The first version of "Odor of Chrysanthemums" (the one read by Ford Madox Ford) was modified to subordinate the role of the Bates children and to render the picture of Elizabeth Bates more complex.

Ford's story is a charming one, and though it perhaps glorifies his genius as an editor more than Lawrence's genius as a writer, Ford's subsequent discussion of just *why* he saw greatness in that first paragraph is still a useful example of how a close reading can illuminate a text.

> "The small locomotive engine, Number 4, came clanking, stumbling down from Selston," and at once you know that this fellow with the power of observation is going to write of whatever he writes about from the inside. The "Number 4" shows that. He will be the sort of fellow who knows that for the sort of people who work about engines, engines have a sort of individuality.... This man knows what he wants . . . .

"It appeared round the corner with loud threats of speed." . . . Good writing; slightly, but not *too* arresting . . . . "But the colt that it startled from among the gorse...outdistanced it at a canter." Good again. This fellow does not "state." He doesn't say: "It was coming slowly," or—what would have been a little better—"at seven miles an hour." Because even "seven miles an hour" means nothing definite to the untrained mind. It might mean something for a trainer of pedestrian racers . . . . . . . But anyone knows that an engine that makes a great deal of noise and yet cannot overtake a colt at a canter must be a ludicrously ineffective machine. We know then that this fellow knows his job. [ . . . ] He knows how to open a story with a sentence of the right cadence for holding the attention. He knows how to construct a paragraph. He knows the life he is writing about in a landscape is sufficiently constructed with a casual word here and there. You can trust him for the rest.

Indeed, Lawrence's use of the illuminating detail, the use of quick, deft strokes of vivid description and dialogue to evoke a terrible evening in the lives of a colliery family, confirm the trust Ford Madox Ford had in Lawrence's talent as a writer. And Lawrence *was* writing about his subject "from the inside." The setting of "Odor of Chrysanthemums"—a colliery town so dreary that the miners pass through it "like shadows" and even the natural world it touches has become "ragged" and "forsaken"—has its source in Lawrence's own experience. The life of the Bates family also derives from Lawrence's experience. Family life in this story, as in *Sons and Lovers*, is coldly violent in its intimacy. It is a kind of trap in which relationships manage to be simultaneously distant and smothering.

"Odor of Chrysanthemums" is essentially a story about human beings trapped in their own isolation even while they are involved in what are evidently the most intimate kinds of relationships. Much of the story appears to be concerned with exploring the hostile nature of the relationship between a joyless miner's wife, Elizabeth Bates, and her irresponsible husband, and it clearly enlists our sympathies on her behalf. The end of the story, however, opens a new dimension; Elizabeth Bates's recognition that she has been forever separate from her husband—that he has lived as a stranger at his own hearth—expands our understanding of the situation and allows us to see that isolation and essential separateness involve not only everyone in this story but also imply a general condition of mankind. Mrs. Bates's horrified discovery of the "utter isolation of the human soul" reveals and enlarges the story's thematic center by forcing us to review the whole, and to think again about the characters who populate the tale: the woman who is "insignificantly trapped" between the colliery train and the hedge; the young boy, John, almost "lost in darkness" at the end of the family table; the cautious and secretive neighbors; Walter Bates's mournful mother; Elizabeth Bates's own father, who wishes to remarry because, as he says, "What's a man to do? It's no sort of life for a man of my years to sit at my own hearth like a stranger" (p. 1730); and, of course, Walter Bates himself, who dies as he lived—underground, trapped in a small airless space, in the dark, literally untouched by earth, his workmates, his children, or his wife.

In "Odor of Chrysanthemums," as in *Sons and Lovers*, Lawrence's presentation of working-class life is poignantly realized while at the same time it avoids sentimentality or patronizing stereotypes. Its closely observed details, its Midlands dialect, and its authentic atmosphere all suggest that Lawrence wishes to portray the Bates family in a "realistic" mode. But in "Odor of Chrysanthemums," as in all of Lawrence's fiction, everything in the text functions on the level of metaphor even while appearing to be "realistic" in its delineation of detail and scene. Thus, the ubiquitous chrysanthemums, the shadowy miners, the opposition of train and hedge, and the darkness of the Bates living room are—first— "realistic" details which are in service to the lives of characters in the text, but they are also metaphors which suggest a world of meaning beyond these characters. The manner of Walter Bates's death, for instance, is as symbolic as the "cold, deathly smell" of the ragged chrysanthemums—a smell which has presided over all of the isolated moments of the Bates's lives and, Lawrence implies, will continue to preside over the Bateses yet to be born.

Lawrence grew up in a colliery town, Eastwood, and in a colliery family. His father, Arthur, was a comparatively uneducated and unsophisticated man who was, like Walter in the story, inclined to drink away significant amounts of the family's skimpy funds. Lawrence's mother, Lydia, felt separate from Arthur and, as seen in *Sons and Lovers*, devoted herself almost entirely to the upbringing of her children who, she devoutly hoped, would not turn out like her husband. Lawrence's biographer, Harry T. Moore, has said, "She hated her husband and, just as extravagantly, she loved her children. These children became a battleground in the parents' war .... She fought fiercely to give them good lives: her sons would not go into the mines, her daughters would not become servants. And through the galling poverty of those years she made intense sacrifices for them, particularly in furthering the education of David Herbert—or Bert, as the family called him." Although "Odor of Chrysanthemums" is quite clearly based on Lawrence's own family life and the characters of Elizabeth and Walter are based on Lydia and Arthur Lawrence, the major incident in the story is modeled on the accidental death of Lawrence's Uncle James and the reactions of his Aunt Polly.

Lawrence's ear for Midlands working class speech was extremely sharp by the time he wrote "Odor of Chrysanthemums," as was his eye for the gritty presence of the colliery town and the surrounding beauty of the countryside, which he called "the country of my heart." In his early novels and stories, working class speech often reflects a kind of crude unsophistication, but in his later work—especially in *Lady Chatterley's Lover*— such speech suggests emotional and sexual vitality.

Before 1909 Lawrence's reading consisted mostly of the English Victorians, especially George Eliot and Thomas Hardy, and the nineteenth-century French classics. Lawrence began to read his older realist contemporaries—Arnold Bennett, H. G. Wells, John Galsworthy, Edward Garnett, and so on—about the time that he was writing "Odor of Chrysanthemums" Beyond Bennett and, to a lesser extent, Wells, there were very few useful English examples of the kind of people (working-class and lower middle-class) and settings (Bennett's industrial Midlands towns and working London) that Lawrence would make his own in his early work.

Other than the novelists, the most important early literary influence on Lawrence was the language of the English Bible and the Congregationalist hymns that he heard in chapel. Lawrence once said "From early childhood I have been familiar with Apocalyptic language and Apocalyptic image: not because I spent my time reading Revelation, but because I went to Sunday school and to Chapel, to Band of Hope and to Christian Endeavour, and was always having the Bible read at me or to me." In his essay "Hymns in a Man's Life" Lawrence said, "I think it was good to be brought up a Protestant: and among Protestants, a Nonconformist, and among Nonconformists, a Congregationalist." He went on to add that even the great poems which had meant the most to him, such as Wordsworth's "Immortality" ode, Keats's great odes, lyrics by Goethe and Verlaine, and parts of Shakespeare, were "not woven so deep in me as the rather banal Nonconformist hymns that penetrated through and through my childhood."

## Classroom Strategies

"Odor of Chrysanthemums" can be taught in one class meeting. To reinforce the notion that the story is not, finally, merely about family friction, or the sufferings of one embittered miner's wife over an unhappy marriage, it might be best to begin with the end of the tale, and then to move back over the story until the students can see how Lawrence has worked his central theme of the isolation and separateness of human beings into every corner of the text.

Students will at first wish to assign blame for the obvious failure of this marriage. Walter Bates—because of his history of drunkenness and apparent irresponsibility—will be blamed first. Further discussion will call Elizabeth Bates into question, and blame may be assigned to her on the basis of her apparent inability to love, and her late (too late) recognition of an inability to connect with her husband and, by implication, her children. In "Odor of Chrysanthemums," however, the assignment of blame is superfluous. It obstructs the students' ability to see that Lawrence is interested in suggesting something about the human condition, something which is beyond blame. Lawrence, as one critic has noted, "concentrates our interest upon isolation itself, not upon who might be responsible for the condition."

To suggest the metaphorical reverberations beneath the "realistic" surface, it is probably best to begin in the obvious place—with the chrysanthemums. Every student will notice the way they pervade the story, just as they have pervaded the lives of Elizabeth and Walter Bates. Ford Madox Ford has pointed out that "Odor of Chrysanthemums" is not, "whatever else it may turn out, either a frivolous or even a gay, springtime story. Chrysanthemums are not only flowers of the autumn: they are the autumn itself." This autumnal solemnity, and its suggestion of death, has hung heavy over the Bates's lives. As Elizabeth says, "It was chrysanthemums when I married him, and chrysanthemums when you were born, and the first time they ever brought him home drunk, he'd got brown chrysanthemums in his buttonhole" (p. 1732–33). The same flowers comment on the future (Annie notices them in Mrs. Bates's apron as she reaches up to light a lamp, her figure "just rounding with maternity) as well as on the present. When the miners bring in the body of the dead Walter Bates, the room has the "cold, deathly smell of chrysanthemums and when they try to put him down they knock a vase filled with chrysanthemums onto the floor. In death, as in life, chrysanthemums punctuate events with their autumnal implications.

The more obvious metaphorical implications of the chrysanthemums can be followed by a discussion of Lawrence's metaphorical uses of darkness and fire (which suggest death and passion), the concretely realized opposition of the natural and industrial worlds, and the scenes involving Elizabeth and her father, her children, and her mother-in-law. Finally, a discussion of the symbolic suggestions of Walter's death by suffocation (see above) and Elizabeth's revelation of her isolation and disconnectedness during the ritual washing of her husband's body will serve to reveal the metaphorical implications which are active beneath what at first seems to be a simple "realistic" story of a terrible night in a mining family's life.

### Topics for Discussion and Writing

1. Discuss the metaphorical implications of the story's title. What do the chrysanthemums represent in the story?
   [See paragraph 3 of Classroom Strategies for discussion.]

2. What are the apparent reasons for the failure of the Bates's marriage? Can this failure be entirely accounted for by examining their social and economic condition, their parents, their apparent assumption of conventional sexual roles, the difficulties of bringing up children, the demands of being a miner or a miner's wife, etc.? Does Lawrence imply that there is something inherent in the human condition which thwarts their ability to achieve a successful marriage?
   [Although Lawrence quite clearly presents the social and psychological factors which might wreak havoc on this marriage, he also strongly suggests that isolation is basic to the human condition—it affects everyone—and, consequently, limits the possibilities of all relationships.]

3. What is the significance of the scene between Elizabeth and her father?
   [See paragraph 5 of Classroom Strategies.]

4. How does our view of Walter Bates change by the end of the story? What was it at the beginning?
   [See paragraph 5 of Backgrounds.]

5. How does Lawrence develop qualities of "realism" in the story? How is Lawrence's use of metaphor and realism similar to Tolstoy's? Mann's? Lessing's?

## Further Reading

See also the reading suggestions in the anthology, p. 1728.

Balbert, Peter and Marcus, Phillip L. eds. *D. H. Lawrence: A Centenary Consideration.*
Collected essays.

Black, Michael H. *D. H. Lawrence, the Early Fiction: A Commentary.* 1986.

Bloom, Harold, ed. *D. H. Lawrence.* 1986.
Collected essays.

Boulton, James T. "Lawrence's 'Odor of Chrysanthemums.'"
*Renaissance and Modern Studies* 13, 1969, pp. 4–48.

Cushman, Keith. *D. H. Lawrence at Work: The Emergence of 'The Prussian Officer' Stories.* 1978, pp. 47–76.

Ford, Ford Madox. *Portraits from Life.* Boston, 1937.
An interesting, if exaggerated, discussion of Lawrence's "discovery" and Ford's reaction to "Odor of Chrysanthemums."

Ford, George H. *Double Measure: A Study of the Novels and Stories of D. H. Lawrence.* New York, 1965.
A solid discussion of "Odor of Chrysanthemums" which emphasizes the story's major theme of isolation. See especially pages 68–71.

Harris, Janice Hubbard. *The Short Fiction of D. H. Lawrence.* 1984.
Offers perceptive and well-documented analyses of individual stories, arranged chronologically in eight thematic sections.

Herzinger, Kim A. *D. H. Lawrence in His Time.* Lewisburg, Pennsylvania, 1982.
A study of English literary and intellectual culture during the early years of Lawrence's career, including a discussion of contemporary reactions to his early work.

Jackson, Dennis and Jackson, Fleda Brown, eds. *Critical Essays on D. H. Lawrence*. 1988.

Kalnins, Mara. "D. H. Lawrence's 'Odor of Chrysanthemums': The Three Endings." *Studies in Short Fiction* 13, 1976, pp. 471–79.
*and*
————, ed. *D. H. Lawrence: Centenary Essays*. 1986.
Contains an essay by John Worthen on the Eastwood connection.

Lawrence, D. H. "Nottingham and the Mining Country" in *Phoenix: The Posthumous Papers of D. H. Lawrence*, edited by Edward McDonald. New York, 1936.
Lawrence's own discussion of Eastwood, the model for the town in "Odor of Chrysanthemums."

Littlewood, J. D. F. "D. H. Lawrence's Early Tales." *Cambridge Quarterly* 1, 1966. pp. 107–24.

McDonald, Edward, ed. *Phoenix: The Posthumus Papers of D. H. Lawrence*. 1936.
Contains Lawrence's own description of Eastwood, the model for the town in "Odor of Chrysanthemums."

Moore, Harry T. *The Priest of Love: The Life of D. H. Lawrence*. New York, 1974.
The most useful full biography of Lawrence.

Moynahan, Julian. *The Deed of Life: The Novels and Tales of D. H. Lawrence*. 1963.
"Odor of Chrysthemums" is discussed on pp. 181–85.

Niels, Edward H., ed. *D. H. Lawrence: A Composite Biography*. 3 vols., 1957–59.
An interesting primary-source biography using letters and documents by Lawrence and those who knew him.

Preston, Peter and Hoare, Peter, eds. *D. H. Lawrence in the Modern World*. 1989.

Collected essays.

Sagar, Keith M. *D. H. Lawrence: Life into Art*. 1985.
Examines letters, manuscripts, and primary documents to discuss the genesis of Lawrence's art in his novels.

Smith, Anna. *Lawrence and Women*. 1978.
Assembled essays with a specific focus.

Widmer, Kingsley. *The Art of Perversity*. Seattle, 1962.
Widmer presents an interesting, if standard, discussion of "Odor of Chrysanthemums," pp. 22–24.

# T. S. ELIOT

T. S. Eliot is probably the best known and most influential twentieth-century poet writing in English. He believed that great writers represent their time, and his own poems, plays, and criticism have given modern Western society a characteristic voice. When we read "Prufrock" we find ourselves engaged with a vulnerable, self-conscious presence which has become so central to twentieth-century literature that it is hard to imagine the modern consciousness without him. *The Waste Land*, with its insistent depiction of a civilization in fragments and its dramatic litany of the symptoms of the collapse, is, for many, the central statement of modern culture's obsessions and fears. Eliot did not stop, however, with the bleak vision of these earlier poems. The *Four Quartets'* "Little Gidding" attempts to redeem the earlier despair; it is a redemption conjured out of the language itself, grave and endlessly fascinating. The range of Eliot's vision and the power of his language make the poet a dominating presence in modern literature.

## The Love Song of J. Alfred Prufrock

### Backgrounds

The opening three lines of "The Love Song of J. Alfred Prufrock" raise significant questions as to just exactly what kind of poem it is. The "I" of the first line does not at first present any particular problems; it appears to be the shadowy, wispy figure of J. Alfred Prufrock. The "you," however, is a different matter. Is it the reader? If so, then the poem is a monologue: the speaker alone, addressing an audience of readers. The monologue depends on its honesty; we tend to believe that what the speaker has to say, especially about himself, is true.

But perhaps the "you" is another person in the poem, someone whose silent companionship calls forth Prufrock's poetic speech? If so, then the poem is a dramatic monologue, and we are invited to look beyond the spoken words for sources of psychological motivation. In such a case we are not dealing with a private self, but instead with a self on public display, subject to the usual distortions and camouflages associated with the social self. But who then is this "you"? Eliot himself said that it was an unidentified male companion. But it has also been suggested, with considerable plausibility, that the mysterious "you" is simply Prufrock's public self, which can be differentiated from the sensitive, thinking inward Prufrock who is the "I" in the poem.

In any case, what we clearly have in the poem is a central figure driven by a psychic unrest toward action (to break away from a meaningless life? make a proposal of love? upset the universe?), yet dissuaded from action by a psychic terror of the unfamiliar, the new, the upsetting. So the poem dramatizes in its narrative, its images, even its rhythms, a tug of war between impulses of restlessness, anticipations of a movement toward a goal, enticements vaguely erotic and sexually arousing (like light brown hair on the woman's arms), and impulses of escape through anesthesia (the etherised patient), through acceptance of defeat ("And would it have been worth it after all?"), and through nostalgia for more primitive states characterized by uninhibited instinctual drives. In one part of himself, Prufrock longs for the fatal interview with its moment of truth; in another part of himself he fights it with every ounce of his rational and rationalizing brain. Such a sketch is far too simplistic to contain the poem, but it may serve usefully as a scaffold for approaching it.

Prufrock's world has three main features. It is trivial and full of trivialities like marmalade and tea. It is in part a metaphor or symbol of Prufrock's own frustrated interior consciousness. And it is, in addition, a sort of Dantesque Inferno. The Dantesque qualities are not to be overlooked. The epigraph (and we should always pay close attention to Eliot's epigraphs) is from *The Divine Comedy* and suggests the degree to which the landscape of the poem is to be seen as hellish and the speaker of the poem as one of the damned. From the first stanza, with its sinister litany of "half-deserted streets," and "sawdust restaurants with oyster-shells," through the feline "yellow smoke that slides along the street," and so on, we are aware that the modern city has become one of the circles of Hell for Prufrock—as in the poetry of Baudelaire, whose Paris is also a derivative of Dante's Hell.

If the first few stanzas of "Prufrock" use a modern cityscape to mirror interior psychic states, the remaining stanzas elaborate the triviality of Prufrock's existence in that setting. It is a setting shorn of heroes; Prufrock is "not Prince Hamlet, nor was meant to be." Should he rise from the dead, like Lazarus, the response would be indifference. He not only cannot answer the "overwhelming question," he cannot even ask it. Questions of real depth can only lead to speechless ellipsis. In an environment where the only great issues are issues of etiquette ("My necktie rich and modest"), who would dare "Disturb the universe?"—and what would "they" say if someone did? Since the women "in the room" can reduce even so extraordinary a figure as Michelangelo to a subject of tea-party conversation—he can guess what short work they would make of *him*.

Shrunk to the dimensions of the world that up to now has contained it, Prufrock's life is "measured out" with "coffee spoons"—has become a meaningless round of meaningless activity; after "tea and cakes and ices" he wonders if he has the "strength to force the moment to its crisis." The "crisis," we suspect, is *any* moment of significance, but Prufrock seems to situate it specifically in a proposal to a woman. Somewhere in this suffocating void then, there is a woman whom Prufrock wishes to approach, perhaps seriously—for this is a "love song," after all. But the possibilities of success are almost nil. Prufrock's prospects are dimmed by his own shyness, by his morbid consciousness of "them," and by the ways of a world over which he cannot even presume to have control. His fantasies and desires, his vision of the romantically heroic self that he longs to be, are inevitably intruded upon by the "real world," a world in which he grows old and wonders if he dares to "eat a peach." In his fantasies, he may have "heard the mermaids singing." He cannot, however, "linger in the chambers" of his romantic wishes for very long before "human voices"—the voices of the world he actually inhabits—drown him and his fantasies together.

Eliot wanted, as he once said, "an expression of *significant* emotion, emotion which has its life in the poem and not in the history of the poet." The way emotion could be born inside the poem, without turning loose what were merely personal—and therefore idiosyncratic and trivial—emotions, was through an "objective correlative":

> The only way of expressing emotion in the form of art is by finding an "objective correlative"; in other words, a set of objects, a situation, a chain of events which shall be the formula of that particular emotion; such that when the external facts, which must terminate in sensory experience, are given, the emotion is immediately invoked.
>
> —"Hamlet and His Problems"(1919)

"Prufrock," especially, presents Eliot's use of this method to good advantage.

Eliot quite consciously left few biographical clues behind him. As yet we have no published collection of letters, and there are no diaries, memoirs, or autobiographical writings to work from. Hugh Kenner has called him "the invisible poet," and Eliot himself was pleased to be called "Old Possum."

We do know that he was, from the first, much disturbed by the conflict between his supersubtle and refined intelligence and what he apparently felt were the demeaning distractions of his physical life. Similarly, the sanctuary of the inward self was felt to be under constant stress from the insistent social and material facts around him—shabby streets, sickness, the social round, the dance of courting. He was inhibited and perhaps afraid when in the presence of women; yet he desired them, and the resulting struggle often left him feeling inadequate, irritated, and distressed. All of these impressions find their way into "The Love Song of J. Alfred Prufrock" and suggest some of the reasons for the poem's tonal interplay of self-mockery and despair.

In "The Love Song of J. Alfred Prufrock" we find adaptations of Dante, Baudelaire, and Jules Laforgue, whose presentations of interior landscapes of atomized consciousness were particularly important to Eliot during the period in which he wrote the poem. He was also influenced by the dramatic monologues as well as the crisis-ridden personae of Browning and Tennyson. Henri Bergson's notion of life as a succession of psychological states, memories, and roles has possibly left its mark on the poem, as have Dostoevsky's portrayals of characters with significant psychological disabilities, and Henry James's analysis of the unlived life, especially in "The Beast in the Jungle" and "Crapy Cornelia" Influences from the seventeenth-century English metaphysical poets (particularly Donne), and the nineteenth-century French Symbolist tradition may likewise be traced.

### Classroom Strategies

"The Love Song of J. Alfred Prufrock" will take a full class period, since you will likely be inclined to discuss not only the poem, but the characteristics of modern poetry generally. Even if other modern poets—from Baudelaire through Rilke and Stevens—have been covered, you may feel the need to review or qualify earlier remarks and to make direct applications to Eliot. Beginning with "Prufrock," in which some of the problems of reading Eliot appear in reasonably simple form, seems much the best approach to take, no matter whether you teach all three poems or not.

When approaching "The Love Song of J. Alfred Prufrock," familiar though that poem has now become to most teachers, it is worth remembering that early readers of the poem often found it obscure and incoherent. Arthur Waugh, father of Evelyn Waugh, reviewed it with the verdict that "the state of Poetry is indeed threatened with anarchy which will end in something worse even than 'red ruin and the breaking up of laws.'" Most students coming to Eliot for the first time are "early readers." For many, establishing the "I" and the "you" will be the most helpful step. Although it can plausibly be argued that Prufrock has no fixed identity and, additionally, that the entire poem takes place not in the real world but in his tormented subconscious, students will grasp the poem more clearly on a first reading if they view the speaker of the poem as a middle-aged man named Prufrock, and the "you" as the reader. The first line then becomes an invitation to go with the speaker on his outward and inward journey. The point that what we "see" in the poem has more to do with Prufrock's consciousness than with any material facts can be established on a second reading by the implications of lines 2 and 3. The evening is "like" an anesthetized patient because Prufrock himself is "like" one. Students are likely to understand this poem long before they comprehend it. With a bit of help they will enjoy it immensely.

### Topics for Discussion and Writing

1. What kind of a poem is "The Love Song of J. Alfred Prufrock"? Is it a monologue? A dramatic monologue? An inner monologue? What difference does it make?
   [See paragraphs 1–3 of *Backgrounds* for discussion.]

2. How is description—especially of the cityscape—used in "Prufrock"?
   [See paragraphs 5–6 of *Backgrounds* for discussion.]

3. What sort of person is Prufrock? What does his full name suggest about him? What is he afraid of? In what ways is his life trivial or meaningless? To what extent is the title of the poem ironic?
   [See *Backgrounds* and *Classroom Strategies*.]

# The Waste Land

## Backgrounds

Experience shows that students attempting to cope for the first time with the flurry of allusions, the imbedded meanings, the tone, and the structure of *The Waste Land* are soon out of their depth. You will be well advised to read as many of the commentaries listed below as you have time for.

*Underlying Myth*: It is important, first, for students to understand a background that the poem takes for granted. The following summary by Cleanth Brooks of the myth that underlies the poem is perhaps the clearest to be had:

> The basic symbol used, that of the waste land, is taken . . . from Miss Jessie Weston's <u>From Ritual to Romance</u>. In the legends which she treats there, the land has been blighted by a curse. The crops do not grow and the animals cannot reproduce. The plight of the land is summed up by, and connected with, the plight of the lord of the land, the Fisher King, who has been rendered impotent by maiming or sickness. The curse can be removed only by the appearance of a knight who will ask the meanings of the various symbols which are displayed to him in the castle. The shift in meaning from physical to spiritual sterility is easily made, and was, as a matter of fact, made in certain of the legends.

Eliot once remarked of Joyce that his use of the *Odyssey* as background in Ulysses gave him "a way of controlling, of ordering, of giving a shape and a significance to the immense panorama of futility and anarchy which is contemporary history." Where Joyce used Homeric myth as a parallel, Eliot used anthropology (Jessie Weston's book, behind which lies Sir James Frazer's immensely influential *The Golden Bough*) as well as a succession of key works in the Western literary tradition. In this way he transforms the original anthropological vegetation myth into one that has symbolic application to the modern world.

*Voices*: Eliot's original title for the poem was taken from Dickens, "He Do the Police in Different Voices." And, indeed, there are many different voices in the poem, many different speakers. Some have names (Tiresias, Madame Sosostris), most have not—but are clearly "characters" in the poem. There is the sledding "I" of lines 8–18; the grave "I" of lines 27–30; the "hyacinth girl" (35–41); the friend of Stetson (60–76); the nervous speaker and her respondent (111–38); Lil's friend and advisor who tells her story (142–72); the Spenserian/Marvellian speaker (173–201); the object of Mr. Eugenides's desire (207–14); the "typist" (252); the visitor to the church of St. Magnus Martyr (257–65); the three "Thames daughters" (292–95, 296–99, 300–305); and the (apparently) single voice of Part V of the poem.

All of these different voices are, however, absorbed into the one comprehensive voice of the poet through which the other voices speak. Eliot himself named Tiresias (who clearly speaks lines 215–56) as the "most important personage in the poem, uniting all the rest. . . . What Tiresias *sees*, in fact, is the substance of the poem." It is a good choice: Tiresias—witnessing prophet, seer of past, present and future, with experience as both man and woman—connects the fragments of a civilization scattered through time and space. In Tiresias (see the *Odyssey* X and XI, and *Oedipus the King*) past and future are always present, contained in a single consciousness. Had Eliot left the matter open he would have allowed us to assume that the all-comprehending voice in the poem was his own, an idea which he probably thought presumptuous.

*Tone*: Despite the competing voices of the poem, it sustains a singular tone—urbane, grave, dry, abrupt, poignant, slightly sinister, and suffering, vibrant with something very like Old Testament prophetic despair. This is the tone of the poet in the poem, who does not take lightly what he sees.

*Structure*: The poem means to appear as disjointed as the world it describes, and we are left to put the pieces together, to make sense of them, just as we are in the "real world." Most poetry, like most fiction, is linear: one stanza leads to the next with a kind of inevitability, and the poet usually takes pains to lead the reader from one part of the poem to the next. Words and stanzas rush—and then, and then, and then—to an inevitable conclusion. The "meaning" of *The Waste Land*, on the contrary, is lodged in the spaces between the lines, where the suggestions of the poet and the responses of the reader mix to make sense of the material at hand. The central theme of the poem is the breakdown of civilization, the resulting death-in-life which is a consequence of that breakdown, and the difficulties of cultural regeneration from this death-in-life. Each of the five sections (or movements) of the poem cleaves closely to this theme.

Section I, "The Burial of the Dead," introduces the reader to the underlying myth of the poem; presents the first image of the waste land; offers the controlling images of water and dryness; explores the difficulty of being aroused from death-in-life; and suggests the false avenues—such as the occult—that might be taken to establish meaning in an otherwise meaningless world.

Section II, "A Game of Chess," again gestures toward the notion of death-in-life, but this time by exploring the failure of love due to emotional impotence; the emptiness of marriage, shown especially through the rejection of offspring; and the suggestion that nature itself has become perverted or artificial.

Section III, "The Fire Sermon," again presents the failure of love, but this time by emphasizing the emptiness of sexual relationships outside of marriage; it explores the automatism of lust, and the "mind-forg'd manacles" (see Blake's "London" [p. 577]) which debase societies and individuals alike.

Section IV, "Death by Water," though extremely brief, enforces the notion that the forces of life (water) easily become the forces of death (by drowning). We are left uncertain whether the death is regenerative or sterile; whether it is real or an image reflecting the speaker's longing for oblivion.

Section V, "What the Thunder Said," continues to insist on the harsh, stony, wasted landscape of the present, but also offers the prospect of regeneration and inner peace through the avenues of giving, sympathy, and self-control. The incantatory "Shantih shantih shantih," which comes directly after the thunder speaks, literally *means* something like the "peace that passeth understanding," but it has also been thought to suggest the sound of the much-desired rain.

*The Comparison of Past and Present*: Past and present in the poem are meant to be simultaneous; they are both contained in the poem's central consciousness. Eliot, like Yeats, was aware in his work that present experience is merely the sum of past experiences. Thus the past may allude to a similar condition in the present, serving as a prophetic warning to contemporary readers:

> What is the city over the mountains
> Cracks and reforms and bursts in the violet air
> Falling towers
> Jerusalem Athens Alexandria

Vienna London
Unreal

(372–77)

Or it may emphasize the comparative decadence of the present. Eliot uses direct quotations, half-quotations, parodies of well-known texts, and allusions through tone, rhythm, and imagery to register the existence of a once vital tradition which has either been corrupted, forgotten, or ignored in the modern present. A few significant examples of various kinds follow:

Lines 1–7: Lines meant to bring to mind the vital, regenerative April and the pilgrimage to a holy place in the "Prologue" to Chaucer's *Canterbury Tales*.

Lines 31–34, 42: From Wagner's opera *Tristan and Isolde*, a story of tragic passion, the lines evoke a kind of passion no longer available in the modern world, and also, however, an enhanced awareness of the aridity of *mere* passion, which is further hinted by the image of desolation and emptiness in line 42.

Lines 60–68: Baudelaire's "unreal city," Dante's souls awaiting transport to the various circles of Hell, Joyce's Dublin graveyard scene in *Ulysses*, and Blake's vision of London in his poem, "London," are used here to suggest the infernal quality of modern life in the modern city.

Lines 77–110: The opening is a parody of Enobarbus's speech describing Cleopatra in Act II, Scene ii of Shakespeare's *Antony and Cleopatra*, and it registers a comparison between a gloried past and a tawdry present. In Shakespeare, the queen is a kind of magical goddess, and her barge and the surrounding seascape suggest harmony with the natural world. In Eliot, the scene is a sexual and natural waste land; the woman can muster no magic without the most artificial aids, and she is surrounded by painted images of rape and violence. Yet here too a melancholy hint remains of the destructive capacities of passion and of the *likeness* of that world to ours.

Line 172: Eliot's use of Ophelia's mad farewell in Act IV, Scene v of *Hamlet* makes even more sinister the pub story told about Lil and Albert, and provides ironic commentary on the "sweet ladies" involved.

Lines 173–84: Spenser's image in his *Prothalamion* of the "sweet Thames" covered with flower petals for an impending double marriage stands in stark contrast to the modern Thames described by the speaker.

Lines 266–78, 279–91: Again, Spenser's *Prothalamion* is invoked in order to contrast the sweating, polluted river of the present with the sparkling, "sweet Thames" of the past.

Lines 306–311: These lines combine the words of St. Augustine, recalling his youthful days of "unholy loves," with those of the Buddha, denouncing desire in his *Fire Sermon*. Carthage, like London, was a commercial center and was, as London might be, destroyed. Conceivably, Virgil's *Aeneid* is also suggested here: Carthage was the site of Dido's funeral pyre, again a monument to passion which ends in death.

After reading *The Waste Land*, one of Eliot's friends declared that it was his "autobiography." But the autobiographical elements of the poem are so deeply imbedded, and we know so comparatively little about Eliot's life, that to unearth what is strictly personal in the poem will probably take years of rather difficult excavation.

Some personal facts are relevant. During the final period of the poem's composition, Eliot's troubled marriage with his wife Vivien was collapsing. She suffered one of her many nervous breakdowns in 1921, and her crises, combined with the strain of his monotonous clerk's job at Lloyd's Bank and a persistent lack of funds, drove Eliot to a breakdown of his own later in that year. He wrote much of the poem during a period of recuperation at Margate ("On Margate Sands. / I can connect / Nothing with nothing") and in Lausanne. Vivien had suffered from bouts of mental illness ever since their marriage in 1915. They had been married under rather mysterious circumstances and without the blessing of his pious and still influential parents. Contemporary rumor suggested that Eliot, in the "awful daring of a moment's surrender / Which an age of prudence can never retract," had "compromised" Vivien and then felt obliged to marry her, but this has never been verified. Whatever the case, Vivien's behavior, especially during her bouts of nervous illness, alarmed Eliot and others. One account describes her this way: "She gave the impression of absolute terror, of a person who's seen a ghost, a goblin ghost, and who was always seeing a goblin in front of her. Her face was all drawn and white, with wild, frightened, angry eyes. . . . Supposing you would say to her, 'Oh, will you have some more cake?' she'd say, 'What's that? What do you mean? What do you say that for?' She was terrifying." Very possibly her accents can be heard in lines 111–38 of the poem.

Like all other Europeans and a large number of Americans, Eliot found World War I and its exhausting aftermath a sign that civilization as it had been lived for 500 years or so was collapsing. Images from the war, or having to do with war, infiltrate *The Waste Land* at every point: the dehumanization of the people of London; the continued references to collapsing or inverted towers and bridges; the "rats' alley" (a term used to describe the trenches as well as urban blight); the allusions to the Russian Revolution in lines 367–77; and the vision of the waste land itself. The Great War had changed everything, and Eliot's poem registers that change and suggests its effects.

In an essay on Philip Massinger (1920), Eliot writes: "Immature poets imitate; mature poets steal; bad poets deface what they take, and good poets make it into something better, or at least something different. The good poet welds his theft into a whole of feeling which is unique, utterly different from that from which it was torn; the bad poet throws it into something which has no cohesion." Though these comments may be thought to be self-serving, there is no doubt that Eliot's own use of his predecessors is transformative.

The direct influence of Ezra Pound on the final version of *The Waste Land* must not go without mention. In January, 1922, Eliot showed the manuscript of the poem to Pound, who remarked that it was impressive enough "to make the rest of us shut up shop." Even so, he felt it could be improved; he slashed out whole sections of the poem, tightened others. The poem we have is, in fact, so heavily indebted to Pound's editorial skills that it is almost a collaboration. Eliot's dedication of the poem to Pound, *il miglior fabbro* ("the better craftsman"), is as justified a dedication as ever appeared on a work of literature. The nature and extent of Pound's editing can be viewed first-hand in the *Facsimile and Transcript of the Original Drafts* of the poem, edited by Eliot's second wife, Valerie.

### Classroom Strategies

*The Waste Land* will take a minimum of two class periods, and perhaps more. Students will not follow Eliot's poems effectively without your aid and generosity—generosity in establishing their general meaning (without sounding pedantic) of individual allusions, lines, images, and symbols. *The Waste Land*, especially, can be turned into a kind of poem-encyclopedia—a great off-putting puzzle—if you do not keep the whole poem continually in focus.

How do you teach *The Waste Land*? Two warnings may be useful:
—Do not attempt to go through the poem line by line, allusion by

allusion, reference by reference. Students will be impressed by Eliot's knowledge, and no doubt by yours, but they will miss the poem altogether and worry overmuch about which of Eliot's allusions is to appear on their next exam.

—Do not pretend that the poem is simple once one has some sort of "key," or that there *is* a key. Eliot himself once told a group of students at Harvard that *he* thought everything about it was pretty clear; he was reportedly disturbed by their laughter.

Some suggestions of procedure may also be helpful:

1. Begin with "Prufrock." Some of the difficulties of Eliot's poetic method in *The Waste Land* clear up in advance for students on their encounter with this poem.

2. Place *The Waste Land* in the context of modern thought and writing—its major themes, images, techniques—already encountered by the student in previous assignments. Useful contextual remarks on the modern era will be found in the general introduction to the period (pp. 1375–84), which students should be asked to review.

3. Make sure the underlying myth of the poem is understood (see *Backgrounds: Underlying Myth*). If you are well-grounded in the Arthurian legends you will find they buttress the discussion, since students usually have some knowledge of these legends and of quest narratives in general, owing to the proliferation of films and books such as J. R. R. Tolkien's *Lord of the Rings* or Frank Herbert's *Dune*. Easily called up too are the many quest narratives students have met with earlier in this anthology: The *Odyssey*, *The Divine Comedy*, *The Canterbury Tales*, *Don Quixote*, *Gulliver's Travels*, *Candide*, *The Death of Iván Ilyich*, and *A Portrait of the Artist as a Young Man*, to mention only a few. The particularities of the myth as used by Eliot will be new to the class, but not the basic form of the quest.

4. Emphasize that the poem's "voices," however numerous, belong to a presiding, comprehending consciousness (which may be called either Tiresias' or Eliot's) and that the story told by each voice contributes to Eliot's overriding theme.

5. Analyze briefly the way the fragments of the poem hang together and make its central themes resonate. Since each section of the poem emphasizes something different, yet contributes to the emotional and intellectual effect as a whole, it will be wise, early on, to discuss what each section individually is about, but without going into detail.

6. At about this point, if time can possibly be managed, it pays to let the class "hear" the poem in Eliot's own rendering of it on Caedmon records or cassette tapes, with its grave Anglo-American twang. This will not only enhance the fascination of the poem, it will also register unforgettably the myriad interconnections of sound and sense within the poem and provide a dramatic background for the next procedure.

7. Pick one section for extremely close examination. Section II, "A Game of Chess," is perhaps the easiest to deal with in this way. Section III, "The Fire Sermon," also offers comparatively easy opportunities for close scrutiny. Section I, "The Burial of the Dead," and the concluding Section V, "What the Thunder Said," generally strike students as the most difficult.

8. Discuss the range and character of the poem's criticism. The way that Eliot manages the devaluations of the present by implicit comparisons with the past can best be demonstrated by looking at lines 77–105 in Section II, lines 173–202 in Section III, and lines 266–91 in Section III. To convince students of the persuasiveness of this technique, you might consider invoking the way politicians imply a decline in the current conditions by evoking past stabilities, or the way teachers condemn present educational standards by comparing them to the standards in place when they were in school. The point is not that any of these speakers, including the poem's speaker, expects to recapture the past. It is simply that the past, seen as golden, makes a persuasive point of reference for inciting improvements in the future. In *The Waste Land*, however, one must remember also that the past functions as evidence that basic human frailties do not greatly change.

*Topics for Discussion and Writing*

1. What is the underlying myth of *The Waste Land*? Where does it come from? In what other works do we find it? How does the poem use it to comment on our world?
   [See *Backgrounds: Underlying Myth.*]

2. Discuss the use of different speakers in *The Waste Land*. How does their use mirror the disjointedness of modern experience? In what way is Tiresias important?
   [See *Backgrounds: Voices.*]

3. How does Eliot compare past with present in the poem? To what purposes?
   [See the appropriate section in *Backgrounds* and suggestion #8 in *Classroom Strategies.*]

4. Describe the controlling images of *The Waste Land*: water and dryness, the seasons, etc. How do they interrelate in the poem?

5. Define the attitudes toward love and sex expressed in the poem. How do they relate to a waste land?

## Little Gidding

*Backgrounds*

As with each of the *Four Quartets*, "Little Gidding" is written in a form that its author liked to think of as analogous to Beethoven's late quartets. It has five movements: an introduction and a statement of theme; a lyrical development of that theme with a meditation on it; a metaphorical journey which suggests the theme of exploration; a shorter lyric; and a summary of the whole which echoes the opening movement.

The first movement is set in midwinter at Little Gidding, a seventeenth-century Anglican religious community, a time of year which suggests the coldness of old age and oncoming death, a time when the "soul's sap quivers." But the first movement emphasizes the possibilities of renewed life, a springtime which, for the speaker, must take place outside of time—it is "not in time's covenant." Pentecostal fire gleams in the poem in the same way the "brief sun flames the ice." Little Gidding, where the eternal ritual of prayer and worship persists and remains valid, becomes symbolic of a place outside of time, a spiritual realm which is "the intersection of the timeless moment," is "England and nowhere," "Never and always." It is the place, the speaker suggests, where all travelers must come and which will "always be the same." Little Gidding exists in an order of reality beyond the world.

The second movement begins with three rhymed stanzas which suggest the hopelessness of mere earthly existence by lyrically detailing the death of the elements—the four Heraclitean elements: air, earth, water, and fire—and the civilization which these earthly elements make up. These are followed by a long narrative section in which the speaker, walking in the "waning-dusk" on fire-patrol during the London blitz of World War II (during which the poem was written), encounters "a familiar compound ghost / Both intimate and unidentifiable." This "ghost" both is and is not the speaker; it is himself and everyone. The meeting is much like that of Dante the pilgrim's meeting with Virgil in *The Divine Comedy*. Thus, the ghost in "Little Gidding" has the "look of some dead master" and is the speaker's guide and kindred spirit. This kindred spirit rehearses the futility, isolation, and guilt which, in the end, are all that life has brought him. He has found that what he once took for "exercise of virtue" came to nothing but the "bitter tastelessness of shadow fruit" because his work and life were not in service to spiritual values.

The third movement attempts to establish a set of values alternative to those cited by the "ghost." Those who once lived these alternative values are our inheritance; they have become for us a "symbol perfected in death," and we, like Little Gidding itself, can be united with them in a common spiritual present.

The pentecostal experience is the central theme of the two-stanza lyric that makes up movement four. It is about the gorgeous terror of being "redeemed from fire [Hell] by fire [the pentecostal flame]." The movement insists that such an experience consumes like love, a love that surrenders all to a spiritual principle beyond us.

> We only live, only suspire
> Consumed by either fire or fire.

(212–13)

The final section echoes all the previous themes and images and attempts to reconcile them. Here, the past is reconciled with the present, the poet is reconciled with his work, "the fire and the rose are one." All takes place in symbolic Little Gidding "on a winter's afternoon, in a secluded chapel" where "History is now and England." The poem, like the life of the spirit, finds that:

> the end of all our exploring
> Will be to arrive where we started
> And know the place for the first time.
>
> (245–47)

"Little Gidding" contains what many find Eliot's best poetry and his most profound and generous thought. The poem finds life in death, spring in winter, the flame in the ice. And it was the last major poem that Eliot would write, finding, perhaps, that the end *was* his beginning.

Eliot was received into the Anglican Church in 1927, an answer to his own despair in *The Waste Land* and the basis for his work in "Little Gidding." The conflict between the life of the spirit and the life of the body found its resolution in "Little Gidding," and in the other *Four Quartets*.

"Little Gidding" is, as we might expect, soaked in the Anglican liturgy—its images and its rhythms. Beyond that, there are explicit references to Dante (especially in the second movement), to the mystical visions of Dame Juliana of Norwich, and to the anonymous fourteenth-century *Cloud of Unknowing*. The influence of W. B. Yeats is evident throughout, most notably in sections having to do with the decrepitude of old age. The major accents in the poem, however, apart from the liturgical ones, come from Eliot's own earlier poems, particularly *The Waste Land* (see lines 64–71, 80–89, and 100, for instance), which quite understandably were at the back of his mind during the writing of "Little Gidding."

### Classroom Strategies

"Little Gidding" will require at least one class period. You might find it useful at the beginning of your discussion of "Little Gidding" to attach it closely to *The Waste Land*, since what Eliot despaired over in *The Waste Land* is resolved in "Little Gidding" through his acceptance of the spiritual life—which in the earlier poem is seen as only a remote, perhaps unattainable, possibility. His vision of a civilization in decline, his insistence on the importance of the past as a comment on the present, his sense that the past and present exist simultaneously—all are found in "Little Gidding" just as they are in *The Waste Land*. The speaker's encounter with the "compound" ghost can almost be seen as the Eliot of "Little Gidding" talking with the Eliot of *The Waste Land*. What needs to be pointed out, of course, is Eliot's change of attitude: the state of civilization may be precarious, but it can be redeemed. The past cannot be reclaimed entire:

> We cannot revive old factions
> We cannot restore old policies
> Or follow an antique drum.

>                                   (185–87)

but it can be reclaimed in our lives by our participating in its best values. In *The Waste Land* Eliot's attitude is one of revulsion; in "Little Gidding" he experiences revulsion, but moves beyond it toward acceptance and love. "Little Gidding," unlike *The Waste Land*, wants to be a generous poem.

### Topics for Discussion and Writing

1. Why does "Little Gidding" take place in midwinter? How does the opening remind us of *The Waste Land*? In what ways does "Little Gidding" constitute an "answer" to *The Waste Land*?
   [See paragraph 2 of *Backgrounds* and *Classroom Strategies* for discussion.]

2. Who is the "compound ghost" in "Little Gidding"? Of what elements is he "compounded"?
   [See paragraph 3 of *Backgrounds* for discussion.]

3. Why is the historical Little Gidding an appropriate setting for Eliot's purposes in this poem?
   [See paragraph 2 of *Backgrounds*.]

### Further Reading

See also the reading suggestions in the anthology, p. 1747.

Ackroyd, Peter. *T. S. Eliot: A Life*. New York, 1984.
A full-length biography.

Behr, Caroline. *T. S. Eliot: A Chronology of His Life and Works*. 1983.

Bloom, Harold, ed. *T. S. Eliot's* The Waste Land. 1986.

Boernstein, George. *Transformations of Romanticism in Yeats, Eliot, and Stevens*. 1976.
Describes similarities and differences in relation to Romantic norms.

Brooker, Jewel Spears. *Reading the Waste Land: Modernism and the Limits of Interpretation*. 1990.

——, *Approaches to Teaching Eliot's Poetry and Plays*. 1988.
Published as part of the Modern Language Association's series, "Approaches of teach world literature."

Brooks, Cleanth. *Modern Poetry and the Tradition*. Chapel Hill, 1939.
Chapter 7 contains Brooks's clear discussion of the underlying myth in *The Waste Land*.

Davidson, Harriet. *T. S. Eliot and Hermeneutics: Absence and Interpretation in* The Waste Land. 1985.

Eliot, T. S. *Selected Essays*. New York, 1950.
"Tradition and the Individual Talent" remains a crucial essay for understanding Eliot's work.

Eliot, Valerie, ed. The Waste Land: *A Facsimile and Transcript of the Original Drafts Including the Annotations of Ezra Pound*. New York, 1974.
An indispensable aid to understanding *The Waste Land*.

——, ed. *The Letters of T. S. Eliot*. 1988.

Gardner, Helen. *The Composition of Four Quartets*. New York, 1978.
An important aid to understanding "Little Gidding."

Gish, Nancy. The Waste Land: *A Poem of Memory and Desire*. 1988.

Gordon, Lyndall. *Eliot's Early Years*, 1977, and *Eliot's New Life*, 1988, New York.
One of the few detailed biographical studies of Eliot.

Harding, D. W. "Little Gidding." From *T. S. Eliot: A Collection of Critical Essays*, edited by Hugh Kenner. Englewood Cliffs, 1962. Pp. 125–28.
The best short discussion of "Little Gidding."

Kenner, Hugh. *The Invisible Poet: T. S. Eliot*. New York, 1959.
Particularly interesting on tone and language.

———, ed. *T. S. Eliot: A Collection of Critical Essays*. 1962.

Longenbach, James. *Modernist Poetics of History: Pound, Eliot, and the Sense of the Past*. 1987.
Draws on contemporary philosphical approaches (Gadamer, Nietzsche, DeMan).

Menand, Louis. *Discovering Modernism: T. S. Eliot and His Context*. 1987.
Discussion of Eliot in the context of modernism.

Schwartz, Sanford. *The Matrix of Modernism: Pound, Eliot, and Early Twentieth-Century Thought*. 1985.
Systematically describes the relationships between twentieth-century philosophers and modernist poets to construct an intellectual-historical model of modernist thought.

Smith, Grover. *T. S. Eliot's Poetry and Plays*. Chicago, 1956.
A highly detailed and thorough investigation of the work, particularly useful on influences and sources.

Spender, Stephen. *T. S. Eliot*. New York, 1976.
A readable short introduction to Eliot, written by another poet of considerable accomplishment.

Sultan, Stanley. *Eliot, Joyce and Company.* 1987.
Contains a discussion of "The Lovesong of J. Alfred Prufrock" and *The Waste Land* as "exemplary shapers" of English modernism.

Tramplin, Ronald. *A Preface to Eliot.* 1988.
Gives a full overview and interpretation.

# ANNA AKHMATOVA
## Requiem

*Backgrounds*

Anna Akhmatova [pronounced Ahk-*mah*-tova] is one of those who testify, who bring to light a painful dimension of social reality in the twentieth century and impel us to a deeper understanding of our era. Like T. S. Eliot denouncing the loss of values in *The Waste Land*, or Kafka portraying the dehumanization of industrial society in "The Metamorphosis," the Russian poet mourns the death of individual freedom and the negation of family ties during the most famous political purges of modern totalitarian society. For each writer, modern society is sick or wounded. Akhmatova's testimony, however, strikes a personal note from the beginning, unlike the more distanced and often symbolic perspectives of Kafka, Eliot, Mann, Brecht, or Beckett. Her readers are immediately confronted by a subjective "I" speaking throughout, whether in individual short poems or a longer cycle like *Requiem*. There are clearly historical reasons for the subjective "I" in *Requiem*, for the cycle refers directly to the poet's own experience during the purge; however, this "I" whose mounting emotions reach out to the reader is not exclusively Akhmatova's own, for it is gradually equated with the voice of her people. Like Dostoevsky and Tolstoy in the last century and Solzhenitsyn in this, Akhmatova is part of a Russian tradition that expects its major authors to be more than subjective individuals, and ultimately to bear witness for the national conscience.

*Requiem* took its current shape over more than twenty-five years. The central (numbered) poems appear to be the first ones written, as if to express her immediate personal shock at the arrest and imprisonment of her husband and son. The first numbered poem is dated 1935, and describes her husband's arrest that year. Numbers Five and Six are dated 1939, the year after her son Lev was arrested for the second time and then imprisoned for the seventeen months Akhmatova mentions in the preface. Number Seven, which announces the son's condemnation, is dated Summer 1939; the following invocation to Death is dated August 19, 1939 (from their home in Fontanny Dom), and Number Nine, which describes her mad despair, is dated May 4, 1940. 1940 appears to be the

---

year in which Akhmatova began to cast her personal tragedy in larger terms, for the Dedication and the two-part Epilogue, which link her fate to that of her people, are dated March 1940, and the tenth numbered poem ("Crucifixion"), which invokes a religious parallel and consolation, is dated 1940–43. Akhmatova herself gave the dates for these poems and for the prose preface (April 1, 1957) and introductory epigraph (1961), as if to reaffirm the historical authenticity of what she says. Nonetheless, she has not forgotten the inner constraints of poetic form, for it seems likely that other poems—written later but reflecting situations earlier in the cycle narrative—were left undated so as not to contradict the sense of chronological development from one stage to another.

In the years when the first poems were written, life was precarious indeed. Manuscripts were often confiscated and examined by the secret police for indications of subversive thinking, and Akhmatova reportedly destroyed the manuscript of individual stanzas of *Requiem* after they were committed to memory. Political censorship had existed for decades and writers did not stop writing, but they often turned to scenes from history, mythology, or the Bible in order to be able to comment obliquely on situations that could not otherwise be addressed. Thus Akhmatova in the thirties wrote an "Armenian" fable in which she took the role of a bereaved ewe asking the shah (and any image of a ruler would evoke Stalin) "Have you dined well? . . . was my little son / To your taste, was he fat enough?" *Requiem*, however, was too open in its condemnation to be published or even acknowledged in Stalin's lifetime, and in fact, the subject of the Stalinist regime is still such a sensitive topic that the entire cycle has never been published in the Soviet Union.

The Epigraph and preface to the cycle introduce Akhmatova to us in three ways: as a person who refused to seek refuge in other countries (she sharply criticized those who did), as a woman waiting numbly outside prison for news of a loved one inside, and as a writer asked by her fellow-sufferers to bear witness to what happened. As the poet begins to speak in the Dedication and Prologue, she evokes their common situation but still sees herself as an individual, a person separate from "my friends of those two years I stood / In hell" to "my chance friends / Of those two diabolical years." It will take the development of the poem itself, and a crisis of mounting personal agony that cannot be faced alone, for the speaker to identify herself with other sufferers in Russia and throughout history.

Religious and patriotic images are present from the beginning. The women waiting before the prison rise each morning "as if for an early service"; other religious references appear in the icon kissed in the first numbered poem, the invocation to "Say a prayer for me" in the second, the swinging censers in Poem 5 and the transcendent cross in Poem 6, and the culminating projection of the bereaved mother's plight onto a biblical level in the last numbered poem, "Crucifixion." A broad sense of Russian history and culture provides another framework transcending current events: age-old "innocent Russia" is the true victim of the present regime (Prologue), contemporary tyrannical murders have an historical precedent (the 1698 execution of the Streltsy in Poem 1), and a projected image of the Russian people of "folk" underlies the lilting melancholy of Poem 5, which echoes both the simplicity and metrical form of a Russian folksong. Shattering as their individual experience is, these women are not alone in either divine or human history.

### Classroom Strategies

*Requiem* can be taught in one period; you may help your students focus their reading if you suggest ahead of time that they read the numbered poems as the diary of a mother who is grieving—perhaps to the point of madness—over the arrest of her son. In class, this personal focus can be situated in the larger perspective of the public poet through examining the preface, and later the frame of Dedication and Epilogue. Although *Requiem* is unique inasmuch as it is the only lyrical cycle in the *Anthology*, it takes its place in the stream of literary works that evoke a moment in history, such as works by Dostoevsky or Chekhov in the preceding section, or by Mann, Kafka, Camus, and Solzhenitsyn in the twentieth century. You may wish to comment on the way the Russian authors especially take it upon themselves to speak for their country, and to ask whether students can think of American authors who do the same. It may bring the poem painfully alive if you draw parallels with the vigils of bereaved mothers in Argentina during the recent military dictatorship: the thousands of women called simply "The Mothers" who gathered each week in the large public square of Buenos Aires, holding the photographs of the "disappeared": their husbands, children, and grandchildren, who were taken by the secret police.

While students will probably be drawn by the image of the grieving mother and imprisoned son, they may have some trouble in linking the perspectives in the "story" poems of the core section. Part of the poem's interest, of course, lies in the rich variation of lyric forms in the different parts, but at the beginning it is probably best to emphasize that these shifting and fragmented perspectives are so many glimpses, over time, into the mind of a woman who is greatly shaken by grief and fear. The Prologue and the first numbered poem are spoken in the first person, using a relatively objective style to describe painful events. In the second numbered poem, however, the pain has apparently dominated the speaker to the point that she is no longer capable of using the subjective "I," but imagines a scene in which she is seen only from outside, part of a strangely alienated landscape. That such alienation is real becomes apparent in the following poem, which returns to the "I" but claims incredulously "No ... it is somebody else who is suffering." In the fourth poem, the "I" restored to her full sense of self looks back on her early carefree life, and compares with it her current misery as she waits outside prison on New Year's Day. In the next two poems she is increasingly fearful as she addresses her son; tinges of madness enter in her confessions of mental confusion, and in images of the stars staring down like predatory hawks. By the seventh poem, sentence has been passed, and she speaks in frantic contradictions of the need to adjust, to kill—memory, or to live, before moving to the eighth poem's invocation to Death, and images of the swirling Yenisei River and glittering Pole Star. She sinks openly into madness in the ninth poem, but only for a moment: madness means forgetting, and it is clear from the poignant images of the latter half of the poem that the speaker cannot and will not forget. The tenth poem, however, marks another significant break in perspective as the poet ceases to speak in subjective terms, and withdraws personally from a scene which is now transformed into the biblical drama. As the epilogues show, the speaker's development throughout the cycle has purged her of a purely separate subjective identity and united her with all those who suffer.

Each poem in the cycle also has its own formal and thematic unity, usually involving the development of a particular dramatic scene. A close reading of two or three individual poems will allow you to discuss them as independent works, and will give students a sense of how Akhmatova varies her style. For example, the prologue is a brief evocation of an historical period whose horror is emphasized through images of contradiction, madness, or inverted proportions; the first numbered poem is more intimate, and focuses on a poignant domestic scene as did Akhmatova's early work; the second numbered poem uses simple folktale imagery and folk rhythms to present a landscape of alienated identity; the seventh poem, "The Sentence," conveys a state of shock through the speaker's alternating and contradictory moods. You will find your own favorite examples, which may also serve to explore more fully a particular important issue.

Most students will have some sense of the secret police systems in dictatorships and totalitarian countries, but they will probably not be acquainted with the geographic references coordinating the setting of *Requiem*. It may be useful to bring or sketch a map of the Soviet Union in order to situate references to Leningrad and the river Neva, and to the Royal Gardens at Tsarskoe Selo close by; to Moscow (home of the Kremlin), to the River Don, to the Yensei River in Siberia, where many concentration camps were located, and to the Black Sea.

### Topics for Discussion and Writing

1. Why does the woman in the preface ask Akhmatova "Can you describe this?" Why is she happy at the poet's response? What aspect of Russian literary tradition is involved in both question and response?
   [See *Backgrounds*, the discussion of the second epilogue and the tradition of the writer as national conscience.]

2. How does the figure of the narrator change over the course of the poem? Does she lose or gain a sense of identity (or both)?
   [See headnote and *Backgrounds* for the poet's identification with the community of suffering women, and with the biblical mother of Christ.]

3. What coherence do you perceive in the numbered poems taken as a group? What themes or strategies hold them together?
   [See *Classroom Strategies* for a discussion of the fragmentation of narrative perspective.]

4. To what extent do the individual poems stand on their own, as independent pieces?
   [See discussion in *Classroom Strategies*.]

5. Why does the tenth numbered poem suddenly present a biblical scene? What previous elements prepare this shift in setting?
   [See headnote and the discussions of religious imagery and narrative perspective in *Classroom Strategies*.]

6. Does the United States have "national writers"? Regional writers? Are American writers and artists expected to act as a "national conscience"? In what way?
[Answers should undoubtedly vary; they should be many.]

7. How are frame and core related in the cycle? Does one develop into the other, or were both conceived at once? Explain.
[See headnote and *Backgrounds* for a discussion of the chronological development of the cycle; this question assumes you will have mentioned that most of the inner poems were composed before the Dedication, Prologue, and Epilogues of 1940.]

8. How effective do you find the poem as a political protest? *Requiem* was not published until well after the purges were over and Stalin was dead; is it, then, totally lacking in influence?
[Answers will vary. Some will be content with intrinsic aesthetic value, others may find the poem too specific and therefore dated. You may wish to suggest—in line with traditional "masterpiece" values—that as long as situations of repression and political censorship exist anywhere, such a poem is potentially explosive in its assertion of civil rights and human values; and that it witnesses movingly to feelings that are timeless as long as children die and mothers grieve, even in a world of perfect freedom.]

## *Further Reading*

See also the reading suggestions in the anthology, pp. 1774–75.

An extremely well-done PBS documentary, "The Story of Anna Akhmatova," is available on videocassette.

Akhmatova, Anna. *Poems.* Translated by Lyn Coffin. 1983.
The introduction is written by Joseph Brodsky, who knew Akhmatova.

*Contemporary Poetry and Poetics.* Fall, 1988.
Several papers from a symposium on Akhmatova appear in this issue (pp. 7–44).

Driver, Sam. "Directions in Akhmatova's Poetry since the Early

Period." *Russian Language Journal*, Supplementary Issue: *Toward a Definition of Acmeism*, spring 1975, pp. 84–91).
Notes as a "new thematics" Akhmatova's increasing sense of "nostalgia for European cultural history."

Ketchian, Sonia. "Metempsychosis in the Verse of Anna Akhmatova." *Slavic and East European Journal*, 25, 1 [1981], pp. 44–60.
Examines the complex layers of reference in Akhmatova's poetry as coordinated with a theme of metempsychosis or the transmigration of souls.

Ketchian, Sonia and Connolly, Julian W., eds. *Studies in Russian Literature in Honor of Vsevolod Setchkarev*. 1986.
Sonia Ketchian agrues that the aspects of a Requiem by Armenian poet Hovannes Tumanian influenced Akhmatova's poem in "An Inspiration for Anna Akhmatova's *Requiem*."

McDuff, David. "Anna Akhmatova." *Parnassus: Poetry in Review*, Spring-Summer 1984, 11 (2), pp. 51–82.
Provides a perceptive, focused, and well-documented overview of Akhmatova's work in the context of political, personal, and literary events.

Rosslyn, Wendy. *The Prince, the Fool, and the Nunnery: The Religious Theme in the Early Poetry of Anna Akhmatova*. 1984.
A discussion of Akmatova's early religious poetry.

*Soviet Literature*, June, 1989.
This entire issue is devoted to Akmatova; it contains many interesting essays and also a translation of Requiem by Sergei Roy (pp. 67–73) that reproduces the poem's metrical and rhyming patterns; Roy also discusses the cultural context of these literary pattersn and how they would have been perceived by the Russian reader.

Terras, Victor. *Handbook of Russian Literature*.
The entry by Sonia Ketchian is a compact and lucid overview of the poet's work.

Verheul, Kees. *The Theme of Time in the Poetry of Anna Akhmatova*.
A detailed discussion of many important themes, formal strategies,

and historical contexts in Akhmatova's poetry, coordinated through their relationship to the concept of time.

(The Driver and Verheul references have much to offer the English reader, in spite of one marked limitation: Russian citations are not translated.)

# KATHERINE ANNE PORTER
## Flowering Judas

### Backgrounds

Katherine Anne Porter, one of the most brilliant literary stylists in American literature, is at once dazzling and resonant. A highly personal writer, she was disgusted by work in which, as she saw it, "poverty of feeling and idea were disguised, but not well enough, in tricky techniques and disordered syntax." Her own techniques are not tricky and her syntax is not disordered, and she may strike students as traditional. But, like that of other modernists, her work was intended to achieve "order and form and statement in a period of grotesque dislocations in a whole society when the world was heaving in the sickness of a millenial change."

As the title suggests, betrayal is at the center of "Flowering Judas." Braggioni, the fat, self-pitying revolutionary, appears to have betrayed the earnest ideals of the movement he leads through his love of luxury and his indifference to his fellow revolutionaries. Laura, the repressed, virginal *gringita*, has betrayed Eugenio—first by refusing his offer of love, then by delivering to him the drugs he uses to commit suicide. She has betrayed the children she teaches; even though she tries to love and take pleasure in them, they "remain strangers to her." Most important, perhaps, she betrays herself by rejecting "knowledge and kinship in one monotonous word. No. No. No," and by disguising her sexual coldness as earnest revolutionary idealism. Laura is afraid; she cannot live; she is "not at home in the world." It makes her, finally, a "cannibal" of others, a "murderer" of herself. When she eats the "warm, bleeding flowers" of the Judas tree in her nightmare vision, she symbolically participates in a sacrament of betrayal.

Porter establishes everything in deft, economical flashes. Braggioni (whose very name suggests his nature) "bulges marvelously in his expensive garments," his mouth "opens round and yearns sideways," he "swells with ominous ripeness," his ammunition belt is buckled "cruelly around his gasping middle" (pp. 1786–87). Braggioni as revolutionary is so completely savaged by this portrayal that it is difficult to take sufficient note of his continuing importance in the movement, and his necessary emphasis on the movement as a whole over mere individual mem-

---

bers of it. The reader must be aware of the extent to which Braggioni is portrayed in the story from Laura's perspective, and although her perspective undoubtedly reveals an important slice of the truth, it is nevertheless distorted by her own ascetic idealism. For Laura:

> the gluttonous bulk of Braggioni has become a symbol of her many disillusions, for a revolutionist should be lean, animated by heroic faith, a vessel of abstract virtues. This is nonsense, she knows it now and is ashamed of it. Revolution must have leaders, and leadership is a career for energetic men. She is, her comrades tell her, full of romantic error, for what she defines as cynicism in them is merely "a developed sense of reality."
>
> (p. 1786)

It is important, then, to notice that the very traits which have led to Braggioni's lewdly obese insolence—vanity, arrogance, self-love, malice, cleverness, love of pleasure, "hardness of heart"—are precisely those which have made him a "skilled revolutionist." He is, on the other hand, a man capable of certain sorts of love; he can sacrifice himself and accept sacrifice from others. He is capable of both revolutionary and amatory action. His ability to love begins with himself and oozes over those with whom he comes into contact.

Laura, however, lives paralyzed, in a waste land of self-repression. Her ideals remain intact, though she must sometimes struggle to maintain them. Her own taste requires fine handmade lace, a revolutionary heresy since "in her special group the machine is sacred, and will be the salvation of the workers." And she is still, significantly, engaged by the faith of her childhood.

> She was born a Roman Catholic, and in spite of her fear of being seen by someone who might make a scandal of it, she slips now and again into some crumbling little church, kneels on the chilly stone, and says a Hail Mary on the gold rosary she bought in Tehuantepec.
>
> (p. 1786)

Yet caught between her revolutionary sympathies and the sympathies of her own past, she finds the experience "no good" and ends by merely examining the tinseled altar and its presiding "male saint, whose lace-trimmed drawers hang limply around his ankles."

Laura's revolutionary activity is equally unfulfilling. She takes messages to and from people living in dark alleys; attends fruitless union meetings; ferries food and cigarettes and narcotics to sad, imprisoned men; she "borrows money from the Roumanian agitator to give to his bitter enemy the Polish agitator." She is found to be comforting and useful, but her revolutionary ardor is of little use when it comes to leading the revolution—for that, Braggioni is needed.

It is only in Laura's dream at the end of the story, a dream brought on by her recognition that by betraying Eugenio she has betrayed herself, that she comes to a horrifying understanding of her condition: her fear of love, of life. She awakes trembling at the sound of her own voice, "No!," and is afraid to sleep again. Porter ends the story here; we do not know if Laura's realization will save her from what she has become. Her dream, which as Robert Penn Warren wrote, "embodies but does not resolve the question," tantalizes us with its implications.

Porter once said, "everything I ever wrote in the way of fiction is based very securely on something real in life." "Flowering Judas" is modelled on an incident which happened to a friend of hers, Mary Doherty, during the Obregon revolution in Mexico. In a 1942 article, Porter wrote:

> The idea first came to me one evening when going to visit the girl I call Laura in the story, I passed the open window of her living room on my way to the door, through the small patio which is one of the scenes in the story. I had a brief glimpse of her sitting with an open book in her lap, but not reading, with a fixed look of pained melancholy and confusion in her face. The fat man I call Braggioni was playing the guitar and singing to her.

In a later interview (1965), she added more information:

> There was a man (you would know his name if I mentioned it, but I rolled four or five objectionable characters into that one man) who was showing Mary a little attention . . . . Goodness knows, nothing could be more innocent. But you know, she wasn't sure of him; so one day she asked me to come over and sit with her because so-and-so was going to come in the evening and sing a little bit and talk. She lived alone in a small apartment. The way I described the place was exactly as it was. There was a little round fountain, and what we call a flowering judas tree in full bloom over it. As I passed the open window, I saw this girl sitting like this, you see, and a man over there singing. Well, all of a sudden, I thought, 'That girl doesn't know how to take care of herself.'

Critics of the story have often noted that the background facts concerning Laura are distinctly similar to those in Porter's own experience: the Catholic upbringing, Porter's having been a teacher in Mexico, her involvement in revolutionary causes there, a stubbornly aesthetic sensibility. It is by no means difficult, then, to establish a biographical basis for "Flowering Judas," but it would be a mistake to lose sight of the degree to which Porter has transformed the raw data of her experience into fiction.

## Classroom Strategies

Students will be so absorbed by Porter's repellent picture of Braggioni that they may only gradually recognize the less appealing side of Laura's character: her negativity and her refusal of emotional attachment. Laura's apparent dedication and self-sacrifice initially present an attractive contrast to Braggioni's insolent exploitation. Before long, however, her repeated withdrawals from involvement, capped with Eugenio's death, establish Laura as a character whose spiritual betrayal is far more profound than the revolutionary leader's corruption. Braggioni is, strangely enough, successful in precisely the same area that Laura is deficient: he overflows with emotions.

One way of launching discussion of these two intertwined elements is to examine the first paragraph in class, emphasizing the off-putting description of Braggioni ("heaped upon the edge" of a chair he over-flows; "sitting there with a surly, waiting expression"; "pulling at his kinky yellow hair"; "snarling a tune . . .") but also the way that Laura avoids the situation, staying away from home as late as she can and then stoically enduring his presence. This palpable tension between two ways of life is developed throughout "Flowering Judas." If students are able to see Laura's characteristic turning-away early in the story, they will find it easier to recognize it's gradually accumulating themes of rejection ("No. No. No.") and self-betrayal, and to understand the final dream sequence in which Emilio calls her both cannibal and murderer.

Pointing out her resistance to Braggioni will not, in itself, be enough to suggest Laura's frigidity and her inability to love. Given Braggioni's nature, who wouldn't feel as she does? It will be important, then to demonstrate that she is unable to give love in any sense: as a divine lover in the Christian sense; as a collectivist lover of her fellow human beings in the revolutionary sense; or as an erotic lover. From her inability to respond to the schoolchildren's affection to her indifference to various suitors (including, possibly, Eugenio), she is engaged in "A negation of all external events," "denying everything" to remain untouched and preserve her immunity (p.1704).

Porter's exquisite and immensely suggestive prose style is hardly a problem; students who will understand nothing else will recognize its brilliance and clarity. Robert Penn Warren's essay, "Irony with a Center," contains a wonderful close reading of a passage from "Flowering Judas" (the paragraphs beginning with "Braggioni catches her glance" and ending with "you will know that Braggioni was your friend" [pp. 1786–87]) which will be of splendid aid in suggesting to students how Porter's prose works.

### Topics for Discussion and Writing

1. In what ways is Braggioni a failed revolutionary? In what ways is he successful?
   [See paragraphs 2–3 of *Backgrounds* for discussion.]

2. What's wrong with Laura? What is the significance of her dream at the end of the story? What has she betrayed? Why is the dream, like the story, bursting with Christian symbolism?
   [See paragraphs 2–6 of *Backgrounds*.]

3. How does the Judas-tree function both as tree and as symbol? Describe the various examples of betrayal in this story.

4. What scenes and details best illustrate the theme of negation?

### Further Reading

See also the suggestions in the anthology, p. 1784.

Bayley, Elizabeth, ed. *Letters of Katherine Anne Porter*. 1990.

Givner, Joan, ed. *Katherine Anne Porter: Conversations*. 1987. The writer's own views.

Lopez, Enrique Hank, ed. *Conversations with Katherine Anne Porter, Refugee from Indian Creek*. 1981.

Machann, Clinton and Clark, William Bedford, eds. *Katherine Anne Porter and Texas: An Uneasy Relationship*. 1990.

Tanner, James T. F. *The Texas Legacy of Katherine Anne Porter.* 1991.
Discusses Porter's work in light of her regional background.

Unrue, Darlene. *Understanding Katherine Anne Porter.* 1988.
A recent, general study.

Warren, Robert Penn, ed. *Katherine Anne Porter: A Collection of Essays.* Englewood Cliffs, 1979.
The essays by Warren ("Irony with a Center," mentioned above) and Welty, and the interview by Lopez are of particular interest.

West, Ray B. "Katherine Anne Porter: Symbol and Theme in 'Flowering Judas.'" *Accent* VII (Spring 1947), pp. 182–87.
An influential essay which emphasizes Christian imagery in the story.

# WILLIAM FAULKNER

Like other great moderns, Faulkner hungered for a mythology. He was content to construct *his* from his home country of north Mississippi, creating a region so firmly rural, so adamantly uncosmopolitan, that a child could be named Wall Street Panic Snopes in vague recognition of the world of big doings, of business and wars and interminglings of nations—a world utterly foreign to characters wrapped up entirely in their own country: enduring it and dying into it. His achievement was to create a fictional world for the American South—Yoknapatawpha, a land both real and imagined, encompassing an Indian past and a black past and present, the fading gentility of the Compsons and the thriving crassness of the Snopes, the eternal soil and rivers which coil and uncoil their histories, together with the wilderness and its legend of bear.

It was perhaps precisely because in the twenties the fixity of Southern life—its reliance on a set caste structure, its unwavering gaze backward to a time of glory—was beginning to waver, that the literary renaissance centered around Faulkner was possible. For Faulkner, the Southern past exercised a compelling influence, yet he was enough at odds with his heritage to be able to step outside, take its measure and commit its conflicts to literature.

## Barn Burning

### *Backgrounds*

"Barn Burning" was originally conceived as the opening chapter of *The Hamlet*. Perhaps because it appears to contradict, or at least qualify, a major theme of that novel—the inexorable rise of Snopesism—it was dropped from the novel, but it soon took up residence, complete in itself, as a short story.

The story has for center the conflict between family, with its "old fierce pull of blood," and a new version of order, a "peace and dignity" separate from and untouched by the tawdry, graceless malevolence so familiar to the story's young protagonist. The conflict is embodied in Sarty Snopes, a boy trapped in a recurrent family history: the family sets up as tenant farmers, some offense is committed, they are accused, they react by burning a barn, a trial ensues, they are sent packing, they go to another part of the state and set up again as tenant farmers, and so on, endlessly. Sarty's father is Ab Snopes, the clan's patriarch, a man of mechanical rigidity, with the "impervious quality of something cut ruthlessly from tin, depthless, as though, sidewise to the sun, it would cast no shadow" (p. 1803), a man who has set a lifetime of puny, "niggard blazes" for his family but who, when crossed, is capable of setting other men's property furiously ablaze.

Sarty is held tight to his father and his family by the ties of blood, the only ties Sarty knows or can know. When his father thinks Sarty might have betrayed the family while on the stand in the trial which opens the story, he strikes him and says:

> You're getting to be a man. You got to learn. You got to learn to stick to your own blood or you ain't going to have any blood to stick to you.
>
> (p. 1802)

Like his cringing mother, his older brother, his bovine sisters, the wagon, the gaunt mules, the battered stove, the broken clock, the worn broom, Sarty is inextricably tied to the never-ending, destructive round of his family's life, carted about when they move, present when the barns burn.

When Sarty and his father go to the plantation house of Major de Spain, however, the boy forgets "his father and the terror and despair both," as he encounters a world of people who are safe from his father's rigid malevolence:

> People whose lives are a part of this peace and dignity are beyond his touch, he no more to them than a buzzing wasp: capable of stinging for a little moment but that's all; the spell of this peace and dignity rendering even the barns and stable and cribs which belong to it impervious to the puny flames he might contrive...
>
> (pp. 1803)

For Sarty, the house registers a world of decency beyond his world; for his father the house registers a world which only humiliates him, and his response to humiliation is, as it always has been, to defile and destroy. His rug ruined, Major de Spain demands compensation, the Justice of the Peace supports him (though hardly to the worth of the rug), and Ab prepares to answer his humiliation in the way he always has. The family cycle has begun its inexorable motion.

This time, however, Sarty warns Major de Spain of his father's intentions. As Sarty runs from the scene, he hears gunshots, and believes his father dead. Sarty has broken free of the clan's cycle of recurrence, but grief and despair overwhelm him, he is alone now in a world where only the "slow constellations wheeled on." He walks away through the dark woods, whippoorwills registering the dawn of a new day, and does not look back.

Although our response to Ab Snopes should be measured first against Sarty's developing sense of decency, the story nevertheless suggests that Ab's iron rigidity and his pyromaniac malevolence have a basis in the social structure of Yoknapatawpha. Ab has a deep sense of "the preservation of integrity," a strong conviction of the rightness of his actions. He cannot tolerate any humiliation which comes from the direction of those in authority, especially when that authority is maintained by systematically subordinating others. As Ab leaves the great house, after having bestowed horse-dung on the Major's rug, he tells Sarty: "Pretty and white, ain't it? . . . That's sweat. Nigger sweat. Maybe it ain't white enough yet to suit him. Maybe he wants to mix some white sweat with it" (p. 1804). That Ab has a ferociously unlovely notion of integrity is undeniable, but his single-minded rejection of authority nevertheless suggests that he is in some measure another of those figures of resistance who criticize the existing social structure by attempting to destroy it. That "Barn Burning" allows for this view of Ab Snopes might have been another reason for Faulkner's dropping it from The Hamlet, since in that book, and the subsequent books which trace the rise of the Snopeses, Snopesism is to be understood as a purely diabolical version of evil.

### Classroom Strategies

"Barn Burning" can be taught in one class period, as can "Spotted Horses." If you are able to teach both, "Barn Burning," because it is less obviously a "set piece," should probably be taught first.

The central issues of "Barn Burning" will be evident to most students on the first reading. Any problems will probably have to do with the story's narrative technique. As always in Faulkner, the design of the story is the design of its telling. "Barn Burning" is told from a third-person limited point of view, the central consciousness being Sarty's. Sarty therefore becomes the measure of what we know in the story even when what he thinks is not necessarily the case. Sarty, for instance, thinks his father has been shot by Major de Spain; as we discover from later books in the Snopes saga, this is not so. That Ab was not shot, however, should not diminish our response to Sarty's grief and terror at the story's end; Sarty *assumes* his father's death and his responsibility for it, and this is what the reader must respond to.

Faulkner's narrative allows him to move rapidly in both space and time; periodically, present and future appear simultaneously. We hear Sarty's voice as a boy in all of its colloquial vigor, both in dialogue and in interior monologue ("ourn! mine and hisn both!"). But we are also allowed to hear a version of the mature Sarty, a Sarty who can look back on the events of the story in an attempt to understand their significance: "Later, twenty years later, he was to tell himself, 'If I had said they wanted only truth, justice, he would have hit me again'" (p. 1802).

The opening paragraph of the story offers a splendid display of Faulkner's narrative gifts; we are able to visualize the country store in which the Justice of the Peace holds court, but we are simultaneously so far inside Sarty that we share in his raging hunger as well as his fear and despair. Faulkner manages this through the use of synesthesia, the merging together of various senses:

> from where he sat he could see the ranked shelves close-packed with the solid, squat, dynamic shapes of tin cans whose labels his stomach read, not from lettering which meant nothing to his mind but from the scarlet devils and the silver curve of fish—this, the cheese which he knew he smelled and the hermetic meat which his intestines believed he smelled coming in intermittent gusts momentarily and brief between the other constant one...
>
> (p. 1798–99)

The end of the story places Sarty in an environment which is again fully realized in realistic terms, but which serves as an almost Dantesque symbolic setting for his grief and loneliness. He is in a "dark woods," alone in the natural world with the wheeling constellations and whip-poorwills, severed entirely from both his family and the peace and dignity represented by the house of Major de Spain. Faulkner uses the traditional imagery of regeneration in this last paragraph: it is spring, day is breaking, and Sarty has no option but to walk down the road toward a new life—one quite different, we have been led to suspect, from the one he is leaving.

1. What kind of narrative technique is Faulkner using in "Barn Burning? What is the point of view? What difference does it make to our understanding of the story that Faulkner uses Sarty as the central consciousness? What would the story be like if Ab, or Major de Spain, were the central consciousness?
[See paragraphs 1–3 of *Classroom Strategies* for discussion.]

2. What is the central conflict in "Barn Burning"? What is Sarty's family life like? How do we know?
[See *Backgrounds* for discussion.]

3. How is Ab's rigid, mechanical quality suggested? Is there any justification for his behavior?
[See paragraphs 2 and 6 of *Backgrounds* for discussion.]

4. What does Major de Spain's house symbolize? Is its symbolic meaning clear?
[See paragraph 4 of *Backgrounds* for discussion.]

5. Why does Sarty warn Major de Spain at the end of the story? Is his action justified?
[See paragraphs 4–5 of *Backgrounds* for discussion.]

6. Does it matter that, in later books, we find out that Ab was not, as Sarty thinks, shot by Major de Spain?
[See paragraph 2 of *Classroom Strategies* for discussion.]

## Spotted Horses

### Backgrounds

"Spotted Horses," a story that was later incorporated in revised form into *The Hamlet*, apparently has its origins in a horse auction witnessed by the young Faulkner from the porch of a boarding house in the village of Pittsboro, Mississippi. The horses up for sale were so wild they were tied together with barbed wire. The story also partakes of a number of traditions, all belonging to the American tall tale as descended from earlier practitioners such as Longstreet and Mark Twain. First of all, it is *told*—not just narrated—by a witness not directly involved in the action, in this case an honest (perhaps too honest for his own material good) sewing machine salesman named Ratliff. The teller uses his own highly colorful vocabulary and idiom. He exaggerates shamelessly, taking things to the edge of natural possibility and just beyond, leaving them in the miraculous for a long breath before setting them back on earth. (Faulkner served as one inspiration for the magical realism of Gabriel Garcia Marquez, another member of a traditional society beginning to dissolve.) The telling renders the narration dramatic, as when one of the passel of ponies encounters a wagon containing the sleeping Tull family:

> They waked up when the horse hit the bridge one time, but Tull said the first he knew was when the mules tried to turn the wagon around in the middle of the bridge and he seen that spotted varmint run right twixt the mules and run up the wagon tongue like a squirrel. He said he just had time to hit it across the face with his whip-stock, because about that time the mules turned the wagon around on that ere one-way bridge and that horse clumb across one of the mules and jumped down onto the bridge again and went on, with Vernon standing up in the wagon and kicking at it.
>
> Tull said the mules turned in the harness and clumb back into the wagon too, with Tull trying to beat them out again, with the reins wrapped around his wrist. After that he says all he seen was overturned chairs and womenfolks' legs and white drawers shining in the moonlight, and his mules and that spotted horse going on up the road like a ghost.
>
> (p. 1820)

The story balances action against inaction; Mrs. Armstid sitting all day in her wagon "as if carved outen wood," against the pony who bursts into Mrs. Littlejohn's house "like a fourteen-foot pinwheel." Thus contrasted, both motion and stillness take on a cartoon-like ferocity.

Closely tied to this contrast is one between predictability and capriciousness: the Texan man tirelessly eating gingersnaps and then looking carefully into the empty box; Henry Armstid doggedly insisting "I bought a horse;" Eck Snopes's son's unfailing luck under the hooves of the spotted horses, who are the very embodiment of chaos—violating the well-ordered world of Mrs. Littlejohn's boarding house and turning the peaceful countryside into a scattering of cries of "Whooy. Head him!"

The story's human embodiment of unpredictability is the notorious Flem Snopes. He appears in the first sentences ("Yes, sir. Flem Snopes has filled that whole country full of spotted horses" [p. 1812]) as a transformative agent of chaos. He is that common feature of the tall tale, the trickster: a creature so wily that he is never caught in the act, but performs his tricks secretly, at one remove, profiting from anything, but most of all from the predictable foolishness of his fellow humans. Flem is a special, hardy breed of trickster: one who is never tricked, never gets his comeuppance. His secret power, as explained by Ratliff, lies in the ambivalence he inspires. He is a repulsive cheat and a crook, but such a good one that he draws admiration even from his prey: "Why, that fellow could make a nickel where it wasn't but four cents to begin with. He skun me in two trades, myself, and the fellow that can do that, I just hope he'll get rich before I do; that's all" (p. 1813). Perhaps because of his rare ability to transcend his circumstances (among other things, to transform himself from store clerk to store owner), Flem is a constant source of pride for his community. What Ratliff believes, and the story demonstrates, is that it is very absorbing to watch just what and how much Flem can get away with.

### Classroom Strategies

Once students have become accustomed to Faulkner's prose style, "Spotted Horses" will not seem as difficult to follow, and it will show them that pure, risible joy is among the satisfactions that masterpieces can supply.

The colloquial vigor of "Spotted Horses" overrides whatever minor confusion that may be caused by its highly colorful dialect. Students may, however, find some of the attitudes displayed by the characters difficult to comprehend. Why are Mr. Armstid and the other men so smitten with spotted-horse mania, since it is obvious that the horses are good for nothing but stirring up dust? Why does Mrs. Armstid bow to her husband's bad judgment (and to Flem Snopes's chicanery)? It can be pointed out that the ponies, arriving from a mythical and impressive Texas, bring with them excitement and a certain glamor—along with the surefire attraction, imparted by the Texas man, of a *bargain*. In contrast to the long-suffering, hang-dog Mrs. Armstid we have Mrs. Littlejohn: a woman fairly bursting with indignation over the folly of menfolk, who defends her domain from the horses by splitting a washboard over one of their foreheads, and who takes capable charge of the wounded Mr. Armstid.

## Topics for Discussion and Writing

1. How does description contribute to characterization in "Spotted Horses"?
   [See particularly the descriptions of Mrs. Littlejohn and Mrs. Armstid in Section VI of the story.]

2. Discuss the contrast Faulkner creates between male foolishness and female steadiness in "Spotted Horses." Does it have basis in fact? (This is guaranteed to raise the temperature of the discussion.)

3. Is the Texas man the same breed of con-man as Flem Snopes? Why or why not?

4. The editor at Scribner's, where "Spotted Horses" was originally published, described it as "a tall tale with implications of tragedy." What are these implications?

## Further Reading

See also the suggestions in the anthology, p. 1798.

Blotner, Joseph. *Selected Letters of William Faulkner*. New York, 1977.
A useful selection of the letters, basic to an understanding of Faulkner's life.

Bradford, M. E. "Family and Community in Faulkner's 'Barn Burning.'" *Southern Review* 17 (April, 1981): pp. 332–39.
Explores Sarty's ties to his clan.

Budd, Louis J. and Cady, Edwin H., ed. *On Faulkner*. 1989.
Assembles essays (chiefly on the novels) from three decades of *American Literature*. See especially "The Symbolist Connnection" by Alexander Marshall III, pp. 269–81.

Ruppersburg, Hugh M. *Voice and Eye in Faulkner's Fiction*. Athens, Georgia, 1983.
A discussion of narrative perspective in Faulkner, with concentration on the major novels.

Skei, Hans H. *William Faulkner: The Novelist as Short Story Writer: A Study of WIlliam Faulkner's Short Fiction*. 1985.
Discusses stories in chronological order with thematic interpretations related to social psychology; the analysis emphasizes narrative strategy, point of view, and the stories' relation to Faulkner's novels.

Vickery, Olga. *The Novels of William Faulkner: A Critical Interpretation*. Baton Rouge, 1959; revised edition, 1964.
An early but useful general study.

Volpe, Edmund. *A Reader's Guide to William Faulkner*. New York, 1964.
A cogent examination of Faulkner's works.

Warren, Robert Penn, ed. *Faulkner: A Collection of Critical Essays*. Englewood Cliffs, 1966.

Watson, James G. *William Faulkner, Letters and Fiction*. 1987.
An imaginative and well-documented study of Faulkner's epistolary style—his "writing practice"—in both letters and fiction.

Zender, Karl F., ed. *The Crossing of the Ways: William Faulkner, the South, and the Modern World*. 1989.
Presents ten interesting essays on the evolution of selected themes in Faulkner's novels; relevant to "Barn Burning" is Richard C. Moreland's "Compulsive and Revisionary Repetition: Faulkner's 'Barn Burning' and the Craft of Writing Difference'" (pp. 48–70).

# BERTOLT BRECHT
## Mother Courage and Her Children

### Backgrounds

With Ibsen, Chekhov, Strindberg, and Pirandello, Brecht belongs on any list of influential modern playwrights. Though his reputation is based on his plays, he was also a talented poet, an accomplished fiction writer, and a crucially important theatrical theorist. It has often been said that the socially committed Marxist in Brecht was at odds with, and often overwhelmed by, his poetic and dramatic powers as well as his temperamental anarchism and zestful cynicism; *Mother Courage* is often cited as a case in point. There should, however, be no doubt as to his commitment to social reform and social justice and his persistent anti-individualism. Equally indisputable are his vitality, his compassion, and his extraordinary use of language in its most vigorous and dramatic forms.

*Mother Courage* is a play in which Brecht's stated intentions and the audience's reactions are almost invariably at odds. Mother Courage is often seen as an heroic figure, as Robert Brustein says, "an image of the 'little people,' beleaguered by forces beyond their control, yet resiliently continuing to make their way." We are inclined to see Mother Courage as a pathetic victim of war and to invest our sympathies in what happens to her and her children. This view of Mother Courage runs diametrically counter to Brecht's intentions, and it made him furious.

Brecht intended Mother Courage to demonstrate how even the most binding and basic of commitments—a mother's desire to protect her children—can be forgotten when it runs counter to the interests of material survival. Even her nickname is ironic; she received it after she had driven like a madwoman through the bombardment of Riga in order to save fifty loaves of molding bread she had in her wagon. Mother Courage has capitulated—to the commercial instinct, to the vicissitudes of war, but most of all to the belief that it is necessary to capitulate in order to survive. The "Song of the Great Capitulation" in Scene Four, although provoked by a small surrender on the part of a young soldier who "won't put up with injustice," encapsulates what has happened to Mother Courage. In the beginning she believed she was "quite the cheese," a special case, with looks and talent and a love for "the higher things." But when the war began, when she found herself alone with two children on her hands, unable to eat, she also found that her earlier ideals were simply so much idealist fluff.

> And before one single year had wasted
> I had learned to swallow down the bitter brew....
> Man, the double-edged shellacking that I tasted
> On my ass and knees I was when they were through.
> (You've got to get along with people,
> one good turn deserves another,
> no use trying to ram your head through the wall!)

(p. 1860)

The "chickadee," the voice of experience, was quite right. Mother Courage had gone:

> marching with the show
> In step, however fast or slow...

(p. 1860)

Mother Courage is the only character in the play who is fully dramatized; only her children and Yvette have anything more than generic names. This is *her* play, and what she does, how she reacts to events, is meant to be the focus of our critical attention. She is, in fact, the only character who functions as anything more than an emblem. Brecht's intention, of course, was to diminish our ability to identify with the characters as if they were "real" people, since identification with them as individuals, he felt, would only interfere with our contemplation and criticism of them. This was the goal of the so-called "alienation effect"— to keep the audience detached from the characters in order to judge them and thus learn from them.

Mother Courage's children, it has been said, represent the cardinal virtues: bravery (Eilif), honesty (Swiss Cheese), and pity (Kattrin). But Brecht wants us to see that, in the context of war, these virtues are all dubious. Eilif's bravery is mere impulsive foolishness, a lust for glory. Swiss Cheese's honesty is incautiously simple-minded. Kattrin's pity is perhaps the only virtue of the three which Brecht sees as positive, because it expresses itself in terms of kindness. But, much like William Blake in *Songs of Innocence and of Experience*, Brecht wants us to be aware that pity is only necessary when there is something to be pitied, and that our job should be to eliminate pity by eliminating the need for it. At the beginning of the play, all three children are with their mother; by the end all three are dead, and they die while their mother is haggling about the price of her wagon, new provisions, or used shirts. Though Mother Courage claims that all she wants to do is to "get through, me and my children and my wagon" (p. 1866), Brecht makes it clear that by making a profit from the war she has inextricably joined it, and that by joining it she betrays her children. In Scene Seven she wears a "necklace of silver talers" that recalls Judas, and announces that war is a "business."

Mother Courage's children die, however, not simply because their mother's attention has been diverted by possibilities of profit; they die as a consequence of their virtues. Swiss Cheese dies because he is too honest to betray the fact that he has rescued the regimental cashbox from the soldiers who have overrun his camp. Eilif dies after he repeats a feat of bravery for which he had been proclaimed a hero. Unfortunately for Eilif, this time he exercises his bravery during a brief armistice and is executed as a looter. Kattrin overhears a plan to besiege the town of Halle; because she cannot stand the idea of innocent women and children being killed she rouses the town by beating a drum and is shot by the soldiers. Brecht wants to insist not only that these virtues cannot survive in wartime conditions, but that they shouldn't be necessary at all. As Mother Courage herself says: "You don't need virtues in a decent country, the people can all be perfectly ordinary, medium-bright, and cowards too for my money" (p. 1841).

Cowardice is, in fact, the only human quality that ensures survival. Mother Courage is, as Robert Brustein says, "the supreme advocate of adaptation and acquiescence." The survivors in the play are those who acquiesce most quickly and fully: Yvette, the camp whore, who ends by marrying a rich colonel; the Chaplain, who switches religious allegiances when it's expedient; the Cook, for whom the war provides a lasting job, ample food, and plenty of opportunities to turn women's heads; and, of course, Mother Courage herself.

The play ends with Mother Courage, alone, pulling her wagon after another regiment as it moves toward another battle. Her wagon is, perhaps, the only one of her children that she has been fully committed to. The war which has gone on for so long will continue for another twelve years, and Mother Courage—and people like her—will continue to cry "Hey, take me with you!"

In *Mother Courage*, Brecht wished to communicate to his audience the real nature of war. He wanted to reveal it as essentially a big-business, profit-making venture which must at all costs be avoided. His purpose was not to create static emotions of pity and fear toward a Mother Courage trapped by unavoidable circumstances of Fate, but rather to instill in his audience both the critical ability to see war as it is—an entrenched social institution which can be alleviated—and a dynamic, long-range anger to alleviate it.

Brecht became a committed Marxist in 1926 and, though he periodically had difficulty following the propaganda requirements of "socialist realism," he believed that his work was more effective in reforming society than anything the party officials had to offer. In 1931 he wrote, "Today when human character must be understood as the 'totality of all social conditions' the epic form is the only one that can comprehend all the processes which could serve the drama as materials for a fully representative picture of the world."

In 1939, when he wrote *Mother Courage*, his political principles had an even more pressing enemy than the bourgeoisie, which he despised. Hitler's Fascist Germany was just about to provoke World War II by invading Poland, and Brecht was living in exile in Scandinavia. The threat of the coming war, the revving up of the military engines, supplied much of the bitterness and cynicism imbedded in *Mother Courage*.

When asked by an interviewer to name the strongest literary influence in his life, Brecht said, "You will laugh: the Bible!" Martin Esslin has pointed out the masterly use he makes of Biblical constructions: "the juxtaposition of contrasted half-sentences, parallelism, repetition, and inversion." Allusions to the Bible and parodies of Biblical events and images are evident throughout his work, including *Mother Courage*.

Brecht was also influenced by the street ballad, a form practiced with particular vigor in Weimar Berlin. Not only did the ballad have its origins in the working and peasant classes, but it was a wonderfully coarse and expressive way to protest what he saw as the overrefined gentility of the German poetic and dramatic tradition.

Brecht was openly influenced by so many different writers that he has been accused, much like T. S. Eliot, of plagiarism and lack of originality. Indeed, he adapted for his own use work by Shakespeare, Christopher Marlowe, John Gay, and Jaroslav Hasek, the Czech satirist whose anti-war novel *The Good Soldier Schweik* foreshadows elements of Mother Courage. Another influence of continuing importance was the nineteenth-century German expressionist Georg Buechner, whom he considered the greatest of German dramatists.

The figure of Mother Courage derives from Grimmelshausen's seventeenth-century *Simplicissimus*, but bears little relation to what happens in that novel other than to reflect its earthy, picaresque qualities.

## Classroom Strategies

*Mother Courage* can be taught in two class periods. One period should ideally be given to discussing Brecht's notion of "epic" theatre, the play's episodic structure, and Brecht's use of "alienation" effects— that is to say, stage practices (like sung ballads in rhyme) that break theatrical illusion and remind the audience they are sitting at a play. Another may be used to examine closely the character of Mother Courage, but you will need to keep a tight rein on the students' likely tendency to read her as a sympathetic and heroic figure of endurance.

The chief problem to confront will be the students' initial difficulty in following the action, or in making overall sense out of a rapid succession of digressive episodes. People come, people go, people quarrel, people barter, people die; the war and its soldiers pass to and fro behind the ever-present wagon in a seemingly endless procession.

Since these are characteristics of the play which are directly related to Brecht's conception of what a play should be, it will be important for you to explain at least the bare outlines of the effect Brecht is after and how he goes about getting it.

*The Episodic Structure*: The play has twelve scenes, or episodes, each self-contained, and each intended to demonstrate a particular aspect of war and its effects. The episodic structure is similar in many ways to the medieval cycle plays which, like Brecht's epic theatre, were essentially didactic. In such a structure, many characters can pass through circumstances rather than become trapped in them. Like other aspects of epic drama, the episodic structure is intended to display its artificiality. Audiences (and readers) should always be aware that they are watching (or reading) a dramatic parable and then, Brecht hoped, learn from what they see.

*The Summaries of Each Episode*: Brecht summarizes what will happen in each episode before the scene begins. On stage, these summaries are displayed on placards or projected on a screen. His purpose was to eliminate suspense, our interest in what is going to happen next, so that we will contemplate the scene intellectually and critically.

*The Use of Historical Locale*: By distancing the play's events in space and time, Brecht hoped to remove the sense of immediacy which led to identification with characters, and to emphasize how the past relates to the present. The Thirty Years War, in which approximately half the German population died, provided a perfect setting for his purposes.

*The Lack of Characterization*: Brecht directed his actors to demonstrate their characters' attitudes, not "become" those characters. He compared this kind of acting to "an eyewitness demonstrating to a collection of people how a traffic accident took place. . . . He never forgets, nor does he allow anyone to forget, that he is not the one whose action is being demonstrated, but the one who demonstrates it." The effect was to alienate or distance the audience emotionally from what was happening on stage, and help them to retain an attitude of critical detachment.

*The Use of Traditional Imagery*: Brecht uses a great deal of Biblical imagery in his work. Because it was unlikely to be shocking or surprising, audiences were able to follow its meaning as well as the ironic use Brecht made of it. He also uses the imagery of the common life: one might note, for instance, the way he uses images of meat and how he relates them to the notion that men are just so much meat that the war will grind up. Scene Two, in which Eilif tells how he made his men "ravenous for meat" and bravely liberated some oxen from the peasants, is dominated by the General's loud shouts for meat. The actual meat in the scene is a scrawny capon provided by Mother Courage, who also— we cannot fail to understand—provided another kind of meat, her son Eilif, to the army.

*The Use of Songs*: Brecht was, naturally, interested in the ballad form because it is so closely tied to the working and peasant classes. He often reserves some of his most crucial declarations for songs. Their use also undercuts the illusion of reality in the play, interrupts the flow of the story, and renders the action strange and unfamiliar, thus further distancing the audience.

To explore Brecht's methods, you might concentrate on one particular scene—Scene Eleven, for instance. Here Kattrin is literally dumb—"a soldier stuffed something in her mouth when she was little"—and symbolically dumb. In war, kindness, which is her great virtue, is silenced. She is nevertheless left alone with the wagon while Mother Courage attempts to buy stocks cheap from the townspeople, who are frightened that they will soon be besieged. The irony of Mother Courage's absence in this scene (and the reasons for her absence) is central to our response to it. The townspeople are quite right to be afraid. Some Catholic soldiers capture a peasant farmhouse in which Kattrin is waiting, and she over- hears them discussing the coming ambush of the town. The captured peasants, afraid for their family in town, pray to God to save their four grandchildren. Their prayer, which is quite moving, may not be heard by God, but it is heard by Kattrin. She climbs to the top of the farmhouse roof and begins to beat her drum in order to rouse the town. The drum, which Brecht used in earlier scenes (along with pipes) to suggest the misguided glorification of soldiering, is used here as an instrument of active resistance to war. For the first time in the play, someone—Kattrin- does not capitulate, does not do the expedient thing. The soldiers, fearing their plot will be revealed, and the peasant farmers, who fear "she'll be the death of us all," attempt to stop her. Their comments are bitingly ironic. The same peasant woman who, just moments before, had asked God for aid, now yells at Kattrin:

Have you no pity? Have you no heart? We're dead if they find out it's us! They'll run us through!

(p. 1883)

The Lieutenant, who returns to see just what is going on, cries out:

If I give you my word? I'm an officer, you can trust my word of honor. She drums still louder. Nothing is sacred to her.

(p. 1883)

Both soldiers and peasants then try to smother the sounds Kattrin makes by making noises of their own, peaceful noises like chopping wood. Kattrin is amazed to see captors and captives working so freneti- cally to prevent her from saving lives. The Old Peasant resists the burn- ing of his house because, as he says, "If the city people see fire up here, they'll know what's afoot" (p. 1884). The world has turned upside down, and even Kattrin has to laugh. She then beats her drum even more fer- vently. Nothing stops her—they threaten to smash the wagon, the sol- diers beat one of the peasants with a pike, they threaten her life. Finally, fresh out of threats, they shoot her. But her action does rouse the town; a cannon goes off, the alarms are sounded and, for the time being at least, the town is saved. Unlike the peasants, the soldiers, the townspeople, and Mother Courage, Kattrin has not survived—but she is, in Brecht's terms, the only truly brave character in the play, and the only successful one.

Robert Brustein has suggested that the most useful way to "see" the play is to see it from the perspective of a belligerent pacifist, one who "loathes military heroism," and finds that "heroic actions invariably stem either from stupidity, insanity, brutality, or simple human error." By establishing this perspective as a given, you should find it easier to convince your students of its value as a social document. Subsequently, by concentrating on Brecht's extraordinary innovations in theatrical technique and his ability to turn those innovations into vital dramatic action, you should find it easier to convince students of the play's value as an aesthetic whole.

### Topics for Discussion and Writing

1. In what ways is Mother Courage a hero? In what ways is she a villain? Which did Brecht intend her to be? How do we know?
   [See *Backgrounds* for discussion.]

2. In what ways does Mother Courage capitulate?
   [See paragraph 3 of *Backgrounds* for discussion.]

3. Mother Courage thinks she can use the war to make a profit and protect her children at the same time. Why does she fail?

4. What is "epic theatre"? How does it differ from conventional theatre? What are "alienation" effects? Discuss some that appear in *Mother Courage*.
   [See *Classroom Strategies* for discussion.]

5. How does Brecht treat locality in this play? How does he treat historical time? Why is the play set during the Thirty Years War?
   [See paragraph 6 of *Classroom Strategies* for discussion.]

6. Eric Bentley says that each of Mother Courage's children represent a cardinal virtue. What are the virtues? What does *Mother Courage* demonstrate about them?

[See paragraphs 5–7 of *Backgrounds* for discussion.]

7. What is the symbolic significance of making Kattrin dumb? What is the symbolic significance of her beating a drum at the end of the play?
[See paragraph 5 of *Backgrounds* and paragraph 10 of *Classroom Strategies* for discussion.]

## Further Reading

See also the reading suggestion in the anthology, p. 1830.

Bartram, Graham and Waine, eds. Anthony. *Brecht in Perspective.* 1982.
A collection of thirteen essays on historical, literary, and theatrical perspectives, including a discussion of Brecht's legacy for German dramatists and the English theater.

Brustein, Robert. *The Theatre of Revolt.* Boston, 1964.
The chapter on Brecht is particularly well-written and enlightening.

*The Drama Review* 12,1 (Fall, 1967).
A special Brecht issue.

Eaton, Katherine Bliss. *The Theater of Meyerhold and Brecht.* 1985.
Considers Brecht's relationship to "epic theater" and twentieth-century experimental theater techniques.

Esslin, Martin. *Brecht, a Choice of Evils: A Critical Study of the Man, His Work, and His Opinions.* 1984.
The revised fourth edition of Esslin's early study of Brecht and his work. Includes a chronology and a descriptive list of works.

Fuegi, John. *Bertolt Brecht: Chaos, According to Plan.* 1987.
Provides a general view of Brecht's work with actors in concrete theatrical situation.

Gray, Ronald. *Bertolt Brecht.* New York, 1961.
A good short introduction.

Kiebuzinska, Christine Olga. *Revolutionaries in the Theater: Meyerhold, Brecht, and Witkiewicz.* 1988.

Lug, Sieglinde. "The 'Good' Woman Demystified" from *Communications from the International Brecht Society*, November 1984: 14 (1), pp. 3–16.
Uses a feminist approach in discussing *Mother Courage* and two other plays by Brecht.

Pike, David. *Lukács and Brecht.* 1985.
Discusses the famous Brecht-Lukács debate over experimental of conventionally realistic form.

Rouse, John. "Brecht and the Contradictory Actor" from *Theatre Journal*, March 1984: 36 (1), pp. 25–41.
Focuses on *Mother Courage* as the main example in a valuable analysis of Brecht's methods when working with the ensemble.

Speirs, Ronald. *Bertolt Brecht.* 1987.
A study of the drama that includes a brief biography and chapters on five major plays, including *Mother Courage* (pp. 91–115).

Willett, John. *The Theatre of Bertolt Brecht: A Study of Eight Aspects.* New York: New Directions, 1959.
Very good on theatrical influences and stage practice, with a useful discussion of Brecht's use of music.

———. *Brecht in Context: Comparative Approaches.* 1984.
Diverse interdisciplinary topics.

Witt, Hubert, ed. *Brecht As They Knew Him.* Translated by John Peet. New York, 1974.
Short memoirs of Brecht.

Wright, Elizabeth. *Postmodern Brecht: A Re-presentation.* 1989.
A valuable study that rejects period-oriented views of Brecht's career and demonstrates the continuing importance of his theoretical pieces and early works.

# FEDERICO GARCIA LORCA
## Lament for Ignacio Sánchez Mejías

### *Backgrounds*

Federico García Lorca is a poet of myth, of emotion, of rhythmic language, of the earth. The most internationally famous Spanish writer since Cervantes, his visionary poetry and his death at the hands of Franco's militia have already made him a symbol of the artist's opposition to the sterility of the modern industrial West, and to the impersonal repressions of the fascist police state. Lorca's imaginative roots reach into the past and the countryside: into the folklore and folk imagery, gypsy legends, ballad rhythms, and pastoral landscape of his native Andalusia. He maintains the mysterious life of nature and the subconscious in the midst of a highly civilized—perhaps over-civilized—society, and seems to speak directly from the life of his dreams and personal emotions. To a reader of Spanish, Lorca's lyric rhythms and the dense, allusive network of his imagery compose a poetic voice unique in modern literature.

Death is the central theme in "Lament for Ignacio Sánchez Mejías," as it is in all of Lorca's work. One critic calls him "the poet of death" and notes that Spain has an ancient popular tradition of the "culture of death" which he continually, and naturally, exploits. The bull has long been the characteristic symbol of death in Spain—as in other Mediterranean cultures—and in the "Lament" it possesses the terrors of darkness that gather around the finality that everyone must face. The confrontation with death is, for Lorca, at its most impressive and spectacular in the bullfight: the "greatest poetic and human treasure of Spain" and "the most cultured pastime in the world today; it is pure drama . . . the only place where one can go and with certainty see death surrounded by the most astonishing beauty."

In "Lament," bulls and bullfighting, death and the spilling of blood, permeate every passage, and Sanchez Mejias's death takes on the power of a religious sacrifice. In Section I, "Cogida and Death," the bull invades Sanchez Mejias's body ("a thigh with a desolate horn . . . . the bull was bellowing through his forehead") and the images of the bullring merge with those of the hospital ("the bullring was covered in iodine") in which Sanchez Mejias lies dying. In Section II, "The Spilled Blood," Lorca invokes the bulls of Guisando, "partly death and partly stone" who bellow "like two centuries / Sated with treading the earth." Later in the same section, as the moment of the goring approaches, "secret voices" shout to "celestial bulls." Overseeing all is the "cow of the ancient world"—mother of bulls, mother of men—who passes her "sad tongue / over a snout of blood / Spilled on the sand."

For Sanchez Mejias, as for Lorca, the bullfight is like a religious ceremony in which priest and congregation alike take part: he has gone "up the tiers / with all his death on his shoulders" and spilled his blood before "a thirsty multitude." The blood—always a symbol of vitality and passion in Lorca's work (the "nightingale of his veins!")—is the medium of sacrifice, a blood so marvelous and potent "No chalice can contain it."

In Section I, the poet encounters the moment of death at the instant of its happening. Section II presents his rejection of it ("No. / I will not see it!") and his simultaneous attempt to universalize it: to give it a meaning beyond itself. In Section III, "The Laid Out Body," the poet attempts to come to grips with death, to accommodate its finality. The section is calmer, more resigned, less hyperbolic. The poet encounters the niggardly meanness of death and asks for answers. There are none, and his final claim—"even the sea dies!"—is cold consolation.

The elegiac occasion gives full play to Lorca's myth-making, surrealistic imagination. That he called it a "Lament" assures us, says one critic, that it will depend heavily on Lorca's personal emotions. And indeed, though Sanchez Mejias is always at the center of the poem, forever praised, its most powerful presence is the despairing and urgent voice of the speaker. It is through the speaker's impassioned response and poetic insistence, his ability to involve the bullfighter in a larger drama of universal feeling, that Sanchez Mejias will be remembered. He may well have been "a great torero in the ring," and a "good peasant in the sierra" but only the poet can make his strength "like a river of lions" and his blood sing "along marshes and meadows." In Section IV, "The Absent Soul," Lorca recognizes the oblivion to which death consigns us, how in death we are forgotten "in a heap of lifeless dogs." And so the poet must sing in an effort to defeat oblivion, even though he knows that his song will be but "a sad breeze through the olive trees."

Ignacio Sanchez Mejias was severely gored in Manzanares on August 11, 1934 and died two days later in Madrid. He was one of the most eminent bullfighters in Spain at the time and a man of surprising talent as a dramatist. His intellectual interests were wide-ranging, a fact which no doubt contributed to Lorca's powerful sense of loss upon his death.

The bullfight—where the bullfighter quite literally faces death in a mounting sequence of dangerous ritual actions—and the *cante jondo*, the traditional music of Andalusia, are the primary cultural influences on "Lament." In one of the most famous of his essays, Lorca attempted to find the essence, the "marrow of forms," of successful art in the "dark sounds" of what the Andalusians call *duende*, the "spirit of the earth," the "mysterious power that everyone feels but that no philosopher has explained":

> The duende is a power and not a behavior, it is a struggle and not a concept. I have heard an old guitarist master say: "The duende is not in the throat; the duende surges up from the soles of the feet." It is not a matter of ability, but of real live form; of blood; of ancient culture; of creative action.

It was in his native culture, in its traditional forms and feelings, that Lorca located the *duende* he wanted to infuse into his own verse.

### Classroom Strategies

"Lament for Ignacio Sanchez Mejias" can be taught in one class period. You may wish to compare Lorca with other poets—Rilke, Stevens, and Baudelaire come to mind—to suggest the range of modern poetry and poetics. Students who are able to read the original Spanish passages printed in the text (pp. 1896–97) should be encouraged to read aloud to the class, and to comment on any rhythmic effects or verbal associations that they feel are lost in translation.

In general, American students will have little understanding of the bullfight as such. The bullfight is *not* a sport; it is a ritual. For Lorca's poem, it is the basis from which the action starts, like the appearance of the ghost in *Hamlet* or Agamemnon's sacrifice of his daughter Iphigenia in the *Oresteia*. Students will be impressed with the play of Lorca's imagination over the event. They will also be impressed by the way the poem follows the stages that psychologists say all of us go through when we encounter death: recognition, refusal, questioning, resignation, and acceptance.

They may not always be able to "follow" the language line-by-line. Lorca's use of archetypal and Spanish imagery in the loosely connected way associated with surrealism will be especially obscure for many. But one of the extraordinary powers of surreal imagery is that it becomes more effective as it accumulates. Surrealism exists to locate and make articulate that place where the conscious intellect cannot go. Lorca's surrealism works in the sense that it soaks in before it is questioned.

Because each section in the poem is different in form and tone, it helps to discuss them separately. With the refrain of Section I students will be on familiar ground, not necessarily from Andalusian gypsy ballads, but from contemporary popular music, where again the refrain serves as a kind of "hook" to arrest the listener's attention. Section II is probably for most students the most immediately accessible; Lorca's refusal to "see" his friend's spilled blood is simultaneously poignant and insistent. For students who are having difficulty with the poem, concentration on Section II will help define its tone, demonstrate its emotional power, and clarify its surrealistic mode of meaning.

### Topics for Discussion and Writing

1. Why is the death of a bullfighter a particularly appropriate occasion for Lorca's lament about death in general?
   [See paragraph 2 of *Backgrounds*, and the headnote to Lorca in the anthology for further discussion.]

2. How does Lorca use images of bulls in the poem? What do they suggest? What other important images are connected with bulls?
   [See paragraphs 3–4 of *Backgrounds* for a discussion of bulls. Teachers might also wish to point out the way Lorca associates the moon (traditionally female, like the "ancient cow" of Section II, and connected with notions of fate) with bulls. Critics have noticed that the moon, its crescent shape perhaps suggesting the bull's horns, presides "with a fatal glow" over Sanchez Mejias's death.]

3. Is there any logical organization apparent in the poem? If so, what is it? How does it bear upon the central theme of death?
   [See *Classroom Strategies*, paragraph 2, and the headnote for further discussion.]

4. What are the conventions of the elegy in poetry? In what ways is this a traditional elegy? In what ways does it differ from the traditional elegy?

5. What is *duende*? Does this poem have it?

6. Compare Lorca's attitude toward death with that of Garcia Marquez in "Death Constant Beyond Love."

7. If you read Spanish, you may wish to read aloud or compare passages from the translation with the section of the original text given in the anthology (pp. 1896–97). Students may also be encouraged to try reading the original text on their own, and to comment on the way the translation has or has not succeeded in grasping the original. Some of the bolder ones may attempt their own translations, which will bring them closer to the text and, at the same time, induce a healthy respect for the difficulties of translation.

## Further Reading

See also the reading suggestion in the anthology, p. 1890.

Adams, Mildred. *Garcia Lorca: Playwright and Poet.* 1984.
Fuller general study.

Allen, Rupert C. *The Symbolic World of Federico Garcia Lorca.* 1972.

Binding, Paul. *Lorca: The Gay Imagination.* 1985.

Colecchia, Francesca. *Garcia Lorca: An Annotated Bibliography of Criticism.* 1979.
A guide to reference material before 1979.

Cannon, Calvin. "Lorca's 'Llanto por Ignacio Sanchez Mejias' and the Elegiac Tradition." *Hispanic Review* XXXI (1963), pp. 229–38.
Demonstrates the "Lament's" place in the tradition of the classical elegy.

Davies, Catherine and Marvin, Garry. "Control of the Wild in Andalusian Culture: Bull and Horse Imagery in Lorca from an Anthropological Perspective" from *Neophilologus* October 1987, 71 (4), pp. 543–58.
An anthropological perspective.

Gershator, David, ed. *Selected Letters*. 1983.

Londre, Felicia Hardison. *Federico Garcia Lorca*. 1984.
Fuller general study.

Lorca, Federico Garcia. "Theory and Function of the *Duende*." In Donald M. Allen and Warren Tallman, editors, *The Poetics of the New American Poetry*. New York, 1973.
One of Lorca's most important prose statements. It goes a great distance in suggesting what Lorca is after in his work.

Lorca, Francisco Garcia. *In the Green Morning: Memories of Federico*. Translated by Christopher Maurer. 1986.

Loughran, David K. *Federico Garcia Lorca, The Poetry of Limits*. 1978.

MacCurdy, Grant G. *Federico Garcia Lorca: Life, Work and Criticism*. 1986.
Brief overview.

Morris, C. Brian. *"Cuando yo me muera . . ." : Essays in Memory of Federico Garcia Lorca*. 1988.
Collects seventeen papers from a symposium on Lorca; the essays are chiefly in English while the poetry is cited in Spanish.

Oppenheimer, Helen. *Lorca, the Drawings: Their Relation to the Poet's Life and Work*. 1986.
Reproduces drawings from different periods in the poet's life along with valuable commentary on their historical context and personal significance; appendices contain Lorca's slide lecture, "Thoughts on Modern Art" and a film script.

Rees, Margaret A. ed. *Leeds Papers on Lorca and on Civil War Verse*. 1988.

Salinas, Pedro. "Lorca and the Poetry of Death." From *Lorca: A*

*Collection of Critical Essays*, edited by Manuel Duran. Englewood Cliffs, 1962. Pp. 100–107.
Discusses Lorca and the Spanish "culture of death."

Stanton, Edward. *The Tragic Myth: Lorca and the Cante Jondo.* Lexington, KY, 1978. Pp. 46–51.
A short but persuasive discussion of bulls, bullfighting, and native Andalusian traditions as mythic elements in Lorca's work, especially "Lament."

# ALBERT CAMUS
## The Guest

### Backgrounds

Camus is known as the great "moralist" of twentieth-century French letters: "moralist" in a very special French sense that describes a philosophical writer who examines the everyday ethical and moral implications of what it means to be human. Despite the technical brilliance of his work in novels, plays, short stories, and essays, Camus is usually remembered first for his pictures of human beings struggling to understand themselves and the critical circumstances in which they exist. Two elements complement each other in his moral vision: the consciousness of the "absurd" (the discrepancy between our desire for meaning and the actual non-sense of material reality), and a subsequent voluntary "engagement" or devotion to liberty and justice "as if" the world made sense. From the starkly brilliant images of *The Stranger* to the labyrinthine half-dialogue of *The Fall*, Camus's fiction asserts an aesthetic dimension that goes far beyond the philosophical and political frameworks often chosen to discuss it. Nonetheless, his enormous popularity with students continues to be based on his moral insight, a context in which they find him vital and even ennobling.

"The Guest" is one of Camus's most successful short stories and contains a number of ideas that obsessed him in all his work. Daru lives alone in a vast landscape which suggests a "total physical and moral isolation." In many ways, it is similar to Beckett's empty landscapes—absurd, stony, inimical to man—but, unlike Beckett's, it is strikingly beautiful. It is, in any case, the only landscape in which Daru does not feel himself an exile. But into this landscape come men, with their "rotten spite, their tireless hates, their blood lust," their political and cultural ties and assumptions. It is these ties that cause Daru the difficulty he must confront in the story.

Balducci brings the Arab to Daru on the assumption that, since Daru is European, he will complete the process of justice set out by Europeans for Arab offenders. The attitude of the *gendarme* toward Daru is one of condescension, the kind of condescension that comes with assumed cultural bonds. Balducci calls Daru "son" and "kid," and simply commands the schoolteacher to act as desired: "You will deliver this fellow to Tinguit. He is expected at police headquarters" (p. 1903). Daru is clearly sympathetic to the natives of his area (he teaches them, speaks the language, distributes food during the drought, and he will treat the Arab as a guest), and it is not his job to deal with prisoners. But, as Balducci says, "If there's an uprising, no one is safe, we're all in the same boat" (p. 1904). His demands of Daru, however friendly, are based on the assumption that Daru will act as a European, that he is obliged to accept the prisoner because cultural bonds are stronger than any individual objections Daru may reasonably have. And, when it comes down to it, Daru *is* obliged, he *is* a European: the four rivers of France on the map in his schoolroom are the appropriate backdrop for his actions as well as his moral quandary. Balducci sees his world as *us* and *them*, and so does Daru ("Is he against us?" [p. 1903]), although his feelings about *them* are mitigated by his sympathies and his own desire not to be complicit in taking action against them.

When Daru tells Balducci that he will have no part in turning in the Arab, it is not because he thinks the Arab has been unjustly treated (he is, apparently, guilty of a murder), but because Daru does want to act in a way that will appear to be *for* the Europeans and *against* the Arabs. Essentially, Daru doesn't want to have to commit himself to any course of action, since any such course will suggest to others that he has political sympathies which he does not, in fact, have.

Daru's situation is impossible: though he hopes to evade misunderstanding, he is bound to be misunderstood no matter which option he chooses. The world he lives in guarantees it. Daru attempts to make a choice *not* to do anything, to let the Arab choose freedom or prison for himself; Daru wants to wash his hands of complicity one way or the other. But a man living in world of "rotten spite" and undeniable allegiances must discover that even not choosing constitutes a choice. Daru has responsibility for the Arab's fate because of his birth and circumstance. He cannot disclaim it.

The end of the story is usually interpreted as an unfortunate misunderstanding, but this interpretation does not do justice to the complexity of Camus's tale. Those who scrawled "You handed over our brother. You will pay for this" (p. 1910), understand Daru perfectly well, though they do not, and cannot, fully appreciate his position. What they understand is that Daru handed over their brother when Daru was born—that the message is written on the map of France confirms why they feel as they do. Daru's solitariness at the end of the story, then, is the solitariness of a man trapped in a universe in which no act is without its moral implications and in which there is no way to elude complicity.

Daru's position may be impossible, as is the Arab's, but this does not mean that he cannot treat the prisoner well as long as the Arab is his guest. Something like brotherhood and a "strange alliance" is established between them, but Daru must recognize that he lives in a world where brotherhood can simultaneously mean betrayal. Still, the brotherhood developed between Daru and the Arab is necessary and heroic. However small a gesture, it is perhaps all that can be done; like the Sisyphus of Camus's essay (*The Myth of Sisyphus*) one must willingly—even joyously—push the boulder up the mountain knowing full well that it will roll back down again.

Camus was born to European parents in Algeria, then a colony of France, and lived and worked there exclusively until he was 27. Friends and family continued to live in Algeria throughout his life. His interest and concern in the Algerian Question, as it was then called, are perfectly understandable. What wasn't understandable to many French intellectuals, including Jean-Paul Sartre (with whom Camus had had a spectacular public quarrel in 1952) and Simone de Beauvoir, was Camus's consistent call for tolerance and understanding, and his refusal to back wholeheartedly any movement which called either for violent rebellion or the restriction of individual freedoms. During the Algerian conflict, Camus was hardly silent—in 1956 he flew to Algiers in order to address both French and Moslem citizens although he was constantly under threat of his life—but he adopted the comparatively safe position of concentrating on the effort to spare innocent civilians: "Truce until it is time for solutions, truce to the massacre of civilians, on one side and the other!" Camus, like Daru, clearly hated having to be put in the position of taking sides. And because he was without question the most powerful Algerian-born voice capable of being heard in France, his position carried with it enormous responsibilities, responsibilities which both those on the Left and those on the Right felt he was shirking or misusing. "The Guest" appears to be, in part at least, an attempt to express the personal difficulties he felt in judging the Algerian situation.

Camus often insisted that he was not an existentialist, and he and Sartre were reportedly surprised, and sometimes disturbed (especially after 1952), at seeing their names constantly linked. At one point they jokingly agreed to sign a statement claiming that neither could be held responsible for the debts incurred by the other.

*Classroom Strategies*

"The Guest" is teachable in one class period and can be linked with a number of other texts in which characters must make difficult moral choices: *Medea, Antigone, Hamlet, Billy Budd* (Captain Vere), *A Portrait of the Artist as a Young Man.*

The major problem that students will have with "The Guest" is selling the story short. Daru's "quiet heroism" is evident, so students will tend to see him as a quiet hero, severely misunderstood and unjustly accused by the Arab rebels at the end of the story. They will compare him with Balducci, clearly a man involved—though not happily—in a master/slave relationship with his prisoner, and find him heroic in comparison. It is more difficult to see him as heroic when we realize that his heroism is not nearly enough; he goes far enough with Balducci to satisfy the letter of the law, and far enough with the Arab to satisfy the demands of his sympathies. He is not heroic because he sets the prisoner free. In the first place, he doesn't free him—he only gives the Arab the chance to take his freedom. Second, the Arab's crime is not a political crime, it is a murder, which Daru (as well as Balducci) finds repellent; it is much to Camus's credit that he hasn't made the prisoner's guilt or innocence an issue. Third, he is complicit, whether he likes it or not, in the system which, perhaps justly, has ensnared the prisoner, but which also, perhaps unjustly, has also ensnared the prisoner's countrymen. Daru is heroic not through heroic action, but by suffering the inevitable fate which awaits man in an absurd universe—and doing it with civility, sympathy, and the desire to be nice.

Students will by no means always understand why the prisoner does not escape during the night, or why he chooses the road to prison rather than freedom at the end of the story. One reason is given in the headnote: the "host's humane hospitality has placed a new burden and reciprocal responsibility on his guest" (p. 1900). There are, however, other possibilities. One has its basis in the master/slave relationship that even a night of humane treatment cannot erase: the Arab simply cannot believe that a European *really* means to set him free. We must remember, as the prisoner no doubt remembers, that Daru still has his gun, just as he still has the power to give or deny freedom at a whim. We know, but the prisoner doesn't, that Daru is uneasy with such power; that he has it whether he wants it or not is, however, undeniable. Teachers may find their position in the classroom analogous to Daru's position. We do not always want the power we have; we may even seek to diminish or deny it. But we give A's and F's and Incompletes, and as long as we stand in front of the classroom we are collaborators in an entire structure of evaluation which it is impossible to disregard.

Another plausible reading is that the prisoner takes the road toward prison because prison is precisely what he deserves. He is, after all, a murderer. If Daru, in his role as a teacher, is interested in "conveying to a fellow human being the freedom of action which all people require" (p. 1900), the Arab may very well be capable of learning it. To freely choose to be punished for a crime he has committed is just as admirable, and perhaps more admirable, than eluding the punishment which is due him.

### Topics for Discussion and Writing

1. Why does Camus set the story on a remote outpost in Algeria, just after a freak snow has isolated it even more profoundly than usual? How does Camus use descriptions of the landscape to confirm Daru's isolation? Do the descriptions of the landscape suggest its beauty? Why?
   [See *Backgrounds* for discussion.]

2. What is the point of Balducci's rather long conversation with Daru? Why does Balducci think he can leave the prisoner with Daru? Why does Daru keep him? Why does Daru say he will not take him to prison? What is Balducci's attitude about this?
   [See paragraphs 3–5 of *Backgrounds* and paragraph 3 of *Classroom Strategies* for discussion.]

3. Why does Daru give the Arab the opportunity to escape? Why doesn't he escape? Why doesn't he take the road to the Arab lands at the end of the story?
   [See paragraphs 4–5 of *Backgrounds* and paragraphs 4–5 of *Classroom Strategies* for discussion.]

4. In what ways is the Arab treated as a guest by Daru? In what ways is Daru a guest in Algeria?
   [See paragraph 7 of *Backgrounds* for discussion.]

5. How can this story be seen as an expression of Camus's personal position on the Algerian Question?
   [See paragraph 8 of *Backgrounds* for discussion.]

## Further Reading

See also the reading suggestion in the anthology, p. 1900.

Amoia, Alba della Fazia. *Albert Camus*. 1989.
An introductory study with a short biography and discussion of individual works organized by genre.

Bloom, Harold. *Albert Camus*. 1989.
A selection of critical essays.

Cruickshank, John. *Albert Camus and the Literature of Revolt*. London, 1959. Reprinted 1978.
A useful general study.

Ellison, David R. *Understanding Albert Camus*. 1990.
A perceptive, readable overview of Camus's work that describes individual works ("The Guest," pp. 194–99) and interprets according to structure, historical context, and themes.

Sprintzen, David. *Camus, a Critical Examination*. 1988.

Suther, Judith D., ed. *Essays on Camus's* Exile and the Kingdom. 1980.
Contains "The Symbolic Decor of 'The Guest' by Paul A. Fortier and Joseph G. Morello, pp. 203–15.

Thody, Philip. *Albert Camus*. London, 1957.
A short but cogent study of the works, including a discussion of "The Guest."

# Masterpieces of the Twentieth Century
## Contemporary Explorations

## JORGE LUIS BORGES
### The Garden of Forking Paths

### *Backgrounds*

Borges is perhaps the most extraordinary labyrinth-maker in contemporary literature; for him everything—the nature of time, of space, of knowledge, of the self, of literary form—is problematic. He looks at the world as a "puzzle" which compels examination even while it resists solution. Nothing can be proved, but nothing can be disproved. Borges combines his immense narrative skill with the qualities of a metaphysic, fantasist, scholar, detective writer, theologian, and ironist. He is very much like the metaphysics in one of his own fictional places, Tlon, who "seek neither truth nor likelihood; they seek astonishment." In all of his major stories, Borges is intent upon making a coherent fictional world almost entirely out of his intelligence and out of his imagination playing over other intelligences.

"The Garden of Forking Paths" is a detective story, but one in which the reader, finally, is the detective, and Time is the solution to the mystery. On the level of plot, the story is reasonably simple: Yu Tsun, a Chinese spy who is grudgingly working for the Germans during World War I, has to transmit an important message to his chief in Berlin. Since Yu Tsun's identity has been discovered by the British, he must transmit the message before he is caught, and he must do so without letting the British know he has done it. He goes to a suburb of London, to the house of a Sinologist named Stephen Albert. Yu Tsun and Albert discuss the nature of a manuscript written by Ts'ui Pen, one of Yu Tsun's ancestors, and then Yu Tsun shoots Albert, who dies instantaneously. In the last paragraph we discover the reason for Yu Tsun's actions; the message he must convey to Berlin is the name of a French city the Germans must attack. The city's name is Albert, and by killing a man of that name Yu Tsun both fulfills his mission and condemns himself to be captured and, ultimately, hanged.

The story, however, is full of coincidences, analogies between characters, and resonances and suggestions of ideas which are more important than the simple plot. The central idea of the story is the labyrinth, which is both the story's subject and its structure. The labyrinth is presented in a number of ways: an actual labyrinth-like walk through English suburban life which Yu Tsun takes on his way to Albert's house; the literary labyrinth constructed by Yu Tsun's ancestor, Ts'ui Pen; and the formal labyrinth of Borges's story itself. The implications of all three are the same: to suggest the infinite possibilities—the "various futures"—of any human action in time, and the consequent shrinkage in the importance of that action when we think of it as just one possible outcome among many. Borges presents a fictional reality which has as its center the death of Stephen Albert at the hands of Yu Tsun; but he implies that there are other conceivable centers, other possible dimensions, other possible times. As Albert tells Yu Tsun, "We do not exist in the majority of these times; in some you exist, and not I; in others I, and not you; in others, both of us. In the present one, which a favorable fate has granted me, you have arrived at my house; in another, while crossing the garden, you found me dead; in still another, I utter these same words, but I am a mistake, a ghost" (pp. 1925–26). The story refutes the notion of present time as the only one which contains "reality," and, therefore, the only significant time.

"The Garden of Forking Paths" effectively blurs most of the categories we use to "know" the world—especially the distinction between reality and fiction. The story begins with Borges blurring the traditional distinctions between author, narrator, and character. We are told in no uncertain terms by someone who appears to be the author of an historical essay that on "page 22 of Liddell Hart's *History of World War I*" we will read about a particular military attack, "planned for the 24th of July, 1916" which had to be postponed until the morning of the 29th because of "torrential rains" (p. 1919). The scholarly authority of the voice in this opening passage—the voice of the historian—suggests that the information delivered belongs to the world of fact, outside of fiction altogether. Further, the matter-of-fact authority of this narrative voice tends to make the sections which follow, consisting entirely—except for a footnote—of

Yu Tsun's narrative, into a revelation important only in that it "throws an unsuspected light" on the postponement of the battle. The "author" of the "essay" reveals no interest whatsoever in the extraordinary qualities of Yu Tsun's narrative itself.

If we look at Liddell Hart's book, we notice that what our "scholar" says is not what Liddell Hart reports: there was such a battle, but there is no mention of its postponement, and the torrential rains did not fall until November. The "author," then, is as much a fiction as Yu Tsun, Stephen Albert, Captain Richard Madden, Ts'ui Pen, or any other character in the story. Even the "editor," presumably the "editor" of the "journal" which published our "author's" scholarly revelation, is exposed as simply another character in Borges's story when he is offended by Yu Tsun's version of Viktor Runeberg's death and then proceeds to comment authoritatively on the "real" events behind that death. The language is heavily loaded: on the one hand, the German agent is identified as a "Prussian spy" who "attacked with drawn automatic," and his opponent is identified both as "Captain" and "the bearer of a warrent" acting in self-defense; moreover, he did not actually kill Runeberg but merely "inflicted a wound" which led to death. Who is to say whether Yu Tsun or the editor is closer to the truth? What we have, then, is a fictional editor taking offense at a fictional account of a fictional death of a fictional spy in a footnote to a fictional historical essay called "The Garden of Forking Paths" written by a fictional author who was created by Jorge Luis Borges in a piece of fiction called "The Garden of Forking Paths."

The ramifications of Borges's story lead us back to the relation between historical events and historical narratives of those events, that is, between reality and fiction. Borges suggests that Liddell Hart left out something important when he rendered the battle of 24 July, 1916, in his history of World War I. And of course he did; Liddell Hart, like any historian, must leave out more than he puts in; he must make selections based on his own fallible interpretation of what is significant and what is not in the series of events he presents as historical "fact." Historians, then, are writers of fiction who use their intelligence and imagination to create a coherent narrative based on reality. The "reality" of that battle ended when it ended; what is left of it is in books like Liddell Hart's, or further emendations like Yu Tsun's tale and even a biased footnote. The disorder and contingency of reality have been replaced by fiction.

Unlike almost all of the other major writers of Latin America—

Gabriel Garcia Marquez, Pablo Neruda, Carlos Fuentes, Alejandro Carpentier, Cesar Vallejo, and so on—Borges's work appears to be adamantly apolitical. (This despite the fact that Borges was briefly a *cause célèbre* in the 1940s because of his public opposition to Peron.) His life has been devoted to books, to writing them, reading them, even cataloguing them, and since his early years—when he was much interested in Argentina's past and its folk literature—his mind has taken up residence in a country without national boundaries. In "The Argentine Writer and Tradition," Borges argues that the real Argentine tradition is "all of Western culture . . . our patrimony is the universe."

Although Borges's reputation in Argentina stresses his poetry rather than his fiction, his influence on contemporary fiction has been exceptional; there is almost no post-modernist writer in any language who is not in some way in Borges's debt.

### Classroom Strategies

"The Garden of Forking Paths" can be discussed in one or two class periods. If two periods are used, the first might be devoted to disentangling the plot and Borges's narrative strategy, the second to disentangling the implications of the plot and the implications of that narrative. At some point, you might chalk a "tree" formation on the board (which mathematics and linguistics students will immediately recognize) to illustrate how various alternative possibilities can exist simultaneously. Students usually enjoy hearing the ancient Chinese riddle about the man who dreamed he was a butterfly dreaming he was a man—who woke up. The question then follows: who is he? Is he a butterfly dreaming he is a man (who was dreaming he was a butterfly) who has just woken up, or . .

"The Garden of Forking Paths" is the kind of story that can make a student's head hurt. Encourage them to see its playing with reality as part of modern fictional techniques: Kafka's *Metamorphosis*, for example, or Pirandello's *Six Characters in Search of an Author*. You may want to draw comparisons with later modern works, such as Julio Cortázar's *Hopscotch*, in which the reader is invited to rearrange the order of chapters, or John Fowles's *The French Lieutenant's Woman*, where the author provides different endings among which the reader may choose. Emphasizing the detective story qualities of the piece, or noting that it bears significant resemblances to many science-fiction stories (stories about parallel times or alternate worlds, for instance), will also help your students enjoy "The Garden of Forking Paths" before they begin to worry about whether they have completely understood it. On the other hand, one of the things that differentiates Borges's piece from a typical piece of science-fiction is the economy and complexity of his narrative. Only a few pages long, it nevertheless dizzies the reader with continually expanding implications and suggestions. You will find that an exploration of the way Borges uses analogies—between events and between characters—makes his narrative economy more evident. The various kinds of labyrinths suggested by the story have already been noted, and the analogies between them should be obvious. It will also be worth noting the following:

1. Ts'ui Pen was murdered by the hand of a stranger, just as Stephen Albert will be, the only one to decipher Ts'ui Pen's novel.

2. Ts'ui Pen closed himself up for thirteen years in the Pavilion of Limpid Solitude to write his novel, and Stephen Albert greets Yu Tsun by saying "I see that the pious Hsi P'eng persists in correcting my solitude?" (p. 1922)

3. Albert reads a section from Ts'ui Pen's novel which has to do with armies marching to battle. He also tries to explain the implications of the novel by describing a scene in which a stranger calls at a man's door and, in one possible outcome, kills him.

4. Stephen Albert—a Westerner who is ostensibly Yu Tsun's enemy —restores the good name of Yu Tsun's ancestor, while Yu Tsun— an Easterner who teaches the languages of the West—kills Albert to prove to his Chief that "the innumerable ancestors" who merge within him are worthy of respect. "I wanted," says Yu Tsun, "to prove to him that a yellow man could save his armies" (p. 1920).

5. Yu Tsun, like his ancestor Ts'ui Pen, is faced with transmitting a message. Both must do so through indirection. Paradoxically, Ts'ui Pen invents something traditionally made for the many—a novel— which can be decoded by only one, while Yu Tsun invents for one—the chief—by addressing the many through the newspapers.

6. Yu Tsun and Richard Madden are paired as spy/counterspy, but both are distrusted aliens who must prove themselves to their chiefs.

# Topics for Discussion and Writing

1. Discuss the ways Borges uses the labyrinth as the central idea and image of "The Garden of Forking Paths."
   [See paragraphs 3 of *Backgrounds* for discussion.]

2. Discuss the implications of Borges's narrative technique in the story. Who is the narrator? In what guise does he present himself? How does Borges blur the traditional distinctions between author, narrator, and character in "The Garden of Forking Paths"?
   [See paragraphs 4–5 of *Backgrounds* and *Classroom Strategies* for discussion.]

3. Discuss analogies between characters and between events in the story.
   [See paragraph 3 of *Backgrounds* and *Classroom Strategies* for discussion.]

4. What kinds of questions does Borges raise in "The Garden of Forking Paths" about the nature of Time?
   [See paragraph 3 of *Backgrounds* for discussion.]

5. What relationship between reality and fiction is suggested in "The Garden of Forking Paths"? What conclusions might we draw about the writing of history?
   [See paragraphs 4–6 of *Backgrounds* for discussion.]

6. What clues are given at the beginning of the story, and how are we misled by them?
   [The name of the person "capable of transmitting the message" is usually interpreted as the name of another agent; the single bullet in Yu Tsun's revolver may suggest that he will commit suicide if captured; generally overlooked is the fact that the Chief in Berlin spends his time "endlessly examining newspapers" while waiting for his agents' reports.]

7. How does Borges base his story in observable documentary facts in order to lend solidity to the idea of alternate worlds?
   [See, in addition of Liddell Hart's book, the following references: the actual town of Albert, located on the Ancre river (near the

Somme) and therefore close to the bloodiest battles of World War I; the existing countries of Staffordshire (west England) and Fenton (east England); the German writer Goethe (see. pp. 461 of this volume); the Latin author Tacitus; a famous Chinese novel, the *Hung Lou Meng*, and the *Arabian Nights*; recognized pottery styles and a real (though lost) encyclopedia from the Ming Dynasty; physicist Isaac Newton and philosopher Arthur Schopenhauer.]

### *Further Reading*

See also the suggestions in the anthology, p. 1915–16.

Alazraki, Jaime. *Borges and the Kabbalah.* 1988.
A collection of essays on various aspects of the writer's fiction and poetry.

Balderston, Daniel, ed. *The Literary Universe of Jorge Luis Borges: An Index to References and Allusions to Persons, Titles and Places in His Writing.*

Bell-Villada, Gene H. *Borges and His Fiction.* Chapel Hill, 1981.
A particularly useful discussion of Borges's use of simultaneous times in "The Garden of Forking Paths." See especially pp. 93–96.

Bloom, Harold, ed. *Jorge Luis Borges.* 1986.
Fifteen essays by different scholars, and a chronology.

Borges, Jorge Luis. *Other Inquisitions,* 1937–1952. Translated by Ruth L. C. Simms. Austin, 1964.
Discussions of "The Garden of Forking Paths" will be aided by reading "A New Refutation of Time" and "The Argentine Writer and Tradition."

Burgin, Richard. *Conversations with Jorge Luis Borges.* New York, 1969.
A useful discussion of Borges by Borges.

Foster, David William. *Jorge Luis Borges: An Annotated Primary and Secondary Bibliography.* 1984.

di Giovanni, Norman Thomas. *In Memory of Borges.* 1988.
Seven essays; includes a 1983 address by Borges on his work, and an anecdotal essay by di Giovanni as Borges's translator.

Rimmon-Kenan, Shlomith. "Doubles and Counterparts: Patterns of Interchangeability in Borges' 'The Garden of Forking Paths.'" *Critical Inquiry* 6, 4 (Summer 1980), 639–47.
An interesting discussion of Borges's use of analogies between characters and between events in the story.

Rodriguez-Monegal, Emir. *Jorge Luis Borges: A Literary Biography.* New York, 1978.
The only full-length biography of Borges in English.

Stabb, Martin. *Borges Revisited.* 1991.
A useful introduction organized by perspectives on Borges's work; includes "The Canonical Texts," "The Critical Trajectory," "Borges in Perspective," and a chronology.

# SAMUEL BECKETT
## Endgame

### *Backgrounds*

Beckett's world is the world of last things—stark, bare, gray from pole to pole—in which characters are bitterly self-conscious, and the activity of life is reduced to mere waiting and game-playing. As Tom Stoppard has said, Beckett redefined the minima of theatrical validity. His world is refrigerated; it tends toward silence, yet he wrote an extraordinary number of plays, novels, short fictions, and poems which examine that silence in a language as suggestive and penetrating as any writer of his time.

The headnote to Beckett points out almost all of *Endgame*'s central obsessions: the dead world inside, the deader world outside; the four barren characters absolutely restricted in both time and space; the notion of life as a game which cannot be won, only cruelly played; the master-slave relationship of the characters, the struggle of body and soul within each of them.

In *Waiting for Godot*, Vladimir and Estragon play games to endure; game-playing structures their wait. In *Endgame*, game-playing, or the game itself, becomes the central metaphor for existence. Games have no meaning outside of themselves (except indirectly); they are morally and practically superfluous; rule-governed; repetitive; independent of the immediate satisfactions of wants and appetites; dependent on the virtuosity of the players, some of whom dominate while others are dominated; confirmative of role and the stabilizing of position. Games create a world of meaning which is entirely self-reflexive, a dead end. One of the most elaborate of all human games is the play, the drama, which provides an actively present metaphor within the larger metaphor of *Endgame*.

*Endgame* is aware of itself as a text performed in a theater, and the characters are aware of themselves as characters on stage; they flaunt their consciousness that the whole business is a performance. Their essential traits are those which have been devised in previous plays: Hamm, another name for an actor, is also Hamlet, who, to quote Hugh Kenner, is "bounded by a nutshell, fancying himself king of infinite space, but troubled by bad dreams"; he is also Prospero, but one whose kingdom is without magic, except perhaps the magic of power. Hamm's relationship with the others is one of domination and cruelty. He is the hammer to Clov's nail; the Prospero to Clov's Ariel *and* Caliban; the King to Clov's Knight; the master to Clov's dog. Both Hamm and Clov continually suggest that they are on stage, alive, only because they have roles to perform in a play, a dramatic game, roles which they cannot stop playing because there is no alternative but to play them. When Clov threatens to leave Hamm, he asks, "What is there to keep me here?" Hamm replies, "The dialogue." Hamm, Clov, Nagg, and Nell say what they say as if they have said the same things many times before. (Note particularly Hamm's story [pp. 1948–50] and Nagg's joke about the English tailor [pp. 1938–39].) The characters are burdened with a blinding self-consciousness of the eternal, repetitive monotony of being trapped in their roles in a game which, when there is nothing outside from which to differentiate it, is meaningless.

When the curtain (if there is a curtain) rises on *Endgame*, it is as if all the characters are just waking up—preparing themselves for another day (another performance) which they hope will soon be finished. The furniture is covered in "sheets, suggesting both storage" (for the night, between performances) and the covering of the dead. Clov opens the play by performing his ritual actions (he must, according to the script, do this *every* performance) until Hamm removes his personal curtain and announces that he is ready "to play." The stage is their shelter and their gameboard; it is the space in which they do their "living."

In this space there is no future, since that can only be a mere repetition of the present, nor a past, except as it persists in memory—the memory, that is, of a life "outside" the stage which now seems only disturbingly ironic when compared to present circumstances. They live in the hell of an eternal present, but outside is the "other hell." The waves of the sea are like lead, the sun is "zero," there is "no more nature" except the characters' natural tendency to grow old and dwindle toward a death that neglects to come.

HAMM: But we breathe, we change! We lose our hair, our teeth! Our bloom! Our ideals!
CLOV: Then she hasn't forgotten us.

(p.1935)

The "little round box" of the universe was once full, perhaps, but now is empty.

Any suggestion of life outside Hamm's kingdom (the flea, the rat, the small boy) terrifies and thrills for the same reason: "humanity might start from there all over again" (p. 1943). Clov, at least, can conceive of a renewal, regeneration, a new play with new roles. But he, like Hamm, can also imagine that new life would only mean a continuation of life as it now exists, a life so checkmated that "a world where all would be silent and still and each thing in its last place, under the last dust" offers itself as a desirable end, the final "pain-killer" to the prison of endless time the characters now inhabit.

Beckett is rumored to have remarked that in *Waiting for Godot* the audience wonders whether Godot will ever come, while in *Endgame* they wonder whether Clov will ever leave. The "small boy," if there is one, intensifies the question, suggesting both the horror and potentiality of new life. At play's end, Clov is "dressed for the road," suggesting the possibility that he intends to carry out his threat and leave Hamm, perhaps to take in the small boy (as Hamm, apparently, once did) and play Hamm's role himself. Or, perhaps Hamm dismisses Clov because he himself intends to take in the small boy, a new player in his game, making Clov no longer necessary. In any case, Clov (who can imagine both "I'll never go" and "I open the door of my cell and go") is still there at the end, "eyes fixed on Hamm." Hamm's final two monologues (p. 1955 and pp. 1959–60), with all of their rhetorical flourish again suggesting scriptedness, are derisive parodies of Jesus's words: they suggest both death and regeneration. Whether regeneration can come in a form other than the play's being enacted again, tomorrow night, is left ambivalent. Hamm finishes where he began, his blood-stained handkerchief over his face, motionless—waiting, perhaps, for the curtain to rise once more.

It has been suggested, by Lionel Abel among others, that Hamm is based on James Joyce—the almost-blind master for whom Beckett worked as a secretary in the late 1920s—and that Clov is based on Beckett himself. Indeed, Joyce (like Hamm) was working on an interminable story, *Finnegans Wake*, during the time Beckett worked with him, and Beckett (like Clov) was very much under Joyce's influence and in Joyce's debt during those years. Even if there is some truth to the claim, however, the play can by no means be read merely as a thinly disguised examination of the conflict between a literary master and his gifted pupil.

Commentators on Beckett often locate him in a tradition which includes Dostoevsky, Gogol, Goncharov, Andreyev, Musil, and Kafka, writers who were interested in the "marginal self," and who find modern men eaten up by consciousness. Dramatically, he has long been included in the "theater of the absurd" with Eugene Ionesco, Jean Genet, and Fernando Arrabal, who certainly belong in such a context, and Harold Pinter, who perhaps does not, but who avails himself of many of the techniques we find in Beckett and the others.

Ruby Cohn has outlined a number of evident allusions, parodies, and influences in *Endgame.* She notes his use of the Bible, especially the Gospel of Saint John; James Joyce, the labyrinth-maker and word-man who may have been a model for Hamm, Shakespeare's *The Tempest* and *King Lear*; Baudelaire, whom Hamm quotes at the end of the play; and Tiresias and Oedipus, blind prophets of suffering.

### Classroom Strategies

*Endgame* can be taught in two class periods. The first should probably examine the thematic implications of the play by exploring the various plausible interpretations which offer themselves to the reader; the second might concentrate on the richness of Beckett's word-play, his humor, and the way his language lends itself to multiple readings.

You might begin by discussing the implications of the stage setting. It is depressingly bare, enveloped in gray light; the off-stage scene is brutally excluded except for the two small windows so high that they can be reached only by ladder. There will be no entrances by persons unknown; the door, which only Clov can use, is so narrow that one actor playing the part of Clov thought of himself as a rat squeezing into its hole. The stage certainly appears to be symbolic, though precisely what it symbolizes it a matter of considerable debate. The headnote (pp. 1928–29) discusses a number of the possibilities: the stage as the inside of a skull, suggesting that Hamm and Clov are two aspects of a single personality and Nagg and Nell are suppressed earlier selves; as a last refuge of those who have survived an unnamed catastrophe (perhaps a Deluge or nuclear holocaust), making Hamm—to quote Katharine Worth—"lord of the ark of survivors, with his human family and a selection of animals"; as a metaphor for the twilight of civilization, in which Nagg and Nell's ash cans come to represent the dustbin of modern civilized values; as an image of Purgatory, or purgatorial consciousness; as a womb, from which the characters are eternally hoping—and fearing—to emerge. Beckett himself has said of his imaginings of life in the womb:

Even before the fetus can draw breath it is in a state of barrenness and of pain. I have a clear memory of my own fetal existence. It was an existence where no voice, no possible movement could free me from the agony and darkness I was subjected to.

Hugh Kenner adds another possibility, describing the stage as a chessboard and the characters' actions as a game of chess, in which Hamm is the king, Clov the knight, and Nagg and Nell are pawns. The point here is that Beckett has constructed his play so brilliantly and ambiguously that, as Kenner has said, "The play contains whatever ideas we discern inside it; no idea contains the play."

Beckett's refusal to assign a definite meaning to his evidently symbolic characters, setting, and dramatic "action," combined with his denial of the rich inner life that students have come to expect from traditional drama, make some students uneasy. But this uneasiness can be turned to your, and the play's, advantage. Just as we recognize the terrifying sense of no exit, we are—like Clov—drawn almost irresistibly to see out, to make the laborious climb up the ladder of vision to a world less claustrophobic, fresher than the one Beckett's characters inhabit. Students may resist the notion that there is "an absence of meaning at the core" of the world. They can, however, imagine it, and with their imagining comes a shock of recognition. The game metaphor is of particular use here: any game which has no reference to anything outside itself, which *is* life rather than a *recreation* in it (or re-creation of it), can be imagined as a kind of Purgatory—repetitive, monotonous, endless.

Students need to be aware of Beckett's extraordinary word-play as well as his humor. Certain scenes might be read out loud in class, with students taking the parts, in order to emphasize Beckett's use of language as well as his humor. The pace of the repartee, which sometimes—though not as often as in *Waiting for Godot*—approaches a vaudeville routine, will become immediately accessible. The opening dialogue between Hamm and Clov (beginning with Clov's "I've just got you up," and ending with his "There's nowhere else" [pp. 1932–33]) will serve you well. Also useful is the repartee beginning on p. 1934 (Hamm: "Every man his specialty") and ending on p. 1935 (Clov: "Something is taking its course"); Nagg and Nell's dialogue (pp. 1936–39) which includes Nagg's joke; and Hamm and Clov's discussion on pp. 1942–44, beginning with Clov's "Why this farce, day after day?" and ending with Hamm's long, bitter speech.

## Topics for Discussion and Writing

1. What is the significance of the stage setting? What does it symbolize? Why doesn't Beckett certify any particular interpretation? [See paragraph 5 of *Backgrounds* and paragraph 2 of *Classroom Strategies* for discussion.]

2. Why is the play called *Endgame*? What do games have to do with it? How does Beckett use play (including *drama* as *play*) in *Endgame*? [See the headnote and paragraphs 2–4 of *Backgrounds* for discussion.]

3. Characterize the relationship between Hamm and Clov. Between Hamm, Nagg, and Nell. Why is Nagg called "accursed progenitor? [See the headnote and paragraph 2 of *Backgrounds* for discussion.]

4. If "waiting" is the controlling verb in *Waiting for Godot*, what is the controlling verb in *Endgame*? [Ending? Gaming? Playing? Finishing?]

5. In what ways does *Endgame* suggest the ending of things? In what ways does it suggest a possible beginning? Can it suggest both? [See *Backgrounds* for discussion.]

6. How is Prospero a useful analogue for Hamm? King Lear? The Biblical Ham? James Joyce? [See *Backgrounds* for discussion.]

## Further Reading

See also the suggestions in the anthology, p. 1930.

Bair, Deirdre. *Samuel Beckett: A Biography.* 1978.
Provides an extensive, if unauthorized, view of Beckett.

Ben-Zvi, Linda, ed. *Women in Beckett: Performance and Critical Perspectives.* 1990.

Although not specifically related to *Endgame*, this collection is interesting as a particular examination of Beckett's dramatic work; it contains 12 interviews with actresses from seven different countries (Part I: "Acting Beckett's Women") and 19 essays using modern critical approaches, arranged in order from fiction to drama and radio-television (Part II: "Reacting to Beckett's Women").

Bloom, Harold, ed. *Samuel Beckett's* Endgame. 1988.
Assembles a range of essays on the play.

Brater, Enoch. *Why Beckett.* 1989.
A brief illustrated biography with 122 illustrations, chiefly photos.

Burkman, Katherine H., ed. *Myth and Ritual in the Plays of Samuel Beckett.* 1987.
Eleven essays including a study by Susan Maughlin based on anthropologist Victor Turner's concept of liminality: "Liminality: An Approach to Artistic Process in *Endgame*."

—————. *Just Play: Beckett's Theater.* Princeton, N.J., 1980.
A thorough study of the dramatic works, particularly interesting on Beckett's language.

Esslin, Martin, ed. *Samuel Beckett: A Collection of Essays.* Englewood Cliffs, N.J., 1965.
Contains a particularly fine essay on *Endgame*, "Beckett's Brinkmanship," by Ross Chambers.

Kalb, Jonathan. *Beckett in Performance.* 1989
An excellent dramaturgical discussion of actual performances as interpretations; includes interviews with eight actors and directors.

Kane, Leslie. *The Language of Silence: On the Unspoken and the Unspeakable in Modern Drama.* London and Toronto, 1984.

Pilling, John. *Samuel Beckett.* London and Boston, 1976.
A general study, useful on the intellectual, cultural, and literary background to Beckett's work.

Sheedy, John J. "The Comic Apocalypse of King Hamm." *Modern Drama*, IX (December 1966): 310–18.

A close analysis which suggests both comic and apocalyptic dimensions in the play.

Worth, Katharine, ed. *Beckett the Shape Changer*. London and Boston, 1975.

Worth's essay, "The Space and Sound in Beckett's Theatre," is illuminating on *Endgame* and his other plays.

# NAGUIB MAHFOUZ
## Zaabalawi

*Backgrounds*

Several years after publishing *Children of Gebelawi*, in which the history of a family descended from Gebelawi was also an allegorical history of religions, Naguib Mahfouz published a collection of stories called *God's World* (1963). If the patriarch Gebelawi (often transliterated Jabalawi) is to be allegorized as God, the almost-homonymic Zaabalawi of *God's World* is at least a close relation. The story "Zaabalawi" can easily be read as a mystic vision of the modern quest for God: as the allegorical rejection of a decadent society that has forgotten religious faith and claims, in Nietzsche's words, that "God is dead." Yet Mahfouz concurrently provides a realistic picture of the middle-class Cairo society he knows best. Although he is not recognized in his native Egypt as a "committed" realist writer—indeed, the more militant younger novelists feel that he has worked too much inside the establishment and become a canonical figure—he has developed his own complex way of representing reality. Mahfouz's criticism of moral weakness or social wrongdoing is not limited to a single dimension: it functions on individual, national, and religious levels. Nor has he gone unscathed. The movie made from *Miramar* was initially banned because it criticized Nasser's régime, and Mahfouz received death threats from religious fundamentalists after publicly criticizing Khomeini's call to murder Salman Rushdie.

Despite his status as the Grand Old Man of Egyptian letters and the first Arabic writer to receive the Nobel Prize in Literature, as of this writing neither *Children of Gebelawi* nor the story "Zaabalawi" has been published in his native Egypt: both works have shocked traditional beliefs about the representation of religious figures.

Allegorical literature is certainly not new with Naguib Mahfouz, but students may find it an unfamiliar mode inasmuch as the best-known Western examples of religious allegory lie further in the past: Dante's *Divine Comedy*, the medieval drama *Everyman*, Spenser's *Faerie Queene*, or Bunyan's *Pilgrim's Progress*. Modern literature—certainly modern Western literature—tends to provide different kinds of symbolism rather than religious allegory, and it presents realistic details more often than personified concepts. One could argue that Beckett's *Endgame* and Solzhenitsyn's "Matryona's Home" are modern versions of religious allegories, but the argument would have to take into account on the one hand a different philosophical basis and on the other a different fictional strategy. Mahfouz's personification of religious history in *Children of Gebelawi*, and the protagonist's quest for a cure in his "Zaabalawi," are clearly closer to familiar models of religious allegory insofar as they employ a set of symbolic characters acting out a drama with specific religious significance.

Yet it would be mistaken to stop here, and to ignore the fact that Mahfouz's stories are firmly rooted in the material world of modern Egyptian society. The religious allegory may itself be an allegory of modern Egypt's struggle to keep its bearings when faced with sudden industrialization, and with what Mahfouz sees as the commercialization of spiritual values. His characters are contemporary individuals trying to survive in urban society, and their acts all have realistic motivations and consequences. The clerk protagonist of *Respected Sir* (1975), for example, gives up love, friendship, and his own personal life in a dogged attempt to achieve the hallowed position of Director General. The narrator of "Zaabalawi" is not just looking for a saintlike figure; he is desperately trying to find a cure for his terminal illness after modern medicine has failed. Everyday life, not an abstract or transcendental other world, is the arena in which these struggles are played out; for Mahfouz, *social* existence dramatizes spiritual fulfillment or its lack.

"But the tragedy of life is a complex, rather than a simple one. . . . when we think of [life] as social existence, we discover in it many artificial tragedies of man's own making, such as ignorance, poverty, exploitation, violence, brutality . . . these are tragedies that can be remedied, and . . . in the act of remedying them we create civilization and progress." Atahaddath Ilaykum (I Speak to You), 1977

Not surprisingly, the story "Zaabalawi" has both social and religious significance. The elusive, otherworldly figure of Zaabalawi exists in a materialist society of ambitious bureaucrats, dilapidated houses, street vendors, policemen, and bars. Zaabalawi's house still exists, although it is no longer inhabited: "time had so eaten away at the building that nothing was left of it save an antiquated façade and a courtyard that . . . was being used as a rubbish dump" (p. 1966). The narrator's illness likewise has a dual interpretation. On the one hand, it is introduced as a physical ailment, a serious condition following a series of minor illnesses that were successfully treated. Most readers would associate this "illness for which no one possesses a remedy" with cancer, and they would find it quite comprehensible that the narrator seeks alternate treatment when medical science cannot help. Many cultures, too, have traditions in which one seeks out holy men to heal intractable illnesses. On the other hand, there are also intimations that the narrator's illness transcends physical definition. The ambiguity of the pain that afflicts him in mid-life (the point at which Dante's *Divine Comedy* begins); the repeated sense that only God (p. 1968–69) or Zaabalawi will be able to cure him; the various hints that "suffering is part of the cure" (1969) and that Zaabalawi cures those who love him (1972), all imply a larger explanation that has to do with spiritual crisis.

Reinforcing this shift from the physical to the transcendental plane is the narrator's progression from interviewing materialistic characters who have completely lost touch with Zaabalawi to others with different values who are closer to the saint. Here Mahfouz employs a sequence of representative figures—the lawyer, bureaucrat, artist and musician—like those in traditional allegories of the human condition (or, given another focus, in the Balzacian novel with its panorama of social types). If the narrator's quest can be read as the search of the soul for God, it also suggests a contemporary Egyptian society which is gradually losing touch with the faith of its ancestors. Some people remember Zaabalawi but don't know where to find him; many don't even know his name; and still others assert that the saint is a charlatan and advise the narrator to turn to modern science to cure his malady (p. 1966–67). The lawyer with whom the narrator first speaks used to practice in the religious courts, but "he left the quarter ages ago" (p. 1965) and devoted himself to making money. It is a scathing portrait, especially in terms of traditional Arab values: Sheikh Qamar wears a Western lounge suit instead of the traditional *galabeya*, he receives clients (including "a beautiful woman with a most intoxicating perfume") in a luxuriously carpeted office with Western-style furniture, he makes it plain that his only interest in his visitors is whether or not they will be profitable, and he virtually dismisses the son of his former friend Sheikh Ali al-Tatawi. The lawyer has moved heart and soul into the modern age, as he makes clear in the verb tense of his description of Zaabalawi: "We used to regard him as a man of miracles" (p. 1966).

Other portraits fill a similar symbolic function. The local sheikh or district officer is more cooperative than the lawyer: he is only half-Westernized ("wearing a jacket over his striped galabeya," p. 67) and once the narrator has ingratiated himself the sheikh helps to the best of his ability. Yet he also has grown away from Zaabalawi ("I myself haven't seen him for years, having been somewhat preoccupied with the cares of the world," p. 1967), and his only help is a map of the physical quarters in which Zaabalawi might be found. Modern technical expertise is not the best route to locate an elusive figure who "may well be concealed among the beggars" (p. 1967), among dervishes, or in cafés and mosques. Neither office-worker has the time for human relationships, as is indicated by their complete lack of hospitality when the petitioner arrives.

In contrast, both the calligrapher Hassanein—who is inscribing the name "Allah" when the narrator arrives—and the composer Sheikh Gad immediately receive the visitor "with unaffected gentleness" (p. 1968) and "understanding and kindness" (p. 1969). Both men also know Zaabalawi well and have done their best work under his inspiration. The arts, it appears, lead one closer to the elusive saint than do commerce or technology, but they remain an indirect route and Zaabalawi is not actually *there*. Sheikh Gad gently reproves his disappointed visitor for complaining that his visit has been of no use, and he reminds him of the value of simple human relationships ("God forgive you . . . ," p. 1969).

The climax at the Negma Bar is both appropriate and problematic. Given the allegorical overtones of Zaabalawi's description, it is not likely that the narrator will meet him in person until the moment of death (p. 1969). Only indirect acquaintance has been possible up to now, and this situation continues when the narrator wakes from a drunken stupor to find that Zaabalawi has been present while he slept. The paradisiacal vision that he enters under Zaabalawi's influence confirms earlier indications of the saint's holiness. Strangely enough, the description of the drinking bout reinforces the vision's otherworldly stature since the narrator must divest himself of earthly consciousness before he can enter the dream of "harmony between me and my inner self, and between the two of us and the world, everything being in its rightful place, without discord or distortion" (p. 1971). On a level of realistic description, the presentation of Mr. Wanas as a hardened drinker who insists that his visitor get drunk with him is a credible explanation for the narrator's losing consciousness. Indeed, Mahfouz believes that the reason the story is banned in Egypt is that he offended religious traditionalists by placing the saintly Zaabalawi in a bar (Islamic religion forbids drinking alcohol).

Yet the stages of this intoxication also suggest the peeling-away of ties to "normal" consciousness that is associated with mystic vision. The wine has an initial fiery effect; with the second glass the narrator loses "all willpower"; with the third glass, he loses his memory, and with the fourth, "the future vanished." Mr. Wanas and the world around him are no longer recognizable; they become an abstract picture, "a mere meaningless series of colored planes" (p. 1971). Ordinary perceptions of space and time have disappeared as the narrator succumbs to a vision of eternity. When the narrator returns to consciousness he is convinced that Zaabalawi exists and is the key to his cure. In the ending pages, the possibility of a material explanation still exists but it has receded into the background. "I have to find Zaabalawi" has taken on a much larger meaning than it had in the beginning.

### Classroom Strategies

"Zaabalawi" can be taught in one class period. Students should have no difficulty with the plot or with the religious symbolism of the quest for Zaabalawi. Compare, if appropriate, *Gilgamesh* or the *Divine Comedy* (both included in the first volume) or the Arthurian romances of the Holy Grail. You may wish to point out the relationship of "Zaabalawi" with Gebelawi (or Jabalawi), and remind students that the story is found in a collection titled *God's World*.

What is more easily overlooked—at least on first reading—is the story's social criticism. Here it may be useful to talk a bit about Mahfouz as an Egyptian writer (the first writer in Arabic to win the Nobel Prize for Literature), and remind students that despite the universal themes addressed in "Zaabalawi," the story reflects a specific cultural setting. Located in Cairo, constantly referring to the context of Islamic religious tradition, it uses the interaction of characters to express a real social dilemma between different generations or ways of life in modern Egypt. No one will find the rude and unfriendly lawyer, Sheikh Qamar, an attractive figure. Your students may nonetheless accept his luxurious office with thick carpet and leather-upholstered furniture as merely signs of upward mobility, instead of an implied critique of Westernized bureaucracy. Examine with them such things as the use of Western or traditional Egyptian clothing to suggest opposing value systems: in contrast with the lounge-suited lawyer, for example, Hagg Wanas wears a silk galabeya and a carefully wrapped turban. (See *Backgrounds* paragraphs 5–6.) The local sheikh comes in for similar criticism, for his gift of a map shows that he thinks in terms of technical expertise when such is clearly not the way to locate the saint. Neither the lawyer nor the local sheikh welcome casual visitors; for them, "business is business" and governs their daily life. In contrast, the warmly hospitable artists (the calligrapher Hassanein and the composer Sheikh Gad) are much closer to Zaabalawi (see *Backgrounds* paragraph 7).

It is possible that some students will be as disturbed as the Islamic fundamentalists to find that the narrator's vision of paradise is reached by drinking himself into unconsciousness in a bar. If so, you will want to examine with them the significant emphasis on the stages of the narrator's loss of consciousness. Everyday categories of time and space are successively demolished in order to reach a mystic vision, a process that may be compared with techniques of meditation to arrive at a special inner consciousness. (See also *Backgrounds*, last paragraph.) On the level of realistic description, moreover, the bar scene makes a logical conclusion for a plot that starts with scenes of self-serving, calculating rationality and technical expertise and works towards an ecstatic vision where rational consciousness is submerged.

### Topics for Discussion
1. Discuss the picture given of Zaabalawi in the course of the story. How does this picture relate to concepts of religion, to society, and to modern society in particular?
2. Why does the narrator want or need to find Zaabalawi? What is "that illness for which no one possesses a remedy"?
3. Discuss the relationship of the lawyer (Sheikh Qamar) and the district officer to Zaabalawi. How do the artists the calligrapher Hassanein and the composer Sheikh Gad differ in their perception of him?
4. How are elements of realism and mysticism combined in "Zaabalawi"?
5. Describe the stages of the narrator's quest for Zaabalawi. Why does the quest culminate in the dream in the Negma Bar?
6. What kinds of people does the narrator encounter during his search for Zaabalawi? Are you surprised at the character of Hagg Wanas?
7. What relationship does Zaabalawi have to art? to commerce? to the police?

### Further Reading

See also the reading suggestions in the anthology, p. 1964.

---

Michael Beard, Michael and Adnan Haydar, eds. *Mapping the World of Naguib Mahfouz.* 1992.
A valuable collection of eleven essays on themes, individual texts, and cultural contexts in Mahfouz's work. Bibliography.

Gordon, Haim. *Naguib Mahfouz's Egypt: Existential Themes in His Writings.* 1990.
Considers existential identity for individuals and for Egyptian society throughout Mahfouz's work; literary analysis and anecdotes stemming from many interviews with Mahfouz. The appendix reviews works in English on Mahfouz (up to 1984). Gordon is an Israeli scholar who praises Mahfouz's universal themes but makes pointed criticisms of Egyptian society.

Mahfouz, Naguib. *Respected Sir*, translated by Dr. Rasheed El-Enany 1986.
Translator's introduction is particularly interesting on the connections between Mahfouz's themes and the evolution of his style.

Ostle, R. C., ed. *Studies in Modern Arabic Literature.* 1975.
Hamdi Sakkout's "Najib Mahfuz's Short Stories" argues for the importance and separate identity of Mahfouz's stories; correlations drawn between selected stories and political events.

# RALPH ELLISON
## King of the Bingo Game

*Backgrounds*

Although Ellison's international reputation rests almost solely on his one completed novel, *Invisible Man*, he is an outstanding figure in the rich tradition of black American Literature. In his stories, as in *Invisible Man*, he examines the black American experience powerfully and specifically, while at the same time suggesting significant implications for the predicament of all human beings caught in a social and economic world that systematically victimizes them and denies them full expression. Ellison's "invisible man"—a character or predicament that recurs in different forms throughout his work—is invisible because society has so many pre-set images of him that any unique personal core simply disappears. It is a psychological as well as a sociological dilemma, and to represent it Ellison's style ranges from the realism of precise historical description to hallucinatory intuitions of deeper structures, all inside the framework of traditional prose fiction. "King of the Bingo Game" shows Ellison to be a brilliant social critic and a masterly craftsman, dedicated to both the revelation of social ills and the artistic expression of them.

"King of the Bingo Game" will first be read as a rendering of the black man's experience in America, but its implications extend beyond. As Ellison once said, in reference to his *Invisible Man*, "All novels are about certain minorities: the individual is a minority. The universal in the novel—and isn't that what we're all clamoring for these days?—is reached only through the depiction of the specific man in a specific circumstance."

The specific man in "King of the Bingo Game" is black, dislocated (he's from the South), anonymous (he is unnamed), broke, hungry, unemployed, burdened by personal responsibilities (his wife's illness) and nightmarish dreams; he is without peanuts in a crowd that can only afford peanuts. The specific circumstance is a bingo game in a Depression-era movie theater, which provides a metaphorical context in which the man can act. The theater suggests the kind of world the man inhabits —dark, populated by nameless and faceless members of a crowd, invisible men; their fantasies are limited to movies and bingo, the only fantasies offered by the people who control them. (The emcee and the policemen, significantly, are white.) It is a world in which, like the beam of the projector on the screen, "everything is fixed": a Hollywood version of reality newly packaged into escapist dreams for the deprived. The projectionists are in control and, the protagonist tells us, if the picture they wanted were to go "out of control" they would "go nuts." The movie being projected is suggestive, too. It provides the early part of the story with a striking image of entrapment and vulnerability: a woman is "tied to a bed, her legs and arms spread wide, and her clothing torn to rags." She will be saved through heroic action by a man who, fortunately, chooses to save her rather than take advantage of her. The movie hero is one of those in control, too; he finds the woman with the "beam of a flashlight," which symbolically links him with the projectionists. There will be no such heroes, especially white heroes, entering through trapdoors to save the nameless black protagonist; he will have to find a way to make his own escape. When the protagonist wins the bingo game and has a chance to spin the wheel of fortune for the jackpot (all of $36.90), he has—perhaps for the first time—the opportunity to control his fate, literally hold it in his hands. Already confused by anxiety and by a drink of whiskey on an empty stomach, he is surprised and frightened to be on stage, in the beam of light himself, blindingly visible. When he pushes the button that will determine his fate he realizes that as long as he keeps his finger on it his fate cannot be determined for him:

> And then he knew, even as he wondered, that as long as he pressed the button, he could control the jackpot. He and only he could determine whether or not it was to be his.
>
> (p. 1980)

It is for him an ecstatic, religious, experience. He feels power, he feels like a prophet, keeper of "the most wonderful secret in the world"—a way to beat the game, beat Fate.

> He was running the show, by God!... Then someone was laughing inside him, and he realized that somehow he had forgotten his own name. It was a sad, lost feeling to lose your name, and a crazy thing to do. That name had been given him by the white man who had owned his grandfather a long time ago down South.
>
> (p. 1982)

Momentarily, he achieves power, forgets his slave name, and creates for himself a new name and identity. The other blacks in the audience jeer at him for getting out of line and interrupting their entertainment; he only pities them for still being caught in someone else's game, still accepting the fate dealt out to them by society. In a practical sense, however, the "King" has changed the rules too radically and control is simply wrested from him by two white men in uniform. His frenetic persistence in clinging to his moment of power ends when something lands "hard against his head." The last paragraph of the story suggests that he has won nothing with his double-zero: the money will surely not be paid, he is probably headed for jail, and Laura may die without medical attention. It is a bleak reminder of a harsh social reality, leavened perhaps by a sense that if the "King" (or others like him) are ever to gain control of their lives, it will be through *not* accepting the image and name others have imposed upon them, and by emerging into real self-consciousness.

### Classroom Strategies

"King of the Bingo Game" can be taught in one class period. You should emphasize Ellison's place in the black American tradition, but should not by any means ignore his place in the Modernist tradition, or his significant relation to nineteenth-century American literature.

"King of the Bingo Game" should not present any tremendous problems for students, though they may choose to debate its validity as a rendering of the black experience in America. Certainly, the major themes of black American Literature—the "invisibility" of being black in a white dominated world, the sense of being a victim of forces beyond one's control, the limited possibilities for success, the struggle for identity and some modicum of control over one's destiny—are all here. Worth noting, too, is the fact that a number of features now associated with black American literature are features made prominent by Ellison himself, especially in *Invisible Man*.

A few questions tend to come up: the relationship of the audience and the hero, the significance of the hero's forgetting his name (some students will assume he's really crazy at this point), and the value to be attached to the ending (whether there is anything positive in what has happened).

Some students tend to overlook the scathing picture of racial manipulation in the game itself: they assume that the audience is both white and black, and don't think about the emcee. Take them back to the passage describing the emcee: "this slick looking white man with his blue sport shirt and his sharp gabardine suit" (p. 1981) who calls the hero "boy" and condescends to him with "jive talk," and to the description of the crowd in which "all the Negroes down there were just ashamed because he was black like them." It is necessary to make this separation clear so that the hero's sense of having advanced a step beyond his peers—who still don't realize that the game of society is rigged for them—can be understood in context.

Other students may lose all faith in the "King's" judgment when he forgets such an elementary thing as his name; for such students, he becomes a "real loser" when his manic refusal to give up the wheel assures that he will never receive the $36.90 he seems to have won at the end. The "name" episode is a real rebirth in two ways, however. First, it is a healthy step for him to reject the name assigned by those who had rigged the wheel of social discrimination—"the white man who had owned his grandfather a long time ago down South" (p. 1982). Second, this long new name is not merely a parody of a name, but an heroic epithet which the hero creates for himself in a kind of celebratory rhythm evoking African ceremonial chants, and following an international tradition of noble epithets given for heroic deeds (Hercules the Lion-killer, for example).

The dual implications of the end are discussed in the headnote (pp. 1976–77) and at the end of *Backgrounds*, above. Although the scale is obviously different, students might be asked to consider if they think that the material and physical ruin of Oedipus is the only consideration at the end of *Oedipus the King*, and if the condition of self-knowledge is not presented in both cases as a (painful) good.

### Topics for Discussion and Writing

1. How would you characterize the protagonist? What is his situation? His background? In what way does he become a "King"?
[See paragraphs 3 and 5 of *Backgrounds* and paragraph 5 of *Classroom Strategies* for discussion.]

2. How does Ellison use the theater at the beginning of the story? What is the significance of the movie that is being shown?
[The theater is a metaphor for black experience and also provides a telling context for the story's dramatic action. See paragraph 3 of *Backgrounds* for further discussion.]

3. What does the bingo wheel mean to the protagonist? Why does he fight so hard to hold on to the button which controls it? Why does he feel so ecstatic when he is pushing the button?
[See paragraph 4 of *Backgrounds* and the headnote for discussion.]

4. Why does the protagonist forget his name while pushing the button? Is this a good sign or a bad sign?
[See paragraphs 4–5 of *Backgrounds* and paragraph 5 of *Classroom Strategies* for discussion.]

5. Relate the implications of the story to some other works with similar themes. Many will have read Joyce's "Araby," where the protagonist at the end sees himself "as a creature driven and derided by vanity; and my eyes burned with anguish and anger." Why do stories about the attempt to discover an identity so often end in apparent failure or disappointment?

6. In what ways does "King of the Bingo Game" reflect the experience of being black in America? In what ways does it reflect a more general experience?

7. How does Ellison blend realism and hallucination to make his point? In what sense is the visionary ecstasy on stage *also* motivated by the hero's physical condition? In what sense does it transcend that condition?

8. Who goes to the movie and the bingo game? Why? How does attendance at the bingo game relate to the socioeconomic picture given at the beginning of the story? (You may start a heated discussion if you ask whether state lotteries fill the same function.)

### Further Reading

See the suggestions in the anthology, p. 1977.

Benston, Kimberly W. *Speaking for You: The Vision of Ralph Ellison.* 1987.
A collection of essays examining the way that Ellison's moral vision in conveyed through the interplay of aesthetic practice and

cultural perception; contains a chonology and bibliography after 1937.

Busby, Mark. *Ralph Ellison*. 1991.
An introduction to the author and his work.

Clarke, Graham, ed. *The American City: Literary and Cultural Perspective*. 1988.
Contains "Harlem on My Mind: Fictions of a Black Metropolis" by Robert A. Lee, pp. 62–85.

Lenz, Gunter H., ed. *History and Tradition in Afro-American Culture*. 1984.
Contains "Ralph Ellison and the Literary Tradition" by Rudolf F. Dietze.

Parr, Susan Resneck and Pancho Savery, *Approaches to Teaching Ellison's* Invisible Man. 1989.
Useful for background material and general strategies for teaching Ellison.

Real, Willi. "Ralph Ellison, *King of the Bingo Game* (1944)" from *The Black American Short Story in the 20th Century*, 1977, edited by Peter Bruck, pp. 111–27.
An analysis of the story in terms of social and individual psychology, with emphasis on identity formation.

Saunders, Pearl I. "Symbolism in Ralph Ellison's 'King of the Bingo Game.'" CLA Journal, 20 (September, 1976).

# MARGUERITE DURAS
## Hiroshima Mon Amour

### Backgrounds

The script that Marguerite Duras wrote in 1958 for director Alain Resnais launched one of the most widely-praised films of all time: "a thousand films in one" that combines a moving love story, an elegy for the victims of Hiroshima, and a grim picture of how everyday human relationships—even inside the same community—are deformed and made vicious by war. One reason for the film's universal appeal is that it interprets a crisis of modern civilization (the second World War in Europe and Asia; the threat of nuclear holocaust) in terms of personal experience. It describes the impossible love of two people of different cultures who have both survived the war—and been changed by that fact.

Like Camus or Beckett, Duras uses the confrontation of individuals to illustrate broader social or metaphysical issues. Like Proust, she evokes the memory of earlier emotions or physical sensations that will shape her characters' lives. These characters are more than individuals: they also represent a crucial moment in the history of two nations. "Hi-ro-shi-ma. That's your name." "Yes. Your name is Nevers. Nev-ers in France." At the end of the film, Duras says, it is "as though, through them, *all of Hiroshima was in love with all of Nevers*." Yet pre-existing differences of nation, race, history or philosophy are put into question, at Hiroshima, by what the writer calls the "universal factors of eroticism, love, and unhappiness," and by the image of a common humanity whose dignity and even survival are threatened by war. Duras illustrates this threat on an individual level with the heroine's pain and humiliation in Nevers, and on a cultural level by the unparalleled destruction of Hiroshima. What does it mean to experience such loss and still live? Does one freeze time at that point, refusing to forget—and does that mean refusing to live? These questions are anything but abstract in the film, where the heroine's buried grief and memories of her first love are brought before our eyes throughout her love affair with the Japanese architect.

The rapidity with which these memories alternate with present time, using quick shifts of scene and perspective to juggle several planes of reality at once, is one of the most striking aspects of the movie. Like the alternation at the beginning between scenes of the lovers and views of hospitals, museums, and demonstrations at Hiroshima, it is a strategic displacement of space and time that recalls the "new wave" cinema and the literary techniques of "new wave" cinema and the literary techniques of "new novelists" like Robbe-Grillet. This technique is known as a *montage* effect (a term derived from photography) in which the panorama of familiar reality is broken up and rearranged to suggest new perspectives and different angles of interpretation. Duras's work after *Hiroshima Mon Amour* makes increased use of such effects, and in France today she is known chiefly as an experimental writer and film director who has broken radically with the realistic tradition still visible in 1959.

Although there is a profound difference between the historical realism of *Hiroshima Mon Amour* and Duras's later work, where the imagination is often left free to wander among unnamed characters and ambiguous contexts, many elements of the later Duras are already evident in this early film. She prefers to focus on female characters, exploring their sense of identity—or lack of it—at moments of crisis or in repressive social circumstances. The sin, for these characters, is to follow what is expected by society, for that is to submit to being a predefined personality. In contrast, Duras offers escape through a kind of creative delirium that breaks artificial restraints and allows existence on a deeper, more spontaneous level. Just as the heroine of *Hiroshima Mon Amour* goes temporarily mad at Nevers, and emerges a changed person, so the protagonist of *The Ravishing of Lol. V. Stein* (1964) fascinates and attracts the narrator with the creativity of her retreat from unhappiness into a world of the imagination, and by her attempt to be someone else. Here and elsewhere, Duras explores the fluid sense of self in characters who display—among themselves—an invisible, irrational bond of sympathetic understanding.

While the focus on love, madness, personal affinities, and a strong personality that cannot submit to society is familiar from Romanticism (see Chateaubriand, p. 579), Duras alters tradition when she de-emphasizes the importance of separate personal identity. Part of the creative madness she describes is an inability to distinguish between identities: just as the heroine of *Hiroshima Mon Amour* cannot distinguish between her body and that of her German lover, and later speaks to the architect as though he were the German, so a sign of underlying personal involvement in Duras's later work is a similar blending of identities. The most famous lyrical passages of *Hiroshima Mon Amour*

("I meet you ... you destroy me ... " "Deform me to your likeness ... ") evoke this loss of personality, a destruction and metamorphosis that become the full subject of the later novel and film, *Destroy, She Said.* Such dissolving of the boundaries of the self has become a peculiarly Durasian theme, reaffirmed in a 1975 interview comment that "a progressive loss of identity is the most desirable experience one can know." It has reminded many readers of Samuel Beckett but—unlike Beckett— Duras chiefly explores female characters, and especially characters whose predicament reflects their society and its shaping influence. She also seems to see the fragmentation or dissolution of personality not just as bleak reality in a meaningless world, but as a necessary step in the move toward a deeper, shared unity (which may not, however, be reached.)

*Hiroshima Mon Amour* was written as a film script for director Alain Resnais, who has several times sought out novelists (including Robbe-Grillet) to establish the many-sided "literary" vision of his films. The script was published separately with an interpretive synopsis and added notes on the characters by Duras. Especially significant are the lengthy "Notes on Nevers" that discuss the heroine's feelings during her first love and madness at Nevers although—as the author comments—these notes were written after the original script and intended as a guide for filming in France; they are thus a further interpretation of an already written script.

Duras's original script called for a long, slow shot of the "Bikini mushroom" at the beginning, after which the lovers' shoulders would appear below. This effect was cut, but the image of Hiroshima dominates the early scenes from the initial grainy, glazed appearance of the writhing bodies to the horrifying scenes that illustrate the Frenchwoman's claim to have seen "everything" at Hiroshima: we follow her gaze as she sees the hospital, the museum, Peace Square, newsreels, the graphic exhibits of atomic destruction and the after-effects of radiation, and modern-day Hiroshima with its tourist shops. From now on, it will be impossible *not* to see the lovers' story as part of a larger whole, a somber framework of eternity where—as Duras explains—"Every gesture, every word, takes on an aura of meaning that transcends its literal meaning."

The characters are never given names: names are unimportant in relation to what has gone on here. (The name "Riva" given in the stage or camera directions refers to the actress Emmanuelle Riva, who played the role of the Frenchwoman.) Duras comments in her notes that the woman is thirty-two years old, and the man a Japanese architect of about forty.

The architect, she says, must be played by "a Western-looking Japanese actor," "an international type," in order to minimize differences between the two, and to stress their love rather than any "exotic" (and thus obliquely racist) encounter. As they talk, we are tantalized by a series of hints: her statement that she too has a memory and has tried to forget, her reluctance to talk about Nevers, her suggestion that "looking closely at things is something that has to be learned." Gradually—with the architect's help, as he intuits that Nevers is the core of the question and leads her to talk about it—we discover what happened at Nevers, and how that experience has marked her, made her one with the survivors of Hiroshima.

A visual clue at the beginning of Part II begins to make the link between present and past, the man in Hiroshima and a dying soldier elsewhere. The tempo speeds up, as we learn that she will be leaving tomorrow after finishing her role in a film about peace. Another piece of the puzzle is added: she was young—and went mad—in Nevers. Gradually throughout the rest of the film, in a progression of questions and answers that is illustrated for the viewers by flashbacks to scenes in France during the war, the two survivors move psychologically closer and closer and we discover what happened in Nevers. They share a common perspective on the absurdity and inhumanity of war: she, in the death of her German lover and her punishment for having loved; he, for having lost his entire family to the atomic bomb. Yet it is not so much her punishment that marks the Frenchwoman as the fact that she is a survivor: "the fact that she didn't die of love on August 2, 1944, on the banks of the Loire [is] . . . this lost opportunity which has made her what she is." The guilt of having survived is one of the chief emotions reported by Hiroshima survivors, and one which presumably the architect shares in spite of his professional success and his role in rebuilding the ruined city. When the Frenchwoman tells the Japanese architect about her first love at Nevers, she is giving him a glimpse into the core of her personality as it is now: in Duras's words, she is giving him "herself as she now is, her *survival* after the death of her love *at Nevers*." Truly, she feels she has betrayed herself in telling the story.

Although *Hiroshima Mon Amour* is clearly an antiwar film inspired by particular historical circumstances, Duras has chosen to emphasize the fictional love story over any "made-to-order documentary." Only thus, she says, will we be able really to "probe the lesson of Hiroshima." Readers who find the script only a love story, however, will have missed the point. The paired loves of Nevers and Hiroshima are equally hopeless, equally alienated from their everyday worlds and doomed to have no future. Many viewers, however, are so caught up in the love story that they insist on hoping for the proverbial happy ending, a wish that attests to the power of this description of unexpected passion. Duras's tolerant response to their hope makes it clear that such an ending is a separate development upon the story we have here: "Certain spectators of the film thought she 'ended up' by staying at Hiroshima. It's possible. I have no opinion." Having taken her to the limit of her refusal to stay at Hiroshima, we haven't been concerned to know whether—once the film was finished—she succeeded in reversing her refusal.

### Classroom Strategies

*Hiroshima Mon Amour* can be taught in one or two periods. If possible, have your students see the film first (either rented or on videocassette), so that they receive the full impact of the initial montage sequence setting the theme, and so they can see (in the second montage sequence) the true balance of the Nevers episode. (Note that Nevers, pronounced Ne-*vair*, has no connection whatsoever in French with the word for "never," which is *jamais*.) You might suggest to the students that they read aloud some of the lyric passages, and try to get a feel for the emotions expressed as well as for the poetic quality of the film in general. Budding writers or cineasts may want to discuss the use of *montage* to present a new point of view.

In one period, you will want to focus on the development of the love affair at Hiroshima (why Hiroshima?) and its significance for the two survivors the most accessible avenues are probably the pairing of the two love stories, and the way the plot foreshadows and gradually reveals the Frenchwoman's secret. Although the easiest way to discuss the latter may be to follow it as a matter of deduction, with hints, parallelisms, and partial answers leading you through, it is also possible to structure it by showing how the architect senses and draws out her story, a process which has been compared to a successful psychiatric treatment in which repressed painful memories are drawn to the surface, relived, and integrated on a conscious level.

If you have two periods, you can move into a variety of important topics: in fact, your students may insist on bringing them up in the first period. In *Hiroshima Mon Amour* Duras has touched on one of the most widespread fears of modern times, the threat of a nuclear war. When she wrote in the fifties, there had already been reports, documentaries, and memoirs about Hiroshima, but—as recent studies of even young children show—anxiety over nuclear war is if anything more common today. Your students will know about the nuclear freeze movement, and the fact that—given our increased capacity for destruction—many scientists see a nuclear war as bringing the end of all life on earth. Under the circumstances, it may seem ironic that Duras is talking about the reactions of survivors: the film provides, however, an opportunity for classroom discussion of how people react to events or possibilities of such magnitude. Related topics include the film's critique of war and its distortion of human relationships; whether or not the protagonists have achieved a special level of insight due to their status as survivors; the criticism of national or racial ideology versus a sense of basic humanity (see the attack in Part I on "inequality set forth as a principle by certain people . . ." races, and classes); and whether any of this relates to the international political situation today.

### Topics for Discussion and Writing

1. What difference does it make to this love affair that it takes place in Hiroshima? (Explain the title.)
   [See paragraph 7 of *Backgrounds*.]

2. Discuss the second "I meet you / I remember you" interior monologue. (p. 2010). How does it sum up the course of events, and express the woman's feelings?
   [This assignment will require more creativity on the student's part, and more flexibility in judging on yours. Paragraph 2 of *Backgrounds* raises the general issue of memory, paragraph 5 speaks to the "You destroy me" aspect, and the student should be able to refer other passages to different parts of the film. The "word" that fades from memory is, in French, the "name" referring to the "thing" that binds us. Note that the end of this monologue differs from the first one, and refers to the heroine's "betrayal" of her cherished memory by talking about it. She now fully recognizes her status as survivor, and that even the memory of her love will ultimately be lost.]

3. How does *Hiroshima Mon Amour* illustrate the "inhumanity" of war?
   [Paragraph 2 of *Backgrounds*. The two levels of Hiroshima and

Nevers are paired: Hiroshima for the bomb damage and after effects of radiation (including the fact that genetically damaged survivors were outcasts in Japanese society); Nevers for the destruction of innocent love, of family ties, and of a community's sense of common humanity.]

4. Do you think the Frenchwoman will change her mind at the last minute? Will she stay in Hiroshima? Does it matter whether she stays or goes?
[Paragraph 10 of *Backgrounds.*]

5. Comment on the statement "I think looking closely at things is something that has to be learned." (p. 1993). How do montage effects help us to "look more closely" in the film?
[Paragraphs 3, 7, and 9 of *Backgrounds*; paragraph 1 of *Classroom Strategies*. The psychological insights gained from actually seeing the past at Nevers well up in the present at Hiroshima; the social criticism implied in contrast of love and death at the beginning, and the ironic contrast of ruined Hiroshima with the banal modern city. You may wish to ask your students what the difference in effect would be if the stories of Hiroshima and Nevers were simply presented as background information at one point, with no jump-cutting in time and space.]

6. In what sense are these characters representative, in what sense individual? Why are they never named?
[Paragraphs 2, 8 of *Backgrounds.*]

7. Comment on the role of memory in the film. Has the French-woman really "betrayed" her memory by telling her story? Why does she think so?
[Paragraph 9 of *Backgrounds.* You may wish to follow the theme of memory through the text in class, beginning with "I wanted to have an inconsolable memory . . . " through the self-accusation and recapitulations in Part V.]

8. Comment on the mixture of fiction and documentary in the film. Would pure documentary have been more effective in probing the lesson of Hiroshima?

[Although the film uses actual documentary footage, and depicts the making of another "film about Peace," Duras believes in the special insights of fiction. See paragraph 10 of *Backgrounds*, and the author's Synopsis preceding the separately published text.]

### Further Reading

See also the suggestions in the anthology, pp. 1987.

Cismaru, Alfred. *Marguerite Duras*. 1971.
An early study that stresses the author's search for identity and offers a good deal of factual information on works up to 1969.

Duras, Marguerite. Preface, Synopsis, and Appendices in the separately-published *Hiroshima Mon Amour*, translated by Richard Seaver. Picture Editor: Robert Hughes. 1961.
A valuable addition to and interpretation of the script, with numerous shots taken from the film.

————. *Destroy, She Said*. Translated by Barbara Bray, followed by interview "Destruction and Language" translated by Helen Lane Cumberford. 1970.
A good example of Duras's themes and cinematic style in her later work, along with an interview discussing her ideas on genre, narrative point of view, characterization, and the necessity of madness.

————. *Outside: Selected Writings*. Translated by Arthur Goldhammer. 1986.
A selection of newspaper articles (many written when she was covering court cases) that demonstrate the author's sympathy for society's victims.

————. *The War: A Memoir*. Translated by Barbara Bray. 1986.
Episodes from diaries describing Duras's experience during World War II; a prefatory note calls *The War* "one of the most important things in my life."

————, and Xavière Gauthier. *Woman to Woman*. Translated and with an afterword by Katharine A. Jensen. 1987.

# ALEXANDER SOLZHENITSYN
## Matryona's Home

*Backgrounds*

Solzhenitsyn's work centers on the effects of modern Soviet society
on its citizens. Many of his characters, Matryona among them, are good
people victimized by their society, who manage to rise above their
predicament and demonstrate an endurance and personal integrity which
cannot be destroyed by circumstances. Awarding Solzhenitsyn the Nobel
Prize for Literature in 1970, the committee reconized Solzhenitsyn for
the "ethical force [with] which he has pursued the indispensable traditions of Russian literature." The choice of the word *Russian* is significant here, since Solzhenitsyn is infinitely more Russian than Soviet. He
·has condemned the Soviet system from the outset of his career, just as he
has condemned what he sees as the corrupt values of the decadent West.
In a letter to the Soviet Writer's Union, from which he was expelled in
1969, he wrote: "Literature that does not warn in time against threatening
moral and social dangers—such literature does not deserve the name of
literature." His unwavering concern for truth and his earnest unwillingness to compromise his beliefs—both maintained at great personal cost—
define his reputation as a major literary presence in the last half of this
century.

"Matryona's Home" involves a favorite Solzhenitsyn theme—the
righteous person forced to deal with corrupt and difficult circumstances.
Matryona is an illiterate peasant who nevertheless faces her circumstances with an almost saintly wisdom; she becomes, in Solzhenitsyn's
hands, a testimony to the good that survives in the best of human beings.

Readers of Tolstoy's *The Death of Iván Ilyich* will have seen something of Matryona's kind of simple wisdom in the servant Gerasim; other
readers may be able to compare Matryona to Dostoevsky's Prince Mysh-
kin in *The Idiot*, Jaroslav Hasek's Good Soldier Schweik, or Isaac Ba-
shevis Singer's Gimpel the Fool. Solzhenitsyn's story will not bear, or
need, a great deal of analysis. In form it is a hagiography—the story of
the life of saint—who, like all saints, is unappreciated, misunderstood,
belittled, bedeviled, taken advantage of, and abandoned. She dies while
sacrificing herself for others. Her story is told with understated directness

by a narrator who, we must understand, knows something about suffering and patience. But even he comes to recognize the spiritual greatness of Matryona:

> ...the righteous one without whom, as the proverb says, no village can stand.
> Nor any city.
> Nor our whole land.
>
> (p. 2046)

Matryona does not need material comforts beyond those necessary for survival; she makes her home available to all the creatures of the earth—itinerant schoolteachers fresh from prison camp, lame cats, mice, cockroaches. Her home is *open* to the natural world and, as always in the pastoral tradition, at her death the natural world mourns her passing.

> The mice had gone mad. They were running furiously up and down the walls, and you could almost see the green wallpaper rippling and rolling over their backs.
>
> (p. 2040)

She owns no suckling pig because she would have had to nurture it only to kill it. She owns no cow because she could not have fed it well enough; her pathetic and filthy goat suits her needs and she does not ask for more. She is supremely competent at the business of survival, though that competence is entirely unappreciated; she weathers sickness, physical hardship, bureaucracy, and the age of machines with uncomplaining dignity. The narrator is in search of "deepest Russia" (p. 2018)—in Matryona, he finds its very core.

Two other central concerns of Solzhenitsyn are evident in "Matryona's Home": the inefficiency and callousness of the Soviet bureaucracy, especially the cooperative farm system, and the inability of the "machine age" to fulfill the essential needs of human beings. The Soviet system is the target of Solzhenitsyn's narrative wrath on a number of occasions in "Matryona's Home." The lack of peat, which Matryona must have for fuel during the insufferably cold Russian winter, is particularly suggestive, because it forces the old women of the village to gather their courage and steal it from the bogs—where it is being kept for more privileged members of the Soviet classless society. Matryona's vain and exhausting attempts to get her pension ("They shove me around, Ignatich," says Matryona at one point, "Worn out with it I am" [p. 2024]) reemphasizes the point, as does her experience trying to get train tickets.

Solzhenitsyn's disgust with the "machine age" takes a number of

---

forms in the story, but the most effective and suggestive is the manner of Matryona's death, which is an anti-machine parable. Matryona is afraid of trains; they have a demonic kind of horror for her:

> When I had to go to Cherusti, the train came up from Nechaevka way with its great big eyes popping out and the rails humming away—put me in a regular fever. My knees started knocking. God's truth I'm telling you!
>
> (p. 2028)

It is ironically appropriate, then, that she should be killed by a train, literally dismembered, as she helps her rapacious and callous relations cart away the pathetic fragments of her own home. The machine she so despised is the agent of her death:

> When it was light the women went to the crossing and brought back all that was left of Matryona on a hand sledge with a dirty sack over it. They threw off the sack to wash her. There was just a mess...no feet, only half a body, no left hand.
>
> (p. 2041)

Matryona's death is the final testament to the inevitable destruction of the simple values which she embodies, and which we are being asked to embrace. Her body, like her life, ends in pieces. The blossoming "red-faced girl clasping a sheaf" cannot survive a system and a way of life which can no longer appreciate her virtues. Once, Solzhenitsyn insists, "there was singing out under the open sky, such songs as nobody can sing nowadays, with all the machines in the fields" (p. 2033).

Like the narrator of "Matryona's Home," Solzhenitsyn spent time (eight years) in a Soviet prison camp. He had been exiled there in 1945 for anti-Soviet propaganda and agitation, after a letter in which he made remarks critical of Joseph Stalin was intercepted by a government censor. After he was released Solzhenitsyn, again like the narrator, took a job as a schoolteacher in rural Ryazan, near Moscow. During his tenure in Ryazan, Solzhenitsyn apparently became friendly with a person who was the basis for Matryona. The train accident which appears in "Matryona's Home" is said to have its basis in what happened to that friend.

"Matryona's Home" was one of the very few works by Solzhenitsyn actually published in the Soviet Union. On its publication, the story was attacked because it was said to misrepresent Russian peasants. They were not, said the critics, greedy and rapacious as are Matryona's relatives in the story. They were, instead, as cooperative as members of a collective farm are supposed to be. Solzhenitsyn was denied the Lenin Prize, for which he had been enthusiastically nominated, and his novel *The First Circle* was rejected. (The novel was finally published in the West, like all of his subsequent works.)

## Classroom Strategies

"Matryona's Home" can be taught in one class period, though the period will be stretched if the teacher provides much background information on the Russian Revolution and the nature of the Soviet Union under Stalin. You may wish to compare Solzhenitsyn's picture of Stalinist society with the more urban and personal experience described in Akhmatova's *Requiem* (included in this volume).

The major problem here will not be to convince students of the "truth" of Solzhenitsyn's tale; they will more than likely be all too happy to accept it as "truth." Because the story answers to most of the myths and preconceptions Westerners already have about Soviet life, the problem will be to make sure that students read it with the same degree of resistance with which they would normally confront any other piece of fiction. Students may well find some of Solzhenitsyn's operating notions—the saintly peasant and the evident superiority of the pastoral life, for instance—difficult to swallow once they are disassociated from his more explicit condemnations of the Soviet system. It will need to be pointed out that for Solzhenitsyn the universal problems of greed, indifference, misunderstanding, and the desire for unnecessary luxury do not by any means disappear beyond the boundaries of the Soviet Union.

## Topics for Discussion and Writing

1. The narrator tells us that he wishes to find "deepest Russia." Does he? In what ways?
   [See paragraphs 3–4 of *Backgrounds*.]

2. What constitutes Matryona's goodness? Would the virtues she exhibits serve her in an urban or technologically sophisticated environment? Does Solzhenitsyn appear to be suggesting that we should return to a life of rural simplicity?

3. How is irony used in the story? What is ironic about the nature of

Matryona's death? What is ironic about the things people say about her after her death?

[See paragraphs 6–7 of *Backgrounds* for discussion.]

4. How is narrative understatement used in the story? Is it effective? What would be the effect of writing about such a saintly woman in inflated language?

### Further Reading

See also the suggestions in the anthology, p. 2017–18.

Burg, David and George Feifer. *Solzhenitsyn*. New York, 1972.
Discusses "Matryona's Home" as purely documentary, perhaps underrating the fictional elements of the story.

Curtis, James M. *Solzhenitsyn's Traditional Imagination*. 1984.
Literary traditions and individual writers (Russian and non-Russian) that influenced Solzhenitsyn's novels.

Dunlop, John B., Richard S. Haugh, and Michael Nicholson, eds. *Solzhenitsyn in Exile: Critical Essays and Documentary Material.* 1985.
Essays on Solzhenitsyn's reception in different countries and on the work itself; documentary and bibliographical material.

Labedz, Leopold. *Solzhenitsyn: A Documentary Record*. New York, 1970.
A collection of comments, reports, reviews, and extracts of documents and interviews. Interesting for Solzhenitsyn's own comments.

Moody, Christopher. *Solzhenitsyn*. New York, 1973.
Contains a short but informative discussion of "Matryona's Home."

Scammell, Michael. *Solzhenitsyn: A Biography*. New York, 1984.
Comprehensive and detailed.

Solzhenitsyn, Alexander. *Solzhenitsyn: A Pictorial Autobiography.* 1974.

Solzhenitsyn, Alexander. *The Oak and the Calf: A Memoir.* Translated by Harry Willets. 1980.

# DORIS LESSING
## Old Chief Mshlanga

### Backgrounds

Lessing is one of the most intensely committed of contemporary writers in English. Individual freedom and fulfilment return over and over again as her chief theme, together with a concern for social justice. Only when human beings are given full members of society, she suggests, will human society be truly harmonious—or sane. These concerns pervade not only the novels and stories set in England, but also the *African Stories* in which black and white characters alike are molded by their position in society. Lessing's own point of view, she notes, emerges from her experience as the daughter of white settlers in Rhodesia, and her African stories describe different facets of the blocked (or budding) consciousness of that socially privileged class.

Although there is a clear historical context for these stories, they demonstrate the *functioning* of colonialism rather than specific locations, people, or events. Lessing writes about a "Zambesia" which is a "composite of various white-dominated parts of Africa and, as I've since discovered, some of the characteristics of its white people are those of any ruling minority whatever their colour." Her British characters are typically alienated from the Africa they colonize: they cling to their British or European identity, and to the habits of their homeland, as an anchor of security in the midst of a country that remains remote and strange. Now and again there are friendships (e.g. between Tommy and Dirk, Mr. Macintosh's bastard son in "The Antheap") or inconclusive attempts by newcomers to set things right (Marina Gile's effort to reprove her neighbors and reform her servant Charles in "A Home for the Highland Cattle"), but these relationships are psychologically demanding, often frustrated, and invariably complicated.

There is a harsh economic history behind the social relationships and final conflict of "The Old Chief Mshlanga." In many ways, the story encapsulates the successive stages of European colonization. In the typical pattern of colonial invasion, commercial companies moved into an area and established *de facto* dominance before their overseas government took official control (sometimes in apparent response to glaring abuses of power). Southern Rhodesia was administered until 1923 by a British Chartered Company that divided all land into "alienated" property (owned and occupied by white settlers, or occupied by Africans who paid a tax to the settler and to the Company) and "unalienated" African property (which could be appropriated by whites if the Company approved). There were native "Reserves" on "unalienated" land, and the Africans who live on such Reserves also paid taxes to the Company. The Company yielded control to the British government in 1923, but in 1930 the new government's Land Apportionment Act effectively reiterated the old distinctions by establishing areas calle "Native" and "European." Africans continued to be pushed off "European" land into "Native" country, and in 1956 Lessing wrote after revisiting Southern Rhodesia that only 46 percent of the land was still owned by Africans. The figure of the old chief Mshlanga thus telescopes a moment of history: a one time ("not much more than fifty years before") he ruled the whole region inside which the Jordan farm occupies a small portion, but now he is reduced to presiding over a single village. Subject to alien laws and a foreign economic system, he and his people are finally pushed off the last segment of their ancestral territory which will be "opened up for white settlement soon."

Lessing's view of African politics is clearly grounded in a European perspective, as she herself recognizes. The focus of her story—despite the title image of Chief Mshlanga—is the evolving experience of a young British girl growing up on an African farm. The protagonist's attitude towards European and African traditions, her confused discomfort as events contradict expectations, and her progressive awakening to the beauty of the African countryside, may all be compared with Achebe's picture of African life in *Things Fall Apart* (included in this anthology).

Like many stories of adolescent coming-of-age (for example, Joyce's *Portrait*, pp. 1633), "The Old Chief Mshlanga" is structured by the various stages of the young girl's gradual insight. At the beginning, she is presented a totally removed from the African landscape and its people; she lives in a fairy tale world of medieval castles, oak trees, snow, and Northern witches. The hot African countryside is unreal and its people an amorphous, faceless mass, "as remote as the trees and the rocks." Even the narrative perspective is external, presenting the protagonist in the third person as "a small girl," "a white child," and a "she" who teases and torments the natives as if it were her inborn right. Mr. Jordan's young daughter is insulated from any contact that might arouse insecurity or fear; she "mustn't talk to natives" and she walks the countryside fortified by two dogs and a gun.

Change and a series of more personal encounters are signalled by an abrupt introduction of the subjective "I." In her own voice, the protagonist tells how she encountered a dignified old man and was put to shame by his pride and courtesy. Chief Mshlanga, she learns later, used to rule the entire country; this extraordinary fact awakens the girl's interest in her surroundings and she begins to experience the African countryside first as a physical reality and second as a heritage to be shared between her own people and the blacks. "It seemed quite easy"—too easy, as she finds when wandering beyond the farm to visit the Chief in his village. Suddenly the landscape is unfamiliar, even menacing, and she is intensely afraid. The women and children of the village do not respond to her questions, she herself does not understand why she has come, and the Old Chief and his attendants are not pleased at her intrusion. Returning home through the newly hostile landscape, the little Chieftainess can no longer pretend to be an innocent bystander; as the land seems to tell her, she is one of the destroyers.

The end of the story comes quickly and painfully. After an argument over crops trampled by the Chief's goats, her father confiscates the animals and threatens the Chief with the police when he complains that the tribe will starve. Proudly reminding Mr. Jordan that the farm and indeed the whole region have been usurped from the tribe, Chief Mshlanga walks away followed by his son, who has been the Jordans's cook. Pride, however, is a less tangible commodity than the settler's acquaintance with the local authorities, and the Chief and his tribe are soon uprooted and moved to a Native Reserve. The young girl's reaction is not fully visible at this point; she merely reports the quarrel and its aftermath and, a year later, visits the decaying village. The people are gone; their houses are mounds of mud topped with rotting thatch and swarms of ants. Conversely, the land is a riot of triumphant colors and lush new growth. The tone of the final paragraph has changed, voicing an older and more distanced perspective which may or may not be that of the narrator—yet it still views the African landscape from outside, and still with a buried question.

### Classroom Strategies

"The Old Chief Mshlanga" can be taught in a single period. The easiest way to coordinate discussion is to begin with the familiar narrative pattern of "coming of age"; in this case, the evolution of the main character towards increased understanding of her African environment. The first page sets up the contrast between a European heritage that is jealously cherished (she reads European fairy tales, medieval romances, and archaizing Victorian literature) and an actual African setting that appears to ber—both people and landscape—quite unreal. "The black people on the farm were as remote as the trees and the rocks. They were an amorphous black mass . . . who existed merely to serve." At this point, you will want to introduce some historical background on European colonization of the eighteenth and nineteenth centuries. This background can be as broad as you wish, with examples from Africa, India, both Near and Far East, and the Western hemisphere, but it will be especially useful to describe Lessing's "Zambesia" in terms of the actual history of Southern Rhodesia (reminding students that Rhodesia is now Zimbabwe). The split between European and African, white and black, that is so much a part of this story has demonstrable historical roots, and the familiar theme of "coming of age" is paired with a poignant description of *what* the child comes to sense: her own cultural alienation, and the irreparable damage done to "her" country by colonization and the forced resettlement of an occupied people. Two comparisons are appropriate here: Albert Camus's "The Guest" (included earlier in the anthology) for another example of the colonial predicament seen through European eyes, and Chinua Achebe's *Things Fall Apart* (included later) as a black African perspective on the same conflict.

The fact that this *is* a European perspective is brought out by the contrast between the title image of the African "Old Chief" and the fact that the narrative recounts the experience of a young settler girl. The presence of the Old Chief is crucial but (in terms of the story) only as a symbolic figure who crystallizes questions the girl is beginning to ask. Ask the students to imagine how the story would seem if told from the perspective of the corresponding (somewhat older) child: Chief Mshlanga's son, who works in the Jordans's kitchen.

You may want to take advantage of recurring themes when you examine significant passages with your class. Lessing has clearly used different descriptions of landscape for symbolic purposes. There is the cold and snowy Northern landscape to which the child escapes in her reading, contrasted with Africa's "gaunt and violent" scenery, the contrast of the Jordan's farm and the well-kept, colorful African village; the bigness and silence of Africa with its "ancient sun," "entwined trees," lurking animals, and "shapeless menage"; and the final scene in which nature has taken over and erased the village after its inhabitants have been sent away. These settings are also linked with different stages of the young girl's awareness. At the beginning, she is armored against fear by her two dogs and the gun she carries; later, she is panic-stricken and lost when walking alone in the immense and alien landscape. The African landscape tell her "You walk here as a destroyer," as an integral part of the colonial presence; it teaches her that she cannot "dismiss the past with a smile in an easy gush of felling." The ending paragraph bring out this sense of impalpable loss in its description of the "unsuspected vein of richness" that persists, buried, in the deserted ancestral ground of the Old Chief's village.

### Topics for Discussion and Writing

1. Why is the story titled "The Old Chief Mshlanga"? In what sense is the story both *about* and *not about* the chief?

2. The narrator mentions "questions, which could not be suppressed" and "questions that troubled me." What might be some of these questions, how and by whom are they suppressed, and at what points in the story do they come to the fore?

3. Discuss the various references to fear in the story, and the way that they are associated with the narrator's awareness of her surroundings.

4. How does Lessing establish the dignity and importance of Chief Mshlanga? Cite several passages.

5. What does the loss of the goats mean to Chief Mshlanga? to Mr. Jordan? What is implied when Mr. Jordan says "Go to the police, then"? Why is there no further discussion?

6. Describe Lessing's use of symbolic landscapes.
   [Note the contrast of North European and landscapes in the opening paragraphs; the untouched landscape during the child's trip to and from Chief Mshlanga's kraal (its beauty and strangeness; the sense of menage); the Jordans's farm with its "harsh eroded soil," twisted trees, and migrant workers' compound that was "a dirty and neglected place"; the harmony of the African village with

"lovingly decorated" huts and the "enclosing arm" of the river; the final scene of the abandoned kraal.]

7. What signs of colonial government are included in the story? Why are they not given more prominence?

8. Discuss the implications of the last scene: the "festival of pumpkins," the exceptionally flourishing plants, the area's "unsuspected vein of richness." What is this richness? Whose point of view governs the ending paragraph? Can you tell?

### Further Reading

See also the suggestions in the anthology, p. 2050.

Bloom, Harold, ed. *Doris Lessing*. 1986.
A collection of essays, arranged chronologically, that discusses Lessing's novels as well as broad issues of ideology and philosophy. In contrast, the editor's introduction sharply criticizes Lessing for emphasizing issues and lacking stylistic mastery.

Gardiner, Judith Kegan. *Rhys, Stead, Lessing, and the Politics of Empathy*. 1989.
Discusses concepts of identity in Lessing's short fiction; contains an interesting analysis of gendered rhetoric used to describe the child in "The Old Chief Mshlanga."

Knapp, Mona. *Doris Lessing*. 1984.
An informative general introduction to Lessing's works, arranged chronologically. Describes individual works and offers a chronology.

# ALAIN ROBBE-GRILLET
## The Secret Room

### Backgrounds

Robbe-Grillet is one of most influential of post-modern novelists and theoreticians. His fiction and theory have influenced French writers such as Nathalie Sarraute, Claude Simon, and Michel Butor; American writers such as John Barth, William Gass, and Donald Barthelme; the Austrian Peter Handke; and a host of others. Reading him requires us to rupture all our previous assumptions about what fiction "means," and to participate in his non-referential world of pure fictionality. Yet this fictional world is not at all "unreal," in Robbe-Grillet's view. Instead, it reflects a modern understanding of the real opaqueness and contradictions of the world in which we live. As Robbe-Grillet says, "If the reader sometimes has difficulty getting his bearings in the modern novel, it is the same way that he loses them in the very world where he lives, when everything in the old structures and the old norms around him is giving way."

It is appropriate that Robbe-Grillet should link a sense of dislocation in the modern novel with the same dislocation in everyday life. The challenge that his works represent to literary criticism is akin to the challenge they pose to contemporary norms and cultural habits, much as it may seem that the enormous technical intricacy of his fiction removes it from real-life considerations. In fact, once you students realize that the elaborately shifting scene of "The Secret Room" replays themes that would be called sadistic or pornographic if published in a newspaper, they may have real questions about the significance of this story and of Robbe-Grillet's work itself. One way of addressing this problem is to begin by discussing the experimental innovations of new-novel technique, and then to consider the ways in which this revolutionary technique causes us to re-examine not just the way we *see* the world, but also the way we think and act in it. The "new novelists" are proposing a metaphysical and social argument, as well as a revolutionary aesthetic strategy. Robbe-Grillet's 1961 essay, "New Novel, New Man," describes preparing the citizen of the future by clarifying that most basic level of social relationships: literally, how we "look at things."

Traditional modes of literary analysis are paralyzed when we come to

Robbe-Grillet, and that is precisely the way he wants it. Following a linear plot or the protagonist's psychological development will not help us in "The Secret Room" as it would, for example, in "Death in Venice," *Portrait of the Artist*, or "The Old Chief Mshlanga." To understand Robbe-Grillet's fictions, we apply immediately to his theories and especially the essays collected in *For a New Novel* (from which the following quotations are taken) provide us with some of the help we require.

Robbe-Grillet makes one basic assertion everywhere in his theoretical writing: that the conventions we ordinarily find in fiction are, in fact, conventional ways of looking at the world, derived from a world view that we no longer share, a world which "marked the apogee of the individual," and in which "personality represented both the means and the end of all exploration." Such a world required that all the technical elements of narrative—"systematic use of the past tense and the third person, unconditional adoption of chronological development, linear plots, regular trajectory of the passions, impulse of each episode toward a conclusion, etc.—tended to impose the image of a stable, coherent, continuous, unequivocal, entirely decipherable universe." Fictions, indeed words themselves, "functioned as a trap in which the writer captured the universe in order to hand it over to society."

For Robbe-Grillet, there are two problems with this conventional mode of literary representation. First, it is not true to our contemporary understanding of reality, and second, it does not help bring about a new order. The contemporary world is "no longer our private property." Nor is it appropriate any longer for human beings to *impress* themselves upon nature, to mold and shape it in their own image. The modern world is "less sure of itself, more modest perhaps, since it has renounced the omnipotence of the person." Where the traditional language of fiction assumed a "nature," and our superior place in it, we can now make no such assumption. For Robbe-Grillet, the world is not "moral." It is neither "significant nor absurd. It *is*, quite simply." This new reality must be explored, but traditional modes of representing reality are ill-suited to the task. Robbe-Grillet's "new-novel" techniques aims to reflect the *is*-ness, the quiddity, of things. He wants to "record the distance between the object and myself, and the distances of the object itself . . ."; this kind of narrative aims to show that "things are here and that they are nothing but things, each limited to itself." Linked to this recognition that things "are" in themselves, separate from us, is the realization that we still *perceive* them from our own angle of vision: hence Robbe-Grillet's emphasis on shifting perspective of what *is*, reminding us that any perceiver is limited and that point of view changes in time. The writer is free to invent, without preconceptions. "What constitutes the novelist's strength is precisely that he invents quite freely, without a model."

The political implications of Robbe-Grillet's position are important. In a world which is no longer "stable, coherent, and continuous," traditional modes of operation—including the ways we relate to others, to things, and to institutions—must be revised. Consequently, the writer revises expectations throughout his career and especially in later work that destabilizes any attempt to find a constant center. The beginning of *The House of Assignations* (1965) announces contradiction as its theme, and thereafter provides merging but contradictory versions of events: different people are given identical defining traits or made to speak identical lines, and short passages frequently do not quite fit into the tentatively established story lines. *Action in Project for a Revolution in New York* (1970) sometimes progresses by verbal echoes, or anagrams of a few key words (*rouge* connected with *rogue, urge, roue, joue*) rather than by logical plot sequence; the narrative persona may shift in the midst of a passage, and that same shift indicates (in French) a sudden shift of gender, too—*he* becoming *she*, for example. *Project for a Revolution in New York* is not a political tract, despite its title, but an experimental revolution of "revolving" nightmare scenes that could almost be taken from pulp novels depicting the depersonalized violence of the modern city—the "New York" of popular mythology.

On the technical side, this increasingly impersonal juxtaposition of elements suggests artistic *collage* processes. Robbe-Grillet was well acquainted with avant-garde artists Robert Rauschenberg and Roy Lichtenstein, and he produced collages himself and also collaborated on a 1978 text with Rauschenberg (*Suspect Surface Traces*). *Topology of a Phantom City* (1975), and Memories of the Golden Triangle (1978) display collage assembly techniques, coordinating a series of texts (some printed elsewhere and by other people) with new prose links, or setting them in patterns of mathematical repetition. *Memories of the Golden Triangle* may be read as any one of several overlapping stories, and each newly-chosen protagonist will suggest a different slant on the same events (like interactions in "real life"). Less technical or impersonal are the underlying themes of all these works: the murders, rapes, torture, anxious pursuit, and general violence portrayed throughout variations on the basic detective-story form. Here the political significance is more ambiguous. On the one hand, these sado-erotic fantasies (already present in "The Secret Room") can be interpreted as the aggressive free play of an author's libidinous imagination; on the other, as parodic recognition of similar pervasive themes in contemporary culture, whether in fiction, advertising, newspaper reporting or—most recently and most strikingly—in MTV.

The "new novel," then, reflects this new state of affairs. It reflects the is-ness, the quiddity, of things, since it is by firmly establishing their *presence* that "objects and gestures establish themselves." The only reality we can discuss, without becoming complicit in an outmoded system of explanatory references ("whether emotional, sociological, Freudian, or metaphysical"), is a reality which simply *is*. In his work, Robbe-Grillet wants only to "record the distance between the object and myself, and the distances of the object itself (its *exterior* distances, i.e., its measurements), and the distances of objects among themselves, and to insist further that these are *only distances* (and not divisions)." He wants to do this because this kind of narrative establishes that "things are here and that they are nothing but things, each limited to itself." Linked to this recognition that things "are" in themselves, separate from us, is the realization that we still *perceive* them from our own angle of vision: hence Robbe-Grillet's emphasis on shifting perspectives of what *is*, reminding us that any perceiver is limited and that point of view changes in time.

The most obvious influences on "The Secret Room" are films, paintings, and popular fiction, especially thriller fiction. Robbe-Grillet's associations with film-making and film-makers (particularly Alain Resnais) are many and obvious. The images of "The Secret Room" are snapshots, and *Snapshots* is the title of the 1962 collection in which "The Secret Room" appeared, but they are snapshots given movement by their juxtaposition, creating a kind of montage effect. One critic has noted that whereas traditional fiction "renders the illusion of space by going from point to point in time," Robbe-Grillet's fiction—like a film—renders time "by going from point to point in space." The overall effect of the cinema on Robbe-Grillet's fiction is clarified by thinking of his narrative point of view as a camera eye captures what there is to see without necessarily linking what it sees in space *or* time. Readers will recall the extent to which Eliot, Pound, Joyce, and Beckett use similar techniques.

Robbe-Grillet's "verbal art" also emulates "painterly style"; "The Secret Room" pays artistic homage to the Symbolist painter Gustave Moreau. Robert Rauschenberg, Jasper Johns, and René Magritte have also strikingly influenced his recent fiction and one senses that Marcel Duchamp's success in transforming our perceptions of objects by revising their context equally left its mark. The painterly notion of collage is evident in "The Secret Room" and elsewhere in his fiction. Finally, the notion that a single "scene" may be presented from a number of perspectives simultaneously, or almost simultaneously, was one of the crucial discoveries of painters such as Cezanne, Braque, and Picasso. It also finds its way into writing by Andre Gide, Gertrude Stein, Wallace Stevens, Jorge Luis Borges, Lawrence Durrell, and many more.

"The Secret Room" begins as a painterly description from which human characteristics are absent; the stain is a "rosette" and not blood, and it stands out against a "smooth pale surface," not a body. It is a theatrical setting, and "space is filled" with colonnades, an ascending staircase, and a mysterious silhouette fleeing in the distance. The body itself—when finally recognized—is described with excessive surface detail as if the painter's eye registered only the shapes and textures of flesh, hair, velvet, and stone. Human emotions are depicted as compositional elements: the victim's mouth is open "as if screaming" while the murderer's face reveals a "violent exaltation." Thus far, the scene is a static tableau about which the reader receives progressively more and more information, but Robbe-Grillet invests it with puzzling movement by describing the victim as both wounded and intact, and the caped figure in four different, incompatible poses. First seen near the top of the stair and facing away, the murderer has next moved several steps back and appears on the first steps, turning to look at the body. Later he appears standing only a yard away from her, looking down, and finally he is kneeling close to the woman as she breathes convulsively, is wounded, and dies. It is as though time has moved backwards, reviewing the stages of the murder and flight before they become fixed on the artist's canvas. Beginning and ending as a painted scene, "The Secret Room" extends the spatial reality it describes by attributing movement and different position to figures on the canvas. One of Robbe-Grillet's earlier works, it already demonstrates the writer's ability to offer the most precise details within a calculatedly ambiguous and disturbing perspective.

### Classroom Strategies

Despite the complexities noted above, "The Secret Room" can be taught in one class period, though its implications—once discussed—might require more time to examine. Students will have problems with

"The Secret Room"; first, that they don't understand what to expect on the basis of the initial painterly description. None of the usual clues are present: no indication of plot, no character interaction, no hints about the direction of the story. (You may wish to contrast the informative beginnings of "The Guest" or "King of the Bingo Game.") Try pointing out that this *lack* is precisely the point: the sole focus is a minutely described, yet mysteriously evocative *setting*—the "Secret Room" of the title. What secret does it hold? How well does it keep its secret.

By the third paragraph it is clear that someone has been killed in this room. The following paragraphs describe the murderer fleeing the scene, and the scene itself is more fully described. Still, there is an uncanny emphasis on physical details and a lack of information about the deed itself or the motive for it. At this point you might ask the students to imagine a murder scene, with the caped figure as murderer/torturer and the woman as victim, just as Robbe-Grillet has presented it. Then have them imagine that the entire action has been filmed from beginning to end. Next ask them to suppose that someone selects four frames from that film, and places them side-by-side without regard to chronology, enlarges each so that we can see every detail, and then paints equally large pictures—identical to the cinema frames—on canvas. Finally, this someone describes in prose what those paintings look like, without telling us until the very end that he or she is describing a series of paintings, not the "real" murder scene itself. This is not a strategy that is particularly fair to the sophistication of Robbe-Grillet's narrative technique, but it is an analogy that makes his method less alien to some students.

Short though it is, the implications of "The Secret Room" will require some reference to its author's literary theories. If you are unaccustomed to discussing theory in class, you may well be surprised at how interesting it can be to students, especially when combined with a short example of that theory (successfully? unsuccessfully?) put into practice. Besides, the implications of what Robbe-Grillet has to say extend prose fiction to politics, social assumptions, psychology, and personal relations—aspects of experience which students, late in the term, often tackle with some eagerness. In any case, students are usually quite willing to have their assumptions questioned, since it is during their college years that they are questioning the assumptions of everyone and everything around them. Ignoring Robbe-Grillet's theories while teaching "The Secret Room" can turn out to be more confusing, and considerably less interesting, than offering them for student consideration.

One of the more interesting topics for discussion will be the degree to which the story seems to depart from the theories. Insofar as Robbe-Grillet means to turn our attention toward the object, he certainly succeeds, but if we understand that he believes in creating "objective literature—in the sense of creating a literature which is impassive, impartial, and entirely uncluttered by subjectivity—he just as certainly fails. A couple of examples might illustrate this point: in the story's third paragraph we are told that the victim's body "gleams feebly, marked with a red stain—a white body whose full, supple flesh can be sensed, fragile, no doubt, and vulnerable" (pp. 2062–63). Later we are told of her "full buttocks, the stretched-out legs, widely spread, and the black tuft of the exposed sex, provocative, proffered, useless now" (pp. 2063). Not only is this material blatantly sensational, it is also filled with subjective judgment and evaluation. How would a fully "objective" narrator know that the flesh was "supple," "fragile," or "vulnerable"? And who, exactly, "senses" these things? The phrase "no doubt" immediately suggests the possibility that there might *be* a doubt, even as it registers that the narrator's opinion is contrary to such a possibility. To whom, exactly, is the victim's exposure "provocative"? And who judges that her sex is being "proffered," or decides that it is "useless now"?

The point here is not so much that Robbe-Grillet's theory is not really "objective," however, as that a fully "objective" narration is always impossible. And that it is impossible is something that Robbe-Grillet knows perfectly well. How, then, are we to interpret the non-objective "objectivity" of "The Secret Room": as unconscious self-betrayal, as a parody of thriller novels and *film noir*, as an exposure of sexual and erotic stereotypes, or simply another layer of representation.

### Topics for Discussion and Writing

1. How does this story differ from conventional narrative fiction? Contrast with a story of your choice.

2. What is Robbe-Grillet's theory of fiction? How does it apply to "The Secret Room"?
   [See paragraphs 2–6 of *Backgrounds* for a discussion of theory, then paragraphs 7 and 8 of *Backgrounds* and paragraphs 3–5 of *Classroom Strategies* for application to "The Secret Room."]

3. What four stages (or scenes) can you discern in the course of the

story? Do they make any logical sense? What impression is made *on the reader* by having events presented in this sequence? How would the effect be changed if a single version of events was presented in chronological order?

4. In what ways is the narrative technique of the story affected by cinematic techniques? Painting techniques?

5. Why does Robbe-Grillet use such loaded images of sexual victimization and violence—images that remind us, moreover of much popular films and fiction? To what extent do you believe that this sensationalism is intentional?

6. How far can one proceed in interpreting this story? Is there a point at which simultaneous interpretations become possible?

7. "The Secret Room" is dedicated to Gustave Moreau. Discuss the painterly qualities that you notice in Robbe-Grillet's description. On the basis of this story, can you visualize the picture as Moreau might have painted it?

8. Edgar Allan Poe stated that a good short story should achieve a "unity of effect or impression," or "a certain unique or single *effect*." To what extent has Robbe-Grillet succeeded in this task?

### *Further Reading*

See also the suggestions in the anthology, p. 2062.

Bogue, Ronald L. "The Twilight of Relativism: Robbe-Grillet and the Easure of Man" in *Relativism and the Arts*, edited by Betty Jean Craige, 1983.

———. "A Generative Phantasy: Robbe-Grillet's La chambre secrte from *South Atlantic Review.* November, 1981, 46 (4): pp. 1–16.

Gibson, Andrew. "One Kind of Ambiguity in Joyce, Beckett, and Robbe-Grillet." *Canadian Review of Comparative Literature/Revue Canadienne de Littérature Comparée.* September, 1985, 12 (3): pp. 409–421.

Heath, Stephen. *The Nouveau Roman: A Study in the Practice of Writing*. London, 1972.
The chapter on Robbe-Grillet discusses the relationship between author and reader.

Morrissette, Bruce. *Novel and Film: Essays in Two Genres*. 1985.
Makes Robbe-Grillet the chief example in a discussion of modern cinematic vision.

Nelson, Roy Jay. *Causality and Narrative in French Fiction from Zola to Robbe-Grillet*. 1990.
Contains a discussion of Robbe-Grillet's narrative technique.

Oppenheim, Lois, ed. *Three Decades of the French New Novel*.
Contains several essays on different aspects of Robbe-Grillet's work as well as a round-table discussion on the new novel in which the author participated.

Robbe-Grillet, Alain. *For a New Novel: Essays on Fiction*. Translated by Richard Howard. New York, 1963.
A crucial set of essays, extremely clear and concentrated, for understanding Robbe-Grillet's work.

Stoltzfus, Ben. *Alain Robbe-Grillet: Life, Work and Criticism*. 1987.
A brief introduction.

————. *Alain Robbe-Grille: The Body of the Text*. 1985.
A discussion of the erotic and sadistic aspects of Robbe-Grillet's writing that recapitulates and develops the writer's own views.

# INGEBORG BACHMANN
## The Barking

### Backgrounds

"The Barking" comes from Bachmann's second collection of short stories, *Three Paths to the Lake* (in German, *Simultan*), published in 1972 and written over the same years that she was working on the novel cycle *Todesarten* (*Ways of Death* or *Death Styles*).

Characters from *Ways of Death* reappear in *Three Paths to the Lake*, and there are cross-references between the stories which make it clear that Bachmann intended to provide a panorama of modern Austrian society from a perspective that questioned social relationships of gender and power, and the role of language in establishing identity. The consummate skill that she had brought to her earlier hermetic poetry reappears in the later prose fiction with its oblique and terrifying pictures of human beings—especially women—unable to express or recognize themselves as complete individuals. The generally bleak picture of personal relationships in a covertly fascist society does not go unchallenged; it is criticized either by implication or occasionally by example. For Bachmann, the writer has both a role and a responsibility to effect social change; in a 1971 interview she commented that "society could be brought to a new form of consciousness by a new kind of writing. Of course one can't change the world with a poem, that's impossible, but one can have an effect on something. . . ." Her influence on later German-language writers and her growing international reputation attest to the impact of Bachmann's "new kind of writing," a consciously modernist style that articulates the twentieth century's "new experiences of suffering."

Readers exploring Bachmann's work may be puzzled by references to the second story collection under different titles: *Simultaneous* and *Three Paths to the Lake*. The 1989 English translation of *Simultan* takes its title from the last (and longest) story in the book, "Three Paths to the Lake," rather than from the first, "Simultaneous." "Simultaneous" ("Word for Word" in English translation) describes the spiritually dispossessed situation of a simultaneous interpreter named Nadja. Nadja exists in a linguistic limbo, an empty space of exchange in which she transmits equivalent meanings for other people's words while living "without a single thought of her own." Another projected title for the collection was *Women from Vienna*, reflecting the fact that all five stories describe different middle-class Viennese women who are, as Mark Anderson says, united "by what is missing from their lives." In one way or another, these women represent an alienation from reality that contrasts sharply with the precise description of apparently trivial details in their daily lives.

These are not isolated cases: instead, all five stories are linked by scattered references to figures appearing in other stories (and in *The Franza Case*) so that a broader pattern of social repression and inarticulate suffering begins to emerge. (This technique of cumulative cross-reference is found in novelist Honoré de Balzac's great nineteenth-century panorama of French society, *The Human Comedy*.) Beatrix, the narcissistic protagonist of "Problems, Problems" who lives to sleep late and visit the beauty parlor, resents her cousin Elisabeth Mihailovics, whose murder by her husband is described in "Three Paths to the Lake"; she also asks the beauty parlor attendant about young Frau Jordan—seen characteristically not as an individual but as "the wife of that Jordan." In "Three Paths to the Lake," a successful news photographer named Elisabeth Matrei recalls the different (complex and disheartening) aspects of love in her life; we hear at one point that one of her lovers mentioned living with "a woman from Vienna, an unbelievably ambitious woman, a simultaneous interpreter," and elsewhere that another character worshiped the actress Fann Goldman (a character in the *Ways of Death* cycle). Elisabeth herself feels deprived of speech, a spectator at the events she reports and unable to say what she really feels: "hasn't it ever occurred to anyone that you kill people when you deprive them of the power of speech and with it the power to experience and think?"

Such themes of loss and alienation are already present in Bachmann's earlier prose: the title story of her first collection, *The Thirtieth Year*, presents a narrator who reviews a life of spiritual passivity as he enters his thirtieth year and recovers from an automobile accident. Formerly "everything he did was on approval, on the understanding that it could be cancelled," but now he is no longer on the threshold of unlimited possibilities. "He casts the net of memory, casts it over himself and draws himself, catcher and caught in one person over the threshold of time, over the threshold of place, to see who he was and who he has become." The route to self-discovery dissolves in ambiguity for the narrator of *Malina* (1971), the only completed novel in the cycle *Ways of Death*. *Malina* is narrated until near the end by a writer who has a complicated relationship with two men who are conceivably also aspects of her artistic personality. Ivan is her lover and emotional reference point; Malina, dryly analytic, shares an apartment with her and encourages her to analyze her feelings. By the end of the novel, the narrator has lost Ivan and simultaneously her anchor in concrete reality. She disappears "into the wall" and the novel concludes with Malina's denial of her existence. What has happened? "An I tells its story to the end," ("Ein Ich erzählt sich zu Ende").

A complicated pattern of discovery and loss of identity is similarly visible in "The Barking." The two protagonists share a mutual discovery in the course of their conversation about Leo Jordan: discoveries about each other, about themselves, and about Leo Jordan. Franziska (the diminutive of "Franza") comes to question her husband Leo's behavior towards his mother, towards his cousin Johannes, and eventually towards herself as she recognizes that she too is afraid of him. It is a very cautious questioning and only the beginning of judgment, fro Franziska (like olf Frau Jordan) is taught to believe that "Leo was just too good to her" (p. 2074). First, she is merely amazed and hurt that Leo, a psychiatrist "whose very profession obliged him to uphold a neutral and scientific attitude toward homosexuality . . . would go on and on about his cousin as though he had somehow, through his own negligence, fallen prey to works of art, homosexuality, and an inheritance to boot . . ." (p. 2073). Even later, when she hears that old Frau Jordan gave away her cherished dog Nuri because Leo didn't like it, she accuses both herself and Leo of cruelty: "What kind of people are we?" We never see the results of her growing comprehension, for Leo has forestalled her and the couple will soon part: "other things came to pass, events of such hurricane force that she almost forgot the old woman and a great many other things as well" (p. 2079). Unlike Franziska, old Frau Jordan does not allow herself to analyze or judge her experience. She cherishes the memory of another child, Kiki, but she represses painful recollection of Leo's childhood behavior. On the surface, she constantly effaces herself while praising her exceptional son; random thoughts, however, tell another story of a vindictive and grasping man who has abandoned his mother, is incapable of close relationships, and may have sent an inconvenient relative to the concentration camps. Old Frau Jordan is incapable of openly judging the contrast between her own sacrifices and Leo's blatant neglect, and defends herself from disillusionment by insisting that "Leo is such a good son!" (p. 2070). When the pressure becomes too great, she recedes into hallucinations of barking dogs that blot out her real-life anxiety. Yet her buried resentment surfaces in different ways: in an implied criticism when Elfi replaces Franziska ("How many wives was that now anyway . . . . . The barking was so close now that for an instant she was certain that Nuri was with her again and would jump at him and bark" [pp. 2080–81]); in self-abasing comments ("your dumb old mother can hardly read anyway" [p.2081]); in our discovery that her accusation of Frau Agnes, whom she accuses of having taken ten schillings, probably displaces an earlier incident she tries to forget—"the day when the last ten schillings had disappeared and Leo had lied to her" (2081–last).

Throughout the story, the indirect focal point is Leo Jordan. Bachmann has very cleverly shown (rather than merely stated) how thoroughly these Viennese women are defined by the invisible priority of the men on whom they depend. Leo is the subject of all their conversations, and a dominant figure without ever being present. His destructive impact is clearly connected with Bachmann's equation of patriarchy and fascism; Leo's authoritarian use and intimidation of others for his own purposes, his alienation from human relationships that would imply equality, and his scorn of women and homosexuals, are all reminiscent of Nazi beliefs. Bachmann evokes the Nazi connections especially strongly in the passages concerning Leo's homosexual cousin Johannes and the study of the concentration camps. Leo Jordan's attacks on Johannes (like his criticism of his first wife) have a suspicious and even guilty air. Johannes had paid for Leo's education, but "Leo was reluctant to be reminded of his mother and his former wives and lovers who were nothing to him but a conspiracy of creditors from whom he would escape only by belittling them to himself and others" (p. 2073). We learn from old Frau Jordan's "roundabout way of saying things" that Leo very likely denounced his cousin either out of spite or to protect himself. When his mother learns that Dr. Jordan has written a book on "The Significance of Endogenous and Exogenous Factors in Connection with the Occurrence of Paranoid and Depressive Psychoses in Former Concentration Camp Inmates and Refugees," she is worried and recalls a mysterious "other thin" that turns out to be Johannes' detention in a concentration camp for a year and a half. Simultaneously, she notes that her son "knows how to defend himself" and that "it meant a certain amount of danger for Leo, having a relative who . . ." (p. 2076). Franziska, ironically, interprets the old woman's statement as referring to the wartime danger of having a relative in a concentration camp; more likely (especially given the references to barking which begin at this point) Leo had protected himself first by denouncing his cousin. Does Johannes have a "paranoid and depressed" suspicion that such might be the case? If so, it would be important for Dr. Jordan to put such psychoses in scientific perspective.

One of the pleasures of reading "The Barking" lies in its indirect, enigmatic discourse and the opportunity it offers to reconstruct different characters from a variety of clues. Although the headnote refers to a fuller picture of Dr. Jordan in *The Franza Case*, it is more rewarding to read "The Barking" in terms of the information given by the story itself. We know, for example, by the end of the story, that both women are dead, but we do not know precisely when or how they died. We can only guess why Leo and Franziska separate; Leo may be involved in another affair that has become serious, or he may be irritated by Franziska's signs of independent thinking. The language itself provides clues to the character's psychological identity. Thoughts reported in a stream-of-consciousness style reveal not only information but also attitudes and anxieties: Franziska, secretly purchasing a radio for her mother-in-law, reassures herself that she "broke into the meager savings she had set aside for some sort of emergency which would hopefully never arise and could only be a minor emergency at any rate" (p. 2072).

Students are sometimes puzzled by the last paragraph, which seems to have little to do with the plot except to make sure that the Pineider taxi service is paid. Yet this paragraph serves as a kind of pendant to the rest of the story. It is not necessary to know that Dr. Martin Ranner (according to *The Franza Case*) accompanied his sister to Egypt where she died in a paroxysm of self-reproach after being raped by strangers; or that her feeling of self-worth, already severely damaged by Dr. Jordan's insidious attacks, was completely destroyed by this last assault. The last paragraph does not provide this information, but it does complete several themes and acts a a partial counterbalance to the bleak picture of old Frau Jordan's increasing paranoia and death. We learn several things: first, that Franziska is dead and her brother has a strong reason never to see Leo Jordan again; second, that Leo Jordan's destructive example is not the only way of life in contemporary society: Dr. Ranner values human relationships and assumes ethical obligations beyond what is strictly necessary (this may be Bachmann's "utopian" side, although it is diminished by the fact that only the men survive); and third, that Leo Jordan had probably acted true to for by refusing, over several months, to pay the taxi service incurred by his former wife on his mother's behalf.

"The Barking" can be taught in one class period. If your students have read the story carefully and have no immediate questions, you may want to move directly to discussion on the barking itself and its function as a psychological barrier between old Frau Jordan and a reality she cannot face. Some may well ask you about the last paragraph, which leaves you starting at the end with a description of the underlying themes that come together at this point. It may be easiest, however, to begin at the beginning, with the description of old Frau Jordan and what we learn about the other characters through her eyes. As soon as her relationship to Franziska is established, it will be useful to introduce the various discovery patterns that are developed throughout the story. The image of Leo Jordan can then be brought out as the hidden, yet dominant, reference point that illustrates Bachmann's attack on the damage done to women and other marginalized figures by a patriarchal (or fascist) society. There are a number of useful themes or passages to consider with the class: the various examples of old Frau Jordan's self-criticism, humility, fear (and buried resentment) of her son; the several stages of Franziska's recognition that "the Leo she came to know through the old woman was a completely different Leo from the man she had married" (p. 2071); the enigma of Leo's relationship to Johannes and his study of concentration-camp psychoses; Leo's personality as an embodiment of fascism; the various passages describing dogs and barking. Discussion should be easy to elicit throughout this story, whether as comments on individual passages, on the differing reaction of Franziska and old Frau Jordan, on Bachmann's view of patriarchy and fascism, or on the recent rise of political groups with neo-Nazi sympathies.

## Topics for Discussion

1. What is the significance of the barking? What function does it serve for old Frau Jordan? When (and in what context) does she first mention hearing dogs barking? How does Nuri fit into the context?

2. Why is the story titled "The Barking" and not "Old Frau Jordan" or "The Jordan Family"? Give some examples of barking in the story and relate them to the plot.

3. Discuss the way that the characters' language (especially unspoken

thoughts) reveal their psychological attitudes.

4. Discuss Leo Jordan's relationship to his cousin Johannes.

5. Discuss Bachmann's equation of patriarchy with fascism, using examples from the story.

6. Is Leo Jordan a good psychiatrist, in your opinion? Explain.

7. What responsibility—if any—does old Frau Jordan bear for her own fate?

8. Describe the various ways in which Franziska tries to help her mother-in-law. How do they put her into conflict with her husband?

9. How does Franziska come to see her husband in a different light? (Cite and discuss specific examples.)

### Further Reading

See also the reading suggestions in the anthology, p. 2070.

Achberger, Karen. "Introduction" to *The Thirtieth Year*. 1987.
Situates Bachmann in twentieth-century German literature; concise discussion of the short stories.

Frederiksen, Elke, ed. *Women Writers of Germany, Austria, and Switzerland: An Annotated Bio-Bibliographical Guide*. 1989.
Includes a brief discussion of Bachmann's work.

Frieden, Sandra. "Bachmann's *Malina* and *Todesarten*: Subliminal Crimes" from *The German Quarterly* 56 (1) January, 1983, pp. 61–73.
Considers Bachmann a precursor of German "inner-directed" novels; discusses the psychoanalytic overtones of her style.

# GABRIEL GARCIA MARQUEZ
## Death Constant Beyond Love

### *Backgrounds*

We read García Márquez for the sheer pleasure of his inventiveness, the explosiveness of his language, the lushness of his imagination. His short fiction often has the magic and energy of a good children's story, and he creates in his readers something that very few writers, even good ones, manage: wonder.

Senator Onesimo Sanchez sells illusions. He has made the same illusory promises every four years in the "illusory" village of Rosal del Virrey, a town so dreary and sordid that "even its name was a kind of joke, because the only rose in that village was being worn by Senator Onesimo Sanchez himself . . . " (p. 2086). As in all his previous campaign visits, he brings with him the illusory props of political promises: rented Indians to swell the crowds, music and rockets, cardboard facades of make-believe red brick houses, an ocean liner made of colored paper, artificial trees with leaves made of felt, rainmaking machines, oils of happiness which will make things grow in the sterile landscape of the village. But this time, Onesimo Sanchez can only go through the motions. His awareness of his imminent death outweighs all other considerations. When he meets himself in the darkness of his own self-knowledge (in part derived from Marcus Aurelius), Sanchez recognizes that "whether it's you or someone else, it won't be long before you'll be dead and it won't be long before your name won't even be left" (p. 2092). He finds himself unable to sympathize with the rented Indians, barefoot on the saltpeter coals of the blistering village square; he looks upon the villagers with disdain because they are still willing to believe in his carnival of illusions, his fictional world. What Sanchez now realizes is that his marvelous world of illusions, even though it is backed by the force of money and political power, cannot defeat the reality of death, of nature, of the absolute and final solitude of every man.

On this final visit to Rosal del Virrey, Senator Sanchez encounters Laura Farina, who appears to him wearing a "cheap, faded Guajiro Indian robe" and, though her face is "painted as protection against the sun," it is such that "it was possible to imagine that there had never been another so beautiful in the whole world" (p. 2089). She embodies that which he uses to fend off the pressure of reality: beauty and love. Like the rose that he has carried with him to that sordid village, Laura's beauty promises to defeat the sterility of the landscape; her love promises to defeat death itself. But nature, and death, cannot be eluded. At the story's end, Senator Sanchez holds her "about the waist, sank his face into woods-animal armpit, and gave in to terror. Six months and eleven days later he would die in that same position, debased and repudiated because of the public scandal with Laura Farina and weeping with rage at dying without her" (p. 2092). The controlling notion of "Death Constant Beyond Love" is suggested by the blunt insistence of its title, which reverses the claims of Quevedo's "Love Constant Beyond Death," and acts as a kind of newspaper headline announcing the final discovery of Senator Onesimo Sanchez.

One's first impression of "Death Constant Beyond Love" is that it functions very close to allegory—Death, Nature, Love, Beauty, and Illusion seem to be functioning in the upper case—while at the same time it retains some of the qualities of the tall tale. Though both of these elements are certainly present in the story, its method is in no way easy to describe. García Márquez's characteristic style—magical realism—provokes something that all good fiction provokes, a recognition of the infinite suggestibility of language, but does so in particularly observable and enchanting ways. García Márquez has said that everything he writes has its source in something that actually happened and that fiction is "reality represented through a secret code." One of the most observable tendencies of García Márquez's magical realism is to use the "secret code" of his language to lead the reader—within a sentence, from sentence to sentence, from paragraph to paragraph—to places that no reader could have expected to be. He has said that his "real inclination is to be a conjuror," and indeed, the effect of his writing is to levitate the reader, to lift him out of the world of his expectations, and let him float giddily for a moment before finding ground again.

"Death Constant Beyond Love" demonstrates García Márquez's use of the techniques of magical realism. We can see how García Márquez suggests possible stories beyond the one he is telling, while at the same time he deepens our understanding of his central character:

> Senator Onesimo Sanchez was placid and weatherless inside the air-conditioned car, but as soon as he opened the door he was shaken by a gust of fire and his shirt of pure silk was soaked in a kind of light-colored soup and he

felt many years older and more alone than ever.

                                                                    (p. 2086)

This we might break down as follows:

Senator Onesimo Sanchez was placid and weatherless inside the air-conditioned car,

[In what way can someone be weatherless? The word certainly suggests calm, but it is a calm which is almost unnatural, almost artificial. This "weatherlessness" could be attributed to the air-conditioning, but it further suggests that Sanchez is, by his own choice, unaffected by the unpleasant world of hot weather and, by implication, shabby poverty through which it is his duty to ride. The suggestion is that to be "weatherless" is to be somehow separated from life in Rosal del Virrey. The opposite, then, would also be true—to enter into the weather suggests a fundamental connection with life there.]

but as soon as he opened the door he was shaken by a gust of fire

[We expect "hot air" or its equivalent here; we get "fire," perhaps because it is more elemental and attacks our own senses more aggressively. The word "shaken" first suggests a physical response, but by the end of the sentence it can be seen to suggest an emotional or spiritual response as well.]

and his shirt of pure silk

[He is rich; he shines in the blistering heat. The shirt suggests that the Senator is used to separating himself from the conditions in which his constituents pass their lives.]

was soaked in a kind of light-colored soup

[The weather attacks him; it has a life of its own, its own magical properties and effects. The word "soup" is particularly suggestive. The peculiar pungency and viscosity of "soup," in this context, compels the reader to participate in Sanchez's sensations. If we assume that this "soup" is *caused* by the weather, rather than being an aspect of the weather itself, we immediately translate "soup" into "sweat." But to say "Onesimo Sanchez sweated profusely" would hardly suggest the energy with which García Márquez wishes to endow the atmosphere of Rosal del

Virrey.]

and he felt many years older and more alone than ever.

[Sanchez's feelings appear to derive from his transition from "weatherlessness" to his immersion in the hot, soupy, and sordid world of Rosal del Virrey—that is, from rose to Rosal, from illusion to disillusion. These feelings of age and solitude are inescapable for Sanchez in his life just as they are inescapable in this sentence.]

Magical realism, in the hands of García Márquez, is a wonderfully supple kind of writing. It penetrates objective reality to reveal the mysterious and poetic qualities which underlie the daily lives of the people and communities it describes; his characters have an aura of woeful futility combined with a wonderful innocence that lends them much of their essential charm and virtue as fictional creations.

"Death Constant Beyond Love" is, like all of García Márquez's fiction, very much a story of Latin America. The geographical, historical, cultural, political, and climatic texture of Latin American life is central to any discussion of García Márquez's work; it is only necessary to compare his work with that of Borges to note the extent to which this is true. It might even be said that magical realism, as a mode of writing, is inextricably bound to Latin America, where the influence of French and Spanish surrealism combined with a desire to use the magical myths of an indigenous tradition to re-examine, indeed transform, an imperfect "colonial" reality.

García Márquez's political concerns are manifest in "Death Constant Beyond Love" just as they are in almost all of his work, including *One Hundred Years of Solitude* and, especially, *The Autumn of the Patriarch*. He is a very active socialist, but one who insists on a socialism appropriate to the cultural and historical conditions of Latin America. "I think the world ought to be socialist," he has said, "that it will be, and that we should help this to happen as quickly as possible. But I'm greatly disillusioned by the socialism of the Soviet Union. They arrived at their brand of socialism through special experiences and conditions, and are trying to impose in other countries their own bureaucracy, their own authoritarianism, and their own lack of historical vision. That isn't socialism and it's the great problem of the present moment." Many of the traditional concerns of socialist writing—the exposure of political corruption and oppression, the condition of the common man, the effects of power and money, among others—are evident in García Márquez's work, including "Death Constant Beyond Love."

Almost everyone who has read García Márquez has noted the affinities between his work and that of William Faulkner. There is the epic creation of an entire fictional world—García Márquez's Macondo and Faulkner's Yoknapatawpha—complete with geography, history, and whole populations of extraordinary characters; there is the lyrical magic of their language, including the tendency to become excessively lyrical. García Márquez has said that he found Faulkner's world—the southern United States—"was very like my world, . . . created by the same people . . . . When I traveled in the southern states, I found evidence—on those hot, dusty roads, with the same vegetation, trees, and great houses—of the similarity between our two worlds. One mustn't forget that Faulkner is in a way a Latin American writer. His world is that of the Gulf of Mexico."

García Márquez has also said, however, that Faulkner's influence was "really screwing me up" and that his problem was "not how to imitate Faulkner but how to destroy him." Although García Márquez couldn't "destroy" Faulkner, he could move in his own direction; his style is now entirely his own.

García Márquez claims that he "began to long to write," and in fact did write his first stories, under the influence of Kafka's "The Metamorphosis" Certainly, García Márquez's use of metaphor and his tendency to insist that his metaphors be taken literally, and our sometimes befuddled attempt to discover an absolute "meaning" beneath the text, remind us of Kafka.

### Classroom Strategies

"Death Constant Beyond Love" can be taught in one class period. Students will probably experience it as a kind of dessert after a term full of main courses. If students have any particular difficulty with the story it will very likely have to do with their resistance to taking it seriously. García Márquez's stylistic conjuring combined with his insouciance will probably distract those students who persistently struggle to find "meaning" in the text. The "meaning" is, of course, there—but it emerges like a rabbit out of a magician's hat. Students who resist magic will resist "Death Constant Beyond Love."

To break down this resistance it might be useful first to discuss García Márquez's magical realism, and emphasize its difference from fantasy, from the tall tale, and from surrealism. Reminding students of Kafka's "The Metamorphosis"—with its apparent discrepancy between narrative tone and the extraordinary events being described—might aid them in resolving their problems with the techniques of magical realism.

You might then emphasize Onesimo Sanchez himself: as a would-be dictator, in full control of the means by which the illusion of his benevolence can be foisted on his public, who is nevertheless foiled by death (the allusions to Marcus Aurelius might be useful here); as a human being not unlike ourselves, who must face the knowledge of his own imminent death; as a man who attempts, and fails, to reduce the terror of self-knowledge through erotic passion. Budding Freudians in the classroom will want to play with the clear suggestion of Thanatos here, García Márquez's merging of Sanchez's movement toward death with his desire for passion—especially since the object of his passion is Laura Farina, the very embodiment of earth.

### Topics for Discussion and Writing

1. What is the importance of the title of the story? What does it tell us about the story's central thematic concerns?
   [See paragraph 3 of *Backgrounds* for discussion.]

2. García Márquez has said that everything he has written has been about solitude. In what ways is "Death Constant Beyond Love" about solitude?
   [See paragraphs 2–3 of *Backgrounds* for discussion.]

3. What is the symbolic importance of the rose, the chastity belt, the campaign props, and Laura Farina herself?
   [The rose, campaign props, and Laura Farina have been discussed in *Backgrounds*. The chastity belt worn by Laura Farina would appear to suggest, ironically, that Sanchez's final attempt to find love, and to fend off death, extracts a literal price. The route to beauty and love, then, is blocked by a padlock—a padlock which can be removed only when he turns one of his heretofore illusory promises into a reality.]

4. What similarities and differences can be found between García Márquez's fictional techniques and those of William Faulkner?

Franz Kafka? Charles Dickens? How are these techniques similar to those found in the *Odyssey*? How can magical realism be characterized?

[See paragraphs 4–11 of *Backgrounds* for discussion.]

5. How does García Márquez link death with nature and illusion with beauty in the story?

[See paragraphs 2–3 of *Backgrounds* for discussion.]

## Further Reading

See also the suggestions in the anthology, p. 2086.

Apuleyo Mendoza, Plinio. *The Fragrance of Guava.* Translated by Ann Wright. London, 1983.
A series of interviews with García Márquez.

Bell-Villada, Gene H. *García Márquez: The Man and His Work.* 1990.
A general description aimed at a broad audience.

Bloom, Harold, ed. *Gabriel García Márquez.* 1989.
Collects eighteen essays on style, themes, and cultural contexts; chronology and bibliography.

*Books Abroad.* The summer, 1972 issue is dedicated to García Márquez.

Byk, John. "From Fact to Fiction: Gabriel García Márquez and the Short Story" from *Mid-American Review* 1986 6 (2), pp. 111–16.

McGuirk, Bernard and Richard Cardwell, eds. *Gabriel García Márquez: New Readings.* 1987.
Twelve essays plus the 1982 Nobel Address.

McMurray, George R., ed. *Critical Essays on Garbiel García Márquez.* Boston, 1987.
Fifteen reviews plus fourteen articles and essays on a range of García Márquez's work.

McNerey, Kathleen. *Understanding Gabriel García Márquez.* 1989.
A useful introduction with comments on the different works;
includes a short biography stressing cultural context and a bibliography.

Minta, Stephen. *Gabriel García Márquez: Writer of Colombia.* 1987.
An introduction to the English audience.

Ortega, Julio and Claudia Elliot. *Gabriel García Márquez and the
Powers of Fiction.* 1988.
A general collection that includes five essays and the 1982 Nobel
lecture.

Shaw, Bradley A. and Nora Vera-Godwin. *Critical Perspectives on
Gabriel García Márquez.* 1986.
Nine essays on a wide range of topics with considerable textual
analysis.

Williams, Raymond L. *Gabriel García Márquez.* New York, 1984.
An introductory study.

————. "The Visual Arts, the Poetization of Space and Writing: an
Interview with Gabriel García Márquez" from *PMLA* 104 (2)
March, 1989, pp. 131–40.

# CHINUA ACHEBE
## Things Fall Apart

### *Backgrounds*

"Literature, whether handed down by word of mouth or in print, gives us a second handle on reality." Achebe's belief in the social importance of literature emerges clearly in this sentence from the polemic essay "What Has Literature Got To Do with It?" Literature for him is not an ornamental fringe benefit of civilization; to the contrary, it provides a necessary critical perspective on everyday experience. By illuminating contexts and choices, literature—both traditional oral literature and the modern printed text—educates us to the meaning of our own actions and offers greater control over our social and personal lives. Achebe continues: literature works by

> enabling us to encounter in the safe, manageable dimensions of make-believe the very same threats to integrity that may assail the psyche in real life; and at the same time providing through the self-discovery which it imparts a veritable weapon for coping with these threats whether they are found within our problematic and incoherent selves or in the world around us.

Thus far, Achebe's description of the educational role of literature could be attributed to many writers in the realistic tradition: Flaubert, Dostoevsky, Ibsen, Solzhenitsyn, or Freud. Nor would his point of view be alien to other writers for whom literature expresses a kind of knowledge: the poet William Butler Yeats, for example, whose description of cultural disintegration ("things fall apart; the centre cannot hold") is borrowed for the title of Achebe's first novel. Yet the particular reality that Achebe describes is located at a specific point in history: a modern Africa whose rich variety of ethnic and cultural identities is further complicated by the impact of European colonialism.

Since the publication of *Things Fall Apart* (1958), Achebe has assumed a leading position as representative and interpreter of African culture at home and abroad. To a European audience that was accustomed to stereotypes of primitive savages in "darkest Africa" (e.g. the murderous Kali-worshippers or loyal servants of Kipling's *Gunga Din*), he has emphasized the complexities of a different society with its alternate set of traditions, ideals and values. Achebe was enraged that *Time* magazine would call Joyce Cary's *Mister Johnson* "the best novel ever written about Africa" when Cary depicted Africa as a stagnant and impoverished culture whose "people would not know the change if time jumped back fifty thousand years. They live like mice or rats in a palace floor; all the magnificence and variety of the arts, the learning and the battles of civilisation go on over their heads and they do not even imagine them" (cited by Achebe from *Mister Johnson*). He was dismayed that Africans themselves would internalize this kind of attitude and emulate a supposedly superior white European civilization. In "The Novelist as Teacher" (from *Morning Yet on Creation Day*), Achebe reports how a student used European seasons to describe African weather, writing about "winter" when he meant the period in which the harmattan wind blows. If he didn't use the European terms, the student explained, everyone would call him a "bushman"! Achebe's mission, therefore, is to educate African as well as European readers, reinstating a sense of pride in African culture "to help my society regain belief in itself and put away the complexes of the years of denigration and self-abasement."

This educational mission is not a simple one, and Achebe has not hesitated to explore the complexities and contradictions of modern African—specifically Igbo—society. Indeed, he has found himself in conflict with several other writers who prefer a narrower or more militant perspective aimed at reconstituting an essentially "African" identity. For Achebe, this quest is ideal rather than practical, and modern African society must recognize that it has been irrevocably marked by the colonial era. He mistrusts absolutes and generalizations about "African identity," no matter how useful such concepts may temporarily be. "You have all heard of the African personality, of African democracy, of the African way to socialism, of negritude, and so on. They are all props we have fashioned at different times to help us get on our feet again." Perhaps the most famous disagreement between Achebe and his peers concerns the debate over the African author's choice of language. Should African writers use the "colonizer's language" (e.g. English or French) or should they use only their tribal tongue in order to build up an indigenous literature and reject any vestiges of colonial influence? James Ngugi stopped writing novels in English and, as Ngugi wa Thiong'o, began to write in his native Gikuyu (these novels are then translated into English for a Western audience). Achebe has a different attitude. His language is an "African English" expressing a particular cultural experience, and he sees

"a new voice coming out of Africa, speaking of African experience in a world-wide language. So my answer to the question Can an African ever learn English well enough to be able to use it effectively in creative writing? is certainly yes. If on the other hand you ask: Can he ever learn to use it like a native speaker? I should say, I hope not. . . . The African writer should aim to use English in a way that brings out his message best without altering the language to the extent that its value as a medium of international exchange will be lost. He should aim at fashioning out an English which is at once universal and able to carry his peculiar experience."
("The African Writer and the English Language," 1964.)

In addition to writing the five novels for which he is best known, Achebe has traveled widely and been an active representative of African letters. In 1962 he became the founding editor for Heinemann Books' new publishing line, the African Writers Series, and he has founded and edited two journals: *Okike: An African Journal of New Writing* (1971) and the bilingual *Uwa ndi Igbo: a Journal of Igbo Life and Culture* (1986). Two books of essays, *Morning Yet on Creation Day* (1975) and *Hopes and Impediments* (1988), collect major statements such as "The Novelist as Teacher," "The African Writer and the English Language," "Colonialist Criticism," "Chi in Igbo Cosmology," "Africa and her Writers," "What Has Literature Got to Do with It?" and "An Image of Africa," as well as occasional pieces stemming from debates over African culture. Achebe's conviction of the importance of literature in creating a national identity led him and poet Christopher Okigbo to envisage a series of children's stories that would offer African children a better sense of their cultural heritage. Their Citadel Press was discontinued after Okigbo was killed in the Biafran war, but the novelist has nonetheless written *Chike and the River* (1966), a novella told from the point of view of an eleven-year-old boy, the animal fable *How The Leopard Got His Claws* (1972, with John Iroaganachi), and various adaptations of traditional tales for children. In fiction, poetry, essays, and lectures, Achebe returns to basic themes of human freedom and dignity for, as he says in an essay written during the Biafran war, "if an artist is anything, he is a human being with heightened sensitivities; he must be aware of the faintest nuances of injustice in human relations."

*Things Fall Apart* demonstrates this concern for the quality of human relations on both an individual and a societal level. Whether describing Okonkwo's family, interactions between neighbors and villages, the evolution of traditional Igbo society in response to internal and external pressures, or the arrival of British missionaries and colonial administrators, Achebe has a sharp and often ironic eye for the shifting balances of human relationships. His characters are strongly drawn but they are never simplified, from the briefly-mentioned couple Ndulue and Ozoemena whose mutual devotion amazes Okonkwo (p. 2129) to the complex character of the hero himself. Okonkwo is introduced at the beginning as a powerful and ambitious man who stammers under strong emotion and has recourse to his fists; he is arrogant and even a bully, yet he has an unadmitted tender side that appears in his relationship to his wife Ekwefi, his caring for Ezinma in her fever, and his attachment to Ikemefuna whose death at his hands shatters him for days. Achebe prepares the reader to understand the contradictions in Okonkwo's personality by his extended description of the hero's shiftless father Unoka in the very first pages. Humiliated by Unoka's laziness, shameful death, and lack of title, compelled early to support the entire family, Okonkwo struggles desperately throughout the novel to root out any sign of inherited "feminine" weakness in himself or his son Nwoye.

This insistence on warlike masculine valor corresponds to traditional Igbo values and Okonkwo rises high in his clan as long as these values are predominant. Nonetheless, things are already starting to fall apart. Internal pressures are at work and point to change. Obierika disapproves of the expedition to kill Ikemefuna and he later starts to question the exposure of twins; the osu (outcasts) are not content with their status and will be quick to convert to Christianity; Nwoye is unhappy under Okonkwo's bullying and he will never forget that his father killed his foster brother Ikemefuna. The process is only hastened and distorted by the arrival of British missionaries, administrators, and the new trading stores with their flow of money. Traditional social and religious values—as well as the authority of the villages to govern themselves—are on their way out. In the first two thirds of the novel, Umuofia's elaborately harmonious society has been clearly established; in the last third, Achebe provides a contrasting description of the invasive colonial presence. These portrayals are scathing. Mr. Smith, who succeeds a more accommodating minister in the church at Umuofia, enforces a harsh and rigid view of Christianity: "He saw things in black and white. And black was evil" (p. 2182). The British administrators rule over populace whose language or customs they do not even try to understand and which they see as a kind of exotica about which one writes scientific books. They establish a system of "court messengers" to convey orders, and the court messengers become a second layer of corruption by using their borrowed authority to cheat and exploit the common people. The District Commissioner lies to get the village leaders in his power and throws them into jail until the villagers have paid an exorbitant fine. Okonkwo's passionate resistance to this exploitation and deceit makes him even more of a hero—or would if his society had not changed. The Igbo community is afraid of defying raw power (the same power that has jailed their leaders), and when they meet they cannot decide how to respond. At this point, Okonkwo is ready to act alone, separate from the community that has provided context and reference point hitherto. His enraged execution of the imperious court messenger isolates him completely from the community he has just endangered and it leads him to commit suicide. Suicide is a shameful or taboo death, just like his father's, and this abomination further separates "one of the greatest men of Umuofia" from the clan. On the last page, Obierika's emotional tribute to his friend contrasts bleakly with the suggestion that this tale of flawed epic heroism will be buried in the annals of colonial history as a "reasonable paragraph in the District Commissioner's book, *The Pacification of the Primitive Tribes of the Lower Niger.*

## Language

Certain aspects of Achebe's "African English" are worth mentioning here. The presence of untranslated Igbo words reminds Western readers of the presence of another linguistic culture that has its own frames of thought and separate words for things. Words such as *egwugwu* or *iyi-uwa* are used repeatedly without translation, but their meaning is clear from the context and their very presence in the English text is a constant reminder of the blend of two cultures.

On a less obvious level, there are also Igbo names whose meaning subtly reinforces themes in the story: a buried, yet real, level of significance that is available to those who take the trouble (as the District Commissioner does not do) to inquire about the African language. Footnotes here explain some of these buried meanings: the name of Okonkwo's lazy father Unoka means "Home is supreme"; the doomed Ikemefuna is named "My strength should not be dissipated"; and Nwoye's name (built on the non-gendered root *Nwa* or "child," and already discussed in the Introduction) contrasts with Okonkwo's name, which combines stereotypical attributes of masculinity (Oko) and a non-Christian Igbo heritage (he was born on Nkwo, the third day of the four-day Igbo week). Ikemefuna, taken from his family and later killed by

Okonkwo whom he considers his father, sings his favorite song about "Nnadi"—whose name, pathetically, means "Father is there" or "Father exists" (p. 2113).

Finally, Achebe integrates into his narrative a characteristic aspect of Igbo speech: the common use of proverbs. As he explains in the conversation between Unoka and Okoye, "proverbs are the palm-oil with which words are eaten." (Okoye, leading up to asking for his money, "said the next half a dozen sentences in proverbs.") Proverbs such as "he who brings kola brings life" (p. 2099) or "the sun will shine on those who stand before it shines on those who kneel under them" (p. 2100) or "if a child washed his hands he could eat with kings" (p. 2100) are inserted into the narrative so appropriately that their nature as proverbs may be overlooked, but in the aggregate they illustrate a characteristic aspect of Igbo thought and speech.

Most of the names in *Things Fall Apart* are pronounced basically as they would be in English (e.g. Okonkwo as oh-KON-kwo), once we exclude the fact that Igbo is a tonal language using high or low tones for individual syllables. (Igbo itself is pronounced *ee-bo*.) Nonetheless, it may be useful to have certain pronunciations approximated below where the stress or number of syllables might be in question.

Agbala (AG-ba-la)
Ajofia (AH-joh-fyah)
Chielo (CHEE-ey-low)
Ezeani (EHZ-AAH-nee)
Ezeugo (EH-zoo-go)
Ikemefuna (ee-kay-MAY-foo-na)
Ikezue (EE-KAY-zoo-eh)
kwenu (KWEY-noo)
Ndulue (IN-doo-LOO-eh)
Nwakibie (NWA-kee-EE-bee-yay)
Nwayieke (NWA-ee-EH-kay)
Nwoye (NWOH-yeh)
Obiageli (Oh-bee-AH-gay-lee)
Ofoedu (oh-FOH-eh-DOO)
Okoye (oh-KO-yeh)
Onwumbiko (ON-wum-BEE-koh)
Ozoemena (oh-ZEH-meh-na)
Umuofia (OO-moo-OFF-ya)
Unoka (OO-no-ka)

## Classroom Stategies

*Things Fall Apart* may be taught in three days: more if you wish to include related cultural material. You may want to begin by giving some sense of recent African history, perhaps starting with a map of contemporary Africa and comparing it with a map of Africa in 1939, which shows colonial protectorates covering almost all the continent. (Both maps are easily available in a modern atlas.) There are also movies and videocassettes on African culture, such as those in the "Library of African Cinema" that are suggested for contemporary classrooms. Photographs or African art objects (masks, statuettes, cloth, bowls, metalwork, decorated calabash gourds) that you or your students can provide will also help to convey the artistic presence and vitality of another culture that is opposed, in *Things Fall Apart*, to a European or "progress-oriented" system that is presumably more familiar to your class. As you evoke the particular African society that is about to "fall apart," the novel's title will acquire more and more significance. Comparisons to Yeats's view of modern European history are certainly appropriate, but it may be even more interesting to ask why a Nigerian writer discussing the African colonial experience would find it useful to draw upon a masterwork of English literature.

*Things Fall Apart* is Okonkwo's story, and students will be fascinated from the beginning by this combative, contradictory, and passionate character. Yet he is very much a member of his community, accepting its laws and struggling to achieve greatness according to traditional values. Achebe's hero does not define himself as a rebel *against* society, as do the heroes of so many European and American novels from *René* to *Catcher in the Rye*. In order to understand his character, therefore, and the poignancy of his ultimate isolation, you will find it useful to consider the values of traditional Igbo society as they are introduced at the beginning of the novel. What are the customs and cultural expectations of Umuofia? How does one succeed in this society, and who is left out? What are the important crops; what is the role of war, of religion, and of the arts? How are decisions made in Umuofia, and who makes them? What differing roles do men and women play? What do we learn from the kola ceremony of hospitality and the taking of titles? The dramatic description of Okonkwo's success and Unoka's failure in the first section incorporates a great deal of information about the many dimensions of Igbo society.

Okonkwo is usually presented as a tragic hero, surmounting obstacles that would crush a weaker person, eventually defeated by the same qualities that sustain his greatness. His impoverished beginning as Unoka's son, the complete failure of his crops when he has just borrowed seed-corn from Nwakibie, and his unexpected exile for seven years after an inadvertent manslaughter are all challenges he manages to overcome. Yet there are other challenges to which his response is more ambiguous: his fear and rejection of the gentleness he associates with failure and, most specifically, the killing of his foster-son Ikemefuna (when the latter runs to him for help against the villages) because he is afraid of being thought weak. Students notice how Okonkwo resorts to violence to solve problems, and they are disturbed when he beats his favorite wife Ekwefi and narrowly misses shooting her. If they give Okonkwo credit for caring for Ezinma in her illness and for loving Ekwefi, they also recognize that his son Nwoye converts to Christianity (taking the name Isaac) chiefly because he seeks the security and approval that his father has withheld. Okonkwo's courage and readiness for action are prized in the old Umuofia that sought supremacy among the neighboring villages, but this brand of warlike heroism is obsolete in the new era and certainly ineffective against the power of the colonial government. Time has passed by both Okonkwo and Umuofia: the former dies by his own hand because he is unwilling to change, while the latter is caught unprepared, weakened from within, and unable to do anything but submit. Ironically, it is the District Commissioner who description of the "Pacification of primitive tribes" provides the last words in the book. We must wait for a later book—by the Igbo Chinua Achebe—to rebalance accounts.

## Topics for Discussion

1. Why does Achebe bring in the colonial presence only in the last third of the novel?
2. What motives does Nwoye have for converting to Christianity, and why does he take the baptismal name of Isaac?
3. How does Achebe create an "African English" in this novel?
4. How does the relationship of Okonkwo to Unoka help determine Okonkwo's conduct throughout the novel?
5. What function do the *kotma* or "court messengers" fill in the new society?
6. What strengths and what weaknesses does Achebe show in Igbo traditional society?
7. Discuss Okonkwo's relationship to his wife Ekwefi and his daughter Ezinma.
8. In what way does Obierika represent a transitional figure between the old and new Igbo society?

9. How are the elders of Umuofia shown to be more "civilized" than the District Commissioner or the missionary Mr. Smith?
10. Discuss Okonkwo's status as "one of the greatest men of Umuofia" How does he represent his society, and what is the significance of his isolation at the end?
11. Compare the two white missionaries, Mr. Brown and Mr. Smith, in their relationship to the villages of Umuofia. Is Mr. Brown's approach without danger?

### Further Reading

See also the suggestions in the anthology, p. 2097.

Achebe, Chinua. *Morning Yet on Creation Day: Essays.* 1975.

————. *Hope and Impediments: Selected Essays, 1965-1987.* 1988.

Okoye, Emmanuel Meziemadu. *The Traditional Religion and its Encounter with Christianity in Achebe's Novels.* 1987.
Discusses Achebe's representation of traditional Igbo religion (including the chi) along with other writers' accounts and occasional disagreement.

M. A. Onwuejeogwu. *An Igbo Civilisation: Nri Kingdom and Hegemony.* 1981.
An anthropologist's detailed account of a strongly hierarchized Igbo political, religious, and social system; useful in understanding the traditional Igbo society of *Things Fall Apart.* Drawings, photographs, and maps usable for classroom illustration.

Ubahakwe, Ebo. *Igbo Names: Their Structure and their Meanings.* 1981.
A sociolinguistic explanation of the complex meanings of names in Igbo society, and of the social importance of naming.